nguage Theatres, 1918-1933

X

X Königsberg

Danzig

EAST PRUSSIA

2

S

S

S²
Rostock

MECKLENBURG

S Stettin

ck

I A

S

Berlin

chweig

X

S

S Magdeburg

S

ANHALT X Dessau

S² Halle

S² Leipzig

3 Weimar

SAXONY

X²
Dresden

Görlitz

S

Breslau

S

S

S

POLAND

S

S

X

S

S

S²

S

Chemnitz

S² X

Teplitz

SX

SX

Beuthen

S

S

S

Hof

S X

S

F Bayreuth

X Pilsen/Iglau

Prague

CZECHOSLOVAKIA

S Brünn

Nürnberg

S Regensburg

S

S

urg

□³ Munich

X

Linz

3
Vienna

F X Salzburg

AUSTRIA

Innsbruck

Graz S²

Klagenfurt

S

**Macalester
College
Library**

THE THEATRE OF THE WEIMAR REPUBLIC

Frontispiece. Berlin in the revolutionary winter of 1918–19: an actress takes the political stage. Molly Wessely of the Metropol Theater addressing the crowd on the need to vote for the new National Assembly which would bring the Weimar Republic into being. Photo by Ullstein Bilderdienst.

THE THEATRE OF THE WEIMAR REPUBLIC

John Willett

HM
Holmes & Meier
New York / London

Published in the United States of America 1988
by Homes & Meier Publishers, Inc.

Holmes & Meier Publishers, Inc.
30 Irving Place
New York, NY 10003

Great Britain:
Holmes & Meier Publishers, Ltd.
One Hallswelle Parade
London NW11 ODL
England

Book design by Marilyn Marcus

The paper used in this publication meets the requirements
of the American National Standard for Permanence of Paper
for printed Library Materials, Z39.48-1984.

Library of Congress Cataloging-in-Publication Data

Willett, John.
    The theatre of the Weimar Republic.

    Bibliography: p.
    Includes index.
    1. Theater—Germany—History—20th century.   I. Title.
PN2654.W55   1988   792'.0943   87-19773
ISBN 0-8419-0759-5 (alk. paper)

Manufactured in the United States of America

In memory of Wal Cherry
With thanks

Contents

PART II
STAGES OF A REPUBLICAN THEATRE

PART III
WEIMAR AND AFTER

PART IV
BASIC DETAILS OF THE WEIMAR THEATRE
AND ITS AFTERMATH   213

PART I

The Road to Weimar

1

The German Nation and Its Stages

Getting Interested: Some Recollections

I first came across the German-language theatre just fifty years ago, when Adolf Hitler's National Socialist regime had already driven men like Max Reinhardt, Ernst Toller, Bertolt Brecht, and Erwin Piscator into exile. Hitler's own country, Austria, was still relatively free, though far from being a democracy; and Reinhardt still dominated the Salzburg Festival which he had founded with Hofmannsthal and Richard Strauss in 1921, even though his creative interests now lay mainly in the United States. Visiting that festival as a schoolboy, I had no inkling of the cultural achievements of the Weimar Republic other than perhaps in architecture, but it was still possible to see Reinhardt's two perennial festival productions: Hofmannsthal's *Everyman* on the cathedral square—a quasi-religious experience of considerable power—and the first part of Goethe's *Faust* in the Felsenreitschule or rock arcades behind the festival theatre, which by comparison with Shakespeare seemed noisy and uneventful. My German in those days was not yet up to much—certainly not up to Goethe—but I did get strong impressions from two Nazi productions which I saw while driving through southern Germany: a provincial *Parsifal* where the Heldentenor (or heroic tenor, a term one no longer hears much) stood silent and motionless during the grail scene for what I recall as being forty minutes, and a *Tartuffe* in—I think—Stuttgart which had been made into an anti-Semitic piece.

3

In Vienna, where I spent some six months after leaving school, the feeling of cultural conservatism was then very strong: at the many concerts and opera performances to which I went I never heard a note of music by the Vienna School of Schönberg and Webern; the one writer I met was Hermann Graedener (who was highly esteemed by the Nazis); and only later at university in England did I learn that Freud and Wittgenstein even existed. Though the Burgtheater was supposed to be one of the great German-language theatres, for me it was dominated by the bawling of the actors and the dingy unimaginativeness of the sets and costumes designed by such as Alfred Roller—once a significant figure in art nouveau but now long stagnant; in the National Library I studied dozens of his designs at the instigation of my teacher Josef Gregor. Decades afterward I would discover that the two chief dramaturgs of the Burgtheater, Buschbeck and Ratislav, held their jobs uninterruptedly from the last days of the Habsburg empire till after the Anschluss of 1938, when Hitler annexed the country to the plaudits of the vast number of local anti-Semites; one of the new words I heard on my first visit in 1936 being *Saujud*—a popular term for "filthy Jew"—which was certainly a help in understanding the Nazi culture of those days, though not Goethe perhaps.

What a dramaturg might be I did not know, for the notion of having a professional play reader, adapter, possibly even playwright or translator regularly responsible for everything to do with play texts, scripts, and program contents was long unknown in the English-language theatre. Nor did I realize that in most German theatres over the same period dramaturgs would have come and gone repeatedly, and not simply because of the violent political changes in that country but because the theatre itself had been in ferment. Something of what had been going on in the European theatre elsewhere, however, became evident when I saw the 1936 international theatre exhibition in Vienna. It showed nothing of pre-Hitler Germany of course, and I doubt if I spent much time looking at the Nazi exhibits, since they have completely slid from my memory. But the Czechs were a revelation, with the surreal cabaret revues of the clowns Voskovec and Werich, and the wealth of modern stage designs from Prague and Bratislava; and later, at the time of the disastrous Munich Agreement, I was able to see E. F. Burian's D38 company, whose extraordinary fantasy on Czech folksongs was the first piece of pure theatre I ever met. The Russian section was confined to relatively recent work, among which Akimov's *Hamlet* looked striking, but by then I had got to know Gregor's richly illustrated book on the heroic years of the Soviet theatre (which he had experienced) and envied my friend the artist Derek Hill, whom I saw off from the Nordbahnhof on his way to study theatre design in that country.

All this at least prepared me for my first encounter with the writings of Brecht and Piscator, which were my real introduction to the German theatre of the Weimar years. Even today these two great advocates of an "epic theatre" tend to dominate my view of that period; the impact which they made on me as a student was considerable, and its effects survived the Second World War strongly enough to lead me to write at some length about both of them. This then was the kernel of that slowly developing knowledge of the subject, which in due course has resulted in the present book. What happened, in brief, was that in 1977 I was invited to West Berlin for a conference in connection with that year's major exhibitions, specifically the one organized by Cologne University and the Kreutzberg arts department on theatre in the Weimar Republic (whose lavishly illustrated catalogue remains important). A year later I was in Australia for some five months, teaching the same subject to final-year drama students at the University of New South Wales, where we covered a good deal of ground from the Expressionists to Brecht's political *Lehrstücke,* his special form of didactic stage cantata. When on my return to London Mrs. Ilse Wolff the publisher asked me to write a short textbook on it I thought that I had at least got the hang of the subject and could probably do so on the basis of my teaching material.

But of course I could not, because it was not possible for me to set it down immediately, as I had hoped, in such a way as to give a simple outline of the Weimar theatre as I then knew it; and when finally I started thinking about it so many questions arose in my mind that I had to start in rather more detail, making use, for instance, of the generously given resources of the Cologne Theatre Museum. Instead of teaching the readers, as I had been asked to do, I now had to teach myself. Part of the trouble is that since the sharp break in continuity created by the Third Reich the Germans themselves have been like archaeological excavators, digging up the fragments of a buried civilization, and they have hardly yet been able to look at that civilization as a whole. What is strangely lacking therefore is any German overview of the subject, or even of the bare facts involved. This is why, however inadequately, I have provided appendices giving overall (if far from complete) résumés of the more important or interesting productions of the German-language theatre after 1916, and a key to the many theatres involved, along with their principal directors, designers, and dramaturgs; such concentrated guides are sadly lacking at present, and I just hope that others will come along to do the job more completely.

The reason for starting them just before the revolution of 1918 is plain enough, for it was in 1916, with the first expressionist performances, that the German cultural upheaval reached the public. But the same résumés also run on to the end of the Second World War, and this is because the Weimar theatre was not simply snuffed out when Hitler came to power in 1933, hard as the Nazis tried to ensure that it was. The stages, the personalities, and, through them, the tradition continued right through the twelve years of the Third Reich, not only among the exiles who for one reason or another—race, politics, or ideological and ethical fastidiousness—left after February 1933, but also within the new National Socialist theatre apparatus. The divided development which followed explains much both about the Weimar years and about the East and West German theatres of today. The nature of the divisions has changed, but the very existence of a divided tradition made it difficult after 1945 for a unified theatre to come about.

A Theatre of Urgency

One of the complicating factors has been that by 1933 the Western interest in the new German theatre—which was never all that strong—had largely evaporated, and its innovations were being smugly treated as old hat: there was, for instance, around that time a remarkably silly parody of a Brecht Lehrstück by the anthropologist Geoffrey Gorer in *Punch*. Hence when outstanding German theatre figures began going into exile not even their professional colleagues in the English-speaking world seemed to regard their achievements as having been all that important. As for people outside the theatre, wherever one chooses to look back at those difficult years—at Brecht's visits to London and New York, at Piscator's frustrated ventures in Paris, at Toller's suicide in a New York hotel, at Reinhardt's growing isolation from live theatre on the East and West coasts alike—the ignorance and insular indifference which we showed now seems amazing. In German studies, in drama and in theatre history, the Western critics and academics of that time appeared to be writing off the Weimar period as trivial, decadent, and slightly perverse; and this made it difficult for following generations to find out what its culture had really been like.

Right into the 1950s the same lack of interest and understanding prevailed over the whole field of the arts. Even within postwar Germany the evidence for studying the pre-Nazi period was difficult to come by; and with Hitler's defeat things had not altered much, though at least it was no longer suppressed. It was only once the national recovery was well under way that things started changing. The seeds of this new development lay in the intense concern felt in many countries—but nowhere more so than among the younger German writers and academics—about Germany's fatal progression between the two world wars, from a Socialist-inspired democracy of high humanitarian ideals to an insane regime of immeasurably systematic evil and cruelty. The ups and downs of German democracy before 1933 soon became passionately exciting, and all the more so because two rival attempts were once more being made to develop a workable Fascist-proof system. It was as part of this process that critical opinion at last became alerted to the power and originality of those modern German art movements that had been crushed by the Nazis during their fifteen years of unrestricted power. Brought back from museum reserves and obscure foreign collections, the pictorial Expressionism of the years 1910–22 soon came as a revelation not only to both Germanies but right across the world. A revival of the literature followed. There were even signs that the pre-Nazi tradition was still alive, particularly in the theatre, where Brecht was just beginning to be recognized as an international influence when he died in 1956. And yet such developments might once again have been dismissed by the outside world had it not been for a growing sense in England, France, Italy, and (to a slightly lesser extent) the United States that the society of pre-Hitler Germany was in many ways akin to our own. This had not been the case before the Second World War; but throughout Western Europe the new existential pessimism of the 1940s and 1950s, the removal of sexual taboos, the widespread inflation, the emergence of an intellectual proletariat, and even the superficial fashions for leather garments and the color black seemed only too compatible with a sympathy for the Weimar years.

The process is still under way, though we have learned a lot more about the modern movement in Germany since then and have found stimulation and excitement not only in Expressionism but also in such later Weimar developments as *Neue Sachlichkeit* (see pp. 96–97), political theatre, photo-montage, and agitprop. Even now fresh discoveries are being made about those years, their lessons being applied more effectively, our appreciation of their legacy still expanding. Nor can we forget the origins of this whole development in the special claims made on us by German history. Easy as it has been in other countries and periods to treat cultural movements separately from their sociopolitical background—even while agreeing in principle that they are somehow connected—in the case of Weimar Germany it is absolutely impossible. Quite explicitly, many aspects of Weimar culture were related to social objectives and influences, and it is this that has helped give it its unique fascination today. For you cannot overlook the fact that these artists were working and living on a thin crust of liberal civilization, under which the more sensitive could repeatedly feel the vibration of terrible things to come.

Nowhere is this better seen than in the case of the theatre, which in so many ways in Weimar Germany was geared into its time. Obviously theatre is a many-sided art, balancing creative and interpretive genius, bending and stretching the vernacular language, responding more directly than any other to the feelings of its audience and always being most vulnerable to fluctuations in the economy. But in the society of the Weimar Republic it also had special features. Thus it was to a great extent governed by public authorities and subject to local or regional administrations. Its fusion of the visual, the structural, and the musical was more natural than in the non-German theatre, its technological basis more advanced, its concern with political issues more frequent and a good deal more open. And nowhere except in revolutionary Russia did the theatre have to contend with such violent and often tragic events in so short a time. True enough, the real test of the Weimar theatre's relevance to us lies in certain inspired works, ideas, performances, productions—or rather the glimpses which we can still get of these, and which even now seem like electric flashes. But in so close a concentration of different factors there is a continually rewarding subject for study. The very urgency which so often underlay its productions touches the nerve ends of those who once again know they are living in a precarious world.

Germany Becomes a Force

Such special aspects of the theatre in Germany go back at least to the time of Bismarck, when Prussia established its dominant position in the German-speaking lands, pushing the immense Austro-Hungarian Empire into second place, defeating Napoleon III in a brilliantly conducted *Blitzkrieg* and setting up the Second German Reich in 1871 under a largely militarized ruling caste. The extent of those German lands tends perhaps to be overlooked nowadays, when English in a variety of forms has emerged as the major global language, but you have only to look at a linguistic map to see that there were German-speaking areas dotted all over eastern Europe as far as the Volga basin, with

Technology for a modern theatre. The world's first electrically lit stage, built for the Munich Electrotechnical Exhibition of 1881, a year before the premiere of Wagner's *Parsifal* at Bayreuth. Photo by Tom Willett.

important German theatres established not merely in what now constitutes the two Germanies, Austria, and Switzerland, but also in modern Czechoslovakia, Poland, and the USSR. Both geographically and quantitatively, Germany's was the leading European theatre during the Wilhelmine period (as the years of the Second German Reich came to be called); and like the world which it reflected it was shaped by the unique system that Bismarck set up.

Faced with the problem of unifying a culturally and linguistically homogeneous but politically and administratively fragmented empire, the Prussian chancellor ruthlessly centralized the real power with little pretense of democratic freedom, representative government, or regional devolution. Yet the twenty-five lesser German kingdoms, principalities, and free cities which he absorbed in this way were left culturally independent, in command of their old court or municipal theatres and orchestras and also of the universities and the school system. In this almost paradoxical division of responsibilities the theatre benefited both ways. That is to say that the patronage structure remained untouched, so that the tradition of local and regional theatre, along with the companies themselves and their directors, was not interfered with; indeed of all European countries, only Italy retained so evenly spread and so decentralized a theatre system, and so intense a local commitment to the arts in general. At the same time the great economic and industrial advances which resulted from German unification helped the theatre to modernize itself and reach a new audience.

So of sixty-seven major public theatre buildings in the subsequent Weimar Republic more than two-thirds were built under the new Reich. Technically too the country's belated industrial revolution (by which the German economy now overtook first France, then Britain) meant that its stage equipment became the most advanced in the world, thanks in particular to the leap forward in steel production (by more than eight times between 1880 and 1910), along with the corresponding boom in heavy engineering and the development of the great electrical firms, Siemens and AEG. Moreover, the new class of technologists, practical scientists, bankers, and managers which was thereby created was itself interested in the theatre and in the arts in general, providing stimulators and supporters and thereby helping to offset the still rather sterile influence of the ruling court officials. For although the courts had been responsible for the general pattern of theatre distribution in Germany their artistic influence right up to the fall of the empire in 1918 was conservative, with two striking exceptions. In Thuringia, in the tiny principality of Saxe-Meiningen, the Grand Duke George II returned from the war of 1870–71 to set up a remarkable troupe of actors known as the Meiningers, under Ludwig Chronegk. Almost simultaneously Richard Wagner, backed first by Ludwig II of Bavaria, then by a vast international subscription, was building a festival theatre at Bayreuth for the performance of operas of a new kind. Between them these two pioneers were to transform more than one aspect of theatre, with effects that are still felt.

Following the relegation to second place of the Austro-Hungarian empire after 1866, there was a changed relationship between the theatres in Vienna and those in Berlin, which by the end of the century was becoming recognized as the theatrical capital of all Germany. Previously, while it had been common enough for the Vienna Burgtheater (the Habsburgs' imperial court theatre) to engage actors from Germany, there was not much to tempt leading Austrians to work for its opposite number in Berlin. Partly because of the Prussian capital's new prosperity, partly in response to its emergence as an exciting theatrical center, a two-way traffic now developed, by which Berlin drew many of its best-known actors from Austria while *Intendanten* (or artistic directors), stage directors, and dramaturgs (or literary advisors) from Berlin would go to work in Vienna. Much of this interchange can be associated with the young Austrian provincial actor Max Reinhardt, who arrived in Berlin in the 1890s, laid many of the foundations for the modern theatre, and twice switched the main focus of his activities back to Vienna, once voluntarily, the second time not. Thanks to him the distinction between the two rival traditions of German-language theatre became very largely blurred.

Bismarck's last contribution to the renewal of the German theatre was one that primarily affected its audience, though later it was to help create the framework for the Weimar Republic itself. This was his policy toward the rising class of industrial workers, whose welfare he at first tried to promote while suppressing every effort on their part to take political responsibility themselves. More relentlessly muzzled than any comparable movement in Western Europe, the SPD, or German Social Democratic party, nonetheless saw its popular vote quadruple over this initial period, while when the

Second International was formed in 1889 (as an association of the entire European Left) the SPD would have been the strongest party even if it had not had the Austrian Socialists to back it up. Numerically, though not yet in terms of parliamentary representation or access to power—in 1906 Socialists were forbidden even to teach gymnastics to schoolchildren, and of course they could not hold commissions in the army—the Socialist movement was the Reich's outstanding single political force. Writers might protest against this utterly frustrating position, but their protests could not yet reach the stage; and the groundswell of less articulate resentment had to be dammed up for action later. In the meantime the existence of so great a body of antiestablishment opinion, a society within a society, with well worked-out alternative beliefs—almost a way of life—of its own, was soon bound to play a part in the reception of the arts. Where Ruskin and Morris had first claimed art to be a basic human right, the German Left grew strong enough to open up fresh practical channels of popular access, above all for its own working-class supporters.

A Continent of Change

Like German socialism and its moves for greater cultural democracy, the new artistic movements which helped form the Weimar theatre were to a great extent international ones initiated outside Germany. Naturalism, originating in the visual arts as a more detailed and painstaking development of the Realist movement of the midcentury, was introduced to the theatre most powerfully in the 1880s by the plays of Ibsen and the Paris productions of the young André Antoine's Théâtre Libre. Symbolism, which took off from Mallarmé in poetry and Gauguin, Moreau, and Redon in painting, was in part a reaction against the positivist and materialist side of late nineteenth-century naturalism, and it started to reach the theatre in the form of Strindberg's and Maeterlinck's plays from about 1890 on. Maeterlinck's were realized in the Paris Théâtre de l'Oeuvre by Lugné-Poe and subsequently by Stanislavsky's Art Theatre in Moscow; Strindberg's, however, were at first restricted to his own chamber theatre in Stockholm, (though his earlier naturalist works were played in France). The literary cabaret, too, which found its way to Germany around 1900 and permeated some sections of the theatre, took off from the foundation of Rodolphe Salis's Le Chat noir in Paris two decades earlier. Those historical changes, in other words, that made themselves felt after 1870 may have decided the pattern of the German theatre and given it its new practical resources. But overlapping them there was a wider artistic upheaval which had other roots. Only one of the movements in which it manifested itself was specifically German; this was Expressionism, which was not to reach the main body of the theatre until the Wilhelmine era was nearly over.

Right back to Romanticism the German theatre absorbed outside movements in its own way. "If there have been three events in the past 150 years," wrote the Weimar theatre's most farsighted critic, Herbert Jhering, after the

Second World War, "which made a revolutionary impact on the European novel and the European theatre, they are *Werther, Crime and Punishment* and the operas of Richard Wagner."[1] Debatable as this choice might seem to anyone brought up in France on Proust, *Pelléas,* and *Madame Bovary,* or in England on *Wuthering Heights, Ulysses,* and the Diaghilev ballet, it is a characteristic German view and one that seems natural enough in the light of the values being established before 1914. For, unlike the wider theatrical movements, these owed much to specifically German pioneers, of whom Schopenhauer, with his concept of a blind irrational Will in a primarily evil and painful world, largely set the tone for the two more influential figures who followed him: Nietzsche and Wagner. Throughout the whole world of the arts Nietzsche's impact was electric, partly because of the prophetic quality of his writing, with its very modern note of intelligent despair and isolation, but also because of his view of the primitive, Dionysiac element in tragedy and its passionate message of *Wahn, Wille, Wehe*: frenzy, willpower, pain. This element he saw as conveyed largely by music—a pre-conceptual form of communication, so Schopenhauer had maintained—in a theatrical setting that resembled "a lonely mountain valley: the stage architecture seems like a glowing image in the clouds."

It was Schopenhauer's view of music, along with Nietzsche's call for a "rebirth of the German Myth" and "return to the *Ur*-home" by means of a new form of non-naturalistic, nonmoralistic tragedy, that came to a head in Wagner's music dramas with their claim to be a *Gesamtkunstwerk,* or "total work of art." Hitherto unparalleled anywhere in the scale and grandeur of their ambitions (as displayed in the Bayreuth festivals from 1876 on), his enormous operas stood in conscious opposition to the realistic, thinking, critical theatre and found a subdued echo in the work of Maeterlinck and other symbolists. Musical impact apart, their primary influence on the new theatre was felt behind the scenes of those big court and civic houses whose technicians now found themselves having to learn ways of coping with swimming Rhinemaidens, giants, dragons, conflagrations, and other spectacular problems from the neopagan world of Wagnerian myth. Such demands pushed stage technology to its limits, and as Wagner's works came to be performed all over Germany the theatre's mechanics and lighting became increasingly resourceful.

Naturalism Comes to Germany

Two years before Wagner opened his theatre at Bayreuth, the new Meiningen company of actors arrived in Berlin for the first of several visits. They were at once unconscious heralds of Naturalism—giving that city its first introduction to Ibsen on 3 June 1876, and also to his fellow Norwegian Björnson—and exponents of a previously unknown scrupulousness in performance. For Chronegk, the Meiningers' director, was in the habit not only of paying close attention to details, whether of individual speech or of crowd movements, but

A pioneer of realistic production: Ludwig Chronegk, director of the Meiningen company from Saxony, photographed in 1881–82, five years after their first guest season in Berlin.

also of rehearsing for four weeks or so, part of this time in the play's set. The designer, and for a while the Intendant, was the grand duke himself, who was an art-historically trained draftsman of professional standard. He, too, insisted on a high degree of accuracy in his props and costumes and saw that the actors' poses and groupings were visually right. He is supposed to have ensured that, before any dress rehearsal, each actor was given a drawing to show him exactly how his costume should be worn. Another innovation was that performances took place with the house lights down and the auditorium in darkness. As a result, Berlin became aware not merely of the importance of such perfectionism but also of the nature of ensemble acting and the true role of the director.

Admittedly the relevance of this to the new movement in the drama was not immediately clear—for the Ibsen in question was the early *The Pretenders*, and it was Shakespeare's *Julius Caesar* rather than any more recent work that most impressed the Berlin audience. Indeed the Meiningers' tours were almost entirely confined to the classics; Schiller first, with Shakespeare's works providing about one-third of all the company's guest performances up to 1890. It is said, too, that their productions were not varied enough, and after Chronegk's death they stopped touring. Nevertheless they were a great contrast to anything else that could be seen in Berlin, particularly at the Prussian royal theatre. For where George II of Saxe-Meiningen, despite being an aristocrat and a guards officer, was genuinely mad about theatre, the imperial Intendant Botho von Hülsen, another ex-soldier, was a courtier and little more. When in 1883 the royal theatres came to celebrate his fifty years of service it turned out that these covered both service in the army and service to the theatre. For to the emperor the duties involved seemed of one and the same kind.

On that self-congratulatory occasion the harshest criticisms of the Berlin court theatre (which later became the State Theatre and was destroyed in the Second World War) came from two critics in their twenties, Paul Schlenther and Otto Brahm. These two young men had seen the Meiningers and attended the first Berlin performance of Ibsen's *Pillars of Society* in 1878; subsequently Schlenther saw *Ghosts* in a single closed performance, while there was also a production of *A Doll's House* in 1880. But once their contemporary Antoine had founded the Paris Théâtre Libre in 1887, the Berlin Ibsenites decided to follow suit and start a "Free Theatre" of their own. On the same day as the first Ibsen production at the court theatre—it was *The Woman from the Sea*, and Ibsen, now living in Germany, attended and was personally applauded—there were ten such rebels who agreed to launch the new undertaking. On 5 April 1889 they met to constitute it formally. Among the group were the twenty-eight-year-old journalist Maximilian Harden and the newly established publisher Samuel Fischer, as well as Brahm, Schlenther, and others from the fringe of the Berlin theatre. They now formed the Freie Bühne (a title copied directly from Antoine), consisting of a private society that would hold ten Sunday afternoon performances a year in the Berlin Lessing Theatre. There were 354 members two months later, over a thousand in the following year. A magazine was started with Brahm as its editor, and given the same title as the society.

Their first performance was of *Ghosts* at the end of September 1889, Mrs. Alving being played by a former Meiningen actress largely under Brahm's direction. Then came the first major work of a new playwright, Gerhart Hauptmann's *Before Sunrise*, which Brahm had just read; and this quick and perceptive choice established the society as the main German outlet for the new socially conscious drama, comparable with its French prototype in every way but one: lack of a theatre of its own. Hauptmann soon became a member of the group (in replacement of Harden), and more of his plays followed, notably *The Weavers* in March 1892. Tolstoy's *Power of Darkness* and Strindberg's *Miss Julie* and *Father* were among other plays performed. Part of the Freie Bühne's aim was of course to get such works past the censorship, which under the Wilhelmian Reich was universal and severe; and this meant that when *The Weavers* became licensed for public performance a major reason for the society's existence was removed. It was further undermined by the foundation of

The founder of German naturalist theatre: Otto Brahm of the Freie Bühne society, photographed in Berlin in 1891 shortly before his historic production of Gerhart Hauptmann's *The Weavers*. From 1894 to 1904 he ran the Deutsches Theater, then moved to the Lessing Theater for the last eight years of his life.

the Volksbühne, or People's Stage, which will be dealt with in the next section, while a third blow fell when Brahm moved, as we shall shortly see, to a full-time theatre. The society managed to survive for some years, actually giving a performance (a repeat of *Before Sunrise*) as late as 1909. But from 1893 on its productions were sporadic, and in ten of those years there was no performance at all.

The task was widening, as was the serious theatre audience, and as a result two new institutions emerged to take up the challenge. These not only saw the modern theatrical movement up to the fall of the Prussian monarchy but would carry on right through to the end of the Weimar period. They are thus the real start of our story.

Josef Kainz from Vienna, the great new actor of the Deutsches Theater, in his role as Hamlet in 1894, when the twenty-one-year old Max Reinhardt played the First Gravedigger for Brahm. Photo by Ullstein Bilderdienst.

2

Bases for a Modern Stage, 1890–1914

Brahm at the Deutsches Theater

In Berlin, as the Freie Bühne sagged into inactivity, Brahm took a ten-year lease on the Deutsches Theater, starting in the summer of 1894. Seating about a thousand, it had been built in the 1880s by a stout and successful (though now forgotten) popular playwright called Adolf L'Arronge, who ran it as a well-financed private theatre with a repertoire of classics in the wake of the Meiningers. Now it became in effect a full-time wholly professional extension of the Freie Bühne, whose close association with Gerhart Hauptmann and generally pioneering role in the promotion of Naturalism it took over. Brahm's most famous achievement as its Intendant was the first public staging of *The Weavers*, whose concern with the hardships of the Silesian home weavers and their cries of protest had already made it a revolutionary play for the German Left. This led William II—no friend either of socialism or of modernism in the arts—to give up his box at the theatre and have its royal coat of arms removed. Eleven further plays by Hauptmann were performed in the ten years of Brahm's management, including the Peasant War play *Florian Geyer*, the family tragedy *Das Friedensfest*, the lowlife comedy *Der Biberpelz*, its successor *Der rote Hahn*, and the verse play *Der arme Heinrich*, in which the playwright was already moving toward Symbolism. Balancing these were ten works by Ibsen (including *Ghosts*, now likewise freed by the censors, *John Gabriel Borkman*)

17

and *The Power of Darkness*, as well as such lesser German-language naturalists as Anzengruber and Wolzogen. At the same time Brahm continued L'Arronge's policy of performing the classics; indeed, he opened his tenure of the theatre with Schiller's *Kabale und Liebe*, for which his predecessor had left him some excellent performers. Notable among them was the thirty-six-year-old Austrian Josef Kainz, who had once or twice played with the Meiningen company.

Kainz, who is generally seen as being among the very greatest German-language actors, is one of those men whose face, like that of Baudelaire, springs out of the old photographs because of its extraordinary modernity; he looks as if he could be living now. Never particularly imposing, he seems to have combined quick intelligence and sensitivity with spontaneous temperamental force and an astonishingly clear, swift, flexible voice.[1] He was indeed a new type of player, whose contribution to the reform of the practical stage (wrote Joseph Gregor) paralleled that of Ibsen to the drama.[2] Or as Max Reinhardt saw it, after having played the First Gravedigger to Kainz's *Hamlet* in November 1894: "old and new style, idealism and realism, in an extraordinary blend."[3] Emmanuel Reicher too, whom Brahm had recruited for the company as he recruited Albert Bassermann and the twenty-one-year-old Reinhardt, impressed the latter with his "startling photographic naturalness," almost too modern for a classical play. Given talents like these, a new unpompous attitude to the performance of Shakespeare and Schiller seeped through the company to become one of the striking features of Brahm's regime; and it accorded with what he wanted, the reinterpretation of the classics in a naturalist light. He himself—"the little man with the lofty thinker's forehead and the big sarcastic mouth,"[4] as Reinhardt saw him—was not a director but a drama scholar, a dramaturg. And this perhaps was his trouble, particularly once the Berlin theatre began moving outward from Naturalism toward other things.

Brahm, said his cantankerous ex-colleague Maximilian Harden, never discovered a new writer after 1889, nor did he ever perform Strindberg, Wedekind, or Shaw, though he remained a theatre Intendant till his death in 1913. He engaged directors like Carl Hachmann and Emil Lessing, but neither press nor public paid much attention to their names; sometimes the programs only listed a stage manager. He knew what actors he wanted and took an active part in rehearsals, it seems, but largely in the form of discussion with the actors. Nor was the standard of design at the Deutsches Theater considered at all remarkable during his years there. After a while the actors themselves started falling away; thus Kainz returned to Vienna for good when Brahm's ex-partner Paul Schlenther went to become Intendant of the Burgtheater there, while the leading actress Agnes Sorma left in 1898. Admirably scrupulous and serious within these limitations, Brahm clearly had little sense of humor, leading Harden to complain of "the drab sobriety of his pedantry."[5] Nor is there anything to suggest that he had much awareness of the *fun* of the theatre; thus in Harden's words:

> His luke-warm little soul preferred the novel with attenuated dialogue, especially a story from the gloomiest depths of misery which he himself had never known.

This trustee and business manager for a capitalistic group brought out plays whose chief merit was the scourging of the capitalistic social order and the demoralizing abuses it carries daily in its wake. Because this policy filled their purses, his backers did not object.[6]

I quote this unkind verdict because it seems to be the earliest comment on a situation that was to be repeated with other progressive theatre leaders both in Germany and elsewhere. It may help to explain why L'Arronge in 1903 was unwilling to extend Brahm's lease, and why the Deutsches Theater conducted so brilliant a campaign against photographic greyness in the decade that was to follow.

Theatre for the People

In relaxing the ban on such plays as *The Weavers* and *Ghosts* the Prussian police had in mind the high ticket prices at the Deutsches Theater and the aristocratic nature of its audience. But although the worst of Bismarck's anti-Socialist laws were repealed in 1890, this did not mean that William II was any less hostile to socialism than had been his grandfather, the first emperor. Access for the underprivileged to subversive theatre was certainly not supposed to be part of the deal. Just this, however, was implied by the first moves toward a People's Theatre, or Volksbühne, at the end of the 1880s. In those days the Socialists and their sympathizers were still cut off from normal political meetings and confined to their discussion clubs, and it was in one of these in Berlin that a group under Bruno Wille set to work to realize the Volksbühne idea. Citing the relevance to the workers of writers like Tolstoy, Dostoevsky, Ibsen, and Zola, he and his supporters proposed the formation of a Freie Volksbühne on the model of its bourgeois precursor, the Freie Bühne of Brahm and his friends. "For that section of the People," said Wille's manifesto in the Berlin Socialist daily on 28 March 1890,

> which has been converted to good taste it is important not only to be able to read plays of its own choosing but also to see them produced. However, public performances of plays embodying a revolutionary spirit are normally frustrated by capitalism, unless they turn out to be money-spinners, or by police censorship. This does not apply to private societies. For instance the Freie Bühne society has been able to produce dramas of that tendency.[7]

At a public meeting two thousand strong the group invited members to join under the slogan "Art for the People" *(Die Kunst dem Volke)*, which is still the movement's motto today.

Based on much the same idea of a repertoire, and with Brahm himself as one of its first advisers, this new, outwardly nonpolitical society was a theatre club on a vastly enlarged scale, with a huge new audience whose members paid only fifty pfennigs per performance (as against seven times as much under the Freie Bühne). Here the leading spirits, so far as one can judge, were a mixture of left-inclined writers, like the realist Julius Hart and the journalists Curt Baake and Conrad Schmidt, and self-educated artisans and workers very

Theatre for a new audience. The Berlin Volksbühne, or 'People's Stage', was founded in 1890 under socialist influence, and eventually built its own Berlin theatre in 1914. Its motto 'Art for the People', here seen inscribed above the colonnade, reflects its debt to the ideas of William Morris and Louis Lumet, which in no other country were realised on such a scale. Photo by Ullstein Bilderdienst.

much of the kind who associated with Morris in England. Wille himself was an SPD member, while anarchists like Gustav Landauer and Erich Mühsam (both to be involved in the Munich Soviet Republic and later murdered by nationalists) were among his friends. Like all left-wing organizations this FVB (as the Freie Volksbühne was called) was bedevilled by splits that now seem of no great relevance to its ultimate significance for the German theatre. Despite this flaw the whole people's theatre movement continued to gather momentum right up to 1914, and just because it was little concerned with launching fresh developments in play construction or staging it acted not just as an extension of the normal European theatre audience but as a solid weight helping to anchor much of the Berlin theatre to the Naturalist period.

Though there were campaigns for people's theatre elsewhere in Europe, no other was comparable with this. In France, where the movement was also strong, there were some stirring essays by Romain Rolland (collected as *Le Théâtre du Peuple*, 1913) but the actual results boiled down to an open-air theatre in the Vosges with the now forgotten Maurice Pottecher staging local plays. Rolland, however, did write his *Danton* and other revolutionary dramas under its impetus; nor is it irrelevant that he was so resolute an advocate of Franco-German understanding, for the whole drive for a people's culture before 1914 was directed not only against the established society but also against nationalism and war. Inside Germany there were attempts to start similar groups in the provinces, initially Hamburg, Hannover, Kiel, and Bielefeld; there was also a Vienna FVB from 1906–11 under Stefan Grossmann of the Socialist *Arbeiterzeitung,* which started with Sunday matinees (and would become a semicommercial affair employing much younger men like Jhering, Fritz Kortner, and Berthold Viertel). For a few months the actual German Social Democratic party, or SPD, held officially aloof, but after its Erfurt Congress of 1891 it acknowledgèd theatrical naturalism to be a useful ally and the theatre an aid to self-improvement of the workers. Franz Mehring, one of its leading thinkers, became the FVB chairman for four years, and though the society's actual commitment to socialism subsequently became a good deal looser, its link with the party was never broken. What is more, it and its provincial equivalents banded together with the workers' amateur dramatic societies to form (at Magdeburg in 1908) what became the DATB, or German Workers' Theatre League, another body that carried over into the Weimar period.

Those issues that variously divided the Berlin Volksbühne movement at different times had been built into the people's theatre concept from the start. The first, which surfaced almost at once with Bruno Wille's resignation from the SPD in 1891, was: to what extent should the society stand outside the class war? Were the members educating themselves for political ends, or as part of the great German tradition of *Bildung*—the notion that high culture had an educational value in itself? Wille and others of the founding group believed the latter, and when he lost the chair to Mehring they split away to form an initially smaller society called the Neue Freie Volksbühne, or NFVB, with a separate membership. Next, was either society going to stage its own productions, or was their main function to get members cheap seats for productions by existing managements? It was Wille's NFVB whose leading members most clearly had theatrical ambitions of their own, though in fact both societies alternated between these two approaches according to the nature of their arrangements with other managers and the amount of funds available for their own initiatives. As the total membership leaped ahead, so the number of different theatres cooperating went up too, with the result that the movement became more of a consumers' price-cutting organization—something that both societies were at one time or another accused of being.

Again, in choosing plays—in particular, difficult or controversial plays that the society itself would have to produce—what was to be the criterion? Was it to be "excellence," as judged by critical opinion and the (only partly proletarian) selecting committee, or was it to be political content? Over and above that there was the problem which troubled Mehring and other Marxists: the danger that an unvarnished picture of real life would merely engender an attitude of hopelessness, and the consequent need for Naturalism to go further and discover "that higher love of the truth that would make it depict what is evolving, as it has to be."[8] All these were differences that not only accounted for the ups and downs of the internal debate before 1914 but continued after the 1918 revolution and the emergence of a separate Communist party. Such issues remain part of the perpetual argument within all cultural groups on the Left, up to the present day.

The program originally was both Naturalist and educative, each play being the subject of a preliminary lecture. Most of the plays (sixteen out of twenty in the first two years) had already been given by Brahm's Freie Bühne, and, as with that body, they were presented initially in Sunday performances by arrangement with different theatres, starting with the Ostend (subsequently Rose) Theatre in Berlin's East End, which had opened in the 1880s as a would-be People's Theatre playing the classics. Ibsen's *Pillars of Society* was the first production (followed by four other Ibsen plays and Zola's *Thérèse Raquin* in the first season); the second was Hauptmann's *Vor Sonnenaufgang. Kabale und Liebe* by Schiller was the first classic to be staged. Ibsen himself attended the production of a play by Hermann Bahr in February 1891 where the actors and directors were mostly those used by Brahm. Thereafter police harassment led to the abolition of the lectures, and the split took place in October 1892.

Despite this division, if one looks through the ensuing programs of both VB societies, a common core of the same type of drama can be seen right up to 1914: Ibsen, Tolstoy, Hauptmann, and other German naturalists such as Sudermann and Anzengruber; then, among the classics, Schiller and Kleist, followed by Shakespeare, with Goethe and Grillparzer close behind.

In 1906 a group of 190 workers attending an adult education course were asked which plays had made the strongest impression on them. It is not clear whether this referred to performance, reading, or both, but four plays by Schiller scored 112 votes between them, and *The Weavers* and Gorky's *Lower Depths* 61, while 14 other votes went to Goethe's *Faust*.[9] Certainly the proportion of workers was higher in the FVB than in the breakaway NFVB, and to some extent the fare provided by the two organizations reflects this. Thus it was the FVB that first offered its members Schnitzler, Shaw, Wilde, and Wedekind, with the NFVB tending to follow suit a year or so later, while the Dutch Naturalist (and Socialist) playwright Herman Heijermans was primarily a choice of the FVB. Both societies simultaneously introduced their audience to Maeterlinck (in 1907–8) as also to a triple dose of Strindberg (in 1911–23), and in 1901–2 took them to Büchner's *Danton's Death,* one of the great twentieth-century German rediscoveries. It was the NFVB, however, that began turning to light entertainment with Flotow's *Martha* in 1898–99, and although this may have been in a desperate attempt to hold the membership, which had previously been well below that of the FVB, operettas of that kind played a large part in its program—even in the years when its membership figures were most buoyant.

Briefly what happened was that after an initial period of struggle the breakaway society, with its aim of politically indiscriminate "excellence," starting soaring ahead as soon as Brahm's tenure of the Deutsches Theater came to an end. For the NFVB had had a booking agreement with Max Reinhardt during his first spell as an independent Berlin producer, and when in 1905 he took over the Deutsches Theater (following a stopgap season under Paul Lindau) Reinhardt transferred the agreement. Thenceforward the NFVB members could get cheap tickets for the most exciting theatre in Germany, and this naturally attracted a rush of new subscribers. Difficult as it is to compare the available figures, the NFVB had clearly overtaken the FVB by 1907–8, when it had 18,000 members (or enough to fill about twenty theatres simultaneously). Thereafter it rose to 37,000 in 1910 and 50,000 in 1911–12, by which time the original FVB had settled at around 18,000. It also seems to have been less exclusively proletarian than the latter, which in 1894 is supposed to have had only about 4 percent of members from outside the working class.

Such figures may well be very inexact, but they show what seem to be indisputable trends. At all events the growing prosperity of both halves of the movement not only encouraged a certain reconciliation but put the NFVB's treasurer (the plumber Heinrich Neft) in a position to start planning to build the organization's own theatre. This was something that Mehring and the SPD had opposed, apparently on the ground that political tasks were more important. But the members were tired of Sunday matinees and wanted a permanent home for the VB's own productions. The result was a renewed alliance between the two organizations and the building of a two-thousand seat modern theatre, which eventually opened in December 1914, in the fifth month of the First World War. This was put under Emil Lessing, previously Brahm's principal director.

I have devoted some space to the Volksbühne because it became, for better or worse, a major factor in the Berlin theatre until the Nazis eventually suppressed it, and indeed was the only institution of its kind in the world. Its immediate effect on the development of the German theatre was more or less negligible, apart from the sponsoring of certain now-forgotten authors and the revival of *Danton's Death* (which had been one of Wille's aims from the outset); and this is hardly surprising, given that it was mainly a client of other managements. What was really exciting about it, however, at least before 1900, was the total involvement of its unsophisticated audience, which led André Antoine to say that it was worth the trip to Berlin to experience that, while Ibsen was heard to exclaim on his visit in February 1891, *"Das sind Hörer! Das sind Hörer!"*[10] (What listeners, what listeners). In this important respect it was entirely new.

Perhaps this freshness wore off, and a certain assimilation into the ordinary theatregoing public began to take place after the first decade, though it should be remembered that the Socialist element remained largely separate from and hostile to bourgeois society until overtaken by the hysterical patriotism of 1914. But even if that is so, the commitment of this great audience to Naturalism and to the classics remained clear, and along with Brahm's own operation at the Lessing Theater (where he went for the last eight years of his life after losing the Deutsches Theater) it perpetuated a tradition of what later critics were to term "Berlin realism." This deep-seated conservatism is what kept the Deutsches Theater's foundations steady despite all Max Reinhardt's flights of fancy after L'Arronge allowed him to take over. For as we shall see in the next chapter, Reinhardt's link with the Volksbühne continued up to 1918, since he also managed its new theatre for the four war years, rent-free. And

Opera technology and its possibilities for the theatrical imagination. Karl Lautenschläger's first revolving stage in the Munich Residenz-Theater in 1896. Eight years later Reinhardt applied it spectacularly in the Deutsches Theater, Berlin. Photo by Tom Willett.

from 1910 on he was to be increasingly concerned with planning new forms of theatre for the mass audience.

Symbolism and the New Stage

Behind the predominantly Naturalist surface so evident in Berlin, the possibility of a freely imaginative theatre was already being explored in other cities. Aligned in many ways with the Symbolist movement—and particularly its concern with atmospherics and with expressive color allusions—such experimentation was now made theatrically practicable by a series of new developments in the stage apparatus, above all by the introduction of electric lighting. Up to the mid-1880s, the great majority of theatres had been lit by gas. Thus Bayreuth in 1882 still had to use gas lamps to carry out Wagner's wishes for a symbolic use of light in Parsifal (he died a year later without seeing the new possibilities). But, following Edison's invention of the filament bulb in 1879, theatre lighting by electricity spread rapidly; in Germany it was demonstrated at the Munich electrotechnical exhibition of 1881, then installed in theatres in south Germany and Austria in 1883 and made compulsory in Prussia in 1891. Alongside this came a whole series of mechanical inventions, many of them by the remarkable band of stage technicians or engineers turned out by the Darmstadt Technische Hochschule. Largely intended to meet the demands of grand opera, they included multiple stage lifts, sliding stages which could shunt a set bodily off into the wings, various types of cyclorama that would obviate the need for flies and gauzes and, first installed by Karl Lautenschläger for *Don Giovanni* in Munich in 1896, the revolving stage.

The main concern of these resourceful experts was to allow for the use of more solid, practicable sets instead of the blown-up scene paintings that had served opera so far. But because under the German system of decentralization opera and drama so often had to use the same stage, their innovations, along with the very generous backstage space which most of the Wilhelmine theatre buildings provided, were also made available to the directors of plays. What this meant in practice was that after the turn of the century it became possible to get away from flat stage paintings and build a practicable set which could be quickly and frequently changed. Alternatively the stage could be kept extremely simple, without footlights and without fussy bits of gauze and other hangings to conceal the lights above. Either way, everything was now open to the experimentally minded, including the possibility of changing the actual architecture of the stage, proscenium, and auditorium; space itself was there to be manipulated into new shapes. As for the rapidly proliferating electric spots, floods, arcs, projectors, and dimmers, they were an immediate stimulus to those who saw a close relationship between color and music, on which a new type of fluid, less naturalistically constricted theatre might be based.

The first man of the theatre to pay serious attention to such developments was the Geneva director Adolphe Appia, whose book *La Mise en scène du drame wagnérien* was published in Paris in 1895, when he was in his early thirties. Though his own productions were few and far between, and hardly ever took place in properly equipped theatres, he was horrified by the realization of Wagner's ideas as seen at Bayreuth and accordingly, from the alternative solutions he thereupon conceived, went on to write *La Musique et la mise en scène:* a theoretical work which, while written in French, was originally published in German in Munich in 1899. By then the *Ring* had been restaged at Bayreuth, but there were still no lifts, the stage was raked (at a gradient of one in thirty-three) and the first Fortuny cupola or embryo cyclorama had not yet been invented. "Without question," wrote Appia later, "the master situated his work in the traditional framework of his period; and if at Bayreuth everything in the auditorium expresses his genius, everything the other side of the footlights contradicts it."[11] This Wagnerian inconsistency challenged the Swiss artist on the one hand to question the whole concept of the "total work of art" (which he termed "a dangerous aphorism")[12] and to establish a new hierarchy of the component elements, while on the other making his own sketches for a more modern form of production. Meanwhile, at Bayreuth Wagner's widow Cosima rejected his criticisms as childish. It was only in her grandson's day that they were to bear fruit.

Appia's hierarchy applied not merely to Wagner but to the theatre as a whole. First and foremost came the actor and his movements, then the stage space, the lighting, and finally the stage "painting." This "painting" he

Adolphe Appia's principles applied in the staging of Claudel's *L'Annonce faite à Marie* in the Hellerau Festival Theatre in 1913. Mary Dietrich played Mara, Eva Martersteig Violaine.

wanted to see banished from the theatre along with the footlights. What he had in mind by 'painting' of course was the element of illusion hitherto provided by the scene painter, as against the "practicable" steps and levels which could be used to define stage space and guide movement. Color and variation of atmospheric emphasis were to be achieved by different kinds of light, which he saw as having a mysterious affinity with music. At the center of it all was the actor, whose living reality must not be obscured or interfered with by any kind of illusion (so much for all the developing aids to Naturalism) but shaped and enhanced. In this emphasis on the central figure rather than on the meaning of the actor's words or of his actions, we may see the source of Appia's friendship with his fellow Swiss Jaques-Dalcroze, the founder of eurhythmics, whose work was to be so influential in the new mid-European school of expressive dance now originating near Ascona in southern Switzerland. Their shared ideas relate, as Denis Bablet has acutely pointed out, to the whole new awareness of the body exemplified in the dancing of Loie Fuller and Isadora Duncan, the figure compositions of Hodler, and the revival in 1896 of the Olympic Games.

In 1911 Jaques-Dalcroze moved his school (or institute) from Switzerland to the new German garden city of Hellerau outside Dresden. Here Appia's scenic ideas were effectively realized for the first time, in collaboration with the resident designer Alexander von Salzmann, in a production of Gluck's *Orpheus* in 1912 and 1913. The surviving photographs show a high, quite elaborate yet formally clear-cut structure of steps and levels, backed by tall plain curtains hanging in folds. Between stage and auditorium there is no barrier or change of level. Much the same principle was followed in October 1913, for the German premiere of Claudel's *L'Annonce faite à Marie*. To Jaques-Dalcroze here was at last "the real musician who knows how to situate emotion, and to arouse emotion by means of space." Bablet quotes Appia's ultimate ideal:

> Sooner or later we shall achieve what I'd call the Room pure and simple, a kind of cathedral of the future whose immense, free, transformable space will house the most varied manifestations of our social and artistic life and be the place above all others where the art of the drama will flourish, with or without spectators.[13]

The Hellerau theatre, itself a brilliantly simple space designed by Heinrich Tessenow, seemed to be heading this way.

Changing Dimensions for Actor and Audience

Gordon Craig, whose influence on the German theatre was less radical in the long run but more direct, was brought up among actors and for eight years acted in London as a member of his stepfather Henry Irving's company. He switched briefly to full-time drawing and engraving, then started combining his talents in the role of director-designer, first in mainly amateur productions of early opera (by Purcell and Handel), then in the professional theatre when his mother and uncle, Ellen and Fred Terry, mounted London productions of *Much Ado about Nothing* and Ibsen's *Vikings*. These were seen by Count Harry Kessler, one of the international aristocracy's last great avant-garde patrons, who in 1902 had become director of the museum in Weimar and cultural adviser to that city's grand-ducal court. Impressed by Craig's dramatic use of lighting, by the simplicity of his stage—no flies or wings and only minimal footlights—by the beautifully designed props and the carefully graduated grays of the Viking costumes, Kessler talked about Craig to his friends. One of these was the Austrian playwright Hugo von Hofmannsthal, whose adaptation of Otway's *Venice Preserved* was to be produced by Brahm with his new company at the Lessing Theatre. In the summer of 1904, therefore, Craig arrived in Berlin to design the sets for this and make illustrations for Kessler's edition of its text. Published in Weimar by Kessler's Cranach Press, the resulting book was followed the next year by the first edition anywhere of Craig's theoretical work, *The Art of the Theatre*. In Berlin, too, Craig met Isadora Duncan, then performing there, whose art and person were to play a large part in his life during the two years that followed.

Like Appia, whose work he got to know only in 1914, Craig had in mind an ideal theatre where accuracy of detail (à la Meininger) would no longer matter and where all movement, whether of the actor or of the lighting, would have the fluency of music. At the heart of this, once again, was a conception of stage space shaped so as to dramatize the human figure. Such ideas were conveyed partly in the pages of Craig's magazine *The Mask*, which he began publishing from Florence in 1907, partly through the productions on which he worked—though his sets for *Venice Preserved* were apparently far too un-

realistic for Brahm and were greatly modified. Thirdly, however, Craig, like
Appia, often expressed his ideas in freely speculative drawings; and it is here
that we find his great visions of flights of steps, square-cut San Gimigniano-
like towers, heavy chiaroscuro, and tall screens dwarfing isolated figures.
Many of these visions were quite unrealizable, and even in his Moscow
Hamlet of 1912 the screens were a mechanical disaster. But as a model for a
more imaginative theatre his images were to be influential right up to the
present day.

Craig's base in Germany was effectively the Grand Duchy of Saxe--
Weimar, where Kessler not only published his work but exhibited it in the
museum; he also introduced Craig to the great artist-architect-designer Henry
van de Velde and tried to interest him in the latter's plans for a new Weimar
theatre.[14] Outwardly a product of the style known as *Jugendstil,* or Art
Nouveau (of which Van de Velde was Europe's outstanding exponent), this
building would have had an elegant curved facade and a technically advanced
stage; it was to be run as a summer festival theatre by Gustave Lindemann and
his wife, the actress Louise Dumont. There were however also other centres of
the Jugendstil, notably Darmstadt, where the young architect Peter Behrens
was working for the Hesse court till 1903, and above all Munich, Berlin's main
cultural rival before the First World War. Behrens, too, held ideas very similar
to those of Appia and Craig, conceiving an ideal theatre which "would be a
holy shrine for all art"[15] with no barriers between stage and audience, no flies,
no proscenium arch, no element of illusion, but a thrust stage with the
audience seated in an amphitheatre: his intention was that the actors should
primarily be seen in relief. This was one of the principles taken up by his
friend the Munich theoretician Georg Fuchs, whose book *Die Schaubühne der
Zukunft (The Theatre of the Future)* was published in 1904, the year before
Craig's. Here, too, we find a reaction against the illusionist peep-show stage
and the notion of a stage space which would be "as favorable as possible to the
movements of human bodies."[16] What Fuchs's imagination saw, unlike Craig's
or Appia's, was a stage on three levels where perspective would be dispensed
with, and those bodies would be ranged flatly like the figures in Puvis de
Chavannes's frescoes or the Ravenna mosaics. As actually realized in the new
Munich Artists Theatre in 1907 by the theatre architect Max Littmann, it
consisted of a forestage, a main stage with an inner arch, and a shallow upper
stage with a panoramic backcloth on rollers. The same Littmann, who had
built the Berlin Schiller-Theater in 1905 as a second stage for the Prussian
Royal theatre, also designed the new Weimar National-Theater following the
court's rejection of the Dumont–Van de Velde scheme. Dumont and Lindemann thereupon moved to Düsseldorf, which they turned into a major
theatre center with their new Schauspielhaus and its acting school.

The ideal theatre as conceived in these remarkable imaginations was
never built, though Van de Velde continued nagging away at it, eventually
producing his low temporary building for the Cologne Werkbund exhibition
of 1914. This had a deep stage thrusting forward into the auditorium, as well
as a large built-in cyclorama, and was capable of being divided into two
smaller stages and a main central one to facilitate scene changes. But though
much more ambitious than the Jaques-Dalcroze theatre at Hellerau (which was

The painter as dramatist. Oskar Kokoschka's visualization of an episode in his short play *Murderer, Hope of Womankind*, for a temporary stage in the Gartenschau art exhibition in Vienna, 1907. Photo by Tom Willett.

designed by that garden city's architect Heinrich Tessenow) it seems a lot further from Appia's original vision. What mattered above all was that such radical ideas were now being circulated, and they ranged all the way down from Appia's "cathedral" and Behrens's "shrine" to the rough hessian costumes designed by Craig. Nowhere were they so eagerly received as in Germany, even though at first they found a warmer welcome in the southern half of the country than in Prussia; nor was there anywhere such a skilled band of leading stage technicians to make them practically feasible. In particular the possibility of a much freer handling of light and color was in the air.

Implications for the Playwright

We can find such concepts resumed in Hans Brandenburg's pamphlet of 1919 *Das Theater und das Neue Deutschland*, published by the Munich-based League for the New Theatre, that included Behrens, Fuchs, Dehmel, the dance teacher Rudolf von Laban, Osthaus of the Folkwang Museum, Bruno Taut the architect, and Gustav Wyneken the progressive educationist: in other words the cultural avant-garde of the 1900s. Written by a close associate of Laban's, it is a kind of revivalist manifesto arguing that theatre, like music and philosophy, is specially accessible to the German spirit *(Geist)* and that times of national humiliation (e.g., the Napoleonic wars and the defeat of 1918) are favorable to its resurgence. But already the new possibilities had begun to stimulate some of the more advanced playwrights, whose stage directions were reflecting this well before the established theatre started accepting their plays. Thus on the one hand we find those directions growing much shorter, with far less tediously elaborate details of the staging and the action—something that Craig always felt should be ignored by any self-respecting stage director. On the other we find such instructions as this, from the first scene of Reinhard Sorge's *Beggar* in its 1912 edition: "From somewhere above, the beam of a spotlight falls slantwise across the stage, showing the whores sitting gossiping on the low leather sofa."[17] Strindberg, too, wanted a "cone of light" for *The Dream Play* in 1907, though he was refused it as being too "music-hall," while in Kokoschka's *Murderer, Hope of Womankind,* (whose hastily compiled text was staged in the temporary theatre of the second 'Kunstschau' exhibition in Vienna in the summer of 1909), The Man is described thus: "White face, blue-armored, headband covering a wound, with the host of warriors, wild heads, grey and red headcloths, white, black and brown clothes."[18] Published in 1914, but written earlier, Georg Kaiser's *Burghers of Calais* likewise specifies a symbolic use of lighting in its last act.

There were artists with whom this new kind of visualization went even further, partly perhaps as a result of the revived interest in Goethe's color theories in his *Farbenlehre.* This work, which interested Schopenhauer as well as the secretary of the Weimar Nietzsche Archive, Rudolf Steiner, is made unique by its comprehensive association of specific colors with different feelings, its suggestion of color harmonies and discords analogous to those in music, and its whole opening up, from the point of view of an endlessly curious lover of the arts, of the idea of light not only as energy but as a vast and rewarding field for analysis. Some of its creative implications are to be seen in an extreme form in Wassily Kandinsky's *Yellow Sound* of 1909, the only one of his four such texts which was actually set to music (by his Russian friend Thomas Hartmann):

> Vague chords serve as a prelude. . . . On stage is deep blue twilight, which gradually grows darker. After some time, a small light appears center. A chorus is heard off stage, the bass voices gradually becoming distinct. A deep voice: "Stone-hard dreams . . . and speaking rocks. . . . Earth with riddles of fulfilling questions. . . . The sky's motion. . . ." Five shrilly yellow giants, with birdlike creatures flying around them; a man walking as in a dream downstage; small figures crossing over a hill. . . .[19]

At the end of this experimental line stood the notion of a transrational, entirely abstract synesthetic Gesamtkunstwerk in which all the component arts would be ordered by a higher creative principle, realized in practice by electric light.

Nor perhaps was it entirely chance that such a visionary approach should develop alongside the Utopian ideal of a mass theatre devoted to great communal celebrations. Even in its most political form the movement for a huge public theatre, like the Socialist iconography of the years around 1905, had its nonmaterialistic side as well as its propagandist concern with the education of the workers and its intention to capture (bourgeois) "art for the people." In a variety of such ways the German theatre was looking ahead and showing itself willing to break new ground—by modifying the conventions of its drama, for instance; developing new relations with its audience; and modernizing the structure and equipment of its playhouses. Meanwhile in Berlin at least the backwardness of the royal theatre and the rigid naturalism of Brahm still served as major obstacles to change, nor was there anything very Utopian about the actual choice of plays in the two rival branches of the Volksbühne. The synthesis only came with Max Reinhardt, whose peculiar achievement it was to take over the Deutsches Theater from Brahm, ransack every possible source for new gadgets and new ideas which might suit it, ensure that they worked, and, finally and most amazingly, make them pay. How he managed this we will see in the next chapter, after first going back to review his starting point as a young director in 1902.

The new generation. A group of Brahm's Deutsches Theater actors photographed at Salzburg in 1899, shortly before Max Reinhardt (here seen unsmiling in the centre, with his future wife Else Heims just below and to the right of him) broke away to form his own ensemble. Future members included are Richard Vallentin (second from left), Friedrich Kayssler (bare-headed, half hidden at the back) and Eduard von Winterstein (next to Kayssler, wearing straw hat). Photo by Ullstein Bilderdienst.

3

Reinhardt, the Bridge to the 1920s

One of the great problems for theatre historians is that it is so much easier to study those pioneers like Stanislavsky and Brecht, who tried to define their principles on paper, than those who, like Reinhardt, never bothered. "Particularly nowadays," said Reinhardt to a Norwegian audience in 1915, "I find that more is said *about* art than *through* art,"[1] and it is a sad indictment of our tendency to concentrate on the first type of statement that this great director's role in German—indeed in world—theatre should nowadays be so underrated. But try to feel yourself back into the European climate at the beginning of this century, and you find yourself standing on a crust of serious, frequently high-minded naturalism with a great field of new ideas like an untapped source of energy beneath it. From this in 1902 Reinhardt took off like a rocket, powered by the new fuel, which he knew how to use, yet carrying parts of the old surface with him, to reach a brilliant apex just before the war, then glide in circles down into the changed landing ground of the Weimar Republic. Never any kind of theoretician, he claimed to "approach the stage as an actor, not as a literary man. I view plays as an actor,"[2] but this often-quoted remark was doubtless made in order to stress his difference from his teacher Brahm. In fact he was quite a phenomenally able master of every aspect of theatre and a most careful analyst of the script before him. What he made of it was indeed a "total work of art," though one very remote from

Wagner's concept. For he reintroduced something that, true enough, is very dear to the actor; and that is the element of *play*.

Reinhardt's wish was for a theatre where audience and actors alike would enjoy themselves, partly as a relief from the gloomy social plays being performed at the Deutsches Theater and in the programs of both wings of the Volksbühne movement. "How did you come to change from acting to being a director?" an interviewer asked him later, to which he replied:

> It was really an accident. . . . It happened to be the heyday of Naturalism in the theatre. I was continually performing in tattered clothes covered with grime and filth. Evening after evening—this is God's truth—I was having to eat sour cabbage on stage. Just once in a while I wanted to act something less hideous and depressing.[3]

It was thus to let off steam that he and some young colleagues began performing irreverent parodies of the high drama, first at a café near the theatre, then as a sporadic cabaret under the name Schall und Rauch (Noise and Smoke)—a title borrowed from Goethe—and finally, when this proved successful, from autumn 1901 in a small theatre of their own. This was in a converted ballroom originally built by Peter Behrens for the Hotel Arnim on Unter den Linden (a wide Berlin street corresponding roughly to the Champs-Elysées in Paris). Decorated in jokey Jugendstil style, it was managed under Reinhardt's instructions by his friend Berthold Held, one such instruction being that the proscenium should be a parody of a Greek temple, with steps leading down into the audience. Reinhardt nominated a number of the actors to be engaged, including Rosa Bertens, Emmanuel Reicher, and Viktor Arnold as well as Friedrich Kayssler, his accomplice in the original group. He himself had to remain in the background until he had formally given notice to Brahm's company at the Deutsches Theater, something that he did not do until it became clear that the new enterprise would succeed.

From Cabaret to Revolving Stage

As a teenage student in Vienna Reinhardt had been introduced to that city's particular masterpieces of lighthearted, verbally and visually imaginative theatre: the nineteenth-century comedies of Raimund and Nestroy. Though these were always to be important ingredients in his artistic personality, they were less immediate, and much less accessible to the Berliners than the brand-new fashion for cabaret, which was even then being imported from France. There Le Chat noir had just shut its doors in Paris after nearly twenty years as the home of literary cabaret with its mixture of satire, insolent denunciation of the bourgeoisie, *misérabilisme*, sentimentalization of low life and Parisian (slum) nostalgia. Aristide Bruant, the greatest exponent of this genre, had retired. But in 1900 Otto Julius Bierbaum, a contributor to the Munich satirical paper *Simplicissimus* (whose publisher Albert Langen was Björnson's son-in-law and Ibsen's friend; such were the crosscurrents at this moment), published a set of *Deutsche Chansons* as material for a German version of the same thing. Written by a distinguished group of poets, many of the songs in this collection were used by the small cabarets which now began to spring up, starting with Ernst von Wolzogen's Berlin Überbrettl (a "superstage" on the analogy of Nietzsche's Superman) and the Munich Elf Scharfrichter ("eleven executioners," masked actors in black, with axes) who started performing in a traditional Munich inn on 12 April 1901.

Schall und Rauch thus came in at the beginning of a short-lived spate of highbrow light entertainment of a kind that had not been seen in Germany before. If Erik Satie had worked for a time at the Chat noir, Schönberg now wrote music for a number of the *Deutsche Chansons* (including Gustav Falke's "Nachtwandler" and verses by Wedekind and Bierbaum himself) and was also briefly and rather disastrously Wolzogen's accompanist. Poets of the caliber of Richard Dehmel, Arno Holz, and Rudolf Alexander Schröder contributed to the genre; Oskar Straus and Leo Fall composed songs; Christian Morgenstern parodied D'Annunzio for Wolzogen's first program. Admittedly the two first and best of these enterprises came to an end around 1903–4, but they had imitators who carried on—in the Munich Simpl under Kathi Kobus; in the Bad Boys (Böse Buben), Carl Meinhard and Rudolf Bernauer with the composer Leo Fall; and in Berlin under the composer Rudolf Nelson, who was to be a successful producer of revues in the 1920s. They also set the example for two later literary cabarets of a rather different kind, Kurt Hiller's Neopathetisches Cabaret of 1910, where the young Expressionist poets first read their works, and Hugo Ball's Cabaret Voltaire in Zurich in 1916, which was the origin of the dada movement.

More immediately they provided the first platform for a unique writer-performer who joined the Elf Scharfrichter for their initial eighteen months. This was Frank Wedekind, son of a German doctor in Turkey and an American mother, who had been brought up in Switzerland, worked in advertising and the circus, and arrived to live in Munich by his wits and talents in 1895. As a singer of his own ballads, Wedekind was clearly amazing: nasal, sharp, penetrating, he rolled his *r*'s and (in Heinrich Mann's words) "could hardly tolerate himself, let alone his audience."[4] This same "demonic" quality—a specifically German concept, meaning hypnotic, sinister, possessed—also underlay the plays which he had been writing for some years. Formally not all that unconventional, these were directed against conventional behavior and conventional inhibitions, particularly in sexual matters. But where *Spring Awakening*, the first of them, deals with the realities of youth in the 1890s (all except for its protoexpressionist last scene), in the two Lulu plays and *The Marquis of Keith* the characters move in a half-world of artists, impresarios, and charlatans whose social pretenses and position repeatedly turn out to be a sham. Like the black humor of which Wedekind was a pioneer (in songs like "Der Tantenmörder," or "Aunty's Killer") the menacing ambiguity of such dramas was not only highly theatrical but most apt for a comfortably expanding society that was uneasy about its future.

Following the first six months or so in the little Schall und Rauch theatre the literary skits and sketches (several of them by Reinhardt himself) started to give way to one-act plays, and in the summer of 1902 it was decided to turn

The author of the *Lulu* plays with two leading Reinhardt actors at a charity performance of his work in aid of the new Kleist Foundation in 1912. From right to left, Wedekind, Gertrud Eysoldt, Kayssler and the dramaturg Ludwig Levin. (This was the foundation that would later give its annual prize to such dramatists as Barlach, Brecht and Zuckmayer.) Photo by Cologne University Theatre Museum.

it into a regular theatre. It was at this point that Reinhardt met his new dramaturg Arthur Kahane in a Vienna café and talked to him at length about his ideas, a conversation set down by Kahane in his memoirs more than twenty years later and sometimes misleadingly presented as a formal statement of 1901. "What I have in mind," this begins, "is a theatre that gives people pleasure once more. That transports them from the grey gloom of their daily life into a pure and cheerful atmosphere of beauty."[5] Such a theatre would not deny Naturalism but would develop it further, "beyond the stink of the poor and the problems of our society," for "the theatre has only one purpose: theatre. And I believe in a theatre that belongs to the actor."[6] For his sake, then, this theatre should maintain some features of the commedia dell' arte, particularly the chance to improvise. Moreover "nobody is an actor till he's proved that he can play Shakespeare": "I want to play *Shakespeare*, and am absolutely sure this is right. . . . The classic authors must be performed freshly; they must be performed as if they were writing today, as if their works were present-day life."[7] In Kahane's recollection Reinhardt goes on to describe his intention to have two theatres close to one another, a big one for the classics and a more intimate house where "a small ensemble of the best actors" would perform modern "chamber plays," like the Rosé Quartet—which was made up of the four leaders of the Vienna Philharmonic Orchestra—playing in the small hall of the lovely Vienna Musikvereinssaal. Probably he did already have both kinds of theatre in his sights, though at the moment he only controlled the second. But according to Kahane he was also speaking even then of a huge festival theatre like a Greek amphitheatre, a "house of light and dedication" with no curtain, perhaps even no sets, just the active confrontation of the actor and his text with the vast popular audience.

The "highest art of our time,"[8] Reinhardt is supposed to have said, was that of Tolstoy, following whom he named Strindberg, Hamsun, Maeterlinck, Wilde, Wedekind, and Hofmannsthal as leading deviants from Naturalism. Six out of these seven were indeed performed in his first two seasons, though Hamsun was not played for several years, by which time Shaw and Schnitzler were both well established in Reinhardt's repertoire. Letters to Held during the summer holidays show the young impresario busy reading scripts and planning to stage Wilde's *Salomé,* along with something by Hermann Bahr and Wedekind's new play *King Nicolo,* a light work involving a good deal of masquerading and a fairground scene. The stage itself was to be further transformed by changing the proportions of the proscenium opening and reducing to a minimum the use of painted flats, which "give the thing a flimsy, improvised air better suited to the previous year."[9] Three outside technicians had been approached for advice, particularly one of the Brandts (an outstanding dynasty of stage engineers who had dominated the German opera scene since the midnineteenth century). Gustav Knina was evidently expected, and possibly a lighting man from Budapest. "We must keep our eyes open for first-rate technical staff," Reinhardt added, meantime recommending Polonius's principle of "Give every man thine ear but few thy voice: Take each man's censure, but reserve thy judgement." Despite this directorial reserve, good public relations demanded that manufacturers and others should be told of the new theatre's aims, for "if all goes according to plan the result will be something out of the ordinary whose novelty and peculiarity will cause quite a stir."[10]

Thus modernized, the former cabaret stage reopened on 19 August 1902 as the Kleines Theater, the Little Theatre, and as soon as the relevant police license came through, began staging full-length plays. Among these, three were immediately significant: the single performance of *Salomé,* Reinhardt's first production as a director, with the young Gertrud Eysoldt and an imaginative use of spotlights—a play then restricted by the censorship but soon to be taken into the repertoire; then Wedekind's *Earth Spirit,* first of the Lulu plays whose production led Kayssler to tell the dramatist (on a postcard): "Do you know what you did tonight? You slew the Naturalist dragon of 'truth to life,' and brought the element of *play* to the stage. Long may you live!"[11] Finally on 23 January 1903 came the great success, the first German production of Maxim Gorky's Naturalist masterpiece *The Lower Depths,* directed by the actor Richard Vallentin with Reinhardt playing Luka. This ran eventually for five hundred performances, and its evident possibilities encouraged Reinhardt to inaugurate the proposed larger theatre in midseason. Negotiations for establishing the Theater am Schifferbauerdamm seem already to have been under way, and even before the Kleines Theater opened the owner's sister had been keen for it to be leased to Reinhardt. Accordingly he was able to take it over as his second—or in point of size, first—theatre on 13 February, renaming the nine-hundred seat building the Neues Theater, or New Theatre. Its

Eysoldt, Reinhardt's first Lulu, seen as Nastya in his crucial success at the Kleines Theater, the 1903 production of Gorky's *The Lower Depths*. This was directed by Richard Vallentin, who named his son Max to commemorate it. Photo by Cologne University Theatre Museum.

opening productions were of conventional enough plays by Thoma, Anzengruber, and the quite forgotten Felix Dörmann; then on 3 April came the second of Reinhardt's own productions, Maeterlinck's symbolist essay in medievalism, *Pelléas et Mélisande,* originally written in 1892 but best known to us through Debussy's opera of ten years later. Meanwhile *The Lower Depths* ran on, filling the till while requests for guest performances, whether abroad or in the German provinces, began to come in.

   For two more seasons Reinhardt operated the two theatres in tandem, establishing his methods and gathering the nucleus of his team. This included Held and his own younger brother Edmund as administrators, Kahane and Felix Holländer as dramaturgs, and Eysoldt, Bertens, Reicher, Arnold, Kayssler as the core of a brilliant ensemble. His repertoire meanwhile continued to expand on the eclectic lines already indicated, till by the autumn of 1905 it ranged from Tolstoy's *Fruits of Enlightenment* (1869) and Strindberg's *Miss Julie* via Wilde, Shaw, and Schnitzler to German classics like *Minna von Barnhelm* and *Kabale und Liebe,* and finally on to the *Medea* and Hofmannsthal's *Elektra* (both this and *Salomé* being made into operas by Richard Strauss, in 1909 and 1905 respectively). What really made Reinhardt's reputation, however, was the first of his Shakespeare productions, *A Midsummer Night's Dream*, in the Neues Theater on 31 January 1905. Here the novelty in his interpretation lay in the fact that, while taking its approach from the Mendelssohn music, it centered on a naturalistic conception of the forest, into which Puck and the fairies—or elves, as the German version called them—fitted as natural denizens, brown, leafy, blown hither and thither, rather than as an intrusive corps de ballet in conventional tutus. Yet neither this nor the contrasting low- and high-life scenes—the hut full of comic artisans or the baroque palace with its grandees (and fifty-four assorted retainers)—made so profound an impression as the director's inspired use of the new stage technology: Knina's solidly built forest, the realistic grass, and above all the twists and turns of the new revolving stage.

The revolve had been installed in the Neues Theater following the end of the first full season, and Reinhardt's evident intention was that it should be kept under wraps, then used immediately for the opening productions of Ibsen's *Pretenders* and *The Merry Wives of Windsor*.[12] Along with it there was to be a well-lit "Fortuny cupola" (or cyclorama) for the sky; "those damned soffits must be got rid of once and for all." A big lift should be installed upstage and an orchestra pit put partly under the stage; stage trolleys, too, he saw as very important. Above all there must be more light, even if the electricity supply had to be adapted to take the increased load; new spots (from gallery and orchestra pit), more banks of lights, extra footlights, and so on. It is very clear that Reinhardt knew what he wanted to do with these greatly improved technical reserves, and he asked for a fair-sized model of the new turntable "with all that goes with it" to be made so that he could put it on his circular office table. Clearly he was not monopolistic about such techniques, and the revolve might equally well have been unveiled in *The Pretenders* or used by Vallentin for *The Merry Wives of Windsor*. But it was Reinhardt who was most eager to use it and had worked out how to do so (as reference to his 'production book' will show). So history, like the Berlin public at the time, rightly associates the entertainingly visible flexibility of the new staging with the first of Reinhardt's many productions of *A Midsummer Night's Dream*.[13]

Great Years of the Deutsches Theater

Shakespeare's perennially wonderful work proved to be crucial. For the 1905 production helped decide L'Arronge, despite Reinhardt's youth (he was then thirty-one) and the competition of other applicants, to accept him as the next lessee of the Deutsches Theater in succession to Brahm. Within months Max and his brother Edmund had raised the money to buy L'Arronge out, and from then on he was in charge of the privately financed theatre that Brahm had already made outstanding in the German-speaking world. To begin with he presented much the same sort of program as he had been giving at the Neues Theater: that is to say he opened with Kleist's *Kätchen von Heilbronn*, followed by his own production of *The Merchant of Venice* (again exploiting the revolve); a triple bill which included Synge's *Well of the Saints;* then Hofmannstahl's *Oedipus and the Sphinx*, followed at the end of April by *Tartuffe*. Forced by the terms of his license to give up one of his three theatres, he released the Kleines Theater to Victor Barnowsky while carrying on at the

Tilla Durieux as Oberon in Reinhardt's original *Midsummer Night's Dream* in 1905. Her first husband, the art dealer Paul Cassirer, had her painted by Renoir and published the magazine *Theater.* Her second husband would later be Erwin Piscator's main backer. Photo by Ullstein Bilderdienst.

somewhat closer Neues Theater (Schiffbauerdamm) with a program that included Shaw's *Caesar and Cleopatra* and closed with a piece of pure froth directed by himself, Offenbach's operetta *Orpheus in the Underworld.* But two largish theatres were still too much for him, and within a year he had got rid of the Neues Theater in favor of the new Kammerspiele (or Chamber Theatre, on the analogy of chamber music), which he was able to set up in the former dance hall next the Deutsches Theater; it is still there in East Berlin today. This two-hundred seat house, with just three steps between stage and audience, was originally to have been built by Henry van de Velde, but for unknown reasons the plan fell through. It opened on 8 November 1906 with Ibsen's *Ghosts* (with Kayssler, Agnes Sorma, and Reinhardt's great discovery, the Montenegrin actor Alexander Moissi), initiating a season that included *Spring Awakening* (which ran for 321 performances), *Man and Superman,* two more Ibsens, another Maeterlinck, and a revival of Hauptmann's rather tedious *Friedensfest.* Together these two adjoining theatres in the Schumannstrasse were to be the backbone of Reinhardt's Berlin undertakings for the next quarter of a century.

Quality, variety, timing are three cardinal theatrical virtues, but it is never easy to say exactly how they are achieved, and as a result Reinhardt's genius at this crucial point is hard to pin down. First of all there was his ability to see things as a whole, whether he was considering an entire production or the interpretation of a particular part: it was no longer to be a sum of naturalistic details. This began normally in his holidays when he would sit down with the play and compile a very full *Regiebuch* or "production book" covering every aspect. Here, for instance, is the first scene of act four of the *Dream*, as visualized for the 1905 production:

> The moon slowly vanishes, and black gauzes come down obscuring the set. (The stage rotates.) The interior of the hillock comes downstage. It portrays a bower completely lined with flowers and foliage. We begin to see the full length of a bed of flowers on which Bottom and Titania are reposing. Two little elves stand on duty at its head carrying glow-worms as lights. B and T are covered with a blanket of roses. The black gauze is raised, and through the second gauze we see the whole picture in a magic twilight. Two more elves, kneeling at the foot of the bed, remove the blanket. Titania and Bottom get up and walk out of the bower left. A procession forms: first the horseman, then four elves bearing lights, then Bottom and Titania, followed by three more elves. The procession moves slowly through the wood. The stage rotates back to its previous position (the scene before).
> Bottom seats himself against the treetrunk to left of the lakeside path. Titania settles beside him. The elves sprawl on their tummies in the grass facing the two lovers, and hum.
> Bottom gets up, Titania takes his arm. They walk round the clearing.
> Bottom casually picks a blade of grass and eats it. Searches in the grass, picks another blade and eats that.
> Bottom seats himself as before, yawns audibly.
> The elves softly leave. First light of dawn.[14]

The whole process, as described by him in an undated note, would start with one or more readings of the text. "Sometimes it takes off at once. . . . Visual images come pell-mell. Sometimes one has to read it a number of times before seeing a way." Then he would begin mentally casting the main parts and making the necessary compromises between actor and play; "never an exact fit." Finally "a complete vision, both optically and aurally":

> You see every gesture, every move, every piece of furniture, the light; you hear every cadence, every crescendo, the musicality of the phrasing, the pauses, the changes of tempo. You feel every inner impulse, realise how it is to be hidden and when it should be revealed; you hear each gulp, each breath. The way the partner listens, every noise on and off the stage. The effect of the lighting. And then you write it all down.[15]

All this without knowing exactly why. The reasons for everything would emerge later.

Next came his work with the actors. His great gift here was his ability not only to help the actor to a similarly complete view of his part, but to give him/ her a sense of security—an awareness that the director knew exactly what he wanted and was confident of the actor's ability to provide it. By all accounts he had great patience, could appreciate the most varied talents, knew how to use the ideas and emotions that surfaced in rehearsal, and could *show* the actor how best to solve a given problem in terms of his, the actor's, particular capacities. This combination of understanding and communication was a major reason for the willingness of so many fine players to work in his ensemble, often in secondary or minor parts. Other attractions were the sense of variety created by his practice of casting against type, his double casting of the main parts in certain plays (so that a totally different pair of actors might take the same part on alternate nights) and of course the very eclectic nature of the repertoire, which continued to range from Greek tragedy to nineteenth-century operetta. About the speaking of the text, too, he had new ideas, for while he loved beautiful voices he saw the sudden pause as "the most important thing in speaking," so that he could call for "complete dissolution of punctuation. Comma: undramatic, academic, bookish. What *is* dramatic is a full stop in the middle of a sentence."[16] Add to all this his concern with the whole psychology of the actor and the character portrayed, and we can understand the verdict of Bernhard Reich, who felt that while Brahm at the Lessing-Theater was still perfecting methods initiated before 1900, "a new century of acting began with Reinhardt."[17]

An acting school was set up at the Deutsches Theater under Berthold Held's direction; among other memorable figures of the Weimar theatre it trained Kortner, Granach, Salka Viertel, and the Communist director Hans Rodenberg. From 1904 too there was a review called *Theater* published by Paul Cassirer at Reinhardt's instigation, with the poet/translator Christian Morgenstern as its editor. For this Reinhardt wanted contributions from Appia (whom he had evidently not yet read), Richard Strauss, Otto Wagner the Vienna architect, artists like Corinth and Ludwig von Hofmann, and a number of playwrights headed by Strindberg. Shortly before the Deutsches Theater opened he went to see Craig in his Berlin studio, "to get a few ideas"[18] as Craig put it; other reports say that he tried hard to get Craig to design him a production—on five different occasions, according to Carl Niessen. Up to the spring of 1906 however he made use primarily of the new German artists and sculptors: Corinth for *Salomé,* Karl Walser for *The Pretenders,* the sculptor Max Kruse for *Elektra,* Slevogt for *The Merry Wives of Windsor,* Leo Impekoven for *Pelléas et Mélisande,* all this culminating in the opening of the Kammerspiele with *Ghosts* designed by the Norwegian proto-Expressionist Edvard Munch, at that time based at Weimar under Kessler's patronage. Thereafter Reinhardt turned more to the designers or even the technicians (as with Gustav Knina for *A Midsummer Night's Dream*), finally finding in the Rumanian-born Ernst Stern a highly versatile draftsman and decorator with whom he could collaborate on a production from start to finish. Stern had made lightning sketches for the Elf Scharfrichter, and began his work for Reinhardt with Offenbach's *Orpheus in the Underworld* at the Neues Theater on 13 May 1906. Similarly with his other artistic partners, who, Hofmannsthal apart, tended to become subordinate figures without much independent status or repute: Einar Nilson the composer, for instance, or the writer Karl Vollmoeller, who made the adaptations of the *Oresteia* and Gozzi's *Turandot* and scripted that masterpiece of high kitsch *The Miracle.*

"On the artistic side," wrote Reinhardt to Held six weeks before opening at the Deutsches Theater, "a lot depends on luck, but technically we have got to be absolutely secure by the time the season starts, and we cannot admit any obstacles in this respect!!"[19]

There are two aspects to Reinhardt as a master of stage technology, and they show him as fully comparable with Piscator after him. The first was his seemingly tireless attention to detail, including such matters as the backstage lavatories, the beating of the carpets, and the washing of the floor. Nothing was too small for him to notice and pass on to his aides for action. The other was his gift for relating the most mundane technicalities to his idea of the eventual production; he truly did treat the theatre apparatus like a musician his instrument, and he used it to full effect. Not only were his technical directors inventive—Knina, for instance, devising a powerful but flexible new system of lighting for the cyclorama and patenting a method of lifting and tilting a great part of the revolve, while Franz Dworsky seems to have been the first to use inflatables as part of the set—but he, too, could suggest similar innovations: proposing, for instance, as early as 1905 a mobile cyclorama that could be wheeled clean out of the theatre.[20] The results could be seen in the new tempo given to the plays of Shakespeare, the staging of works by Maeterlinck, "which all other theatres were sure could not be materialised;"[21] finally, on 11 February 1911, the solution of that most intractable of problems, the second part of Goethe's *Faust*. No wonder the rising generation of playwrights felt free to pose new demands.

Reinhardt of course worked under very different conditions from those obtaining today. In those days a play with thirty or more characters could make money in a two-hundred seat theatre; moreover, in all his published correspondence before 1918 there is no reference to any kind of trade union. Even so it is not easy for the modern reader to realize that he ran his entire operation without any sort of subsidy. It is true that he had private backers, both individual and collective, but they wanted interest on their money and had nothing to gain (in the way of publicity, tax benefits, or other modern incentives) by losing it. Quite simply he had to make art pay. This he managed by various means: for a start by charging high seat prices and paying his actors what Reich later said were the lowest wages of any German theatre. From tours, too, the actors got no extra benefit; the fees all went to the Reinhardts and were a valuable source of theatre income. He was lucky in that the German audience saw the classics as part of Bildung, the necessary equipment of any completely formed citizen, but he was, as Reich also says, perhaps the first such manager to see that these same classics could be made positively profitable, by presenting them in new forms and in readings that related to the modern world. This final integration of the artistic and technical aspects of the theatre with its basic economics was due in part to Max Reinhardt's having a business manager with whom he was on the closest terms, his younger brother Edmund, who remained in that capacity till his death in 1929; "the real head of the theatre," Alexander Granach called him.[22] Certainly the elder Reinhardt made compromises, and Stanislavsky was among those who criticized him for them; certainly, too, he became personally rich. But if his reconciliation of art and economics often seemed an

Reinhardt masters the arena stage. His staging of Karl Vollmoeller's mime *The Miracle*, here seen in London at the Olympia exhibition hall in winter 1911–12. Photo by Ullstein Bilderdienst.

awkward balancing act, it was none the less brilliantly performed. Never has it been done better than in his new company's greatest years.

Reinhardt Looks Outward

Such were the varied talents and interests of the man who took the Deutsches Theater to its peak of fame before the First World War, setting the standards against which German theatre was to be measured till Hitler made unpersons of him and many of his colleagues. Into this he threw his driving energy, himself directing something like a play a month during the first two or three years. In the repertoire itself there was no great change; it simply expanded along the lines already set, that is to say, primarily Shakespeare and the German classics; the Scandinavian and German naturalists; Nestroy, Aristophanes, and Goldoni for light relief; and finally modern plays by such as Wedekind, Shaw, Schnitzler, and Hofmannsthal. The acting talent expanded to match, Alexander Moissi, for instance, developing from his raw, awkward beginnings to become one of the chief box office draws, while Tilla Durieux, Paul Wegener, Rudolf Schildkraut, and Werner Krauss joined the earlier nucleus, with Albert Bassermann, too, coming over from the Lessing-Theater and Kainz himself appearing as a guest in 1909. Soon it was performers such as these, and the chance to compare and discuss them, that excited the audience rather than any further technical innovations. And because the company was increasingly in demand for tours and guest seasons—Budapest and the Munich summer festival in 1909, Vienna in 1910—the management started picking out those productions which looked most like succeeding there, sometimes against expectation. So the pseudo-oriental mime piece *Sumurûn* by the otherwise obscure Friedrich Freksa and the light composer Victor Hollaender, after an insignificant start in the Kammerspiele, became one of Reinhardt's greatest hits, playing in the London Coliseum and subsequently at the Casino Theatre in New York. Its massive earnings are supposed to have enabled Reinhardt to pay back all his backers' investment.

Around the same time he appears to have been losing some of his enthusiasm for the Kammerspiele concept in favor of those ideas of mass theatre which were now very much in the air. As he told an interviewer later, he had designed his little chamber theatre in 1905 for an élite who would form the ideal audience in close communion with the play; even the critics were to be excluded. This could be achieved so long as it was an invited audience perhaps, but the wealthy Berliners who came later were not what Reinhardt had had in mind. So instead he decided that "the best audience for an actor is the big audience, the broad emotional mass,"[23] or, as he put it a quarter of a century later, that "the audience's quality rises with its quantity."[24] Though he may well have had this ideal before him all along as Kahane suggested, it was only in the summer of 1910 that he decided to try to stage *Oedipus Rex* in the three-thousand-seat Munich Musikhalle; and having done so, ran it for a month in Schumann's forty-five-hundred-seat circus in Berlin (for an estimated profit of 270,000 marks),[25] more or less repeating the experiment with the *Oresteia* the following year. Meanwhile the *Oedipus* production, extras and all, went on to play in similar spaces in Moscow, St. Petersburg, and other foreign cities.

This first assault on the mass audience culminated in the London premiere of *The Miracle*, produced by the showman C. B. Cochran and mimed to the music of Engelbert Humperdinck (the one who lived from 1854–1921 and has been described by Nicholas Slonimski as a "composer of fairy operas in an infantilized Wagnerian idiom").[26] Its production took place on Christmas Eve, 1911, at Olympia, another home of the circus, which could seat around ten-thousand people. With one thousand extras, five hundred chorus, and an orchestra of two hundred (so the reports say) it ran for over a month. Subsequently it played in Vienna and many German cities, then later toured the United States with Lady Diana Cooper—no actress, but a famous and always newsworthy beauty who figured in such episodes as these:

24. The face of the Nun becomes distorted in speechless horror. She stands up suddenly with shaking knees in order to protect her child with pleading gestures.
25. The figures remain immovable.

26. In wild terror, the Nun lifts the child wrapped in rags out of the crib, presses it passionately to her and flees as if pursued by the furies
27. A nuns' choir sings fervently.[27]

This was the production that made Reinhardt's name internationally known, to be mentioned in the same chic breath as that of Diaghilev. In 1924 it ran for almost three hundred performances in New York, and the ensuing American tour lasted five years.

Though the Reinhardts were always very secretive about their accounts, there seems little reason to suppose that it was simple economic necessity that drove them in search of such huge audiences. Certainly the more permanent arrangements which they started planning in 1914 would have meant an enormous capital outlay both in Berlin and in Salzburg, where Reinhardt was already proposing to establish a festival. For in order to create his already publicized "theatre of five thousand" in Berlin, he arranged in February of that year to buy the circus building from the Schumanns. This lay just off the Friedrichstrasse next to his former Neues Theater, and the price was expected to be around a million marks. The outbreak of war that summer, however, led all building operations to be postponed, so that the actual purchase only took place some six months before the 1918 armistice, by which time Reinhardt appears to have envisaged it as a German National Theatre (such being the name under which he bought it). Its realization as the Grosses Schauspielhaus belongs in the next chapter.

At the same time, however, he was winning the support of the Austrian emperor for an even more ambitious scheme. This would have meant the construction of a three- to four-thousand-seat theatre, linked by colonnades to a small theatre for intimate operas and a full-time "High School for Theatre Art," all to be built in the grounds of the old episcopal summer residence at Hellbrunn outside Salzburg—in itself a magical place. Both projects involved the same architect, the quasi Expressionist Hans Poelzig, whose designs at that time had something of the ectoplasmic quality that might be expected from giant jelly molds.[28] Perhaps fortunately, only that in Berlin materialized, and the eventual Salzburg Festival—launched in 1920 by Reinhardt, Hofmannsthal, and Richard Strauss—was confined to the center of the town and a more modest scale.

By any normal standards Reinhardt should have been somewhat distracted from the Deutsches Theater proper by such plans to "create the possibility of attracting broad circles of the population who at present are excluded from the theatre by economic considerations." Nor should it be forgotten that he was already catering for Volksbühne members and actually ran that organization's new Berlin theatre from 1914 to 1917–18 with a program incorporating, beside the expected classic and Naturalist items, others whose titles have a more patriotic ring: Reicke's *Blutopfer (Blood Sacrifice)*, Emil Gött's *Edelwild (Noble Game)*, Schmidtbonn's *Volk in Not (People in Need)*. Moreover, he himself directed eleven of the twenty-seven productions mounted there, featuring such new actors as Conrad Veidt, Emil Jannings, and Ernst Lubitsch. And yet it was just in the years around 1912 to 1917 that the Deutsches Theater made its most considered attack on the theatre repertoire, devoting substantial parts of several seasons to establishing the claims of

Wedekind, some of the less-known German classics, and Strindberg as dramatists who could never in future be ignored. So four plays by Wedekind were given successively in the summer of 1912; *Danton's Death* and Lenz's *Soldiers* were part of a series of "German Plays" in 1916; while the touring of Strindberg's *Dance of Death* and *Ghost Sonata* to Sweden gave that playwright a measure of overdue honor in his own country. Just before the war, too, there was a Shakespeare cycle of ten plays, which occupied the whole of the first half of 1914; nor did the war stop Reinhardt's theatre from playing the great "enemy" playwright both at home and on its tours to neutral countries. Finally from the end of 1917 to May 1919 came the series of new German plays, many of them Expressionist, under the general title of "Young Germany."

Reinhardt has before now been criticized for neglecting the plays of this new movement, which was already important in poetry and painting and would for a few years come to dominate the new republican theatre. And it is true that he was not keen on such works; indeed he took a poor view of "literature" generally and seems only to have enjoyed the company of writers when, like Hofmannsthal or Noel Coward, they had proved acceptable in high society. However, while the earliest Expressionist productions were due to progressive provincial theatres, even these were late off the mark, and the Young Germany series was not more than a year or two behind them. Thus of Georg Kaiser's plays *The Burghers of Calais* was published in 1914 (when he was already thirty-six) and performed at Frankfurt in January 1917; *From Morn to Midnight* was published in 1912 and performed at Falkenberg's newly opened Kammerspiele in Munich in April 1917; Walter Hasenclever's *Son* was written in 1913, then staged in Prague and Dresden in 1916; Ernst Barlach's *Dead Day,* started in 1907, was published in 1912 and first staged in Leipzig in 1919. This unusual time lag put the realization of theatrical Expressionism some five or six years behind the earliest public readings by the poets in the Neopathetisches Cabaret in Berlin. Admittedly a number of such productions— including the Young Germany series—were on a club basis, and it was only once the censorship was swept away by the Revolution that the new plays could become accessible to the general public. But at least Reinhardt and his dramaturgs made a systematic attempt to introduce the movement, and although one or two of their productions (like that of Reinhard Goering's verse play *Seeschlacht,* or *Naval Encounter*) were staged in an inappropriately naturalistic way, nevertheless Ernst Stern's designs for Sorge's *Beggar* and for Else Lasker-Schüler's *The Wupper* were a clever pastiche of expressionist angularity and distortion. Moreover, not only had the Deutsches Theater paved the way for Expressionism by its Wedekind and Strindberg productions; from 1911 to 1914 it had also staged four of the most characteristic plays of Carl Sternheim, whose terse dialogue and subversive sense of comedy make him count as one of the movement's pioneers.

Escaping from the Times

Despite all this there was a growing feeling already before the war that the Reinhardt theatres had passed their peak, that there was something unprincipled about their hedonism, and that his whole operation had got too big. The semblance of a star system was beginning to make itself felt; once a premiere was past the outstanding players would too often be replaced by less interesting performers. There were rather too many tours for the maintenance of the highest standards, while for a critical young actor like Kortner, just making his way out of the ranks of the extras, the intrusion of middlebrow kitsch started to jar. Thus the watered-down religiosity of Hofmannsthal's *Everyman* seemed unacceptable; likewise *Sumurûn* and *The Miracle* "made me throw up."[29] Though rehearsals with Reinhardt remained fascinating, Kortner was by no means the only new recruit to find his lieutenants uncongenial, and in the postwar years the very brilliance of the productions became distracting. "This liberating revolutionary play," said Kortner of the Vienna production of Schiller's *Kabale und Liebe*, "was neutralized by too much baroque."[30] Similarly in *The Merchant of Venice*, one of Reinhardt's showpieces, "all the characters were enchanting, jolly, overweening, in love, charming, melancholic. I could see no reason for finding any of them much better or much worse than the others."[31]

Looking back at what evidence we still have, there does sometimes seem to be a fatal cuteness, as in the fairy episodes of *A Midsummer Night's Dream*, and it too easily took the form of a prettied-up baroque. The humor, too, clearly could be strained; photographs show the stock comic actors like Wassmann, Diegelmann, and Hermann Thimig apparently working their guts out to be funny. The relaxed attitude of the great comics was lacking.

Whether any of this would have mattered if the new postwar projects had gone as planned, it is impossible to say. But the mass theatre was not a success, as we shall see; the growth of the cinema proved distracting and in Reinhardt's view demoralizing to his actors; moreover, the level of entertainment tax seemed to him unjust. It is also true that after 1918 the Deutsches Theater was no longer the only theatre worth going to for the smart Berliner; and although it still recruited amazing new talent (ranging from John Heartfield the designer to Elisabeth Bergner, the Austrian actress), new directors and new theatres suddenly began coming up and were better able to excite a republican audience. In the event Reinhardt largely withdrew from Germany in 1920, leaving his Berlin theatres to be managed for the next nine years by (successively) Felix Holländer, Karl Rosen, and Robert Klein. He himself went off to Austria to get the Salzburg Festival started—the first international music festival of the modern kind, and one that certainly appealed less to the broad masses than to the cosmopolitan new rich—then to set up two new theatres in beautiful rococo spaces in Socialist Vienna. The first of these, the old imperial ballroom in the Hofburg, saw what some consider to have been his finest production, Goethe's early play *Stella,* with William Dieterle and Helene Thimig. But his hope of heading the Burgtheater was never fulfilled, and instead he took over the Theater in der Josefstadt, which he opened in 1924 with a program of Schiller, Goldoni, Hofmannsthal, and Strindberg, and carried on with light comedy and international successes till the Nazis annexed Austria in 1938. Occasionally he directed a production in Berlin, then in 1929 he briefly returned to the helm there and saw his theatres through the worst of the economic crisis, before handing them over once more when the Republic was about to fall. Later, as we shall see, he moved to the United States, where he died before the end of the Second World War.

What Reinhardt did for the German theatre has never been repeated. By imagination—artistic, technical, financial—and obsessive dedication to quality he made it one of the wonders of the pre-1914 world. Nothing that it achieved afterward escaped his influence; those players, directors, writers, and designers who had not been through his organization found themselves inspired by it or measured against it, and with the emigration of the 1930s his touch stretched to the London and New York theatres and on to Hollywood. But as Kortner put it in his memoirs, prior to the outbreak of the First World War "we were lulled by a sense of security that is nowadays unbelievable," and certainly this was true of Reinhardt himself:

> But once the loss of the world war led to a complete collapse which seemed to tear people up by the roots, leading them to expose their innermost selves and develop new perspectives, both political and philosophical, then Reinhardt could no longer sense the ground on which he stood. . . ."[32]

With the new postwar Austrian nostalgia, the overexploitation of Mozart, "the cheerful and pious genius of Salzburg" as Reinhardt termed him,[33] and the odd touch of showbiz religiosity, he was really doing something else: *acting* a security that no longer existed. Perhaps he had begun doing so even before the war.

All the same one cannot feel anything but admiration for a production like *Jahrmarktsfest zu Plundersweilern* (or, *At Plundersweilern Fair*), which he staged in the Deutsches Theater with a cast including Ernst Lubitsch, Else Eckersberg and Werner Krauss.[34] For who would have thought of making a play of this slight sketch, which the twenty-four-year old Goethe wrote in nine pages of irregular rhyming couplets? It is pure theatre of the kind which Reinhardt could brew up just as much to amuse his actors (and himself) as for any other reason. Here a kind of ringmaster stands by his traveling theatre talking to the local doctor as his clown potters around, then the doctor is summoned to the main fair, and as he walks through the crowds—peasants, children, musicians—the revolve turns to show the town square with the market in full swing and hucksters offering their wares: a Nuremberger selling toys, a Tirolese milliner, two disgruntled gypsies with nothing to sell. Others do their turns; a dancer, a Harlequin, a sweep's boy from Savoie who sings, a ballad (or Moritat) singer with a morally instructive picture to sing about, then the clown selling patent medicines. At that the ringmaster announces that the theatre is about to start, the crowd throngs round, the revolve turns back again, and the little curtain goes up on a puppet show, where the story of Esther and Ahasuerus is acted by live puppets moved by strings. In the interval the ringmaster brings out more medicines and ointments to sell. Then in scene 2 the villain is hanged and Esther exits, reciting:

> My husband must have fallen asleep—
> Sooner be lying with your sheep.

> Whatever comes he'll see it through.
> If you've no sheep a pig will do.

By then darkness has fallen; slowly the crowd wanders home with candles and lanterns; in a distant alleyway harlequin and dancer embrace. Finally a shadow-play man with his hurdy-gurdy and silhouettes narrates the tale of the Creation in seventeenth-century style to the refrain "Orgelum, orgeley." He finishes with the appearance of the pagan god Mercury to put things straight after the Flood, and the last of the party breaks up:

> DOCTOR: Well then, we should be all right.
> UNMARRIED LADY: I take my leave.
> MAGISTRATE: But you'll be back tomorrow night?
> GOVERNESS: I'd say once is quite enough.
> DOCTOR: Every day there's something tough.
> SHADOW-PLAY MAN: Orgelum, orgeley
>   Dudeldumdey.

Here, surely, is not just another ingratiating Reinhardt rococoction but a pointer to the carnival scene in Brecht's *Galileo*. Only, instead of bringing us to the height of the spectacle and the disclosure of a crucial point, Reinhardt and Goethe end on an old story and a dying fall. And rightly so, for this performance took place on 21 May 1915, some nine months after the invading German armies had swept into France.

PART II

Stages of a Republican Theatre

Expressionism comes to Berlin's 'theatre for the people.' Paul Legband's production of *Gas* by Georg Kaiser, with sets by Karl Jakob Hirsch and a large cast including E. Stahl-Nachbaur as the Millionaire's Son and Rudolf Lettinger as the Engineer. Photo by Cologne University Theatre Museum.

4

Revolution and the Establishment of Expressionism

Theatre as Release and Renewal

If the Republic itself was the product of the First World War—and of Germany's defeat in that war—so, too, was its theatre. Looking back thirty years later, Herbert Jhering wrote of his beginnings as a Berlin critic in 1918:

> The theatre only needed to be relieved of the pressures of war, and plays and productions came sizzling out of it. Everything that had been accumulating in the censor's cupboard now shot up like a cloud of steam when the valve is opened."[1]

Similarly the English writer Huntly Carter—Britain's best contemporary commentator on the European theatrical avant-garde of those days—was amazed by

> the extraordinary vitality of the German theatre, and its astonishing achievement in placing before the public a spiritual interpretation of each crisis as it arose and in experimenting with new species of plays and new forms of technique, especially stagecraft. Looking at England and France we saw two countries making merry over victory, and leaving their spiritual institutions, including the theatre, to look after themselves. In Germany we saw a vanquished nation, stricken to the heart, using the theatre as a powerful instrument of refinement, and an unerring guide to the way out of the terrible chaos.[2]

Though the new German theatre was not to be all that unerring a guide, as we can now see, many writers and directors in those days were dedicated to making it one, on lines laid down by the author who was to continue dominating its classical repertoire as he had already done that of the Volksbühne. For it was Friedrich Schiller who in a famous lecture of 1784 had discussed theatre's function "as a moral institution," claiming that the stage was

> the common channel which allows the light of wisdom to emanate from the better, more thoughtful elements of the people and fan out in gentler beams so as to permeate the whole state. More accurate concepts, clarified principles, purer feelings flow thence through the people's every vein; the fog of barbarism and dim superstition vanishes and the darkness yields to the triumph of the light.[3]

Optimistic as such a judgment may sound to us today, there was something heroic, as well as theatrically brilliant, about these people's effort to reeducate and renew their country in a period so crucial for Germany—and for the world.

It is easy to forget how very short a period it was. Germany's revolution, which put an end both to the war and to the Wilhelmine empire that had waged it, took place in November 1918, roughly a year after the Russian October Revolution and eighteen months after the fall of the tsar. Formally, the Weimar Republic was established in July 1919, Weimar being where its constitution was worked out: a symbolic choice precisely because of that city's association with Schiller and Goethe. In January 1933 Adolf Hitler became chancellor and proclaimed the Third Reich—thereby putting an end to the new Weimar theatre after an effective life of no more than fourteen years. For four of those years the country was plagued by unsuccessful uprisings and rocketing inflation. For nearly half its life, too, it was handicapped by being a cultural as well as a political outcast from Western Europe, subject to travel restrictions and unable (for instance) to import American films till 1923. Only for some four years, from 1925 to 1928, was it able to enjoy economic and political stability and normal international relations. Then came the economic crisis and the four-year prelude to Hitler. As a result, the story of its theatre, too, falls into similarly distinct sections to which we shall devote this and the next three chapters: that is to say, the Revolution and its immediate aftermath; the period of disillusionment and economic crisis; the four stable years sometimes known as the "golden twenties"; followed by the final spell of politicization and polarization in the theatre as in many other aspects of German life.

Though the divisions between these periods were not hard and fast, they did roughly correspond to the main changes in the type of play being written and produced; to the fluctuating economic situation of the theatre "apparatus"; and to the consequent changes in its structure. Where other aspects of the Weimar theatre were concerned, however, there was at the same time a certain continuity. In particular the actors, directors, and designers didn't simply disappear from the scene every three or four years, but continued to do their best to grapple with the new plays and the new conditions. So from here on I propose to set aside any detailed consideration of the performance aspects of the new plays and leave them to be dealt with in a later chapter covering the Weimar period as a whole. This means that whereas up to now I have tried briefly to cover every element of the prewar theatre which helped shape that of the Weimar Republic, for the fourteen years of the Republic itself I shall be separating the most socially sensitive aspects from others where the theatre seems more autonomous. The former embrace its creative side and demand chronological treatment; the latter are more ephemeral and more concerned with interpretation. Finally there will be a general account of the relationship of this whole story to the German theatre as it continued to exist under the Nazis and in exile after 1933. Then perhaps we can judge its relevance to the English-language theatre today.

Expressionism and the New Spirit

That new feeling of spirituality and redemption which so struck observers like Huntly Carter in the early 1920s arose on the one hand out of the growing opposition of artists and poets to the war and to the persons and classes who had made it. Starting as soon as 1915 with individual protest and breakdown in army barracks or at the front, a bitter hatred of militarism accompanied men like George Grosz and Ernst Toller back to civil life and/or convalescence, and found a focus in a number of courageous magazines of which Franz Pfemfert's Expressionist *Die Aktion* was the most influential. By late 1916 the bloody and inconclusive fighting around Verdun and the stagnation of trench warfare was stimulating a more generalized resistance to the war spirit right across Germany, and this new humanitarianism was echoed on the public (if as yet powerless) plane of the Reichstag by the splitting off of an Independent Social-Democratic party, or USPD, opposed to further Socialist support of the war. With the Russian Revolution of March 1917 and the fall of tsarism one of the principal motives for that support was removed; then with the Bolshevik October Revolution six months later a still nominally Social-Democratic party (though one detested by the German SPD) showed that it was possible to halt the fighting. That summer and autumn saw groups of 'Activist' writers and intellectuals making their own localized efforts to stimulate opposition, mostly outside any parties but in the name of Man *(der Mensch)*, Humanity, and Brotherhood. The strength of such vague slogans should not be underrated: the movement was much wider and more vocal than anything yet seen in the other warring countries. It was not matched even in Russia, since there the dissenting intellectuals had a mass antiwar party to which they could hitch their ideals and saw less need to act on their own.

The new spirit in Central Europe can on the other hand also be seen as part of the still rising movement of Expressionism, of which Activism had become the dominant national branch, with its highly charged rhetorical poetry whose prewar pioneer had been Franz Werfel. For while this latest trend in the arts had not hitherto penetrated the theatre, (so that the new poets had generally been unable to get their plays performed), from 1917 on it started developing into a major German dramatic movement. Beginning with the first productions of Hasenclever's *Der Sohn* in the autumn of 1916—productions that were not in themselves Expressionist apart from the performance of Ernst Deutsch in the title part—this passionate, ecstatic, often contorted school of playwriting became associated first with the Activist opposition to the war, then with the new republican arts establishment and the socialized Prussian State theatre. In a sense it superseded both the Naturalist drama of the late nineteenth century and the eclectic theatricality that followed; but in two respects its role was very different. For, first of all, it related much more closely and clearly to the historical events and the change of ideological climate; and secondly it was part of a movement that was at once more all-embracing and more specifically German than anything that had gone before. Where Naturalism could never be seen as the achievement specifically of the Hohenzollern Empire (given the important contributions of the Scandinavians and the French), Expressionism is rightly identified with that empire's decline and demolition.

Just where to situate the beginnings of Expressionism is always a problem, but in the other arts they certainly lay before the First World War. Expressionist writing can be fairly said to have constituted a school from 1910, the year when Herwarth Walden began his magazine *Der Sturm* (with Kokoschka as a regular contributor) and a group of young poets gathered around the Berlin Neuer Club and its 'Neo-Emotional Cabaret' under the twenty-five-year old Kurt Hiller. It was then, too, that the breakaway artists' body called the Neue Sezession held the first representative show of Expressionist painting and the art critics began using the term in its definitive sense, though its two main centers in Dresden and Munich had already established their distinctive styles by then and the prototype of Expressionist graphic art—Munch's *Der Schrei*, the movement's characteristic "cry" or "scream"—actually dated from 1892. In January 1911 *Die Aktion* started publication, initially as a rival to the better-known *Der Sturm,* featuring the Neuer Club poets and some of the subsequent Dadaists, then later developing into a focus of Activism and opposition to the war. With the theatre, however, the situation was very different in that, although some of the first Expressionist plays were by then being written or had actually been completed, the theatre "apparatus" had still to be won over before anything like a movement could get under way. Thus the only such works to reach the stage before 1916, (and the first, private production of Hasenclever's *Der Sohn*), were Kokoschka's *Murderer Hope of Womankind,* which was performed outside the framework of the theatre proper, and three of the ten-year-older Carl Sternheim's satires on bourgeois life which Reinhardt staged between 1911 *(Die Hose)* and 1914 *(Der Snob).* At that point nobody yet thought of their cynical and well-heeled author as an Expressionist.

It was the war, then, that gave birth to the concept of a distinctive theatrical Expressionism, to be associated with the new writing, painting, and graphics, not to mention the emergence of an Expressionist architecture in which Poelzig's theatre projects figured prominently, while his colleague Bruno Taut published an "architectural play for symphonic music" entitled *Der Weltbaumeister (The Master Builder of the World,* Hagen, 1920). And this may well have been because the writers in question were seen by the wartime authorities as potentially subversive and thereby (as often happens) constituted a challenge and a stimulus to all enterprising theatres. Sternheim's *Die Hose* was at first banned because the (female) lingerie of the title was thought indecent; this was circumvented by changing the name. His *1913*— which was in no sense a revolutionary or antimonarchist play—could not be performed till after the war; moreover, he imposed his own ban on *Tabula Rasa*. *The Son, The Beggar,* and, more understandably, Reinhold Goering's *Naval Battle* could only be given in closed or club performances. *From Morn to Midnight,* another politically innocuous work, could not be staged in Prussia. However, with the emergence of a growing antiwar movement involving a number of *Die Aktion* contributors and other Expressionists, such plays started to attract a curiosity and in due course an enthusiasm over and above their merits. Fritz von Unruh, whose *Ein Geschlecht (A Breed)* was staged just before the end of the war, was a former Imperial Guards officer who had twice been court-martialed for his writings; Hasenclever, Toller, and the young Zuckmayer were known as Activist poets; Sorge and August Stramm were both war victims, like the Expressionist painters Franz Marc and August Macke. No wonder, then, that Expressionism came to be borne forward on the final wave of antiwar feeling which came crashing down on a defeated empire and its capital in the autumn of 1918. For it seemed for a while to embody not only the traumas and resentments of a time and a generation, but also their hopes.

There are various strands in the Expressionist message, and several of them date from those earlier years. There is the emphasis on *Pathos*—which does not mean "pathos" in our sense but a heightened emotionalism—and the "station-drama" structure, which presents the hero's life as some kind of road to Golgotha. There is the notion of a complete break away from society (society in such a context being the society of the Wilhelmine middle class), from one's family, and above all one's father, where the father figure clearly stands for a rigid family tradition and discipline such as some of the Expressionist writers had themselves been painfully subjected to, or more broadly, for the absolute authoritarian ruler of Imperial Germany. There is also for some writers the conception of the "new man," who will be born better able to cope with the modern epoch and its problems; the question then is how will he come about and what kind of person will he be. On top of all these elements, which often involved a degree of self-dramatization bordering on narcissism, there were features that became particularly intense during the war years, notably Expressionism's lofty concern with Humanity at large, with the hero's mission to reorganize and lead it, and sometimes also with a messianic ecstasy such as the idea of such a mission can inspire. In addition there were less basic, almost technical, features relating to the means of expression adopted, for instance the use (particularly by Kaiser and Sternheim) of abruptly condensed language, or the prevalence of unidentified, generalized or symbolic characters called simply The Man, The Son, The Stranger, and so on. Of course some of these characteristics can also be found among the movement's precursors: in Strindberg's *Road to Damascus*, for instance, or even in *Parsifal*. But it was only in the middle of the war that they came together in such a way as to make a recognizably new drama whose spiritual charge could electrify a varied audience irrespective of any differences of creed.

As well as the productions of Kokoschka and Sternheim just mentioned there had been others that helped prepare the German theatre for the new movement: Reinhardt's realization of the second part of *Faust*, for instance, and the whole wave of Strindberg productions in Germany around 1913–16. Likewise the rediscovery of Büchner's terse, tragic, episodic *Woyzeck* (given in a somewhat heavy production by Viktor Barnowsky at the Lessing-Theater in 1913) was crucial, while Wedekind was a persisting influence. But it is very noticeable that for a time it was not Berlin but the provincial theatres that began pioneering the new plays, starting at the end of 1916 and continuing until well after Berlin finally began to follow suit at the end of the war. On the one hand there were the new private theatres, which began springing up in the big cities in the five years or so before 1914; on the other a certain number of the old court or municipal theatres which were exceptions to the general stagnation of such generally feudal institutions. It is not difficult to see why the first of these became interested in Expressionism: men like Arthur Hellmer, who cofounded the Neues Theater in Frankfurt in 1911, or Otto Falckenberg (once of the Elf Scharfrichter cabaret), whose Munich Kammerspiele had been founded the same year, were glad to offer something new and attuned to the changing times, and similarly with the Dumont-Lindemann regime at the Schauspielhaus in Düsseldorf, the Kammerspiele in Hamburg (founded by Erich Ziegel in 1918), the Albert-Theater in Dresden, and Alwin Kronacher's Altes Theater in Leipzig. What is less easy to understand is why older subsidized theatres like those in Darmstadt, Dresden, Mannheim, Frankfurt, Leipzig, and Stuttgart should also have gone the same way, particularly when even the Deutsches Theater hesitated to put its toe in the water, as it were, until Christmas 1917. Between them however these variegated bodies not only gave first performances to such Expressionist playwrights as Hasenclever, Unruh, Kornfeld, Kaiser (fifteen of whose plays were presented by Hellmer alone from January 1917 onward), Reinhard Goering, and Hanns Johst, but came to constitute something of a close-knit network across which the leading Expressionist actors, directors and designers moved from job to job.

It was in the provinces too, therefore, that the distinctive style and spirit of Expressionist performance was worked out. One center was the Rhine-Main area, with Frankfurt, Mainz, Darmstadt, and the Mannheim National-Theater all within a twenty-five-mile radius, and a group of practitioners including Hartung, Weichert, and Zeiss, directors; Unruh, Kornfeld, Edschmid, and (later) Bronnen, writers; Hellmer the theatre manager; Ludwig Sievert the designer; and Bernhard Diebold the critic. There was Dresden with Kokoschka and Hasenclever (who had both arrived as army convalescents); Carl Zeiss and Berthold Viertel, directors; Ernst Deutsch and Heinrich George, actors, and the leading Expressionist theoretician and animator Kurt Pinthus; there was also the very radical Dresden painters' Sezession, while Leipzig was only seventy miles away. Finally there was Munich, with Erich Ziegel, till he moved to Hamburg, and Falckenberg as directors; Zoff and Zarek as dramaturgs; Feuchtwanger, Johst, and the young Brecht as writers (though the jailed Toller was never performed there); also Otto Reigbert the designer; and a galaxy of actors including Albert Steinrück, Dieterle, Granach and (after the Revolution) Elisabeth Bergner.

Virtually all these became figures of national, if not international importance, and between them they gave theatrical Expressionism its physical and visual shape. So the critics came to contrast Richard Weichert's first public production of *Der Sohn* at Mannheim in January 1918—at a time when Hasenclever's play was still banned in Dresden, Munich, and Cologne, though not in Berlin—with Holländer's at the Deutsches Theater a year later, very much to the latter's disadvantage. For despite the brilliance of his cast, which included Deutsch and the amazing Werner Krauss, Reinhardt's aide misguidedly gave a naturalistic interpretation of this in itself preposterous and adolescent play. By contrast Weichert and his designer Sievert had set the twenty-year-old Son (he has no other name) in the middle of a black-and-white set, concentrating their lighting on him, cutting some of the rhetorical excesses, and stylizing all movement, gestures, and speech. Above all they gave the story enough drive and rhythm to make the whole production seem consistent and convincing.

The Explosion of Man

"Don't you feel" asked Pinthus in one of his various high-pitched paeans to the new poetry—the "Speech to Young Poets" published in the Kurt Wolff almanac for 1918—"that the drama is going to be the most passionate and effective way of expressing your poetry? . . . Perhaps it will come closest of all to what we have termed Expressionist. Here Man [*der Mensch*] explodes in the presence of Man."[4] This is the feeling that underlay Herbert Jhering's retrospective view that "the dynamism that was missing from the revolution was to be found in the theatre."[5] For while the German Revolution of November 1918 seemed to consecrate Expressionism and turn it into an ideology-cum-aesthetic for the first years of the Republic, the specifically political enthusiasm the Revolution generated was a good deal more restrained. For in fact it was not so much a spontaneous Socialist or pacifist rising as a practical result of the collapse of a defeated high command which would have been prepared to restore parliamentary rule and ditch the emperor even without such popular pressure. Despite that "stab in the back" legend which the military leaders subsequently promoted, the Revolution's two most solid achievements—the cessation of hostilities and the abdication of the imperial family—were decided on even before a Socialist administration had begun to operate or any revolutionary forces were in a position to dictate policy. Nor, as it turned out, were the high expectations of the writers to be fulfilled. Two years later, in his introduction to the classic Expressionist anthology *Menscheitsdämmerung* (*Twilight of Humanity*, a variant on the title of Wagner's opera), Pinthus spoke of his contributors as "doomed yearners, left with nothing but their hope in Man

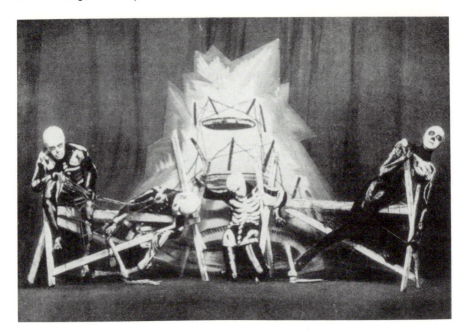

Acts 4 (above) and 5 of Ernst Toller's Expressionist first play at the 'proletarian' Tribüne theatre in September 1919, with Fritz Kortner (below, centre) in his first big Berlin part as the First World War Soldier. Thereafter he played leads at the Staatstheater for much of the 1920s, as well as in Pabst's Lulu film. Photo by Cologne University Theatre Museum.

and their belief in Utopia."[6] For the moment, however, they still had them, and it was these, along with the practical and administrative changes in the operating of the arts, that now gave Germany something of the feeling of a new renaissance.

The spontaneous revolutionary forces, such as they were, were at first located neither in the USPD nor in the bulk of the old prewar SPD (who together constituted the provisional government of 10 November) but in new Soviet-style councils that had formed themselves in the armed forces and now sprang up all over Germany. Developing into a whole extraparliamentary system, they moved into what appeared to be a power vacuum (for the Reichstag was not in session) and were joined on two levels by the artistic and intellectual activists. Not only had these latter sometimes been chosen by their wartime comrades to serve on the Workers' and Soldiers' Councils and the congresses in which they came together, but similar councils also began to be elected by the public theatres and a number of Councils of Intellectual Workers were set up on the lines of that formed in Berlin by the Activist leader Kurt Hiller (former animator of the Neo-Emotional cabaret of 1910–13). None of these new revolutionary organs was able in the end to assert itself against the secret understanding between the army and the Socialist leaders by which there was to be no question of establishing a Soviet system, and once the Republic had been formally constituted they all died out. Nonetheless, enough of the younger writers, theatre people, and their friends became involved one way and another in the movement towards a peaceful, internationalist civilian Germany for the theatre itself to be affected, at least for the first two or three years. True, there would be a corresponding reaction as soon as it became clear how little headway that movement was actually going to make, but in the first few months there was a genuine excitement and a sense of change. And this expressed itself in some unprecedented theatrical events.

Whereas in Soviet Russia Meyerhold's Theatrical October only began in 1920 and depended at first on the adaptation of foreign plays, the theatre of the German revolution started a year earlier with the premiere of an indigenous pacifist-revolutionary play. This was Ernst Toller's *Die Wandlung* (The Transformation), whose twenty-five-year-old author was then serving a five-year jail sentence for his part in the short-lived Munich Soviet Republic, which had been bloodily put down that spring. Produced as the second offering of a new left-wing management at the little Tribüne theatre in Berlin, it showed the "stations" or *via crucis* of a Jewish (hence supposedly "alien") intellectual like the author, who plunges into war to prove himself a German, is wounded, and, haunted by skeletons and cripples, goes through various roles—sculptor, medical student, prisoner, orator—till he is prepared, in a last scene outside a church, to burst out in a long speech to the People calling them to become *Menschen*—human beings—once again and march off hand in hand singing after him such words as

> Brothers, stretch out your crippled hand,
> Flaming joy intone!
> Striding across our free land
> Revolution! Revolution![7]

What lent real force to this loftily Utopian and self-dramatizing text was the combination of a director, Karl-Heinz Martin, who gave full value to its tensions, pauses, and screaming explosions, as well as to the macabre distortions of the many incidental figures, with the powerful acting of Fritz Kortner and the economically achieved grotesqueness of Robert Neppach's Expressionist sets. The play ran for 115 performances and not only put Kortner instantly into the first rank of Weimar actors but also established Toller for a time as something close to a Socialist messiah in the theatre, several of his plays subsequently being staged in the new Russia. (These included two which Meyerhold himself would direct in the winter of 1922–23.)

The Tribüne had been planned as a primarily Expressionist theatre by Kortner and Martin when they were still at the Hamburg Kammerspiele. They were joined on its board by the writer Rudolf Leonhard, one of Hiller's Berlin Council of Intellectual Workers who was now trying to set up a League for Proletarian Culture on the model of the Russian Proletkult. Its three-hundred seat theatre was in a Charlottenburg students' hostel, where it remained through the period. Among others involved were Hans Rodenberg, John Gottowt, and Julius Gellner among the actors and Friedrich Mellinger and László Vajda as successive assistant directors; and its first, much less successful program had included a one-act play by Leonhard's friend Hasenclever. As for the Proletarian Theatre which Leonhard's League went off to sponsor separately after differences with the Tribüne's management, it only staged one production; this was of a play called *Die Freiheit (Freedom)*, by an entirely obscure writer named Herbert Cranz, and took place in a concert hall. Directed again by Martin, this dealt with a group of soldiers imprisoned for mutiny who are offered the chance to escape and are at first reluctant to take it till reminded of their collective political duty. It was not a success in the eyes either of the critics or of the organizers, and the first Proletarian Theatre thereafter dissolved, leaving the name to be picked up a year later by a new group headed by Toller's contemporary, the young director Erwin Piscator.

Piscator, though these same sponsors of Proletarian Culture can be found among his supporters, came from rather a different stable. Like Toller he was one of those who had had their life transformed by their front-line experiences, and had found an outlet in the magazine *Die Aktion*. Returning to Berlin after a brief involvement with the Soldiers' Councils in Belgium, he quickly met up with the local Dada movement, which had come together at the beginning of 1918 under the guidance of the poet-doctor Richard Huelsenbeck. This represented yet another wing of the antiwar movement; initially a group of youthful deserters, convalescents, and students of various nationalities who came together on the neutral territory of wartime Zurich and centered on the Cabaret Voltaire set up there by the Munich dramaturg Hugo Ball and his wife, the chanteuse Emmy Hennings. Too often regarded primarily as an art movement, Dada, with its cabaret-style programs of songs, scenes, and happenings (including items by Wedekind, dances by the Laban group, and Kokoschka's play *Sphinx und Strohmann*) had from the first had a strongly theatrical side, and on Huelsenbeck's return to Berlin the group which formed around him there soon started diversifying into revolutionary politics on the one hand and theatre proper on the other. So Piscator, after directing one or two of the group's art gallery performances, joined the new Communist party (or KPD) on its foundation at the end of 1918, along with the writer Franz Jung and the artists George Grosz and John Heartfield. Walter Mehring, the Berlin Dada poet, began turning out the *chansons* for which he became famous, and for two years acted as the literary director of the Schall und Rauch cabaret, which Reinhardt now revived, with Grosz and Heartfield designing puppets and sets, and Friedrich Holländer (the drama-turg's nephew) as pianist. Heartfield and Jung both went on to collaborate in Piscator's Proletarian Theatre Mark Two, which he set up as the "stage of the revolutionary workers of Greater Berlin" with the aim of playing in halls around the city and inflaming the revolutionary feelings of the working class.[8]

If Toller's eminently poetical play failed (to all intents and purposes) to outlive the excitement and topicality of its first production, the new plays staged by the second Proletarian Theatre made even less impression except as short-term agitprop. Two of the authors, Lajos Barta and Andor Gábor, were refugees from the recently defeated Hungarian Soviet government; two other plays were written by Jung, who was among that time's more extraordinary political-economic adventurers; and a third by Karl Wittfogel, later to become a specialist in political affairs (first pro- then anti-Marxist) but in those days one of the German playwrights who most interested the Russians. Another remarkable newcomer was the Hungarian constructivist László Moholy-Nagy, who designed an Upton Sinclair play for Piscator soon after first arriving in Germany, where he was about to become one of the leading teachers at the Bauhaus. But perhaps the most significant aspect for Piscator lay in the Proletarian Theatre's relations with the audience. For he worked with some success to root its activities in the regular support of left-wing organizations such as the USPD and the short-lived Communist Workers' party in which Jung was prominent, and the unemployed were admitted free. Meantime the KPD, to which Piscator himself belonged, not only gave no support but attacked him for bringing art down to such a vulgar level, while the SPD police president who grudgingly gave the theatre a license in the summer of 1920 withdrew his permission within a year. The official abolition of cen-sorship, it should be noted, never throughout the whole period of the Re-public seems to have inhibited the state police from stopping a production when they or the military found it objectionable.

Expressionism Rules

While *Die Wandlung* was memorable as a Utopian revolutionary explosion and the two Proletarian Theatres as an attempt to link theatre to the militant working class, the biggest unique theatrical event of this time reflects the farsighted flair of the wizard Reinhardt. This was the opening at the end of November 1919 of his new would-be German National Theatre in the con-verted Schumann circus, which Hans Poelzig had turned in the course of that summer into a great U-shaped auditorium seating three thousand around an

Reinhardt's permanent mass theatre in Berlin, the Grosses Schauspielhaus, opened in November 1919. The architect Hans Poelzig had adapted it from a former circus building. The principal designer was Ernst Stern, who remained when it went down market some four years later.

arena (which could be changed into stalls) backed by a wide proscenium stage with fly tower, cupola, and revolve. Over the audience was a new dome with twelve scalloped concentric rings hanging down like spectacular stalactites. There was no balcony, and under the building was the revived Schall und Rauch. As we have seen, Reinhardt's concern was with the mass audience rather than with any particular political intention, and had arisen in the first place from the quasi Greek ideals of men like Craig and Behrens without apparent thought of the new revolutionary spirit. Nonetheless he cannot have helped seeing how, even after the suppression of the extreme Left risings in Berlin and Munich, his finally realized vision must link up with the concept of a new democratic community. And certainly there were critics who made the connection, as the lights went down and the dome seemed to lift and turn into a starry sky, while Reinhardt's spotlights began one by one to pick out Aeschylus's figures recalling an earlier war. Here, watching some of Germany's finest actors—Moissi as Orestes, Agnes Straub as Clytemnestra, Werner Krauss as Agamemnon, and others of Reinhardt's prewar ensemble— was the new republican society, from the chancellor down, melting into an anonymous mass unbroken by the old theatre's traditional distinctions of level.

This seemed to parallel the early attempts at mass theatre in Moscow and Petrograd, as well as Firmin Gémier's work in Paris at the Cirque d'Hiver and the new Théâtre Populaire in the same years. Yet Reinhardt's *Oresteia* production was not in itself new, and once again from then on he showed himself to be more interested in translating his previous repertoire to the new arena— which indeed presented fascinating problems of acoustics, distance, and dimension for the actor and the director of actors—than in developing that repertoire so as to express the powerful revolutionary romanticism prevailing elsewhere. So in the Grosses Schauspielhaus's first season, while it is true that Reinhardt's productions of Romain Rolland's *Danton* (a play of the 1890s) and *Julius Caesar* (with Krauss, Moissi, Straub, Emil Jannings, and William Dieterle) were attuned to the new spirit, the only example of the new Utopian-Expressionist drama was Hasenclever's 1917 version of the *Antigone*, which Karlheinz Martin was brought in to direct, presumably on the strength of his success at the Tribüne. Similarly in the 1920–21 season when Reinhardt, already disappointed with his theatre's reception, had by then shifted his attention to Salzburg and Vienna. This time the one supposedly Expressionist offering was Georg Kaiser's feeble mock-classical romp *Europa*, which once again Martin directed. Only in the summer of 1922 did Martin stage Toller's newly written *The Machine-Wreckers* with Dieterle, Granach, and Rodenberg in a set by Heartfield, but this historical play about the Luddites suffered by comparison with its prototype *The Weavers* in the same theatre a year earlier and was not a success. As for Toller's conscious attempts at mass pageants for the annual trade union festival at Leipzig, which came nearer to the Soviet model, they only began after that, and it seems that none of their texts have survived.

Transformation of an Establishment

Overlapping these new initiatives, there was what looked at first like having to be a radical reorganization of the whole system of subsidized theatre, since not only the Prussian monarchy in the capital but also the lesser provincial potentates, from the Wittelsbachs in Bavaria right down to the Dukes of Saxe-Meiningen, lost their thrones (though not their estates and fortunes, nor their right to live in Germany). Of the twenty-six theatres previously administered on such people's behalf by more or less educated, mainly ex-military courtiers, twenty now became State or *Land* (i.e., province) theatres, while five were given to the big municipalities. Some private theatres also were taken over. The changeover, however, was not a smooth one, since to begin with the theatres remained nominally the property of the old owners, so that for instance the Hesse Landestheater in Darmstadt near Frankfurt (from which a number of outstanding directors were to emerge) was still known as the Grand-ducal Court Theatre as late as March 1919 and could not yet develop a new policy. Many companies, too, set up their own councils on the national revolutionary pattern, some even drawing up elaborate constitutions which might enforce compulsory trade union membership or assert a right to "worker participation" in matters of artistic policy, another factor which was unsettling and appears to have favored the appointment of administrators and directors of dubious quality. All this might take months to sort out, sometimes with the intervention of the Association of German Stage Workers, the local equivalent of Equity. Very conscious of its new responsibilities to serve what its manifesto of November 1918 had called "the promotion of the lofty ideals of the German theatre,"[9] this generally moderate union wished as many theatres as possible to be taken under public ownership, as indeed did the Volksbühne's new secretary Siegfried Nestriepke, who had hitherto been a political journalist on the Socialist daily *Vorwärts*. By the spring of 1920 such a step had been ruled out by the government-appointed Nationalization Commission, whose policy in all spheres (notably in mining, heavy industry, and large-scale land ownership) was to abstain from any further socialization.

The center of Socialist arts administration lay in Prussia, which remained under SPD control right up to Chancellor Von Papen's dismissal of the Prussian Land government in 1932. Here the Revolution had led to the appointment of a generally progressive corps of advisers under an education minister called Konrad Haenisch, who strongly rejected the former imperial policy of interfering with the arts. "The state," he is quoted as saying, "must no longer consider itself the master of the arts, and its officials at all levels must get used to feeling it a matter of honor and pride to use the resources of the state to serve the artist."[10] His deputy (and subsequent successor) was Carl Becker; his adviser for theatre affairs the lawyer Carl Seelig, who was one of the committee of the Stage Workers' Association and now had to look after the three Prussian state theatres in Berlin, Kassel, and Wiesbaden, simultaneously keeping an eye on the corresponding opera houses in which the music adviser Leo Kestenberg also had an interest. The radical shaking up of the whole structure which these men effected could afford to be more drastic than elsewhere partly because the apparatus in question was bigger and more important than in any of the other Laender, partly because there was no ambiguity about the status of the former regime, which was thoroughly discredited and could be instantly disposed of. So Carl Hagemann became the Intendant at Wiesbaden, Max von Schillings (a nominee of the revolutionary council) at the Berlin State Opera, with Leo Blech and Fritz Stiedry as his main conductors, while in June 1919 Leopold Jessner from the Königsberg municipal theatre was appointed as Intendant of the former court theatre, now known as the State Schauspielhaus or Staatstheater. This last was a consciously political appointment, Jessner being not merely a republican but also a member of the SPD.

The third great premiere, then, following those at the Tribüne and the Grosses Schauspielhaus was Jessner's inaugural production at the Republic's new *Staatstheater*, which opened on 12 December 1919. This theatre had actually started playing in October with a production of Schiller's *Maria Stuart*, in which Kortner, commuting with the Tribüne, played Mortimer. Now, however, came the real test, not only of the Socialist takeover and of the new Intendant's attitude and abilities but also of the cultural identity of the Republic. Jessner had clearly chosen his play with this in view, willingly challenging comparison with its production a year earlier at the Volksbühne. For he had picked *William Tell*, a classic drama of liberation written by Schiller during the Napoleonic Wars and put on by him at Weimar in 1804, a work whose theme was the establishment of a seemingly classless democracy in defiance of emperors and princes. Written in high-flown blank verse without the least personal knowledge of Switzerland or sense of the ridiculous, this unexportable classic has always meant much in the German context, but never more so than in the still revolutionary climate of 1919. Thus when Ruodi the Uri fisherman—one of the forty or so minor characters—cries out that

The tyrant
Is dead, the day of freedom has appeared[11]

it was an instant challenge to all supporters of the old regime and the old imperial theatre. Significantly, however, Jessner had not allowed for the anti-Semitism of those—reputedly in the cheaper seats—who saw in him not just a Socialist but, above all, yet another Jewish theatre director. The result was one of the great twentieth-century theatre ructions, with protestors in the gallery interrupting the actors and conducting a shouting match both with other gallery-goers and with such favorable first-night critics as Siegfried Jacobsohn and Julius Bab. According to Kortner, who was playing Gessler, the imperial prefect—the tyrant in question—actors and Intendant alike were unsettled by this, and it was left to him to counterattack, making his appearance toward the end of the third act with florid face, cracking whip, chainmail cap, and a chest full of medals, to go on bellowing Schiller's apt line *"Treibt sie auseinander!"*[12] or "Break it up!" until the noise stopped. Nothing could be more in the new tradition of theatrical conflict, and when Albert Bassermann as Tell himself later appeared through the curtain to yell, "Chuck the bloody hirelings out!" (or words to that effect)[13] the triumph was complete.

From a short-term point of view what happened that night was that the red, yellow, and black republican flag was successfully hoisted over the Kaiser's theatre, where it would remain flying throughout the 1920s. Jessner's more lasting achievement, however, was to impose his own style and perfectionism as a director in such a way as to change a great theatre from being one of the most boring in Berlin into a house that could stand comparison even with the Deutsches Theater. He could not, of course, instantly make a homogeneous ensemble of a rather miscellaneous collection of actors, but he could and did achieve a dynamic tempo with precisely organized scene changes so as to give a new drive to even the most familiar scenes. The line of his interpretation emerged clearly: "unmistakably revolutionary and anti-nationalistic" wrote Kortner later,[14] while regretting that this meant cutting at least one of Baron Attinghausen's many references to the Fatherland. There was no lifelike picturesqueness or Swiss local color, no "Meiningery," as the critic Alfred Kerr put it. Instead there was something more like symbolism, though symbolism of a stark and streamlined kind. Making a virtue of his theatre's lack of a revolve, Jessner got his designer, Emil Pirchan, to build him three platforms forming three sides of a quadrilateral open to the audience and ringing the main stage, to which broad steps led down so as to constitute a multilevel display stand for the crowd scenes. Equally Appia-like was the use of light and color: warm sunlight for the Tell family, a bright red cloak for the villainous Gessler, gray for the scenes of oppression); all variations within a fixed framework. As to the characters, Bassermann's Tell had something of the stylized dignity of a figure by Ferdinand Hodler; Kortner's Gessler was an ugly bundle of energy and malice. Above all, the cast had a new confidence; the director was clearly in control, and his ensuing productions—a headlong, noisy *Marquis von Keith*, then in November 1920 a *Richard III* again on a permanent stepped-up structure with a powerful use of light, color, and stylized movement—showed the clearness and consistency of his conceptions. Henceforward the Staatstheater was a force.

If the same could be said of the Volksbühne it was true only with respect to the size of the audience. Reinhardt's stopgap arrangement for the war years had come to an end in the summer of 1918, when the reunited Volksbühne societies at last took over their fine theatre and appointed Friedrich Kayssler as their director of productions, recommending him to members as having a "proud, self-reliant, solitary and obdurate natural nobility" and a love of the "dark strivings of the vast mass of the People"[15]: not, perhaps, a very encouraging description. It is true that Kayssler recruited some remarkable actors, including Veit Harlan, Lucie Mannheim, and Heinz Hilpert, while Ludwig Berger's production of *Measure for Measure* just before the November Revolution did much to revive interest in that often underrated play. There were also productions of two important Expressionist plays, which will be considered presently. But generally the critical consensus seems to have been that Kayssler was not himself a creative director, while his two most promising talents, first Berger, then later Jürgen Fehling, soon went off to work for the Staatstheater instead. This did not stop the organization as a whole from expanding vastly, particularly after its formal reconstitution as a single body in 1920. Emerging from the war with some eighty-five thousand members, it had approximately doubled this figure by 1923; by which time it was also running the little Theater in der Köpenickerstrasse (under the title Neues Volkstheater), block-booking seats at several other theatres including the Central-Theater (for operettas) and the Grosses Schauspielhaus, and negotiating for what later became the Kroll Opera. It was still in fact doing a great deal to make the theatre more accessible, though its left-wing critics could complain of its increasingly middle-class membership and preoccupation with light entertainment as well as old-style Bildung. Like several other Berlin theatres it was neither very notably marked by the Revolution nor particularly associated with Expressionism. None the less the wave of new plays after the end of the war was too strong for any theatre to ignore them entirely. From now on the chief Expressionist dramas might be staged almost anywhere.

This was when the Expressionist movement took stock of itself, with a flood of magazines and a succession of anthologies of which Pinthus's *Menschheitsdämmerung* and Alfred Wolfstein's *Die Erhebung* were the most important. Admittedly the term *Expressionism* was loosely used, sometimes meaning almost any aspect of the modern movement, stretching from Cubism to Surrealism (two -isms which were never strong enough in Germany to have an independent existence). But by any reckoning it did constitute a great process of renewal in the arts, even if its spiritual and political sides were to prove somewhat deceptive. One knowledgeable authority has estimated that there were in all about twenty-five hundred Expressionist authors (poets, dramatists, essayists, and prose writers) writing in German, and that one thousand of these were new writers. Whether Carl Sternheim should be included among them is a moot point, since he was not only an older and earlier writer but organized his plays tautly in conventional form without *Pathos* or anything resembling the Expressionist visual imagination. But his very condensed dialogue is not unlike that of Georg Kaiser and what became identified as Expressionism's "telegraphese."

Kaiser himself on the other hand certainly counts as an outstanding

Expressionist, but he wrote his plays in more than one genre and with a tidy-minded mastery and sense of symmetry such as preclude spontaneous passion. None the less *From Morn to Midnight* remains one of the movement's striking masterpieces of "station drama," and after its wartime premiere in Munich it was staged repeatedly, notably at the Deutsches Theater by Holländer in 1919 with Max Pallenberg as the frenetic bank clerk, then two years later by Barnowsky with Granach in sets by César Klein—a production that struck Jhering as a model of how to emphasize the best aspects of such plays and establish, by precise rhythms and good ensemble playing, "the expression on which the scene's construction and composition depend." There was also an effective film version by Karlheinz Martin, starring Ernst Deutsch in ultra-Expressionist sets by Neppach; while Barnowsky later staged the somewhat similar but even jerkier and more angular *Hölle Weg Erde* (or *Hell, Way, Earth*) at the Lessing-Theater in January 1920. There the sets were by César Klein.

Kaiser's much more contrived and schematic *Gas* trilogy was also widely played; with their millionaire and technologist figures and science-fiction themes these plays look forward to Fritz Lang's film *Metropolis*. *Gas I* indeed was one of the plays introduced to Berlin by the Volksbühne. Other, less structurally gifted writers like Hasenclever, Unruh, and Kornfeld were treated more as Expressionist curiosities, while Toller, after *Die Wandlung* had been refused by a number of other theatres, was told its rhapsodic-political successor *Masses and Man* had been poorly received at the Volksbühne in September 1921 despite a visionary production by Jürgen Fehling, which the still imprisoned author had in principle approved. "Such a play," he said, "can only have a spiritual, never a concrete reality."[16] By then he was writing *Hinkemann* (or *Brokenbrow*), to date the most conventional of his plays, with its named characters, prose dialogue, and returned-soldier theme; first staged at the Leipzig Altes Theater in 1923, it was also the most widely successful. This relative slowness of Toller to break through, despite the respect paid both to his convictions and (notably by Alfred Kerr) to his competence as a playwright, suggests that his reputation as a dangerous revolutionary may have discouraged many provincial Intendants before his release in 1924, the year of *Hinkemann*'s Berlin production with Heinrich George in the title part. It was only after this that the provincial theatres seriously took the play up.

Reinhardt's last attempt to come to terms with Expressionism was in a production of August Stramm's *Kräfte* in April 1921; in other words, after handing over the management of his Berlin theatres and shortly before turning his attention to Vienna. Written as it is in an explosive, Futurist-influenced language not far from phonetic poetry, this play was one of the most extreme examples of the movement, and hitherto its author's works had been realized only by Herwarth Walden's Sturm-Bühne. This was a somewhat amateurish fringe group run by one of the Deutsches Theater's speech teachers, Rudolf Blümner, a sculptor-cum-director called Wauer, and the mystical artist Lothar Schreyer, who for a time headed the Bauhaus theatre course. Reinhardt by contrast cast the play with four outstanding actors—in particular there was a great Expressionist performance by Agnes Straub—though at the cost of filing down its jaggedness: "He undid all its compression and concentration and brought it back to normal," wrote his assistant Bernhard Reich.[17] Jessner, too, directed one or two modern works, which he treated with the same dynamic stylization, very Expressionist in spirit, as he applied to Schiller and Shakespeare. With Barlach, whose best plays are so much less Expressionist than his sculpture, this led to some distortion; though in the case of the 1912 play *Superdevil* by the extreme "Black Expressionist" Hermann Essig, the clarity of Jessner's interpretation appears to have rescued an appalling work. At the same time there were new followers of the movement still coming along: Friedrich Wolf, whose drama *Das bist du* was directed by Viertel in Dresden in 1919, or Carl Zuckmayer, who returned from the war to write a first play, *Kreuzweg*, which lasted for only three performances at the Staatstheater in December 1920 (leading Alfred Kerr to prophesy that this author would "never engender a sentence that can be spoken on the stage").[18] The young Arnolt Bronnen, too, wrote *Vatermord*, a return to the old father-son theme, though in far more violent and verbally extreme form. Dating from 1919, it was the subject of Brecht's first attempt at direction in the spring of 1922.

Something to laugh at once more. Berlin revue and cabaret artists in 1920. Left to right, Molly Wessely, Olga Limburg, Trude Hesterberg (founder of the 'Wilde Bühne') and Rosa Valetti (founder of 'Grössenwahn'), backed up by Max Adalbert, Fritz Werner and Paul Morgan (co-founder of the Kabarett der Komiker in 1924). Photo by Ullstein Bilderdienst.

5

Expressionism Runs Out of Steam

End of an Illusion

Disillusionment with the German Revolution was built into the Republic almost from the outset. Though it was only later that the Germans learned of the close understanding between the SPD leaders and the military—President Ebert's private line to General Groener at the high command; his review of the irregular Freikorps under General Maercker on 4 January 1919—it quickly became clear that the majority Socialists would make almost any compromise with the Right to stop the revolutionary movement from spreading further. The first test of this came just a day after the review, when the Left Socialist (USPD) Berlin police chief was dismissed. "Today world history is at stake," noted Count Kessler in his diary following the protest demonstrations which initiated the Spartacist Rising: "not merely the survival of the German Reich or the democratic republic, but the choice between East and West, between war and peace, between utopian intoxication and the plain greyness of everyday life."[1] A week later, with the Spartacists (Communists) defeated and government troops once more in control, the same shrewd and cultivated observer saw the alternatives still more clearly:

> The most horrifying thing would be if all this damage and suffering were *not* the birthpangs of a new time, because there was nothing wishing to be born; if it were just a matter of patching up the fragments . . . The old social democrats are only

out for material improvements, fairer and better distribution, not for any new ideals. But ideals are what the enthusiasts of the far left have set their heart on, nor would anything less justify the immense bloodbaths of the World War.[2]

In the event the choice would come down in favor of plain grayness. But it was a bloody choice and could not have been decided in a worse way. For instead of relying on troops loyal to the new order to suppress the rising, Ebert and his minister Gustav Noske called in the extreme right-wing irregular formations known as *Freikorps*, (some of whom were already using the "Aryan" swastika symbol later adopted by the Nazis), and these brutally murdered the two outstanding Spartacist/Communist leaders Karl Liebknecht and Rosa Luxemburg after their arrest on 15 January when the rising had already failed. A third, Leo Jogiches, was murdered in prison shortly after. This inexcusable butchery, which incidentally left the new German Communist party, or KPD, without adequate leaders for the next decade, was not only shocking in itself but became a precedent determining how all further revolutionary actions would be dealt with. Henceforward the various Freikorps, who continued roaming around Germany and its eastern borders largely on their own anti-Communist initiative for the next four years, were never made subject to the civil courts, but only to army courts-martial, which treated their killings very lightly. In conformity with bad old Prussian tradition, the politicians still gave precedence to an entirely unreformed officer caste, who were repeatedly ready to take action against the Left, while taking none against such right-wing adventures as the Kapp putsch of 1920 (which forced the Socialist government to leave Berlin—something that the Spartacists never came near to achieving) or the Bavarian separatism of 1923. Meanwhile in a number of independent publications like E. J. Gumbel's *Drei Jahre politischer Mord (Three Years of Political Murder)* and the courageous Berlin weekly *Die Weltbühne* this fatal imbalance in the new Weimar democracy was made very clear. This *Weltbühne* (or *World Stage*) was a magazine which had originated under Siegfried Jacobsohn's editorship as a development of his prewar writings on the theatre.

So in February 1919 Ernst Toller's mentor Kurt Eisner was murdered in Munich; a month later there was a wave of house searches and arrests in Berlin, involving some of the Dadaists; in April the Munich Soviet was bloodily suppressed by regular troops and Freikorps (the latter under one of Hitler's subsequent supporters); Toller and Mühsam were jailed for long terms, Gustav Landauer was murdered, and B. Traven went into exile. A year later a "Red Army" set up in the Ruhr during the Kapp putsch was crushed by units who till recently had been backing Kapp; even middle-of-the-road democrats like Rathenau and Erzberger were murdered with impunity; and so on right up to the unconstitutional deposition of the part-Communist coalition governments in Thuringia and Saxony in the autumn of 1923. It must be recognized that the greater part of all the extreme Left moves to extend the original November Revolution, from the Spartacist Rising onward, had no prospect whatever of succeeding; indeed it was a further factor in the Activists' disenchantment that the Comintern in Moscow (particularly Zinovieff and Radek) continued to be so unrealistic in its hopes of spreading the

Bolshevik revolution via Germany to the West. This it still seems to have thought feasible as late as November 1923, when it called somewhat romantically for further risings and a general strike to take place on the anniversary of the Russian Revolution six years earlier. The majority of the German workers, as it turned out, were no longer interested in such ventures, while as for the intellectuals, their attitude had been well expressed by Max Beckmann, whose lithograph *The Disappointed* shows a jaded-looking group yawning over the writings of Liebknecht, Luxemburg, and Karl Marx.

What brought the chaos to a conclusion toward the end of 1923 was the great inflation and its sudden ending. The decline of the currency, itself a result of the country's unsettled state and the postwar reparations imposed by the peace settlement, started to become serious in the course of 1922, then vastly accelerated as a result of the French occupation of the Ruhr mines and industries and the widespread German response of passive resistance. One prewar gold mark, it has been reckoned, was worth 10 marks in January 1920, 100 marks in June 1922, 2,500 marks in January 1923 and about 800 million marks by the time of the stabilization in November. In mid-October Alfred Döblin could describe a visit to the Deutsches Theater, clutching a bundle of million-mark notes with which to pay for his ticket. Though it was raining, he noticed that hardly anyone in the cheaper seats had brought a coat or hat; they couldn't afford the cloakroom.[3]

There was thus some pretext for the Russian leaders to expect a general collapse of the German economy, which would lead to a revolutionary situation. It was only the mood of the people and the abilities of its potential leadership that they so failed to understand. First the value of savings was wiped out, production for the home market (e.g., for theatre audiences) rendered unattractive, the middle class largely destroyed, and the population increasingly polarized into rich and poor; moreover, any remaining confidence in the future swiftly ebbed away. Then came the sudden stabilization, only a fortnight after the last revolutionary effort had collapsed. From that point on the old mark was worthless, new money for investment in short supply, and a rapid rise in unemployment the result. The situation would soon be saved by massive new investment from abroad, but meantime the whole cultural apparatus was affected in much the same way as was industry proper. Utopia had been blown away, and on economic, as well as on political grounds, the theatre was forced to rethink.

Death of Expressionism and the Hunt for Its Successor

The disillusionment of the Expressionists was well conveyed by the Alsatian poet Iwan Goll, who had been associated with Expressionism throughout the war and in 1921 published his classic statement on the death of the movement:

> Once again an art is dying, betrayed by its time. [Expressionism] was the name not of an artistic form but of an *attitude of mind*. Not so much the object of an artistic impulse as the meaning of a particular outlook on the world . . . Challenge. Manifesto. Appeal. Accusation. Entreaty. Ecstasy. Struggle. . . . Ex-

pressionism was a fine, good, great cause. Solidarity of the intellectuals. Parade of
the truthful. But the result alas, by no fault of the Expressionists, is the German
Republic 1920.[4]

This deathbed scene was drawn out over a number of years, taking place in
one art after another. In the visual arts the life had gone out of the movement
already by 1919, which is when younger artists like Dix, Schwitters, and
Moholy-Nagy abandoned its conventions and colors in favour of newer
schools (notably a harsh and unflattering Verism and a Constructivist-inclined
Dada). The poets, too, were writing less rhapsodically; thus Kessler in March
1919 reports Becher as "looking amazingly well and as if transformed; with a
new peasant or bourgeois air of crudeness. Blushing and embarrassed when
talking about his past."[5] During the following year the number of Expressionist magazines began to decline, though Bruno Taut, most Utopian of
the architects, kept his fantastic review *Frühlicht* going into 1922. More elaborate apparatuses like the cinema and the opera, being by nature so much
slower to move, continued to produce Expressionist works (Berg's *Wozzeck* in
1925, Lang's *Metropolis* in 1927) long after the movement was otherwise defunct.

Almost from the first the beginnings of a change were visible in the
cabarets, which sprang into life again between the end of 1919 and the
autumn of 1921. This had never been congenial territory to the full-blown
Expressionist theatre, and even the Neo-Emotional Cabaret of prewar Expressionism featured the light, clear, more or less conventionally formed
verse of poets such as Jakob van Hoddis and Alfred Lichtenstein rather than
the rhapsodic rhetoric and visual distortions of the Expressionist plays. Thus
there was a certain continuity between the literary cabaret of Wedekind's
time, running through the Neo-Emotionals and the Dadaist Cabaret Voltaire,
and the revived Schall und Rauch, which opened on 8 December 1919 beneath
Reinhardt's Grosses Schauspielhaus. Like other such locales of the early 1920s
the new enterprise owed its style largely to the Berlin Dadaist poet Walter
Mehring and the immensely versatile journalist Kurt Tucholsky, two devoted
Francophiles who, like Goll, would soon leave Berlin for Paris. Its actual
director was Rudolf Kurtz, formerly of the Neo-Emotionals, followed by Hans
von Wolzogen, whose father had run the original Überbrettl; the sailor poet
Joachim Ringelnatz also came to perform there. But it was Mehring who
dominated and who introduced the Dada element, with Grosz and Heartfield
designing puppets for the first program's closing antimilitarist number "Ein-
fach klassisch" ("Simply Classic").

In April 1921 Schall und Rauch changed managements and became an
unsophisticated "beer cabaret." By then its main contributors had gone over
to Rosa Valetti's rival Grössenwahn (or "Megalomania") above the Kurfürstendamm's Café des Westens, supposedly the haunt of ambitious writers; this
lasted till the middle of 1921 before changing to pocket theatre. Thereafter
Mehring's main outlet was Trude Hesterberg's Wilde Bühne (Wild Stage) in
the basement of the Theater des Westens in the Kantstrasse, where the poet
Klabund was literary director, and Brecht at the beginning of 1922 made what
seems to have been his only Berlin cabaret appearance. By then the main lines

of the Weimar cabaret had become clear, with Marcellus Schiffer coming in to reinforce the powerful poetic side, Friedrich Holländer and Mischa Spoliansky leading a team of regular composers, and performers like Graetz, Gerron, Ebinger, Hesterberg, Kate Kühl and Forster-Larrinaga, who were also to become prominent in the straight theatre. There seems to have been only one known Expressionist in this milieu: Hans Janowitz from Prague, who was also joint author (with Carl Mayer) of that classic Expressionist film *The Cabinet of Dr. Caligari.*

It was in the course of 1922 that the Berlin theatre world as a whole first began to recognize that Expressionism had had its run. "What is the good," wrote Jacobsohn that May, "of an expressive art if it has no content worth expressing?"[6]—this with reference to one of Jessner's less effective productions. Jhering, too, was already speaking of a "crisis of the repertoire" which needed to be resolved by a new type of play. Tucholsky mocked the Expressionist playwrights by proposing such titles as *The Father as Masturbator*[7], while Zuckmayer complained to a friend that "all this Expressionism makes me so sick."

> Indeed [he wrote later] I was fed to the teeth with "Expressionism." The most recent plays by its star authors struck me as increasingly convoluted and remote from life. I dimly began to see that "man is the measure of everything" in the theatre too. . . .[8]

Likewise, Kortner, who counted his own gradual dissociation from Expressionism roughly from Jessner's *Othello* production in November 1921, looked back at that movement as having been "a breakthrough, an explosion and a pointer. But it is no more a form of theatre than a revolution is a form of state."[9] Gushing out like a "flow of lava" after the First World War, it was, he said, at once the product of the Brahm/Reinhardt tradition and a noisy reaction against it. But only its realization by actors schooled in that tradition, "who knew how to keep on breathing life into its sweeping intensity, how to put sinews in its heightened speech structure and blow the breath of every day into its orgies of sound," had allowed it to survive as long as it did. This view is not unflattering to Kortner's own talents, admittedly, though in the event he took longer than he imagined to shake off the movement's faults. Nevertheless as a summing up of theatrical Expressionism it is not bad.

How far the same type of disenchantment affected the audience is hard to say. But, coincidentally or not, the practical implications of the inflation now began to operate in the same sense. That is to say that first of all the thinking middle-class audience started falling off in the course of 1922, driving unsubsidized managements (particularly in Berlin) to desperate measures in the effort to attract the inflation profiteers. So the Grosses Schauspielhaus for instance in 1922–23 went over largely to more or less obscure operettas and thereafter became devoted to nothing else. Meinhard and Bernauer in 1924 started to concentrate on operettas too; while even the Deutsches Theater played the popular hit *Alt-Heidelberg (The Student Prince),* and the Volksbühne cut down on its serious productions. Elsewhere there was a wave of what has been called "black Expressionism," meaning an extreme form of Expressionistic drama concerned no longer with the Utopian, messianic, visionary aspects of the movement, but rather with extremes of violence and perversion as seen in Bronnen's *Vatermord* and the tortuous sadomasochistic dramas of such writers as Hermann Essig, Alfred Brust, and Hanns Henny Jahnn. Meanwhile most of the recognized playwrights of the movement—Goering, Unruh, Kornfeld, and Hasenclever for instance—were no longer much of a draw and were already seeking other ways. "No more about war, revolution and the salvation of the world," wrote Kornfeld in 1924. "Let us be modest and direct our attention to other and smaller things." And Hasenclever too is quoted as confessing

> We sounded the bells for the tempest of Freedom.
> We were striplings. Now we are Men.[10]

The theatre apparatus itself had to change. So Reinhardt effectively abandoned the Grosses Schauspielhaus to his choreographer Erick Charell for the rest of the decade, while Jessner brought in new forces, of whom the director Jürgen Fehling was the most considerable. At the Volksbühne Kayssler handed over to the more enterprising, if more lightweight Stuttgart director Franz Holl in the course of 1923, while the unpopular Felix Holländer resigned from the Deutsches Theater. Along with these moves came the direct effects of the headlong inflation that year, ending with the Stresemann government's temporarily paralyzing currency reform. Piscator's new venture at the Central-Theater, where he had hoped to build up a left-wing alternative to the Volksbühne, collapsed in spring 1923; the Schiller-Theater, previously run by one Max Paregg on behalf of the Charlottenburg authority, was nationalized as a second stage for the Staatstheater. Meinhard and Bernauer abandoned their serious theatres to Barnowsky; the Volksbühne had to close its own second stage and hand its planned "people's opera" in the old Kroll circus over to the Prussian state. Outside Berlin, too, the Düsseldorf Schauspielhaus temporarily closed, while a number of other privately owned provincial theatres went bankrupt and had to be taken over by their respective municipalities. Not surprisingly, with so much change and uncertainty, the actors themselves were unsettled; there was an actors' strike in the winter of 1922–23, and the Deutsches Theater company are said to have begged Reinhardt to come back.

This was when a fair minority of Berlin actors began grouping together to form their own short-lived companies acting in any available theatre. The chief of these was Berthold Viertel's Die Truppe, with which he directed six productions at the Lustspielhaus in the 1923–24 season, two more being staged by his assistant Heinz Hilpert. Viertel had arrived from Dresden in 1922 to direct *Richard II* at the Deutsches Theater with Reinhardt's finest actors, including Bergner, Moissi, George, Granach, and Eysoldt, but then became resentful at Holländer's introduction of a star system at that theatre. Consequently he set up Die Truppe as a new ensemble, with such actors as Forster, Homolka, Paul Bildt, and (for the opening performance of *The Merchant of Venice*, incongruously designed by two obscure Bauhaus pupils) Fritz Kortner, who had now left the Staatstheater. Similar groupings were organized by Heinrich George (The Actor's Theatre), by the dramaturg-cum-critic

Jo Lhermann (Das Theater), and later by William Dieterle. What was best about these short-lived enterprises was that all of them were looking for something new in the way both of plays and of designers. And in this they resembled the promising new Sunday theatre club which was set up in 1922 by the young Moritz Seeler under the name Junge Bühne or Young Stage and in the six years of its activity was to introduce the work of such writers as Bronnen, Brecht, Zuckmayer, and Marieluise Fleisser. Operating in various different Berlin theatres and always closely watched by the critics, it would play a crucial role over the greater part of the decade.

Both the change of feeling around 1922–23 and the shift of economic climate, as we have described them, were specific to Germany. Nevertheless, like Expressionism itself, they can also be seen as more intense versions of what was happening on the wider European scene. For, looked at in the most simple terms, the whole continent was experiencing a return to normal following the wartime chaos and the revolutionary disorders that had resulted from the fall of tsarism and the faltering of the ruling order in Central Europe. This was visible even in Bolshevik Russia, where Lenin's New Economic Policy in 1921 reintroduced a measure of capitalism after the Civil War was over, while between 1922 and 1924 a number of international agreements went some way toward opening up Germany and Russia first to one another, then to the still relatively stable regimes of Western Europe and the United States. What this meant in practical terms is clear enough if you remember that the previous eight years of isolation had kept the rest of the world ignorant of the new German theatre, at the same time cutting the latter off from all knowledge of the American cinema and in great measure from foreign plays. The Rapallo Treaty of 1922 between Germany and Russia formalized a new relationship between the two pariah countries, with particular implications in the cultural sphere, while the ensuing recognition of the new Republic by Britain and subsequently France likewise marked a greater ease of exchanges and freedom of individual movement.

Though Reinhardt had resumed his tours to the Scandinavian countries in the winter of 1920–21, it seems that his Austrian interests thereafter supervened. At the beginning of 1924, however, he could take *The Miracle* to New York, financed by Otto H. Kahn, for a spectacularly successful run which continued into the next season, encouraging him to return there three years later with *A Midsummer Night's Dream*, *Everyman*, and three more of his best-known productions. Meanwhile one of his former actors, Ernst Lubitsch, who had directed the film of *Sumurûn*, moved to Hollywood in 1923 to become the first of several major German-trained directors in that city. From Russia Stanislavsky had already sent his Moscow Art Theatre company to Berlin at the end of 1921, though at the time his productions seemed very remote from what was expected of a revolutionary society and left little trace. What counted rather was the arrival of Alexander Tairoff and his Kamerny Theater (or Kammerspiele) in the spring of 1923, less than half a year after the first big Soviet art exhibition had been held in Berlin. In addition, there was now a German-led organization responsible to the Comintern whose function was in part the promotion of such cultural exchanges; this was the IAH (Internationale Arbeiter-Hilfe, Mezhrabpom, or International Workers' Aid), which had been set up by Willi Muenzenberg to channel foreign assistance to the Russian "workers' state," with Franz Jung as its Moscow representative and Piscator as chairman of its "Artists' Aid" committee. So far as actual plays were concerned the Russians for their part seem to have had nothing new to offer, but, conversely, there were no fewer than six Toller productions in Moscow, Leningrad, and Tiflis between November 1922 and the end of the following year.

It was in the course of 1923 that the German stage seriously began looking abroad for new plays to do. Of these, Shaw's *Pygmalion* and *Saint Joan*, both played at the Deutsches Theater, were undoubted successes—the latter in a production by Reinhardt, who had temporarily come back from Vienna, with Bergner as the saint—but then Shaw had been in that theatre's repertoire for nearly twenty years, and both *Caesar and Cleopatra* and *Misalliance* had been staged there since the war. Synge too, whose *Playboy of the Western World* was done for the first time in February 1924 by Viertel's Die Truppe under Hilpert, was not new to Germany, nor was Claudel, whose *L'Échange* had been staged the previous year at Frankfurt. However, there were also productions of Chesterton's *Magic*, Maugham's *The Circle*, Crommelynck's *Les Amants puérils* and *The Magnificent Cuckold*, and the two Čapek plays, *The Insect Play* and *R.U.R.*, this last with a set by the Austrian Friedrich Kiesler. The most substantial of the imported novelties were the plays of two newcomers: Pirandello and Eugene O'Neill. Of the latter, *Anna Christie*, *The Hairy Ape*, *Moon of the Caribbees*, and *The Emperor Jones* were all performed without much success at different Berlin theatres between October 1923 and the end of 1924, the last named once again by Die Truppe in a generally criticized production by Viertel with sets by Kiesler and with Homolka as Jones. *Desire under the Elms*, which the same director staged for the Lessing-Theater a year later, fell even flatter, though around the same time it was being successfully enough performed in Russia, Czechoslovakia, and elsewhere. Skimming through contemporary reviews, one detects perhaps a certain reluctance to find much merit in any imports from America, even though O'Neill was one of the English-language writers most influenced by the modern German drama. Perhaps this was part of the trouble, for the trend that seems to have impressed O'Neill most was the Expressionism of Kaiser and Hasenclever, which was no longer felt to be all that exciting in its country of origin. In any case O'Neill made a lot less impact than Pirandello, whose *Così è, se vi pare* (or *Right You Are, If You Think So*) was first played at Barnowsky's newly acquired Theater in der Königgrätzer Strasse in spring 1924, heralding a whole sequence of productions, among which Reinhardt's *Six Characters* at his new Komödie theatre at the end of that year (with Pallenberg as the Direttore) made much the deepest impression. This was pure theatre of a unique kind, flickering between dream and reality, interpreted by a master of theatrical ambiguity so as to convey something quite new.

The Experimental Fringe and Its Limits

If the international return to normality opened the way for fresh influences, it also saw the ending of virtually all those other schools which had contributed

Experimental theatre at the Bauhaus before 1924. This unattributed tableau from Oskar Schlemmer's theatre department reflects the conventions of international Dada. Photo by Tom Willett.

to Expressionism and played comparable roles in the rest of Europe over much the same period. Most notably in France the art and music critics had begun speaking of a "return to order" soon after the end of the war, meaning the conversion of the former avant-garde to a more figurative, decorative type of painting and a clearer, more rhythmical, and populist school of music fusing neoclassicism with the new language of American jazz. Cubism was now practically dead; Italian Futurism and Metaphysical art had run their course even before Mussolini's advent in 1922; Dada, too, came to an end, with the German movement effectively breaking up after 1920 while the French wing headed into Surrealism from late 1922 on. Marcel Duchamp gave up art. "Reaction in art and literature is the line here," noted Kessler during a visit to Paris at the beginning of 1923.[11] The new Surrealist movement never seriously touched Germany, where the decisive new influences now came from Hungary and Russia. Instead there was the two-pronged impact of Constructivism—that is to say on the one hand both the pure three-dimensional abstraction, carried out in various materials and with kinetic elements, and introduced by new arrivals like Lissitzky and Moholy-Nagy—and on the other the more utilitarian version, which Soviet artists such as Popova, Stepanova, and the Vesnin brothers were now applying in stage design, textiles, and similar practical fields. Closely allied to the rationalistic machine art now being propagated by Le Corbusier from Paris (and exemplified there in Léger's paintings), this new movement found its first expression in the Berlin theatre in Kiesler's mechanical-kinetic sets for *R.U.R.*

The bilingual Goll, who from 1919 on lived mainly in Paris, wrote an article in Le Corbusier's magazine to tell French readers that the German theatre was "at least fifteen years" ahead of their own; and perhaps this long start is why Germany never developed much of an avant-garde fringe but could so quickly absorb significant innovations even once Expressionism was over. Only around 1923 was there a spate of "alternative" experimental activity centering largely on the Weimar Bauhaus, where a major shift of direction was now taking place. This was associated with Gropius's appointment that same spring of Moholy-Nagy as head of the basic course, followed shortly after by Kandinsky's arrival from Russia as a senior teacher. Two years earlier a theatre department had been set up there under Lothar Schreyer, a romantic mystic (and undistinguished painter) previously associated with Walden's Sturm-Bühne in Berlin; but the first display of the students' stage work proved a great disappointment, and Oskar Schlemmer had then been put in charge instead. Schlemmer, himself a dancer as well as a fine painter and outstanding sculptor, had staged his own highly abstract *Triadic Ballet* at the Stuttgart Landestheater in 1922 (where he had already designed and choreographed two one-act operas by Paul Hindemith, Germany's leading young neoclassical composer). Holl brought him from that city to the Berlin Volksbühne to design sporadic productions, including *Hamlet* in spring 1925, and would seemingly have given him a permanent job if Schlemmer had not preferred to pursue his more experimental work. This was seen most spectacularly at the first Bauhaus Exhibition in Weimar during the summer of 1923, marking Gropius's new policy of the unity of Art and Technology. For here the Weimar National-Theater performed the *Triadic Ballet* (for which Hindemith subsequently wrote music), while the students' *Mechanical Ballet*, executed to H. H. Stuckenschmidt's music by abstract forms and moving figures, was included with other experiments in the theatre at neighboring Jena. The same occasion saw one of the earliest German performances of Stravinsky's *The Soldier's Tale*, that crucial work of the new "music theatre," under the avant-garde conductor Hermann Scherchen, who had introduced it at Frankfurt in the spring.

Schlemmer put together his book *Die Bühne im Bauhaus* early in 1924.[12] This was a cross-section of the ideas then current in the school, which as yet had no stage of its own, with the result that its work could only be realized on a puppet scale or else filtered into the local theatre. Schreyer plays no part here; nor do the two Bauhaus-trained artists (Franz Singer and Friedl Dicker) who designed Viertel's *Merchant of Venice*. The presiding "signs of our times," rather, are held to be Abstraction and Mechanization, together with the new possibilities of realizing them which "Technology and Invention" would provide. First in the book comes Schlemmer's own work: graphic analyses of theatre and the positioning and movements of the human body in space, followed by photographs of his very striking masked, geometrical, toylike ballet figures and the Dadaistic sets for his improvised Bauhaus shows. Echoing these are similar Dada-type projects by Marcel Breuer and Xanti Schawinsky, then a number of mechanical kinetic shows by Kurt Schmidt, executed by puppets or expressed as sequences of drawings. At the same time Schlemmer also includes a couple of much more radical proposals, which remain forward-looking even today. One such was Farkas Molnár's sixteen-hundred-seat "U-theatre" with a deep thrust stage, a so-called hanging stage above it on a level with the first circle, a mobile suspended cylinder for lighting and acrobatics, and various kinds of gadgets for pumping out synthetic sounds and smells. The other was Moholy-Nagy's concept—once again graphically worked out—of a form of variety show involving what he termed "mechanical eccentricity": that is to say, an elaborately scored mixture of film, music, sirens, clowning, smells, electrically generated thunder and lightning, explosions, phosphorescence, hydraulics, colored light, and mechanical kinetic effects. This was meant to be only the first step toward a "theatre of totality," where the actor might find his features and expressions being blown up on a screen, while phrases of his speech were amplified or his thought processes conveyed by loudspeaker and/or film. The mixed result would be a "completely balanced organism" not unlike the circus, whose exemplary qualities (such as the clowning of Chaplin and the Fratellinis) seemed to Moholy to prove that "the soundest instincts and wishes" were often to be found among "the despised masses—for all their supposed academic backwardness,"[13] a judgment that seems like an updated echo of Behrens, Appia, and Craig.

Meantime Dada, already dead in Berlin, was still a force in the fringe theatres of Paris (to be seen in the work of Tristan Tzara and Georges Ribemont-Dessaignes); a year or two later it also surfaced in the Liberated Theatre and Théâtre Dada of Prague, where the clowns Voskovec and Werich kept its spirit alive long after it was defunct elsewhere. In Germany apart from the Bauhaus it survived mainly in the happenings and largely unintelligible nonverbal public readings of Kurt Schwitters, whose "Merz"—in effect, "rubbish art"—nonsense movement had begun as an offshoot of the Sturm stage and its poets in 1919. For some years Schwitters operated as a one-man group in Hannover, largely spurned by the now sharply political Berlin Dadaists but still in friendly contact with Tzara and Arp. Then in 1922 he formed a lasting alliance with Theo van Doesburg of *De Stijl,* who had come to Weimar in the hope of helping the Bauhaus enter its new technological phase. A tour of Holland ensued, with Van Doesburg, his pianist wife and the Hungarian architect Vilmos Huszár performing Dada programs with phonetic poetry and a mechanical puppet on Bauhaus lines. This experience allowed Schwitters to clarify his hitherto rambling and mainly verbal concept of a Merz stage through constructivist models and drawings bearing a close relation to current Bauhaus ideas. After showing them at the Vienna international theatre exhibition in 1924 he went on to sketch a Merz "Normalbühne" space stage with steps and platforms, a glass stage suspended above, and a rope ladder descending to it from overhead. It was not, however, carried out.[14]

Quite independently of such Bauhaus and constructivist influences, Goll in Paris had been writing a handful of post-Expressionist works of a Dadaist kind which he termed "superrealism,"[15] thus indicating (like Breton and the subsequent Surrealists) his indebtedness to the Franco-Polish poet Guillaume Apollinaire. Léger and George Grosz provided his illustrations; Georg Kaiser was a supporter; Kurt Weill set his poem "Der neue Orpheus" to music; and in

Augsburg at the end of 1920 the two little farces called *Die Unsterblichen (The Immortals)* were favorably reviewed by a young local critic called Bertolt Brecht. Though there is no record of any performance of either of these, Goll's full-length satirical drama *Methusalem oder Der ewige Bürger (Methuselah, or the Eternal Bourgeois)* was scheduled to be performed in Berlin in 1922 under William Dieterle's direction, with designs by Grosz. For unknown reasons this fell through, and instead the play was produced two years later with a different designer and director, to laughter and applause and the warm approval of the critic Alfred Kerr; Goll himself thought this came too late.

All three of those works, along with the "film poem" about Chaplin which preceded them, were modern but practicable texts, largely anticipating Ionesco, whose *Bald Prima Donna* contains dialogue in much the same tersely nonsensical style; Artaud, too, played in Jean Painlevé's Paris production of *Methusalem* in 1927. Once again they call for a modern "theatrical theatre," starting with the use of masks. Thus Goll's foreword to *Die Unsterblichen* states:

> The new drama must call in all the technical methods that are now taking on the effect of the mask. For example we have the gramophone as mask of the voice, the electric advertising sign, or the speaking tube. The actors must wear unnaturally proportioned face masks which allow their characters to be crudely and super-ficially recognised: an unduly large ear, white eyes, legs on stilts.[16]

Again, in the *Methusalem* foreword he argues the case for the new nonsense theatre:

> At the same time illogicality serves to show the tenfold shiftings of a human brain that thinks one thing and says another and carries on hopping from thought to thought without the least evidence of any logical connection.
>
> But if the writer isn't to be a cry-baby, a pacifist or a Salvationist, then he must cut a caper or two to take you back to your childhood. For what does he want to do but give you puppets, show you how to play, and then, when the puppets are broken, shake their sawdust once more into the wind?[17]

Signs of a New Reality

These were years of change, when Expressionism disappeared from the German scene and something else seemed to be preparing to make an entrance. Perhaps it was not yet entirely clear what that something would be, since so much was still in flux: new directors, new types of design, new groupings of actors, new influences from abroad, not to mention unsettled audiences and discontented critics. Yet already there was a nucleus of plays and productions that seemed to point toward the changed theatre which would come with full economic recovery. A jumping-off point had been reached (as indeed proved to be the case for the Republic itself); the Utopian, revolutionary phase was finally over, and although its passing left unhealed wounds and unfulfilled aims, there was, in the arts at least, a great curiosity as

Kaiser's 'People's Play' of the German inflation of 1923. The "Pension" scene of his *Nebeneinander* in the original production by Berthold Viertel, with sets by George Grosz. Photo by Cologne University Theatre Museum.

to what would happen next. Despite the new activities of the avant-garde, the theatre's transformation was neither instant nor total; but enough had been achieved in the way of new work, reevaluation, and reinterpretations to suggest that the German stage would now follow much the same course as had the other arts. Literature, painting, and architecture had already grown less frenzied, harder, more down-to-earth and matter-of-fact; they were less concerned with Mankind and more with individual fates. Thus in 1922 the magazine *Das Kunstblatt* canvassed artists for their views of the "new naturalism" to be seen in the paintings of Dix and Max Beckmann, and within months the crucial Neue Sachlichkeit exhibition was being planned, which would give its name to the new, realistic, socially critical school. Similarly Ernst Rowohlt the publisher dropped nearly all his former Expressionist authors and started turning to books of fact and travel, popular history, and mainly foreign novels. As for the new practicality of the Bauhaus, it was widely echoed across the architectural scene.

In the view of the Berlin audience and critics the first play to embody this unpretentious coolness was Georg Kaiser's *Volksstück*, or people's play, *Nebeneinander* (literally, *Alongside Each Other* or *Side by Side*), which Viertel staged with Die Truppe in the Komödienhaus on 3 November 1923. This was a play very much about Berlin in the inflation era, a colder, more cynical version of his earlier "station dramas." Neatly organized in five acts, each divided into three scenes set in the play's three different milieux, it follows (a) the pilgrimage of a (nameless) pawnbroker who wishes to stop an unknown girl's threatened suicide; (b) the love affair of the girl with a friend of her lockkeeper brother-in-law somewhere in the north German countryside; (c) the shady but successful operations of Herr Neumann, her former seducer, who helps to launch a film starlet to commercial success. The triple ending is tragic for the pawnbroker, who loses his livelihood and kills himself for having "got so involved in the fate of one's neighbor"[18] cozily happy for the girl, as the schoolchildren gather outside to play and sing for her wedding feast, profitable for the seducer, who is left heading for a great career, punctuated by occasional romps with the starlet. The dialogue is terse as ever, but shot through with Berlin dialect and the odd phrase of business English, and very much of its time. "Shut up," says the starlet to her cinema-owning brother, "I'm intrigued by Herr Neumann's *Sachlichkeit*."[19] In Viertel's production the play even began like a film, with the title and cast flickeringly projected on a screen. Sets and costumes by Grosz look characteristically sharp and satirical, though Siegfried Jacobson complained of the lack of a revolve, which meant that in effect the tempo was thrown out each time there was a scene change. Nonetheless he, too, saw the play as a great step forward: "Georg Kaiser," he wrote in the *Weltbühne*, "has tumbled off the cloud which long cloaked him from view, and landed with both feet on the earth."[20] "More open, more mobile, more humane," commented Alfred Döblin, to whom the earlier Kaiser had seemed something of an adolescent even in his forties. "The man is stirring, *incipit vir*."[21] Or as we would say, he had started growing up.

Barlach, too, was not the Expressionist playwright he was once thought to be, though in his case it wasn't so much he who had changed as the understanding of his plays shown by their interpreters, their critics, and their audiences. Though his first play *Der tote Tag (The Dead Day)* had indeed been Expressionist, and was rightly staged as such by Erich Ziegel in Hamburg in 1919, the trouble was that all its successors had been viewed and understood in the same way. To some extent this was due to the force of his sculptures, whose style was quite wrongly linked with that of his writing, even by persons as scrupulous as Jessner and as skeptical as Herbert Jhering. In fact, however, *Der arme Vetter* and *Die echten Sedemunds* were in no way passionate, messianic, rhetorical, self-dramatizing, or contorted, but instead were made up of a largely new mixture of shrewd, realistic, often humorous observation, closely based on Barlach's own North German environment, with flashes of inspired fantasy or oddness. Both these plays describe the complicated network of events on a special day—the first taking place on Easter Day among trippers beside the Elbe, the second at a fair in a small north German town where a menagerie lion is thought to have escaped—events sometimes farcical, sometimes socially revealing, and now and again transforming or maybe wrecking the characters' lives.

Yet when Jessner staged the second of them at the Staatstheater in April 1921, despite having discussed it with the author in his Mecklenburg home he set it on a vast, bare, stepped-up stage such as he had used for *William Tell*. There he stylized the actors' movements, apparently basing their costumes on what he knew of Barlach's sculptures. The effect, to judge from the reviews, was to suggest a visionary play which the author's inconsequential story and richly characterized dialogue had somehow come along to confuse. Barlach subsequently said that he would have preferred a naturalistic production; however, the only critic who understood this was Jacobsohn, who felt that Jessner had mistakenly regarded the author/artist as being up in those clouds "where everything starts to be subject to new and peculiar rules which are arbitrarily termed Expressionist,"[22] whereas he, for his part, would have liked to see Jessner "go ahead blindly and for once tackle the whole of human life." "A play by Herr Jessner, not by me," was Barlach's verdict. "Film tempo and expression: I want no part of it."[23]

Yet with *Der arme Vetter* two years later at the same theatre Jessner's newly arrived director Jürgen Fehling was able to give full value to the story's well-contrasted complexities in such a way as to establish its author as a leader of the post-Expressionist school. This was the production which made Jhering change his view about the relative importance of Barlach's words and his sculptural vision, and admit that there was a productive force in the plays which he had not previously recognized. For Fehling's policy, which deeply impressed itself on Heinrich George, his leading actor, was to grasp the uniqueness and idiosyncrasies of each character, with the result that the many secondary parts on which Barlach depended for his texture of contrasts were (by all accounts) beautifully played, with a careful and sensitive regard to the main thread of events. This world of seemingly ordinary lower-middle-class excursionists, set in evocative designs by Rochus Gliese, was in Paul Fechter's words "half-comfortable, half-uneasy, half-ridiculous and half-ghostly,"[24] while Jhering too saw the whole performance as balancing the concrete and the fantastic. The one serious fault in Fehling's production was the fact that it lasted for four hours, something that Jessner would never have allowed to himself. As for the actual play, Barlach's distinctive qualities for the first time became clear: the imaginative realism, the dry wit, the illogical flow of events, "unfolding, not developing,"[25] as one ancient critic complained, the grasp of life's multiplicity—visual, auditory, psychological—and then, at the end of it all, what Jacobsohn called "a shudder running over one's bones."[26]

It was Fehling, too, who was subsequently able to do much the same for another wrongly categorized work, Else Lasker-Schüler's *Die Wupper (The River Wupper)*, a play likewise about the dramatist's own home territory, written before 1914, originally in the local Wuppertal dialect. This, though not performed at the time of its writing (which she incidentally claimed was done in the course of a single August night), had been treated as an Expressionist play because of the author's frequent, if rather questionable, inclusion among the Expressionist poets. It had originally been staged for a single performance in Reinhardt's Das junge Deutschland series in April 1919 by Heinz Herald with mock-Expressionist sets by Stern. But once again it was not the work it was taken to be, nor was it in any way related to Lasker-Schüler's somewhat arch poems; rather, it was a rich naturalistic chain of events in a specific city, some tragic, some comic, some critically observant of the local society—what the author described to Jessner as "a city ballad with smoking chimneys and railway signals."[27] Once again it was Fehling's great if always reticent talents that brought it to the right kind of complex life at the Staatstheater in 1927. "I've no idea how I came to write that," was her verdict after the premiere, "but let me tell you, Fehling, I meant it exactly the way you did it."[28] Almost by accident, in other words, these earlier plays now turned out to be a distinctive kind of many-layered realist drama, written with wit and fantasy and a strong sense of place and of the particular society attaching to it. And this relates them not merely to the great change of mood and approach now under way in the theatre but to other writers yet to establish themselves in much the same vein: notably Marieluise Fleisser, Carl Zuckmayer, and Ödön von Horvath. With the last named we again find Kaiser's descriptive label "People's Play."

Having lost Fehling to the Staatstheater, Holl's regime at the Volksbühne at the end of the 1923–24 season engaged a new director, in the shape of the now jobless Erwin Piscator. His first production there was of a political play of an unfamiliar, tersely factual kind, subheaded "an epic drama" by its journalist author, which Kayssler had accepted (very possibly on the advice of Arthur Holitscher) but made no arrangements to produce. This was *Fahnen* (Flags) by Alfons Paquet, a visitor to the new Russia, who, like Piscator himself, was involved with the IAH. The subject of this somewhat indifferent but, as it turned out, seminal work was the Chicago anarchist trials of 1886–87, presented in a series of short scenes in a complicated permanent set by Edward Suhr, the Volksbühne's main designer at the time, and given a new "documentary" quality by the use of screens for the projection of posters, news items, and quasi cinematic captions. Piscator himself added a commentator in order to abolish the distance between stage and audience, drawing the latter into the events until the theatre was like a political meeting, which ended in a shower of red flags fluttering down on to the stage. The result was not merely a contract that established Piscator as one of Berlin's most prominent directors for the next three years, but more immediately a deliberately political revue which he got together, outside any theatre, for the KPD's election campaign at the end of 1924. This again used projections (of topical photographs and George Grosz drawings), becoming a model for the agitprop groups which subsequently began to be set up on the pattern of the first Soviet "Blue Blouses." Moreover, this low point in Communist fortunes (for the elections themselves were a disaster for the KPD and the Nazis alike) coincided with a change in that party's view of the arts. For the new chief critic of its daily *Die Rote Fahne (The Red Flag)*, the Hungarian Constructivist sympathiser Alfred Kemény, threw over its previous aesthetic conservatism, while a new Red Group of artists was set up in June 1924 including Piscator, Grosz, Heartfield, and others of the old Dada iconoclasts. Unfortunately this was only short-lived.

Around the same time a new, still virtually unpolitical group of innovators was moving from Munich to Berlin, where Felix Holländer had engaged them for the Deutsches Theater as one of his last acts before leaving. This comprised Bertolt Brecht, his school friend the designer Caspar Neher, the director Erich Engel, who had previously worked in Hamburg (notably with Kortner, who became a close friend) and, slightly apart from this trio,

The new team from Munich. *In the Jungle* at the Munich Residenztheater in May 1923: a play by the twenty-five-year old Bertolt Brecht, with sets by Caspar Neher, directed by Erich Engel. Eighteen months later all three men had moved to Berlin. Photo by Deutsches Theatermuseum.

Carl Zuckmayer who had recently had to leave Kiel after adapting and staging a free version of Terence's *The Eunuch* that featured a giant phallus, a naked actress with orange-colored breasts, and the military figures of Hindenburg and Ludendorff. The central personality here was certainly Brecht, whose *Drums in the Night* had been staged in Expressionist style by Falckenberg at the Munich Kammerspiele in September 1922 and thereafter was played in some forty other German theatres including the Deutsches Theater, where Falckenberg again directed it that December. Having been vainly put forward by Brecht as the right designer for that play, Neher was allowed to design *In the Jungle* under Engel's direction in Munich the following May, then again at the Deutsches Theater, with Kortner as the sinister Malayan, Shlink. *Baal*, too—actually the first of Brecht's plays in time of writing—was staged in Leipzig at the end of 1923 by Alwin Kronacher. Neher knew the play backward and had done many drawings for it, but this time he was not involved.

The state of this very promising alliance in the autumn of 1924, when Brecht and Zuckmayer arrived to take up junior posts with the Reinhardt concern, was that Engel had by then established himself as a leading director by his first two Berlin productions (which included *Danton's Death* with Kortner), and that Neher became his regular partner. For Brecht Neher was indispensable (conversely Neher did his best work when Brecht was most closely involved) as was Engel, too, in those cases where Brecht, a difficult and not infrequently nasty customer, was not allowed to direct himself. Zuckmayer remained a friend and a colleague rather than an ally, but elsewhere Brecht had his provincial supporters like the dramaturg Jakob Geis in Munich and the young writer Melchior Vischer in Frankfurt. Given his friendships with Bronnen and Döblin and the critical support which he always got from Herbert Jhering, he now struck Berlin not just as a new dramatist but more like a new force.

Coming on top of the change in Kaiser, the fresh, realistic interpretation of Barlach, and the discovery by Piscator of the epic and documentary theatre, Brecht's rejection of the well-made plot with its preternaturally logical structure, backed by Neher's stripped-down artistry and Engel's intellectualism, seemed part of a distinctive school. This was not confined merely to Brecht's or Barlach's plays—indeed, it would be four years before any new work of Brecht's was seen in Berlin, unless one counts the single Junge Bühne performance of a revised and shortened version of *Baal*—but also led to a new, less emotive and overheated (or portentous and ossified) way of presenting the classics. Though Jessner had in some degree paved the way by his dramaturgical clarity, cutting ruthlessly back to the main thrust of the story and imposing a largely abstract though still atmospheric vision, it was Brecht's adaptation of *Edward II* that broke new ground by transposing Marlowe's original into the conventions, and to a great extent the language, of his own emergent "epic theatre." This strong, harsh, containedly violent approach was very evident in his Munich production of March 1924 with Neher's plain painted sets; 'I'd never seen history plays staged in such an emphatically simple style', said Asja Lacis, who watched the rehearsals with her husband Bernard Reich, then one of the Kammerspiele's directors.[29] The play, however, seems to have been less effective when Fehling directed it for the Staatstheater that December in a dragging tempo, half-darkness, and sets by Rochus Gliese. (This remained Fehling's only attempt at Brecht.) The unspoken target here for both Brecht and Neher had evidently been the German theatre's interpretations of Shakespeare—whether on Reinhardt's or on Jessner's lines—and indeed the project had begun as a substitute for a partly planned production of *Macbeth*. Much the same thinking was evident at the beginning of 1925 when Engel and Neher staged *Coriolanus* at the Lessing-Theater with the Deutsches Theater company and Kortner in the title part. *Coriolanus* in this interpretation was no contemptuous aristocrat but a passionately ambitious climber; there was no glamorizing of war; the gray, steel-helmeted soldiers were modern cannon fodder with whitened faces like those in the Munich *Edward II*. Later the line would continue on to Jessner's updated antimonarchist *Hamlet* and Piscator's 1926 *Die Räuber (The Robbers)* by Schiller with its relevance to the Left's campaign for expropriating the old princely rulers.

Ambiguity of the Expressionist Heritage

And yet apart from Piscator, who had come from the Dada stable and was a KPD member, all these seemingly new-wave figures had in one way or another tangled with Expressionism—which is why they are still apt to be seen as somehow rooted in that movement. In Kaiser's case the reason is clear enough, for although he was never "Expressionist-Expressionist" (in Alfred Kerr's definition)—that is to say never all that rhetorical in his dialogue or self-centered in his choice of hero—he was for a while at the heart of the Expressionist theatre. Indeed his nameless Pawnbroker in *Nebeneinander* has something of the naive, buffeted, puppetlike quality of the protagonists of such extreme station dramas as *From Morn to Midnight* and *Hölle, Weg, Erde*. Hence it is possible to see the new, populist *Nebeneinander* as still being Expressionist for the first third of each of its scenes, with the old Utopian values each time becoming gradually defeated by the world of 1923. With other such writers, however, it is important to distinguish between what was actually Expressionistic in their work and what simply could be seen as such if put in an Expressionist framework or applied in an Expressionist production. This kind of "guilt by association" (as it were) is what at first hampered understanding of Barlach's two inspiredly realistic early plays, while *Die Wupper* was long seen in the light of the Expressionist milieu in which its author happened to move. Nor should the question whether Barlach's sculpture or Lasker-Schüler's verse was or was not strictly Expressionist affect our judgment of them as playwrights. That Barlach did not wish to be considered an Expressionist writer seems quite clear.

Similarly with Brecht, who as early as June 1918 was telling Neher that "Expressionism is frightful"[30] while working on the first version of *Baal*. Admittedly he had considerable respect for Georg Kaiser, though much less for Unruh, Toller, Rubiner, and Werfel; but if he too is thought to have gone through an Expressionist phase it is partly because of his alliance with Bronnen and partly because of the Munich production of *Drums in the Night*. This was characterized by its contorted acting, its quasi symbolic use of a large red moon, and the expressive distortions of Reigbert's sets; the photographs are still vivid. Yet Brecht himself was aware also of an Expressionist element in all his dramatic work before *Edward II*, and in the case of both *Baal* and *In the Jungle* he made extensive revisions so as to take it out. With *Drums in the Night*, whose final act (in the schnapps bar or gin mill) gave him endless trouble, he lost interest in the play following its great success, though when he did have to revise it for republication some thirty years later he cut down a great deal of the wild poetry somewhat as he had done for the 1926 *Baal*. In other words, whereas Neher, so far as we can now see, never had an Expressionist phase—indeed about the only twentieth-century artist who visibly influenced him was Klee—Brecht's attitude was mixed, so that much later he would be found defending Expressionism against the Moscow German-language critics as a source of new and liberating formal ideas. What the Expressionist example did perhaps help to give him in this way, apart from a license to use the tremendously vivid, almost physical language which first drew Jhering to his work, was that structural principle of "one thing after another," which can be found in the station drama as well as in *Woyzeck* and, before that, in Shakespeare's chronicle plays.

What, then, was still fertile in the legacy of the earlier movement? To start with, the importance attached to language as a motive force, along with the structural freedom that made it possible to return to an epic, by conventional standards illogical, form of narrative. Likewise the fluidity of lighting, which had really been initiated by Reinhardt, though the use of projections to document the narrative was new. What had gone, at least for the foreseeable future, was the Utopianism, the high rhetoric, the cries of "O Man!" and a good deal of the stylized overemphasis of attitude, movement, posture, and facial expression. What had now arrived as part of the changed climate was the coolness, the irony, the realistically set out complexity of human characters and relationships; the tragic, comic, or satirical alertness to paradox. Formally, perhaps, the change at the moment of stabilization was more gradual than we now tend to think. Spiritually and atmospherically it was complete.

Entertainment takes over. The box office annexes the mass theatre. Chorus girls rehearsing for one of Erik Charell's Grosses Schauspielhaus revues in the 1926–27 season. Photo by Ullstein Bilderdienst.

6

The Twenties Strike Gold

Restoration and Money for the Arts

Within eighteen months of the currency stabilization the Republic was set on the new and boomingly prosperous course which it would follow until 1929. The steadying of the mark, the ending of the national state of emergency, the conservative abandonment of separatism in Bavaria and the Rhineland, the Dawes Plan, the economic unification of the country, the new private American loans, the French withdrawal from the Ruhr: coming one on top of the other, these several factors established an entirely new perspective for the country, which now settled down under a combination of right-center national (or federal) government and left-center government in Prussia, the great province which covered some two-thirds of the country including Berlin. To the SPD, which had set aside whatever hope it once had of realizing its Socialist aims, this appears to have been a tolerable enough arrangement; for industry too it became one as a result of the restoration of the economy, which remained entirely capitalist, even the railways being reprivatized. And true enough, the new setup did almost at once begin to look like a return to the prewar Reich in all but name. For the country's first president, the SPD leader Friedrich Ebert, died at the end of February 1925, and the man whom Germany then chose to succeed him was not, as expected, a middle-of-the-road politician but the old wartime head of the army, Field

Marshal Paul von Hindenburg. Admittedly no move was made to bring back the former emperor or his family (who were now vegetating in Holland), nor did Hindenburg query the Weimar constitution, though he did not interpret it in a very liberal sense. But all in all the nationalists, the army, the big landowners, and the industrialists were better placed than they ever had been since 1918. The old ruling houses were assured of their private fortunes, and an antidemocratic adventurer like Franz von Papen could now begin his disastrous clamber to the top.

It was not altogether a good situation for Germany as a whole, but it was just that for the arts. For while on the one hand the new prosperity quickly benefited them by modernizing the "apparatus" and lubricating the box office, at the same time the sense of opposition, social criticism, and satire which had so spurred many of the most gifted practitioners was not allowed to die. The new right-wing establishment in fact was so comfortably settled-in that it could not only afford to tolerate a good measure of sharp sniping from the more uncomfortable artists (like Brecht and Piscator, not to mention the now commercially viable George Grosz), but would pay good money to experience the process. Even the Socialist rank and file were more satisfied with their lot, for the massive unemployment that followed the stabilization—1.5 million at the end of 1923—fell to less than two hundred thousand by the middle of 1925, and two years later the SPD was for the first time able to introduce a system of unemployment insurance. Up till the 1928 elections, which saw considerable gains by that party, the general rule was that the Socialists opposed government policy at home while supporting Stresemann's intelligent and courageous conduct of affairs abroad. This did not stop largely Socialist cities like Berlin and Frankfurt, or for that matter the Prussian state, from going ahead with major communal programs locally. In particular the housing and town planning in those two cities, as also in Stuttgart and Dessau (the new home of the Bauhaus from October 1925) and the fringes of Hannover, were socially and architecturally outstanding.

With the new climate came the recognition of a fresh spirit in the arts which, like its predecessor Expressionism, began as a visual movement and then fanned out—in the manner unique to Germany—to affect a number of other fields. This was *Die neue Sachlichkeit*, the new matter-of-factness, objectivity, or sobriety, which formally announced itself with a painting exhibition at Mannheim in the summer of 1925. *Sachlichkeit* was already a term for any attitude that seemed down-to-earth, economical, and sober, and the "new" version quickly became attached to that functionalism in architecture which had been inspired by Le Corbusier's machine-based ideas. In writing it came to cover reportage, literature of fact, the light but sharp cabaret-influenced poetry of Tucholsky and Erich Kästner (of *Emil and the Detectives* fame); in music the matter-of-fact utilitarianism of Hindemith and the young Kurt Weill, with its search for links with the new technological world. As for the theatre, the situation was more complicated, and the label not so often used. But Sternheim gave it as a subtitle to one of his minor plays (*Die Schule von Uznach*, 1926); the Essen theatre magazine *Der Scheinwerfer (The Searchlight)* under Brecht's friend Hannes Küpper propagated the movement; and perhaps nothing popularized it better than the theme song of Marcellus Schiffer and Mischa Spoliansky's 1928 Berlin revue *Es liegt in der Luft* ("It's in the Air"), which starts, *"Es liegt in der Luft eine Sachlichkeit"*:

> There's something in the air called objectivity,
> There's something in the air like electricity.
> There's something in the air, and it's in the air,
> >   the air [. . .]
> And you can't get it out of the air.
>
> What has come over the air these days?
> Oh, the air has fallen for a brand-new craze.
> Through the air are swiftly blown
> Pictures, radio, telephone [. . .]
> There's the air, just hear it humming!
> Trunk calls, trios in B flat
> In the gaps that are left a picture's coming. . . .[1]

For the media were changing and expanding, new techniques were being pursued (notably in relation to radio, film, photography, and electro-mechanical sound reproduction) while the relevant industries were regrouping and attracting American capital, if only on short-term loan. Under the Dawes Plan for reviving Germany's finances (not least with a view to its international obligation to pay war reparations) 800 million gold marks were supposedly to be loaned, mainly by American banks and finance houses; and in the event it turned out to be twice as much. The great electrical firms, Siemens and AEG, prospered; in the chemical industry I. G. Farben, the vast combine which includes Agfa, was set up in December 1925, while that same year the Parafumet agreement between UFA (under the extreme nationalist Alfred Hugenberg), Paramount, and MGM effectively tied the German cinema industry to Hollywood, giving the latter quota proof outlets in the German cinemas and a call on German directors and actors (thus Murnau, Jannings, and Erich Pommer went to Hollywood in 1926). New cinemas were built, notably the Capitol and Universum cinemas in Berlin, by Poelzig and Erich Mendelsohn respectively. There were a few new theatre buildings, notably the deliberately "West End" Komödie, which Reinhardt commissioned Oskar Kaufmann to design him with old-style boxes and inaugurated with *The Servant of Two Masters* in November 1924; and the new Essen municipal theatre, which opened under Martin Kerb in 1927.

There were several modernizations or reconstructions that installed revolves, lifts, or modern lighting equipment and abolished the raked stage; among the houses affected being first and foremost the Berlin State Opera (1926–28) the municipal operas in Essen and Hannover, the Kroll Opera in Berlin (1924), the Hamburg municipal theatre and the Oldenburg Land theatres in Schwerin and Neustrelitz (1927–28). Arc lights were replaced by high-powered new bulbs; film projection equipment was in some cases added or brought up to date. After 1927, it has been reckoned, most scene changes in the German theatre involved some form of still or moving projection. It is doubtful whether this could yet have been said of any other country.

Reinhardt's Berlin audience of the mid-1920s. His elegant new "Komödie" theatre on the Kurfürstendamm, photographed at its opening in November 1924. Several of its productions were shared with its Viennese opposite number, the eighteenth-century Theater in der Josefstadt, which Reinhardt had taken over a few months earlier. Photo by Ullstein Bilderdienst.

The part of Germany most affected by such developments was Berlin, now firmly a capital city once more and the recipient of stimulating new influences from Russia and the Anglo-Saxon countries alike. In the autumn of 1928 there was a drive by the electricity companies to make it a *"ville lumière"* like Paris, and Brecht and Weill were commissioned to write a song, whose initial text went:

> We've got so much to show
> Which can't be seen at night.
> Unless you have a thousand lamps
> You won't have that much light.
>
> Berlin's a fair-sized town
> The sun is none too bright
> But switch the arc-lamps on, and you'll
> See Berlin in the light.
>
> It ain't a meadow by the stream
> With daisies all around.

It ain't a nook to sit and dream
It is a fair-sized town.[2]

With the provincial centers becoming less prompt to take the initiative in the arts, the capital now saw an influx of major talents. Following the young theatre innovators from Munich came other new dramatists like Ödön von Horváth and Marieluise Fleisser; likewise former expressionists such as Toller, on his release from prison in 1924, Kornfeld (from Frankfurt), and (from Stuttgart) Friedrich Wolf. Of the leading composers, Hanns Eisler arrived in 1925, his teacher Schönberg in January 1926, Hindemith in 1927, while from 1925 on Stravinsky treated Berlin as the principal center for the performance of his works. Indeed the attraction of Berlin for composers and conductors was perhaps stronger than for any other class of artist, for it was above all else the city's musical life that most felt the effects of the boom. And from now on this was to have some important implications for the theatre.

The Demand for Entertainment

If times of economic hardship tend to favor small-scale forms like the cabaret and the poetry reading, more expansive periods are good for those like the opera and the musical spectacular, which demand a costly apparatus. Accordingly during the second half of the 1920s we find the most interesting of the Berlin cabaret artists stretching out into revues or the new musical theatre and playing a role particularly in productions associated with Piscator and Brecht. Meanwhile the bigger theatres were increasingly given over to what the industrial psychologist Fritz Giese (in a book of 1925 devoted to this subject) called *Girlkultur:* for instance the Grosses Schauspielhaus under Erik Charell, the Komische Oper with James Klein's shows like *Get Undressed* and *Donnerwetter—1000 Women*, and the Admiralspalast with the revues of Hermann Haller. Thus the *Berliner Tageblatt* of 7 July 1926 could report that nine theatres were being given up to revue, absorbing a daily audience of about eleven thousand consumers, while during the following season there were no fewer than thirteen revue productions on the large scale. This says a good deal about the Berlin theatregoer and his new demand for well-coordinated titillation, yet not everything that went into these programs was rubbish by any means. Charell, for instance, got Hans Reimann the humorist to write dialogue for his revue *From Mouth to Mouth*, which ran for six months in winter 1926–27, with Ernst Stern as its designer; the cabaret artists Claire Waldoff and Curt Bois (Brecht's favorite Puntila a quarter of a century later) were in the cast. Trude Hesterberg of the Wilde Bühne was in more than one Haller show, while Oskar Schlemmer's *Triadic Ballet* was danced by Harald Kreutzberg in one of the mixed programs at the Metropol that same season. Moreover, what seemed exceptional in the big popular shows was much more characteristic of those "cabaret revues" which now invaded the more traditional theatres, largely superseding the cabaret proper as it had developed since the turn of the century.

These were mainly the work of three men: Rudolf Nelson, who had been

The commercial theatre calls in the avant-garde. Schlemmer's Triadic Ballet as a component of the revue *Wieder Metropol* at the Metropol-Theater in the 1926–27 season. Photo by Ullstein Bilderdienst.

accompanist and musical director of some of the Berlin cabarets before 1914, Friedrich Holländer, the leading composer at the postwar Schall und Rauch and Rosa Valetti's Grössenwahn (not to be confused with his uncle Felix Holländer at Reinhardt's Deutsches Theater); and finally the short-lived lyric writer Marcellus Schiffer, who had made his mark at the Wilde Bühne when Tucholsky and Walter Mehring were writing for it. Nelson by this time had his own Nelson-Theater on the Kurfürstendamm, where he had started presenting the odd small-scale revue, accompanied by two pianos or a small jazz band. But from 1924 on, once Tucholsky had moved to Paris, the Nelson productions, though doubling in frequency, became less remarkable for their texts than for their verve and timing. This was just when Holländer began writing and producing his own revues, which he staged in different Berlin theatres, and these, while primarily serving as West End entertainment, had rather more social and political relevance. Holländer's first show, *Laterna Magica,* which opened in the Renaissance-Theater on 19 February 1926, combined cabaret performers like his wife Blandine Ebinger with recognized actors such as Aribert Wäscher and H. H. von Twardowski (who wrote literary parodies on the side) and the dancer Valeska Gert. *Hetärengespräche (Courtesans' Conversations)* at the Kleines Theater the same year was co-written with Schiffer, one of whose sketches was later set to music by Hindemith to make the miniopera *Hin und Zurück (There and Back)* in 1927. Then came *Das bist Du,*

A golden debut—Marlene Dietrich (right) sings Mischa Spoliansky's duet "Die beste Freundin" with Margo Lion, wife of the clever librettist Marcellus Schiffer, in the 'Neue Sachlichkeit' revue *Es liegt in der Luft* at Reinhardt's new Komödie in May 1928. Photo by Ullstein Bilderdienst.

(*That's What You Are*) with Weintraub's Syncopators, one of the best of the new bands, and the utterly "West End" *Bei uns um die Gedächtniskirche rum (Round About the Gedächtniskirche)* for which Holländer and Moritz Seeler (of the Junge Bühne) together took the Theater am Kurfürstendamm. Meanwhile Schiffer, after collaborating fitfully with both Nelson and Holländer, wrote *Die fleissige Leserin (The Conscientious Woman Reader)* to be staged in the Renaissance-Theater later in 1926, followed in spring 1928 by *Es liegt in der Luft (It's in the Air)* for the Komödie, Reinhardt's new Kurfürstendamm theatre. Besides its Neue Sachlichkeit theme song this show was remarkable for the discovery of Marlene Dietrich, who appeared in it with Schiffer's wife Margo Lion (known as a "cold and challenging" reciter with the Wilde Bühne) and the Austrian Oscar Karlweis. The music was by Mischa Spoliansky, yet another who had come up through Schall und Rauch.

But neither Schall und Rauch, Wilde Bühne, nor Grössenwahn were operating any longer, and the only new foundation to replace them was Kurt Robitschek and Paul Morgan's 'Kabarett der Komiker' (Comedians' Cabaret) which carried on the earlier tradition with a mixture of cabaret proper, music-hall acts and one-act plays, sometimes featuring visiting film stars such as Jeanette MacDonald. There was also a much more sporadic affair in the shape of 'Die Wespen', (The Wasps), a pro-Communist group that from late 1926 on gave performances to working-class audiences in different parts of Berlin. The poet Erich Weinert, the compere Karl Schnog, and the singer Ernst Busch were among its occasional members, while the pianist was Claus Clauberg, formerly of Grössenwahn and the Wilde Bühne; it became more active later.

More significant than either of these ventures in the long run was the activity of a still younger accompanist and musical director called Franz S. Bruinier, who that year began organizing a series of Monday evening performances (or *MA-Abende*) in Berlin. A piano pupil of Egon Petri, he composed settings of poems by Iwan Goll (*Paris brennt, eine ekstatische Szene mit Jazz* [*Paris Is Burning, an Ecstatic Scene with Jazz*]), Walter Mehring, and Klabund. Coming into contact with Brecht apparently in 1925, Bruinier not only helped him transcribe his first primitive song settings but wrote some new ones, evidently with a view to performance by Kate Kühl, whose recitations had been one of the features of Grössenwahn.[3] Like Klabund, however, Bruinier was tubercular, and both men died in the summer of 1928, just as two or three of those same songs were being reworked by Weill for inclusion in *The Threepenny Opera*. Since Brecht had independently written couplets for Blandine Ebinger as well as singing his own songs, he was more open to the cabaret tradition and the corresponding style of performance than any serious playwright since Wedekind.

It was partly the critic Herbert Jhering and partly their own working alliance of the early 1920s that led the public at first to associate Brecht with Arnolt Bronnen rather than with this unpretentious alternative theatre of topical satire, jokes and songs. For at the time it looked as if Bronnen, following the *succès d'estime* of the Junge Bühne performance of his ultra-Expressionist *Vatermord* in 1922, was at last coming into his own. From April 1924 to the end of January 1926 there were no fewer than six Bronnen premieres—all but one of them in Berlin—an average of one every four months, and if it had been true, as Jhering and others thought, that his work would fill the gap left by Expressionism, he now had every chance to prove his admirers right. Alas, they were terrible plays. *Anarchie in Sillian*, or *Verrat* (*Anarchy in Sillian* or *Betrayal*) was not unlike early Georg Kaiser: a four-handed play in stylized dialogue about the tensions, professional and sexual, during a strike at an isolated power station on a rainy night. It ends symbolically, as the nameless Engineer, bleeding and ragged, switches on the distant dynamos, exclaiming, "The time of fog and confusion is over. Now we shall start!"[4] This, like *Vatermord*, was staged by the Junge Bühne, where Heinz Hilpert directed it at a furious tempo, then taken over by the Renaissance-Theater; it also had some important provincial productions.

Next came *Katalaunische Schlacht* (*The Battle of the Catalaunian Fields*), an astonishingly farfetched play about the First World War and the passionate loves and hates bred in battle in a dugout that shelters two brothers and the woman they both love; there are three acts, each ending with the death of one of the triangle. Jessner had agreed to produce this in Berlin after its Frankfurt premiere, but chose instead to give the first performance of the next play, *Rheinische Rebellen* (*Rhenish Rebels*), a work designed to celebrate the Rhine-

The last writhings of Expressionism: Arnolt Bronnen's *Anarchie in Sillian* (or *Verrat*) in Heinz Hilpert's "Junge Bühne" production of April 1924. Left to right: Walter Frank, Maria Eis, H. H. von Twardowski and (recumbent) Franziska Kinz. Photo by Cologne University Theatre Museum.

land's thousand years as part of the Reich; it was banned in the Allied-occupied zone and moved the critic Kurt Pinthus to ask whether Bronnen had become a nationalist. Indeed he had, and in a scene of Lesbian incest in a Coblenz hotel his heroine Gyn, played by the highly emotional Agnes Straub, described her longing for the Germany she had seen: "I drank the land; villages knocked me out; cities came over me like red bulls; mountains thrust into my body."[5] Termed by one critic a *Zeitstück*, or play of the times—an expression just beginning to be used—this strongly cast patriotic thriller was Bronnen's most successful work. A reaction followed when Pfemfert of *Die Aktion* and the Communist dramaturg Oskar Kanehl led a noisy demonstration against his would-be comedy *Die Exzesse (The Excesses)*, which was staged once again by Hilpert for the Junge Bühne. "Incoherent and decked out with obscenities," Alfred Kerr called it. "Who on earth thinks of performing something like that?"[6] Bottom was reached in December 1925, when the same group staged his first play, *The Birth of Youth*, whose script ends in a feveredly erotic rhapsody of boys, girls, and horses that fortunately was cut.[7]

This strange inflation of a manic and already semi-Fascist writer would not have been possible if the German theatre had developed any clear sense of direction. But Brecht, whose opinions were normally clear enough, was preoccupied with the oppressiveness of the great cities and still struggling with his new Anglo-Indian play *Man Equals Man*; Reinhardt was fully occupied elsewhere; and Jessner was hesitant to commit himself. In short the nature of the new post-Expressionist theatre was still undefined. Viertel, who like Jhering placed great hopes in the Brecht-Engel-Kortner-Zuckmayer group, was unsure which way such rebels would jump. "Action is what these young theatre people want," he wrote in 1925,

> action at all costs, extraordinary stories without motivation or preconditions, unsupported by external logic. Their attitude to the world is that of sceptics; they don't believe in a Destiny shielding and supporting bourgeois society. Their god is the irrational, and Knut Hamsun is his prophet. They are trying to follow the inner logic of their blood wherever it may lead them, and they think a story is dramatic if it leads to situations where that blood boils.[8]

This surprising misinterpretation seemed at first borne out by Zuckmayer's early play *Pankraz erwacht oder Die Hinterwäldler (Pancras Awakes or The Backwoodsmen)*—the only one, its author later said, to have been written under Brecht's influence—which was directed by Hilpert for the Junge Bühne in the Deutsches Theater that February. With its Wild West story of incest and murder, recalling to some the novels of Karl May, it, too, was violent and disorganized in a manner akin to Bronnen's, though the two men were never friends. The production succeeded because of its director, who from then on became something of a Zuckmayer specialist, and the acting of Rudolf Forster, but the play itself struck its author as a sad failure, proving to him only that he was not cut out to be a member of the avant-garde. Coming just as his own (and Brecht's) employment at the Deutsches Theater was about to end, this gave him a sense of relief—indeed of pleasure—and that summer he sat down to write a comedy in his native Rhenish dialect about people he had known all his life.

Der fröhliche Weinberg (The Lighthearted Vineyard), as he shrewdly called it, was as much of a landmark as Toller's *Die Wandlung* had been six years earlier. It was genuinely funny: the author laughed while writing it, the actors while rehearsing, and so did the Berlin audience during the run of two and a half years which followed its historic premiere at the Theater am Schiffbauerdamm just before Christmas 1925. Here was a poet and short-story writer whom many still thought of as an Expressionist, writing a *Volksstück*, or people's play, full of party spirit essentially in the line of *Die Wupper, Nebeneinander,* and the more recent Barlach plays: a work based on close knowledge of a given locality, but this time with a much simpler and jollier story—boy and old boy meet girls, dude rival meets comeuppance—written in nonliterary language, the speech and songs of rural life. Many of its features were exactly suited to the ambiguous public taste of the mid-1920s: the sense of landscape, the golden wine, the sturdy, sunburned girls and the strong, drunken men, ready for a brawl at any age; the very basic sexual allusions; the slaughtering of the pig in "a ton of blood";[9] the ridiculing of the two Jewish wine salesmen; above all the ingrained love of country, so remote from the hysteria exhibited by Bronnen's Gyn in relation to the same Rhineland region. There could even be an unconscious analogy between the revitalized old wine-grower and the reemergence of Hindenburg, whose first public appearance after his election Zuckmayer had attended in Brecht's sardonic company.

Triumph of the middlebrow. Carl Zuckmayer's pleasantly bucolic comedy *Der fröhliche Weinberg* staged by Reinhard Bruck at the Theater am Schiffbauerdamm in December 1925, with settings by Benno von Arent, later Hitler's ceremonial designer. An episode from Act 1, with Eduard von Winterstein and Grete Scherk. Photo by Cologne University Theatre Museum.

Brecht said (and I remember this sentence precisely): "At the conclusion of the first quarter of Christendom's twentieth century they brought a man into the city and welcomed him with the highest honors, because he had never read a book."[10]

At the same time a decent democracy permeates the play, which presents the parading veterans of the Kaiser's colonial wars as complete absurdities, mocks the "stab in the back" theory, and drags the would-be Prussian aristocrat Knuzius, with his dueling scar and his call for racial purity, literally through the mire. "Dowries, inheritances and family estates," comments the young bargee when he finally wins the girl from this dude, "all that stuff is finished, we're past that now. We've come up from the bottom and are going to make it on our own."[11]

Der fröhliche Weinberg was never a great play, though it is a very cleverly balanced one, following a delicate line between nationalism and sense of country, between racialism and physical self-awareness, between the light-hearted and the merely hearty. But it embodied a number of lessons which the theatre was only now prepared to learn. The most superficial of these was that the Weimar Republic was ready for comedy, just as it was ready for light entertainment, with the result that a number of previously uncomic writers (including Hasenclever and Kornfeld) began trying their hands at the genre. More importantly, its success showed the demand for a less stilted and unnatural form of serious drama, such as could be identified in three plays by new playwrights, starting with the young Marieluise Fleisser's drily written *Fegefeuer in Ingolstadt (Purgatory in Ingolstadt)*, a rebel's view of adolescent experiences in that Catholic Bavarian town, which was performed by the Junge Bühne on Brecht's recommendation on 25 April 1926. There was also *Krankheit der Jugend (Sickness of Youth)*, a tightly organized play about similar problems in a Berlin boardinghouse setting, written by Theodor Tagger, the recent Intendant of the Renaissance-Theater, under the pseudonym Ferdinand Bruckner. It was first staged in the Hamburg Kammerspiele on 17 October the same year and only reached Berlin about eighteen months later. Finally came Ödön von Horváth's first play, a somewhat artificial drama of adventurous, even murderous men and one woman building a cable railway in the Alps, which was likewise performed in Hamburg and was really only significant as a pointer to the people's plays that were to come.

There was one further lesson which could hardly have been guessed at from the Berlin production of Zuckmayer's pioneering work. Once it got out into the provinces this supposedly entertaining, nonpolitical middlebrow play proved to be very political indeed. Student corporations protested against the caricaturing of Knuzius; Nazi city councilors in Munich called the play "quite unbelievably swinish" for its mockery of "German customs, the German woman, the German war wounded, the German public official";[12] in Halle the opening night was interrupted by student songs and the singing of "Deutschland über Alles"; even in Mainz, where the author had grown up, the inhabitants felt they were being held up to ridicule, and strongly objected to his rather ill-advised use of real local names. Part of the moral, then, was that Berlin theatre audiences were hardly representative of the great German public, hence that there was not much point in the theatre's trying to be nonpolitical when provincial public feeling on both Left and Right was getting so sensitive that the mildest flippancy could blow up into a political event.

Piscator, Brecht, and the "Epic Theatre"

It was during this period that both Brecht and Piscator came to grips with their respective ideas of the "epic theatre." Though not itself part of the prevalent notion of Neue Sachlichkeit, this catchy new label embraced certain elements that were: the principle of montage, for instance, which became the great new structural device of the 1920s; the documentary style; the use of new technologies like photography and sound recording; the analogies between art and sport. Each man chose different aspects of this complex to stress. Brecht in *Man Equals Man* conformed with the new climate by writing a comedy with farcical touches, first imagined in a Bavarian setting as a play about the malleability of identity, then transported to the camps and battlefields of a British India dominated by whisky, beer, and sport. Strung together episodically regardless of length, his cool demonstration of human engineering—a man being "put together like a car"—had its premiere at Darmstadt on 25 September 1926, after which Berlin had to wait some eighteen months while its author kept making changes. Otherwise he had no major new play

1926: examples of the new 'epic' theatre. Above, Brecht's play *Man equals Man* about the malleability of human personality, as first staged at Darmstadt by Jacob Geis with Neher's sets. Below, *Sturmflut,* a play about the Russian revolution by Alfons Paquet, in Piscator's Volksbühne production the same year. Note the use of film; it was the year when Eisenstein's *The Battleship Potemkin* had its German release. Photos by Hessisches Landesarchiv and Cologne University Theatre Museum.

to show, only the shortened and modernized version of *Baal* which the Junge Bühne had produced that February. This single Sunday performance was the only Brecht event to be seen in Berlin in three and a quarter years, and it was not surprising that he agreed in mid-1927 to go and work for Piscator as one of a collective of dramaturgs. He had evolved something like a collective of his own by then, since he had recruited Elisabeth Hauptmann and Emil Burri to help him write and could count on Caspar Neher to visualize his ideas for him. In turn he himself had been drawn into revising Lion Feuchtwanger's *Calcutta 4 May,* one of that writer's two flippant "Anglo-Saxon plays" which now got Berlin productions.

Piscator for his part seems to have picked up the term *epic* from Alfons Paquet's play *Fahnen,* which he staged in 1924. Now it was the same author's Russian revolutionary play *Sturmflut* (or *Tidal Wave*) coming on top of the Communist party pageant *Trotz Alledem (In Spite of Everything),* which led Piscator to identify epic methods with the documentary approach of the latter and the rousing images of the former, conveyed in both cases by a new theatrical use of film not uninfluenced by Eisenstein's *Potemkin.* As he set out to create *The Political Theatre* (the title of the book he was to write in 1929), one of his chief problems was finding the writers who would tailor his chosen plays to fit a mixed use of these and other media whose technology he was determined to master. So long as he remained at the Volksbühne under Holl he had not much luck in his search, though he certainly appeared to be revitalizing that institution, so that Toller, on settling in Berlin, agreed to write him a play for it, set in the Berlin slums. For a while the prospects there looked hopeful: he could call on a splendid team of actors headed by Heinrich George and Alexander Granach, three projectors were installed, and in Paul Zech's play about Rimbaud *Das trunkene Schiff (The Drunken Ship)* (21 May 1926) he could again use film in addition to projected drawings by George Grosz. During that winter, however, a concerted campaign against the Volksbühne developed, partly on the basis of the same inbuilt divisions as had split the original organization in 1892, but partly also because of the KPD's decision to develop a more independent cultural policy, which had already led it to set up an opposition movement inside the workers' theatre movement, the Socialist-led DATB. In March Piscator brought this informal conflict to a head by imposing an aggressively Leninist interpretation on a historical drama by the unwitting Ehm Welk *(Gewitter über Gotland [Thunderstorm over Gotland])* on 23 March 1927. After which he walked out, with widespread support, to start his own theatre.

He managed to get the Volksbühne to agree a deal by which up to four thousand of its members (soon to rise to sixteen thousand) could choose to get as many tickets for the new Piscatorbühne as for all other theatres including the VB's own. At the same time he had secured backing from a newly rich brewer called Katzenellenbogen who was closely involved with the former Reinhardt actress Tilla Durieux. Though this never allowed Piscator to build the technically advanced "Totaltheater" which Gropius designed for him, he was able to equip the old Theater am Nollendorfplatz (which he rented) with the most complex and sophisticated stage equipment yet seen, and with it he put on four revolutionary productions. The first (on 3 September) was Toller's *Hoppla, wir leben! (Hoppla, we're alive!)* an entirely new play about the disillusionment of a released political offender like Toller himself, who comes back to find a general (i.e., Hindenburg) being elected president and his own former comrade serving as one of his ministers. In the excitement of the novel staging, which employed film, radio, and a vast multilevel Constructivist set, the play proper was almost overlooked, though it represented a marked change in Toller's work, partly because of its recognition of the real political situation and partly because it had been adapted to this new kind of production, not only by Piscator and his dramaturgs, (who turned the hero from a student into a worker and trimmed some of the excess romanticism from the language), but also by the author himself, who specified the subdivision of the "Grand Hotel" set in act 3 and prescribed such "film interludes" as this (before act 2):

> Women in professional positions:
> Women as typists
> Women as chauffeurs
> Women as engine-drivers
> Women as police . . .[13]

In addition there was a theme song by Walter Mehring, one of the company's many literary advisers, which was sung by Kate Kühl before act 3. It was composed by the musical director Edmund Meisel, who had recently made his name with a score for Eisenstein's *Potemkin*.

Rasputin by Alexei Tolstoy and P. Shchegolev, which followed on 10 November, involved the advisers much more extensively and was staged almost as a documentary play, with projected texts on side screens and newsreel clips shown on the outside of the hemispherical set. It appears to have been the first modern Soviet play to be seen on the Berlin professional stage, but was generally thought to be less interesting than what Piscator made of it: "a half-way house between imaginative writing and reportage," in Jhering's words.[14] *Schweik*, however, which opened on 23 January 1928, was at once the most radical and the most successful of all Piscator's productions. It was certainly the one which most engaged Brecht, whose not wholly dissimilar play *Man Equals Man* had its Berlin premiere under Engel at the rejigged Volksbühne some three weeks earlier, and this dramatization of his favorite novel left a lasting impression on him. The secret of its success lay primarily in Hašek's immortal military un-hero and the interpretation of that role by Max Pallenberg, one of Reinhardt's greatest actors. But its truly original achievement was its solution of a much wider problem: how to keep so episodic and picaresque a narrative uninterruptedly on the move. The key to this was found by Piscator, who got a pair of treadmills or primitive travolators from a Dortmund engineering firm and had them built into the stage, meanwhile commissioning George Grosz to make drawings for an animated film as background particularly for Schweik's "anabasis," or erratic peregrination towards (and sometimes away from) the front. Brecht and the principal dramaturg Felix Gasbarra radically rewrote the authorized adapta-

Four incidents from Piscator's 1928 *Schweik* production, the most "epic" of them all thanks to the use of a treadmill stage and an animated film by Grosz to keep its changes of scene flowing. Max Pallenberg is seen here as Schweik, with projection screen behind. Items like the latrine (bottom left) are swept on and off as by conveyor belt.

tion to suit these new devices, breaking up its conventional three-act form and producing a true epic script in line with Hašek's montagelike structure.[15]

Finally there was *Konjunktur (Boom)*, the last of the four productions, which opened on 10 April in the Lessing-Theater with much reduced technical resources and a generally unremarkable script by the Viennese journalist Leo Lania, another of Brecht's fellow dramaturgs. Centering on the international oil business (with an excellent "Shell" song by Gasbarra and Kurt Weill as an insertion) it was given a front-page form of presentation with projected newspaper columns. It also provided Tilla Durieux with a major, if somewhat absurd, part and caused a minor politico-artistic scandal when the KPD intervened to soften its handling of Soviet oil interests.

The "Theatre of the Times"

Brecht, who was not yet a Communist, looked back on his eight months at the Nollendorfplatz primarily as an extension of his understanding of epic the-

Success of the "Play of the Times." *Verbrecher* (Criminals) by Ferdinand Bruckner in Hilpert's 1928 production at the Deutsches Theater, on a simultaneous stage by Rochus Gliese, with the new stars Hans Albers (top left) and Gustav Gründgens (bottom right). Photo by Ullstein Bilderdienst.

atre, which he saw as a linear chain of scenes and episodes, brilliantly realized in *Schweik* and shown by *Konjunktur* to be the only possible form for complex modern economic themes. But though he would not forget the new technical adjuncts to these productions, he found them less important as extensions of the story than as a means of breaking the audience's involvement and recalling it to the critical attitude at which he aimed. Piscator, too, saw the productions as epic, but for him this was now an aspect of the committedly political theatre (which had, of course, to be under Communist leadership); i.e., the new technical means were above all to give documentary backing to the story, and the aim must be to get the audience as closely involved in the argument as if it were at a political meeting. Clearly the two men held virtually incompatible views, and perhaps their only common feature was a rejection of the tidy but artificial plot, the three-act structure, and boxed-in set, with its exploitation of people's private lives for emotional tension and catharsis. Not that such considerations were what mattered to the theatregoing public, who had seen fascinating new technical resources being applied to those topical social and political themes that were becoming covered by the term *Zeitstück* (play for the times), a fashionable nonparty concept which now emerged as by no means exclusive to Piscator but a logical part of Neue Sachlichkeit.

Those technical resources were to be experienced only once again on so spectacular a scale, since their unexpectedly high costs coupled with some unwisely expansive decisions bankrupted the company. Katzenellenbogen withdrew, and for the 1928–29 theatre season there was no Piscatorbühne, and its founder reverted to being a free-lance director. Then he returned to the same theatre with a second company and fresh sources of finance. The one production which he was able to stage there—Mehring's *Merchant of Berlin*, an unwieldy, mildly satirical "historic drama of the inflation"—was written for all the previous devices plus one or two new ones (such as the use of stage lifts to emphasize class separations); it was designed by Moholy-Nagy and had music by Hanns Eisler. By then the boom was over, and it had already become clear that the Zeitstück could be staged much less lavishly and still retain its attraction.

During the year and a half between *Konjunktur* and *The Merchant of Berlin* four such plays were successfully performed in Berlin, two of them by an actors' collective called the Gruppe junger Schauspieler, which had sprung up after the original Piscatorbühne's collapse. The two in question were P. M. Lampel's *Revolte im Erziehungshaus (Revolt in the Reformatory)*, a rapidly written dramatization of his book about a Prussian reformatory and its inmates (2 December 1928), and Friedrich Wolf's *Cyankali (Cyanide)* (6 September 1929), a play against the Prussian abortion laws by a practicing doctor. Of the others, Ferdinand Bruckner's otherwise conventional *Criminals* was conceived for a multiple set rather like that for *Hoppla, wir leben!* and staged at the Deutsches Theater (23 October 1928) by Hilpert with a brilliant cast including Lucie Höflich, Hans Albers, and the young Gustav Gründgens; its basic theme was the lack of human understanding shown by German judges. A week earlier Günter Weisenborn's *U-Boat S4,* about a recent American submarine disaster, was put on by the Volksbühne (which Holl had left at the end of the 1927–28 season) for those of its members who opted for the Piscator productions. This, too, recalled Piscator's own methods in its use of film, though on a more modest scale, and there are other signs that they were spreading; thus Jessner at the Staatstheater used projections for *Rheinische Rebellen* in May 1925 and film for *The Weavers* in February 1928, while film strips and projected titles were seen at the world premiere of Claudel's *Christophe Colomb* at the Berlin State Opera in 1930.

Opera for a Changing Society

Aside from the Volksbühne the more established theatres went on much as before, though without making so much impact. At the Staatstheater Jessner seemed much less sure of himself in the new climate; criticized by the nationalists on racial and political grounds, he fought shy of new plays once the Bronnen boom was over. The Junge Bühne gave up the ghost after spring 1927; its leader, Moritz Seeler, went into management and film production. Fehling, once he had directed *Die Wupper* that same year, concentrated mainly on the classics, notably *The Merchant of Venice,* with Kortner as Shylock and

Modernizing the musical theatre and opera. Above, Georg Kaiser's 'revue play' *Zwei Krawatten* (Two Ties), with Albers, Valetti, Marlene Dietrich, the Comedian Harmonists and music by Spoliansky. Below, the Black Bottom scene from Max Brand's opera *Maschinist Hopkins* in its original Duisburg production. Photos by Cologne University Theatre Museum.

Elisabeth Bergner as Portia; this was one of the rare productions of the time, said critics, that did not orbit around her stardom. Georg Kaiser continued writing interesting new plays, including the lighthearted musical comedy *Zwei Krawatten (Two Ties)*, which was composed by Spoliansky and had Albers and Marlene Dietrich in its cast. Zuckmayer wrote two further Volksstücke— about the eighteenth-century Rhineland bandit *Schinderhannes* and the high-wire acrobat *Katharina Knie*—and these were staged by Heinz Saltenburg's management, as had been *Der fröhliche Weinberg*.

The Reinhardt theatres struck up an alliance with those of Viktor Barnowsky (Theater in der Koniggrätzer Strasse and Komödienhaus) and Eugen Robert (Die Tribüne); while at the Deutsches Theater itself Robert Klein took Felix Holländer's old post, with Heinz Hilpert as his outstanding director in the new naturalistic mode. Since Reinhardt himself was fully involved with his Austrian base and his 1927 American tour, Klein and Edmund Reinhardt built their program partly around successful foreign plays, partly around such outstanding players as remained true to his theatres even after they had become stage and screen stars, a policy which may have unbalanced the ensemble but appears to have balanced the books. The result was not very exciting for anybody interested in something more than the acting. And although Reinhardt was still initiating some original ideas, as when he suggested that Brecht should write a revue for him and commissioned Claudel to devise a spectacle which could be set to music by Richard Strauss, where Germany was concerned he did not have the time to see them through.

Perhaps the most spectacular innovations of these "golden" years lay in the field of opera. Once again it was an expensive but stagnant form that was brought to life by the new prosperity, though much of the individual creative work had been done much earlier. The transformation started just eight days before *Der fröhliche Weinberg*, when Erich Kleiber at the Berlin State Opera conducted the world premiere of Alban Berg's *Wozzeck* using the text of Büchner's play. From that moment Berlin became the center of modern opera and of modern operatic production and performance, thanks to the policies of the Prussian state and the Berlin City Council, both of which devoted considerable resources to this, a development which was reflected in several of the big provincial operas and supported by energetic promotion on the part of Universal-Edition, the principal publishers of such works. The State Opera itself was modernized; the privately owned German Opera House went bankrupt at the end of 1924 and was taken over by the city as its Städtische Oper with Bruno Walter as conductor; in 1926 Heinz Tietjen became Intendant of both houses. A third house, known as the Kroll Opera after its original builder, was a joint enterprise of the Prussian state and the Volksbühne. When this opened at the beginning of 1924 it was in effect just a second stage for the State Opera company, but by mid-1926 this division of the latter's resources had been found unworkable. The state government therefore invited the most modernist of the rising conductors—Otto Klemperer, who had championed Janáček and Stravinsky and had a number of successes in the USSR—to become director and appoint his own team. With his friend the austere Ewald Dülberg as head of design, the art historian Hans Curjel as his dramaturg and deputy, and Schönberg's brother-in-law Zemlinsky as his second conductor, he now brought opera from its richly ornate fringe right into the center of the new musical, artistic, and theatrical movements.

The Kroll Opera repeatedly adopted a fresh approach to the normally sluggish operatic medium, and the results could be seen and heard even when the opera being performed was a classic. The interpretation might be new, as with *Fidelio*, where Klemperer's emphasis was on the liberation of the prisoners; or the score might be an unknown one, as with Wagner's first version of *The Flying Dutchman*; or the sets might be extremely radical, as with the *Tales of Hoffmann* in February 1929 (when Moholy-Nagy was the designer); or of course the whole program might be innovatory, as when Stravinsky's *L' Histoire du soldat* was performed in October 1928 in a set by Traugott Müller directed by Brecht's associate Jacob Geis. Whatever the mixture, the Kroll stimulated critical and professional interest, while often angering the Volks- bühne subscribers, to say nothing of those reactionaries and racists who were even more self-assertive in the opera than in the straight theatre. The Kroll in fact was by no means alone in staging new works: thus the notion of a *Zeitoper*, to match the *Zeittheater*, stemmed from Křenek's jazz opera *Jonny spielt auf (Johnny Strikes Up)*, which had its premiere at Leipzig on 11 February 1927, while Kurt Weill's first opera *Der Protagonist* (with a text by Georg Kaiser) was given in Dresden in March 1926, and works by Antheil and Wilhelm Grosz of an even more up-to-date kind were later premiered by the Frankfurt opera under William Steinberg. A railway station, an Atlantic liner, a film studio, a factory: all now figured on the German provincial operatic stage. But Klem- perer was unusually aware of what was going on in the other arts—all the more so when Curjel succeeded Dülberg in his counsels—and he was cer- tainly the opera director most in touch with the sociomusical experiments being tried out each summer by Hindemith and his colleagues of the Neue Musik.

These festivals, first at Donaueschingen, then from 1927 to 1929 at Baden- Baden, were the real workshop of Neue Sachlichkeit musical thinking, and in their concern to resituate music in relation to the economy and technology of the mid-1920s they drew in not only Milhaud and Ernst Toch but all the most advanced composers associated with the new German theatre: Eisler, Wagner- Regény, Walter Goehr, Paul Dessau (then an assistant conductor at the Berlin Städtische Oper), and, above all, Kurt Weill and his wife, Lotte Lenya, who in turn brought their new friend Brecht. The crucial event here was the program of minioperas at Baden-Baden on 17 July 1927. It was for this that Hindemith set Schiffer's clever revue sketch *Hin und Zurück (There and Back)*, writing a musical score that, like the action, proceeds to a central point and then runs back again. Two years later Schiffer would provide a second cabaret-influ- enced libretto, this time for Hindemith's full-length *Neues vom Tage (News of the Day)*, which was performed by Klemperer at the Kroll on 8 June 1929 to a rather mixed reception (a sign perhaps for Hindemith to revert to a more serious style).

But the key work certainly was Weill's early "Songspiel" version of Brecht's *Mahagonny* material, a precursor of the corresponding full opera.

Impact of Hindemith's music festivals. The *Mahagonny* Songspiel (or "Little Mahagonny") at Baden-Baden in 1927, with boxing-ring stage and projected drawings by Neher. On the stool, Lotte Lenya. Weill is at the right rear, just above the seated Hindemith. Photo: Austrian National Library Theatre Collection.

Again, this had started out virtually as cabaret material, appearing with others of Brecht's early songs in his first book of poems that same year, and Weill himself had actually met Brecht as a result of a Berlin broadcast of *Man Equals Man*, which he had had to cover in his capacity as the leading radio critic of that time. Klemperer was fascinated by the little cycle, with Brecht's boxing-ring staging backed by Caspar Neher's drawings and Lenya's dazzlingly unconventional performance, and by the beginning of the 1928–29 season it had been taken for granted that when the full opera was ready the Kroll would produce it. It is even possible that Weill's initial notes on its production were written with the Kroll in mind, particularly given the impression made on Klemperer by Hindemith's *Cardillac* and that work's rejection of the principles of "music drama." Had the Kroll gone ahead with *Rise and Fall of the City of Mahagonny* as Weill intended there would no doubt have been a major scandal, but it would have established the right style of production, and the theatre as a whole would have benefited.

As it turned out, the full opera took longer to write than expected and it was overtaken by events, the first of them being the diversion of the same team's energies to an entirely unexpected task by which they had become seduced in the spring of 1928. This was the provision of a suitable play to mark the start of a new regime at the Theater am Schiffbauerdamm, which had been rented by the young actor Ernst-Josef Aufricht, formerly with

Marieluise Fleisser's antimilitarist satire *Pioniere in Ingolstadt,* which followed *The Threepenny Opera* at the Theater am Schiffbauerdamm in 1928–29, with Peter Lorre and Lotte Lenya directed by Geis in Neher's sets. Photo by Cologne University Theatre Museum.

Viertel's Die Truppe. Aufricht had booked Erich Engel as director, and, after rejecting those unfinished politicoeconomic epics which Brecht had been trying to write for Piscator, seized on Elisabeth Hauptmann's draft translation of *The Beggar's Opera,* a work known to have run for more than two years in London between 1920–22. Brecht and Weill agreed to turn this into a musical play for Aufricht's birthday on 31 August 1928, and the whole operation was performed in less than six months of frenzied work.

The result was *The Threepenny Opera,* which ran for about a year in Berlin, has subsequently been staged all round the world, and remains to this day the most successful mid-European music-theatrical work of the twentieth century. It came at just the right moment, when the failure of the first Piscatorbühne had left a vacuum and a strong element of sharp sociopolitical satire was still acceptable to bourgeois audiences. And its success not only launched Aufricht's management as a new force in the theatre but, at least for a time, gave Brecht and his collaborators such a dominant position within it that he could come to talk of it as "my" theatre. Thus between them they staged Marieluise Fleisser's second, very brilliant play, *Pioniere in Ingolstadt (Army Engineers in Ingoldstadt)*—about the descent of a company of soldiers on her hometown—which Geis directed, with Brecht's new discovery Peter Lorre as the local innocent; this opened on 30 March 1929. A series of Junge Bühne–style matinees was started under the direction of Heinrich Fischer, a close friend of Karl Kraus; these included Cocteau's *Orphée,* directed by Gründgens on 5 January. Lampel's second play, the antiwar *Giftgas über Berlin (Poison Gas over Berlin),* was stopped by the censorship; *The Threepenny Opera* was brought back, and Brecht, Weill, and the rest of the team were put to work writing a similar play with which to open the second season. However, like the first production of the full-scale *Mahagonny,* this only materialized after the whole situation had changed.

The Threepenny Opera hit the German theatre at one of its peak moments, when an open-minded middle-class public was prepared to accept new formal ideas and unexpected shifts of level, and at the same time willing to look self-critically at the life and times around it. The "political theatre" had made its appearance with Piscator, but despite the first stirrings of agitprop it was still a theatre that operated within the conventional Berlin theatre framework, and its appeal was made primarily to the existing audience even though its politics had been cleared with the KPD. Piscator might incidentally renew the theatre's technical equipment, but he was not out to change the "apparatus," the whole social and organizational theatre structure; indeed his ideal throughout his life was to remain that of the old Volksbühne movement. Even less, then, were the politics of *The Threepenny Opera* to be taken all that seriously, despite the aggressiveness of their presentation, and in fact the KPD's *Die Rote Fahne* rejected them as bourgeois flippancy. "In those years," said Elisabeth Hauptmann some four decades later, "we often did things because we simply liked to and it was fun doing them."[16] Likewise Aufricht, in his vivid and amusing memoirs: "Those deeper considerations about *The Threepenny Opera*'s sociopolitical content, to which Brecht himself subsequently contributed, gave the play in retrospect a false significance.[17]

But formally, and in relation to avant-garde theatre as it had hitherto developed, *The Threepenny Opera* was much more radical than anything conceived even by Piscator. For despite certain intrinsic flaws and *longueurs,* not to mention the chaotic circumstances of its actual production, it brought together some of the most interesting new threads in the theatre of the golden years: cabaret songs and cabaret or revue actors (Valetti, Kühl, Gerron, Paulsen), the jazz idiom, the Anglo-Saxon ambience, the designs of Caspar Neher with their use of projections, the new operatic standards of the Kroll, the sociomusical experiments of the Neue Musik, all linked in what could be seen as an epic structure. It was at once light and prickly, avant-garde and popular, in a way that now seems to have been one of the great achievements of the 1920s. It was instructive. It was entertaining. It was urgent. It was fun.

Two ways of reacting to the economic crash. Above, premiere of *The Land of Smiles* by Lehár at the Metropol-Theater, October 1930, with the tenor Richard Tauber (center). Below, the Brecht/Eisler Die *Massnahme* on a concert platform, with orchestra behind and projected text of one of the choruses. Photos by Cologne University Theatre Museum and the Brecht Archive.

7

Politics Take Command

Economies and the Polarizing of Art

The gilt fell off the gingerbread as soon as the economic boom came to an end: a process most conspicuously marked by the Wall Street collapse of 24 October 1929. The short-term loans made to German industry under the Dawes Plan then had to be quickly called in by the American banks who had made them; drastic economies had to be made in all sectors of German life; unemployment doubled by the end of 1931 and went on rising. Finally the Nazis climbed out of six years of almost total insignificance to become the strongest party the Reichstag had ever seen. Irony had it that this process began only some eighteen months after the Socialists had come back into the government for the first time since 1920, with Hermann Müller as chancellor heading a so-called "great coalition" of the democratic parties, and Stresemann remaining foreign minister. Two things in particular made them incapable of giving any lead in the mounting crisis: first the blindly obstinate Allied attitude in the reparations negotiations leading to the so-called Young Plan, which the government accepted in June 1929, and secondly the release of much pent-up nationalism following Stresemann's death on 3 October. The "great coalition" broke up early in 1930, and from then on Hindenburg's remedy was to govern much as William II would have done, nominating a trusted (i.e., right-wing) chancellor, largely ignoring the Reichstag, and ruling by presidential decree.

121

    This chain of events affected the arts in the first place on two levels. The immediate impact of the economic crisis was to reduce expenditure on theatre tickets, just as managements were feeling the competition of the talking cinema and the high salaries expected by its theatrical stars. Reinhardt, who took over the direction of his Berlin theatres once more in 1929 following his brother's death, responded partly by making joint subscription arrangements with his new allies Robert and Barnowsky, partly by his brilliant rehabilitation of popular operettas like *Die Fledermaus* and *Tales of Hoffmann*. Aufricht, on finding his theatre half full at best, with even free tickets being rejected, began a desperate search for a box office success. This led him, too, to try a light opera, an updated and cleverly cast theatre version of Donizetti's *Daughter of the Regiment*, then to put on Jaromir Weinberger's still less demanding *Spring Storms* with Richard Tauber. At the Grosses Schauspielhaus Charell still drew the crowds with the sentimental Austrian musical comedy (complete with a fatherly Franz Josef II) *White Horse Inn*, which later ran for over six hundred performances in London and more than two hundred in New York. On an even more commercial level the long-established Alfred and Fritz Rotter were staging popular musicals in the Admiralspalast and a number of other theatres. "If you want to see what we're in for," wrote Jhering in a booklet indicatively called *Camouflaged Reaction*, "go and see *The Land of Smiles*," Franz Lehár's latest work.[1]
    Yet as the crisis deepened all four of those managements were forced to give up. Reinhardt, disillusioned "with entrepreneurship," tried to hand over the Deutsches Theater and its Kammerspiele in 1932 to Rudolf Beer and Karlheinz Martin and return to Vienna. Charell left the Grosses Schauspielhaus in 1931. Aufricht abandoned the Theatre am Schiffbauerdamm the same year and became a theatreless production company. The Rotters moved their base to Liechtenstein. Others were even worse placed. Thus with the active Volksbühne membership beginning to fall, from 1928 on the VB organization for the first time became dependent on Prussian government help. The Prussian state parliament, however, was becoming uneasy about the growing deficit of the state theatres, which in mid 1929 was seen to have risen by 300 percent in five years, and in the course of 1930 it decided that the simplest and least controversial way of making this up would be to close the Kroll Opera. Since the Volksbühne was in effect the Kroll's cosponsor, given its right to fill half the seats in the house at a reduced price, it could have vetoed this proposal; but because of its own financial problems it allowed itself to be bought off with an annual grant of one hundred thousand marks. So the most forward-looking opera house of the decade, if not the century, was shut down in defiance of protests from Stravinsky, Thomas Mann, and other major artists, and with little acknowledgment of its achievements by its Socialist patrons. This was only one aspect of a process which was largely to stifle modern opera throughout Germany, for (as Peter Heyworth has reported) "between 1928 and 1931 theatre subsidies were reduced from 60,000,000 marks to 35,000,000 marks. . . . Premières of new operas fell from 60 to 28 and the Dresden state theatres went so far as to remove from their repertoire all works on which royalties were payable"[2]—a decision attributed by the

Sozialistische Monatshefte less to a serious wish to economize (the royalties involved being less than two thousand marks) than to a dislike of modern works.

For on the second level the new political evolution was simultaneously accompanied by a sharp cultural backlash, and this accentuated the natural tendency of managers and accountants to economize on whatever was least immediately popular with the public. Already there had been angry controversies—as we saw in the case of Zuckmayer's *Der fröhliche Weinberg*—over plays that offended German nationalism or criticized the army, while even in sexually emancipated Berlin there were passages in *The Threepenny Opera* that had to be cut. But with the death of Stresemann the nationalists became far more vocal, the Socialists weakened, police censorship was reintroduced in defiance of the Weimar Constitution, and from the start of 1930 the new philistinism was given a racial and ideological twist by the Nazis, supported by Alfred Rosenberg's newly organized Militant League for German Culture, the *Kampfbund für deutsche Kultur*, or KfdK. The alleged "cultural Bolshevism" of the modern movement in the arts became an identifiable enemy, or, as the nonpolitical Oskar Schlemmer was to put it in his diary:

> The permanent crisis of standards in art has been exacerbated during the present nationalistic frenzy to the point that now anything different, individual or new is considered un-German, "Eastern," politically suspect.[3]

This new aggressiveness of the philistines showed itself in demonstrations (with white mice and stinkbombs) against the premieres of such works as Brecht's *Rise and Fall of the City of Mahagonny* (in Leipzig and Frankfurt, 1930) and the Hollywood film of Remarque's *All Quiet on the Western Front* (in Berlin at the end of the same year). It became most systematic in Thuringia, where the Nazi ex–civil servant Wilhelm Frick, soon to be Hitler's minister of the interior, was briefly the Land minister for education and culture, purging the Weimar applied art school (which had been the Bauhaus up to 1924) and the walls of the museum, reinstituting corporal punishment in the schools, appointing a race theorist to a professorship at Jena university, and decreeing an ordinance against "Negro Culture,"[4] i.e., in the first place, jazz. But the same pressure was felt in decisions taken nominally not on ideological but on economic grounds. Thus nationalists of all sorts helped to stimulate and concentrate the campaign against the Kroll, which before its final performance on 3 July 1931 had been forced to postpone Janáček's *From the House of the Dead* on anti-Czech grounds and to drop Hindemith's Zeitoper *Neues vom Tage*, because the Volksbühne directors thought it too modern for their members. In such ways economic retrenchment, Socialist populism, nationalist backlash, and racist Nazi ideology worked hand in hand to demolish much that had been new and vital.

At the same time there was a further factor which may have helped spur the process on, but at the same time brought fresh life to the plays and performances of a great sector of the German theatre, stretching from the Berlin Volksbühne and the Deutsches Theater leftward via Piscator and Brecht to the Communist agitprop groups. This was the sharp political polarization which had already begun under the influence of the Comintern's anti-Socialist policy in 1928 and now became intensified by the failure of the democratic parties, the growing repression, and the need to stand up to the Nazis' practice of violence. As the course of the national elections most clearly shows, the tendency from 1930 on was for steady losses by the SPD and the other democratic parties to offset spectacular gains by the Nazis and a more modest if equally unprecedented increase on the part of the Communists. Self-evident though it may seem to us now that the SPD and the KPD together, had they combined in anything like the Popular Fronts of the mid-1930s, could have kept the Nazis from gaining power, the bald figures take no account either of Socialist defeatism and exhaustion or of the KPD's misplaced confidence in the approach of a revolutionary situation. The short-sighted Communist decision, then, to split the old Socialist cultural associations not only seemed understandable at the time but led to that new extension of political theatre which was perhaps the most distinctive theatrical feature of the Republic's last years.

This process had begun with the campaign of spring 1927 against the Volksbühne board brought about by its handling of Piscator and his secession. The "special," i.e., pro-Piscator sections of the membership which were established in response to this became a permanent pressure group some sixteen thousand strong, which favored more radical programs and appointments. Franz Holl having resigned as director of productions after the 1927 Piscator crisis, he was first succeeded by the association's long-standing treasurer Heinrich Neft, who soon came under attack both for his conservatism (it was under his direction that the theatre staged the First World War play *Douaumont* by the Nazi playwright E. W. Moeller) and for his alleged nepotism. Then as a concession to the radicals the board on the one hand appointed Karlheinz Martin as the next director, while on the other hand expelling the pressure group's leaders; these subsequently set up an independent Young Volksbühne organization under Hans Rodenberg, a KPD appointee. The result from 1929 on was a twofold gain for the Left: a more progressive program in the old Volksbühne theatre, plus a new six-thousand-strong association which supported other Left groups and mounted a number of productions of its own.

In 1928 a similar attempt was made to split the Deutsche Arbeiter-Sänger-Bund, or DASB, the main workers' choral organization, by forming an internal opposition. In this case, too, the oppositionists were expelled, to become an independent *Kampfgemeinschaft,* or association of militants, at Whitsun 1931. Likewise in the workers' radio listeners' organization a splinter group was set up. With the workers' theatre movement (DATB), however, the boot was on the other foot, for there the Communist opposition won control in April 1928, forcing the Socialists to form their own breakaway organization. Thenceforward the proliferating agitprop groups (as well as some orthodox amateur companies) came under the direction of Arthur Pieck, son of a leading KPD politician, supported by the Hungarian film theoretician Béla Balázs and the Reinhardt actor Gustav von Wangenheim. A year later this became the most active section of a new Moscow international federation in which both Pieck and later Piscator would play leading roles. Finally, linking these and other Communist arts bodies, came the KPD's new Interest Group for Workers' Culture, or IfA, which was set up as a supervisory committee in October 1929.

The result of these divisions and the separate Communist culture which they helped to establish was that, just when the theatrical structure was under threat both economically and ideologically from the new reactionaries, an alternative "apparatus" was coming into being independently of all existing private or subsidized theatres and of what Hanns Eisler called "the bourgeois concert machine."[5] This was not only encouraging to those artists and performers who felt the lack of positive policies on the part of the moderate Left, but also extraordinarily stimulating to a number of outstanding creative talents such as could respond to the challenge of the new organisms and their need for new forms and new audiences. True enough, the existence of such an alternative weakened the straight theatre by drawing away some of its more progressive figures, and certainly the illusion which it gave of a new revolutionary apparatus looking forward to the revolution itself—along with an aesthetic revolution to accompany it—was hopelessly unrealistic, the eventual cause, in some cases, of paralyzing disappointment. There were those like George Grosz who were too skeptical to accept it—he emigrated to the United States instead—or rejected its ultimately fatal reliance on Moscow both as an aesthetic arbiter and as a firm base on which those who took this option could fall back. Nonetheless for about four years it provided a wonderful framework for Brecht, Friedrich Wolf, Hanns Eisler, the director Slatan Dudow, and the actor Ernst Busch—theatrical innovators who for the first time felt the impact of political events strongly enough to commit themselves to a wholeheartedly Communist theatre, which they wanted to make formally and aesthetically new.

An Alternative "Apparatus"

The opening of this fascinating final period in the history of the Republic and its theatre was marked by a number of symptomatic events of which the chief were Stresemann's death, the Wall Street crash, and the resignation of Lunacharsky, the enlightened Soviet arts commissor. On 15 July Hofmannsthal died; on 19 August Diaghilev followed. "Part of my life has departed with Hugo von Hofmannsthal," commented Count Kessler in his diary;[6] then again on hearing about Diaghilev, "Part of my world has died with him."[7] The German theatre was in fact now almost out of touch with the great pre-1914 Reinhardt tradition with which Hofmannsthal had been associated, while that of Nijinsky, Karsavina, and the Russian Ballet had long since vanished from its reach. Kessler's cultural world of well-traveled aristocratic enlightenment was virtually dead; indeed, he himself would soon be forced to stay outside the country if he was to survive without being jailed. Already two of the older

New outlets for a new theatrical form. The first *Lehrstück* by Brecht and Hindemith at the latter's Baden-Baden music festival in July 1929. Photo by Brecht Archive.

Intendants had given up their theatres in the summer of 1929, when Weichert left Frankfurt to become a freelance, and Hartung abandoned his short tenure of the Renaissance Theatre in Berlin.

At the start of the 1929–30 season both Piscator and Brecht had catastrophic failures which halted further development of any political and socially satirical approach to the established theatre such as had worked so well with *Schweik* and *The Threepenny Opera*. In Piscator's case the crucial production was *The Merchant of Berlin*, whose wealth of visual and technical effects would no doubt have fascinated his audiences of 1927–28 but now fell flat. This was due partly to a change in the first-night audience, who would no longer accept the insulting of a dead soldier's body, which took place in the "Song of the Three Street Cleaners"; partly to the poor functioning of his overworked machinery; partly to excessive length; partly to the anti-Semitic implications of the story. The combined result was to alienate the theatre's new management, which effectively closed the play down and with it Piscator's second company. From then on he reluctantly had to operate under much more austere conditions and outside the circle of major theatres. Though his proclaimed political aims remained unchanged, he could no longer pursue them before a West End type of audience and with capitalist backing. His dictatorial position vis-à-vis his own productions had gone, and with it went something of his pleasure in them.

Just a week before *The Merchant of Berlin* Brecht and Weill had an equally decisive failure with *Happy End,* the musical play that had been tailored on the pattern of *The Threepenny Opera* in an effort to repeat the outstanding success of Aufricht's first season at the Theater am Schiffbauerdamm. Part of the trouble here was that, despite the brilliance of the songs (which some connoisseurs today prefer to those of *The Threepenny Opera*) and the introduction of a remarkable new actor in Peter Lorre, the tailoring was not very conscientiously done. Brecht had not really bothered; the Chicago gangster story, written for him by Elisabeth Hauptmann (masquerading as a fictitious Dorothy Lane), was not adapted to the change in climate; its ending was hastily cobbled together at the last minute, and Erich Engel the director eventually resigned, leaving it to Brecht to sort out the mess. As with Piscator's somewhat costlier disaster, Aufricht's error had been to assume that the audience would gladly pay to see the mixture as before; however, this time the combination of luck, energy and theatrical magic that had confounded Brecht's more sceptical friends a year earlier was all too plainly missing. Underlying this was something else. For Brecht had anticipated matters by himself undergoing a marked change, both politically and artistically. Already in some measure a Marxist, he committed himself to support of the KPD, so far as we can tell, from the spring of 1929 on, when the Berlin police, directed by a Socialist police president, killed some forty unarmed members of a KPD May Day demonstration which they had been ordered to break up. From that moment the fun was over, and with it the golden brilliance. *Salonbolschewismus,* or parlor bolshevism—ancestor of the "radical chic" discovered by Tom Wolfe some thirty years later—no longer seemed a tenable position.

Such was the significance of those two theatrical catastrophes just a few weeks before the economic crisis really struck home. Not that the two cases were exactly parallel. For the difference between Brecht and Piscator now lay in the fact that the former had become absorbed in a very different kind of theatre which could only with difficulty be conceived in terms of conventional stages like those of the Nollendorfplatz and the Schiffbauerdamm. It was this preoccupation that had diverted him from the work on *Happy End,* for even as his political views were hardening he was getting involved with Weill and Hindemith in a cantatalike form of music theatre such as was to be a main feature of the latter's 1929 Baden-Baden festival: the *Lehrstück,* or didactic play or piece; (*Stück* can mean either). Who really devised this new form of play is even now unclear. To Hindemith it represented a logical extension of his concern with *Gemeinschaftsmusik,* or community music, which would educate via the pleasure of performing together; it simply added a further stratum by means of an instructive text. To Brecht and also to Weill it linked most suggestively with their new interest in the Japanese Noh drama, which Elisabeth Hauptmann had begun exploring that year. Already the influence of this austere, ritualistic, participatory form can be sensed in the first two Lehrstücke which Brecht wrote for performance in July 1929: the *Baden-Baden Lehrstück* (or Lehrstück *tout court*) for setting by Hindemith, and the radio Lehrstück *Lindbergh's Flight,* mainly for Weill but with four numbers by Hindemith, who termed it a "collective work." Both pieces are in effect moral-philosophical examinations of the implications—social and personal—of recent transatlantic flights, the one by the young American Charles Lindbergh, who later became associated with the Nazis (leading Brecht to rename the work *Ocean Flight*), the other by the Frenchmen Nungesser and Coli. Both were staged on a concert platform, the former with a grotesque clown interlude brutally answering the problem "does man help man?", the latter so as to represent a broadcasting studio, with the performers in shirtsleeves and a large inscription at the back proclaiming that "doing is better than feeling."[8]

Aufricht having declared a "Brecht-Pause" following the demise of *Happy End* (which remained buried for the next thirty years), Brecht was free to pursue this line of development further. *The Rise and Fall of the City of Mahagonny* was now with Weill's publishers, who arranged for its production by the Leipzig opera, something that seems barely to have interested Brecht except as a stimulus to set down his radical ideas about opera and epic theatre in an important theoretical essay. At the same time the continuing royalties from *The Threepenny Opera* (and its sale to Nero-Film) allowed him a new freedom to experiment. So he proceeded to plan two further didactic works, the one a "school opera" with Weill, based on the Noh play *Taniko, or The Valley-Hurling*, which Elisabeth Hauptmann translated from Waley's version; the other a more political development of this same theme, to be worked out with the young Bulgarian director Slatan Dudow (who had just spent some months in Moscow studying the Soviet theatre) and Brecht's new musical collaborator, Hanns Eisler. Both pieces were intended for Hindemith's next festival, which was due to take place in Berlin in the summer of 1930.

The Weill work became *Der Jasager (He Who Says Yes)*, a straight rendering of the Noh text with two exceptions: the (possibly unwitting) omission of all the action that Waley had condensed into footnotes, and an expansion of its ending so as to stress the boy's acquiescence in his own death—acquiescence on the principle of *Einverständnis*, already posited in the Hindemith Lehrstück and now restated in an added opening chorus. Then together with Eisler and Dudow Brecht adapted this, while still retaining many aspects of the Noh form, to make a story of illegal Communist agitation in China (a subject that Eisler knew of from the experiences of his brother Gerhard), the boy transformed into a Young Comrade who has to acquiesce in his own execution when he, too, becomes a danger to his colleagues. The resulting piece of music theatre, *Die Massnahme (The Measures Taken)*, irrespective how it can be interpreted politically—and the argument about its interpretation has gone on, both in and out of the Communist movement, from that day to this—is an astonishingly powerful piece of work, like a refunctioned version of a Bach passion. In both cases the action—minima. in *Der Jasager*, only illustrative in *Die Massnahme*—takes place on a bare floor or platform in a performance space mainly filled by the orchestra and chorus. The conductor is visible and the audience can remain in the light.

Die Massnahme was rejected by the Berlin festival organizers before they had seen the music, the grounds being clearly political, though this was never admitted. Weill, too, thereupon withdrew his work from the festival, and as a result both pieces were staged outside Hindemith's auspices. *Der Jasager* was performed on 23 June by schoolboys and music students in the Central

Institute for Education and Instruction conducted by Kurt Drabek, later a well-known band leader, and some of the schoolboy listeners from the Karl Marx-Schule in Neukölln were subsequently invited to discuss it. As a result Brecht wrote a second version (not set to music) called *Der Neinsager* in which the moral is reversed: the sickly boy refuses to acquiesce, says no instead of yes, and suggests that the Great Custom of hurling stragglers into the valley needs to be rethought.

With *Die Massnahme* there was an interval of some six months once the first version of the text had been completed before the work was finally performed in mid-December in the concert hall of the Berlin Philharmonie in a single midnight performance by three workers' choirs. The conductor was Kurt Rankl, a Schönberg pupil who later became the musical director at Covent Garden. The actors were Helene Weigel, Alexander Granach, and Ernst Busch, all performers closely associated with Brecht. The director was Dudow, the solo singer Anton Maria Topitz. Eisler himself sang and shouted in the chorus. On 18 January a daytime repeat performance was given in the Grosses Schauspielhaus, with some minor changes in answer to criticisms made in a public discussion chaired by Karl Wittfogel. Both then and later there were complaints about the play's "idealism" (for it still includes the concept of "acquiescence" when the Young Comrade agrees to be shot) and its misconception of Communist tactics, which were attributed to the author's lack of political experience. But there was also widespread recognition of the work's originality and force, as well as what the *Rote Fahne* called its "epochal" significance for the workers' choral movement.[9] As a result, Brecht at the end of 1930 became accepted not only by the party press and intellectuals, who had previously regarded him with geat skepticism, but also by the groups now beginning to constitute the alternative "apparatus" of the theatre. As for the audience which he was now addressing, it was anyway what one conservative critic termed "not very Berlin W."[10] ("Berlin West" was the elegant western districts of the city, as opposed to the working-class eastern districts.) For the first time he respected its opinions.

Collectives and Agitprop

Closely matching the political polarization of the arts, the great change in the structure of the Berlin theatre began with the failure of the first Piscatorbühne in 1928, when the young actors from its Studio formed a collective to carry on producing the Zeitstück type of play on which they had been working. This was the Group of Young Actors (or Gruppe junger Schauspieler), competent professionals of Communist conviction who had been hoping to stage Lampel's *Putsch*, then decided to do his new play *Revolte im Erziehungshaus* instead. No doubt it was their success which encouraged a group of more senior Piscator actors headed by Granach, Busch, and Friedrich Gnass to form themselves into the November-Studio for the production of Mühsam's *Sacco and Vanzetti* about the recently executed American anarchists, though this made less of a mark, and the group seems not to have survived. Following the

First production of the "Piscator Collective," 1929. The travelling pro-abortion play §218 by Carl Crede, in an economical set by Wolfgang Roth. Photo by W. Roth, New York.

Merchant of Berlin, however, and the collapse of the second Piscatorbühne, a whole series of such collectives started to come into being, much as had happened after the stabilization of 1923 (which was the last time that so many actors had been unemployed). Not all the new groups were militantly left-wing, but a lot were—members of that great pool of politically minded actors which had developed around the Volksbühne, the Theater am Schiffbauer-damm and Piscator's two companies (with their appetite for enormous casts). And certainly the liveliest of them were interested in performing some kind of Zeitstück, or play about current social and political issues. Thus there was the Performance Association of Berlin Actors (Spielgemeinschaft Berliner Schau-spieler), which was formed in January 1930 under the direction of Fritz Staudte and Hansheinz Winkler and kept going for over two years; their great success was a play by the otherwise obscure Alfred Herzog about the German army, *The Row about Lieutenant Blumenthal*. There was the Actors' Theatre (Theater der Schauspieler), which included players from the subsidized the-atres like Agnes Straub and performed Theodor Plievier's play *Sharks* under Leopold Lindtberg's direction in May 1932. There was the Workers' Theatre (Theater der Arbeiter), the Berlin Experimental Theatre (Versuchsbühne Berlin), and a nameless group of Volksbühne actors, members of the Commu-nist breakaway union organization RGO, who took time off in December 1931 to perform a recently rejected play by Friedrich Wolf called *The Boys of Mons*. This presented Agnes Straub as "Captain Campbell," a woman transvestite

who is the recruiting officer for an irregular Fascist formation. The director
was Richard Weichert.

The way in which such groups worked, as Klaus Pfützner has described
it,[11] was to find a theater which would let them put on a particular production. The rehearsals would have taken place elsewhere, costing the theatre
nothing; it would then charge the group for rent (say two hundred to three
hundred marks a night), authors' royalties, hire of scenery possibly, and cost
of posters. The group would have to pay wages to any nonmembers, and only
then could it share out its takings in proportion to the individual hours
worked. In some cases a theatre might be rented for a number of productions;
in others the group would play in halls or at political meetings; sometimes it
might, like the Group of Young Actors, be supported by the International
Workers' Aid or some other Communist organization. Even Piscator had to
have recourse to this system in November 1929 when his remaining actors
decided to form a "Piscator collective," in which he would be just one of the
members under the lead of two of his most experienced actors, Erwin Kaiser
and Albert Venohr. Yet although it may have been something of an affront to
his dignity, this drastic reorganization of his shattered company not only
revived it successfully, it took Piscator from his previously ambiguous position in Berlin's West End and put him, like Brecht a year later, into a leading
place in the alternative apparatus. For four months the new collective went on
tour with Carl Credé's pro-abortion play *§218*, a disputatious topical work
akin to Wolf's *Cyankali*, which was presented in such a way that the second
half of each performance became a public discussion. Then they returned to
Berlin, rented the shabby old Wallner-Theater in the East End near the
Alexanderplatz, and, still as a collective, became the third and last Piscatorbühne.

Piscator's concept of political theatre had not really changed, but now he
had to cut his coat according to the collective's cloth, and the old mechanical
and technical extravagances were out of the question. *§218*, which had three
hundred performances, was much the most economical of the productions; it
used a minimal set by Wolfgang Roth, and little-known actors, and was
revived more than once. Plievier's *Des Kaisers Kulis (The Kaiser's Coolies)* was
adapted in the old way from the naval war novel which had recently made its
more or less anarchist author famous; it had a simultaneous set by Traugott
Müller, Piscator's old designer, showing a cross-section of the battle cruiser
Seydlitz at Jutland; Busch and Wangenheim were in the cast, as well as Hans
Rodenberg and the author himself, and since it used film for its battle effects it
had to be staged at the better-equipped Lessing-Theater. Much the most
original of Piscator's own productions in this phase was Wolf's Chinese
Lehrstück *Tai Yang Wakes Up*, a counter-play to the Reinhardt *Chalk Circle* of
1925 with its delicate chinoiserie, showing how the heroine might have fared
in modern industrial Shanghai. Here, following designs by John Heartfield,
the actors carried inscribed banners, which were grouped to shape the stage
picture and could be turned round to form an improvised screen. The play
had been specially written for Piscator's company, and once again it led to a
form of public meeting, with a lecture by a Marxist economist and a final

Friedrick Wolf's "Lehrstück." *Tai Yang Wakes Up* in Piscator's production with his third company at the Wallner-Theater in January 1931. Set by John Heartfield. Photo by Cologne University Theatre Museum.

speech pointing out parallels with the situation in Germany. Opening on 15 January 1931, it was to be the last of Piscator's own productions before he left for the USSR. The same winter the collective performed two modern Soviet plays, one of them directed by Martin Kerb of the Essen Stadttheater, home of the choreographer Kurt Jooss, whose political-satirical ballet *The Green Table* was one of the notable works of 1932. There was also a first play by Ernst Ottwalt, the former nationalist who had joined the Brecht-Eisler-Dudow collective making *Kühle Wampe*. Released in May 1932, this remarkable film was the one that most fully represented the alternative apparatus, for it not only used its actors, featuring an entire agitprop group as well as members of the Communist sports organizations, but was made outside the ordinary commercial channels.

At the Wallner-Theater the "proletarian-revolutionary" Piscatorbühne allied itself once more with the Young Volksbühne, which was founded on 23 November 1930 as a supporters' organization entitled to tickets at prices between fifty pfennigs and 1.70 marks. This arrangement also embraced the Group of Young Actors, who had successfully been touring Wolf's abortion play *Cyankali* round the provinces (like Piscator with *§218*) in the early part of the year, following a run of 100 performances at the Lessing-Theater. "No ensemble in the world could perform this particular play like them," wrote the author.[12] By then they had lost their original leader Fritz Genschow to the

Staatstheater, but still had a Piscator nucleus with Gerhard Bienert, Adolf Fischer, and Renée Stobrawa. The intention was that thereafter the two collectives should coordinate their programs. However, in the course of 1931 the economic conditions became impossible; the Piscatorbühne had to give up the Wallner-Theater at the end of March, after which a group headed by Venohr, Lotte Loebinger, and Heinz Greif toured some of its productions in Germany and Switzerland before going off to work with Piscator on his Russian film. This left the Group of Young Actors, who had meantime been directed in a number of short-lived productions by Lindtberg, Hans Rodenberg, and Max Ophüls. Even when they had a further critical success with Kataev's *Squaring the Circle* at the Berliner Theater in September 1931 they found after five performances that it was not earning enough to pay the Reinhardt concern its rent. The result was that Rodenberg at the head of the still very active Young Volksbühne decided that his organization must mount its own productions, starting on 18 November with the revue *We Are Sooo Satisfied* in the Bach (concert) Hall in the Lützowstrasse. This was performed by a mixed cast including Busch, Lenya, and Helene Weigel, and among the items were the Brecht/Eisler "Ballad of Paragraph 218" (or "Abortion Ballad") and "Song of the SA Man." Ebinger and Friedrich Holländer also contributed.

The cabaret and to a lesser extent the cabaret revue had from the first contained an element of social and policial satire, which in the hands of Mehring and Tucholsky had often been much sharper than that of the Paris *chansonniers* that were their model. As a whole the KPD's critics had tended to dismiss the genre as "petty bourgeois" (the term used by Hanns Eisler of Holländer's very West End *Bei uns um die Gedächtniskirche rum*). But in 1929 Karl Schnog's group The Wasps decided to take it to those working-class audiences whom their precursors had generally neglected, and soon they were joined by new groups like The Pill (drawn mainly from the Group of Young Actors) and Larifari, calling on such committedly left-wing performers as the actors Busch, Gnass, Genschow, and Renée Stobrawa, and the Communist poet-reciter Erich Weinert. Two new cabarets had fixed premises—the Küka (Künstler-Kabarett, or Artists' Cabaret) in a café, and the Katakombe under the Künstlerhaus, both in the West End—and in both of these some of the same talent appeared. The latter was run by Werner Finck and Hans Deppe, the original director of the Group of Young Actors, and later, after Deppe's resignation, actually continued operating well into the Third Reich before being banned in 1935. Out of this last wave of the Weimar cabaret came not only a good part of Weinert's output but songs by Kästner and Edmund Nick. We also owe it those which Eisler now wrote on texts by Tucholsky, Weinert, and "David Weber," a pseudonym for Robert Gilbert—better known as one of the authors of *White Horse Inn,* that immensely successful piece of Austrian imperial nostalgia.

Neither the collectives nor the new Left cabaret overlapped much with the agitprop movement, which was both older-established and less professional, indeed less middle class. This was a much bigger affair, and it had been rapidly developing since 1927, the year when Willi Muenzenberg's International Workers' Aid (IAH) brought the Soviet Blue Blouses group to

An agitprop group (on platform) about to perform at a workers' sports meeting. Shot from the Brecht-Eisler-Dudow-Ottwalt film *Kühle Wampe*, 1932. Photo by Cinemathèque Française.

Germany for a profoundly influential tour. Up to that point the movement had consisted mainly of workers' "speech choirs," or mass pageants in the old Socialist tradition (Toller scripted the Leipzig one for three successive years from 1922, and Wangenheim too was prominent in them), plus a few amateur cabarets. The Blue Blouses, however, set the pattern for a new type of performance by groups eight to ten strong on improvised stages or the backs of trucks, often in the open air, with short, aggressive, challenging sketches, rousing tunes, stylized or gymnastic movements, and uniform working clothes.

The first such was the Young Communist group, which in 1928 took the name The Red Megaphone. This was led by the Reinhardt actor Maxim Vallentin, the son of Richard; a year earlier it had also roped in Hanns Eisler, whose experience as its musical director was crucial for his development of the *Kampflied*, or militant song, which played a central role in his ensuing relationship with Busch and Brecht. The most important perhaps was Kolonne Links (literally, "Column Left") led by Helmut Damerius, which originated in a sports and hiking club, then in 1929 became the official whole-time agitprop group of the IAH, touring extensively in Germany and to German communities in the USSR; it claimed to have recruited sixteen thousand new members for the IAH by its performances (and is the group seen in *Kuhle Wampe*). Other groups were affiliated to organizations like the paramili-

tary Roter Frontkämpfer-Bund, or the Marxist Workers' School (MASch).
Besides these there were dozens more not merely in Berlin but throughout the
provinces, down to factory level. Their job as "class-conscious workers," so
Wilhelm Pieck told them in 1928, was *not to perform theatre* on the stage, but to
help propagate the proletarian class struggle by their stage impact."[13] Admittedly this led to some absurdities—a song called "Proletarian Self-Criticism," a
sketch called "Surplus Value," a program called *Hallo, Kollege Jungarbeiter!
Hello, Colleague Young Worker!*—and much of the satire was stereotyped and
simple minded. But politically it worked, and the IfA could report that a four-
week election campaign in 1930 by nineteen Berlin groups involved 349
performances to some 180,000 spectators, resulting in the collection of at least
twenty-five hundred marks for party funds and the recruiting of 300 members
for the KPD, 120 for the Young Communists, 375 for Red Aid, 260 for the IAH,
and so on.[14] Perhaps no new writers of significance were discovered by this
well-coordinated movement, but there were some serious composers involved
besides Eisler, notably Hans Hauska, Stefan Wolpe, and Josef Kosma. Brecht
seems to have played little or no part, but Friedrich Wolf took a close personal
interest, notably through his new membership of the KPD (he joined in 1928)
and his association with the Stuttgart-based Spieltrupp Südwest.

Stands against Reaction

Within days of the unfortunate premiere of *The Merchant of Berlin* in September
1929, Herbert Jhering reviewed Wolf's first wholly committed play *Cyankali* as
performed by the Group of Young Actors in their second production. Very
perceptively he drew some drastic conclusions for the established theatre:

> The theatre has pushed its outposts so far forward that the well-entrenched front
> line behind them—by which I mean the Staatstheater, Max Reinhardt's theatres
> and the Deutsches Künstler-Theater [the German Arts Theatre recently launched
> by Reinhardt's ex-lieutenant Robert Klein]—will need to follow up if contact is to
> be maintained. Otherwise not only the outposts but the newly exposed front line
> theatres will be in for a sticky time. Because once the assault on the experimental
> theatre has been launched it will soon be the turn of the peaceful, cossetted
> theatre of quality.
> So we have to have an artistic theatre. But it needs to shrug off the indifference
> created by hackneyed conflicts and hollow, bombastic "evenings out." We have to
> have a theatre of entertainment. But it needs to shrug off any plagiarism of old-
> style operetta, old-style comedy. We have to have a "theatre of the times" (Zeit-
> theater). The makings of this exist. It is being successful because it has discovered
> its subjects, its category, its actors. The modified, reborn arts theatre, with its new
> basis, is on the way. The Zeittheater exists.[15]

The interesting thing about the Berlin established theatre in the last years
of the Republic is that it did in fact move a long way toward meeting Jhering's
requirements. Though Klein, it seems, dropped out of the race against the
general reaction (no longer "camouflaged" once Rosenberg's Kampfbund and
the Nazi press got to work), the Deutsches Theater, the Volksbühne, and the
Staatstheater did indeed follow up into more exposed positions, and the

Intermediate form between theatre and agitprop. Gustav von Wangenhein's *The Mousetrap* performed by his collective Truppe 1931 at the Kleines Theater, Berlin, December 1931. Photo by Cologne University Theatre Museum.

encroachments of National Socialism, increasingly connived at by the social and political establishment, were generally resisted by the front-line theatres. Nor for that matter did the commercial cinema give as much ground as might have been expected. During 1930 and 1931, for instance, Fox produced *Cyankali,* Ufa *The Blue Angel* (the Heinrich Mann novel adapted by Zuckmayer and Vollmoeller), and Nero-Film not only Lang's *M* with Peter Lorre but three Pabst films: *The Threepenny Opera, Kameradschaft,* and *Westfront 1918,* both the last two being scripted in part by Lampel. Many outstanding actors of the left theatre performed in these, while an independent company produced the multilingual pacifist film *Niemandsland (War Is Hell)* with Busch, Stobrawa, and music by Eisler.

At least in these two sectors the battle was not yet lost. So at the Volksbühne Karlheinz Martin's opening premieres in winter 1929–30 were about the manipulation of justice: Hans Rehfisch's *Dreyfus Affair* and Karl Maria Finkelburg's *Amnesty,* directed respectively by Martin himself and by Günther Stark. Attacked by the "special sections" for not being radical enough, he responded early the following season with Wolf's *Sailors of Cattaro,* a strong Communist play about a mutiny in the Austrian navy in 1918. Together with *The Kaiser's Coolies* and Toller's *Draw the Fires* this was one of a trio of First World War naval dramas running more or less simultaneously in Berlin; the lead was played by Ernst Busch, who joined the company for two seasons and also distinguished himself in Paul Schurek's *Kamrad Kaspar* (for which Brecht wrote some songs) and Stefan Grossmann's Zeitstück *The Two*

Adlers, about the Austrian Socialist politicians. Along with such new plays Martin directed a number of revivals featuring actors who might equally have been performing for Piscator or Aufricht: Peter Lorre, Lotte Lenya, Ernst Ginsberg, Theo Lingen, Hermann Speelmans, Margarete Melzer (Hans Richter's friend), Leonard Steckel, and others. Among them were not only *Danton's Death* and *The Weavers* but contemporary works of merit like *Der fröhliche Weinberg* and Kaiser's *Nebeneinander*. This whole progressive policy continued up to the summer of 1932, when Martin left and Heinz Hilpert took over. Even then, only half a year before Hitler came to power, there were no spectacular concessions, and some of the same actors would stay on.

Partly incorporated in the Volksbühne ticketing system was the Theater am Schiffbauerdamm, which Aufricht managed by a remarkable piece of juggling. On the one hand Brecht felt closely enough involved to term it "my" theatre; on the other it needed the Volksbühne subscribers and was soon prepared to snap up any chance of bringing in a show that would appeal to them. Thus following the "Brecht-Pause" Hilpert, who was probably the last major director to have emerged under the Republic, staged *Draw the Fires* with Speelmans and Albert Hoerrmann and sets by Neher, opening the same day as *The Kaiser's Coolies* at Piscator's theatre. It was a great critical success, reports Aufricht, but the tickets did not sell: "The realistic Zeittheater of the '20s was dead." Nonetheless he persisted, getting Erich Kästner to dramatize his *Emil and the Detectives* for Martin to direct with a first-class cast, while Hilpert successfully staged Horváth's new people's play *Italienische Nacht* about a social evening in a south German small town complete with republican council, marching Nazis, and irreverent Marxists: a work in the Barlach-Zuckmayer-Fleisser tradition for which Zuckmayer gave Horváth a Kleist Prize for 1931. Kataev's *Squaring the Circle*, however, with Lorre, Lenya, Heinz Rühmann, and Hilde Körber, drew small audiences, nor could a 50 percent reduction in ticket prices fill the house. At the end of the 1930–31 season Aufricht accordingly surrendered this theatre, which thereafter served briefly for a so-called German National Theatre supported by Hans Hinkel, the regional Kampfbund organizer for Berlin, and the nationalist Prussian deputy Koch (who had headed the campaign against the Kroll Opera). This collapsed at the end of 1931 after Hinkel had alienated the actors by calling Reinhardt "Judendreck" (or Jewish crap).[16] Aufricht meantime continued his slightly erratic way, renting the huge Admiralspalast on the one hand for a revival of Molnár's *Liliom* with the new popular star Hans Albers, followed by the Tauber operetta, while on the other hand staging an orchestrally reduced version of *Mahagonny* in an ordinary theatre with Lenya and a primarily nonoperatic cast. The best *Mahagonny* production yet, in Theodor Adorno's view, this opened on 21 December 1931 and ran for more than fifty performances.

At the Staatstheater Kortner in 1928 congratulated Jessner on his fiftieth birthday, remarking that every winter there was a "Jessner crisis," an annual social event to rank with the Press Ball.[17] In the new climate, however, this finally became too much for Jessner. Nationalists attacked "the Jewish element in the Prussian State theatres,"[18] and not long after the renewal of his Intendantship (marked by a new production of *Don Carlos*, with Kortner as Philipp) a makeshift performance of Ferdinand Reyher's *Don't Bet on Fights*— an American boxing play Elisabeth Hauptmann had translated—turned most of the critics against him and forced his resignation. The severity of their verdict, wrote Jhering coldly, had nothing to do with politics:

> Jessner today is neither left nor right. He has outlived his usefulness as an Intendant . . . Jessner the director will find his feet again; there are plenty of tasks for him. For Jessner the Intendant there are none.[19]

For the next two seasons Jessner was temporarily replaced by Ernst Legal from Darmstadt, but he continued to direct a number of plays, including the largely factual *Captain Scott's Expedition to the South Pole* by the ex-Expressionist Reinhard Goering: *Othello* with Werner Krauss as a virtuoso Iago, often directly addressing the audience; also Paul Kornfeld's *Jew Süss* at Aufricht's theatre, with Ernst Deutsch in the title part. Meanwhile Jürgen Fehling directed Barlach's last major Berlin premiere: *Der Blaue Boll (Squire Blue Boll)*, another of his northern small-town plays, though one more suffused with fantasy and mysterious symbolism than *Der arme Vetter* or *Die echten Sedemunds*. Barlach by now had become another target for the nationalist backlash, on account of his markedly unheroic war memorials, which may be why Jessner had hesitated to put this four-year-old play on the program. The more courageous Legal compensated by letting Fehling stage Richard Billinger's peasant play *Rauhnacht*, which pushed Barlach's type of earthiness over the border into the blood-and-soil mysticism favored by the Nazis. The premiere was on 17 December 1931. Seven weeks later came a swing in the other direction when Brecht directed the astonishing third production of *Man equals Man* (at whose premiere in Darmstadt Legal had played Galy Gay) with its use of stilts and jerky, "gestic" speaking—the latter particularly on the part of Peter Lorre in Legal's old role. This had five performances only, being poorly received by the critics and booed by some of the audience.[20]

If Reinhardt's brilliant *Fledermaus* production had been his way of celebrating his return to the Deutsches Theater, the premiere which marked his twenty-fifth anniversary there was less successful. The chosen dramatist was Fritz von Unruh, who after achieving a certain fame with his inflated (and much overrated) Expressionist plays had got a good name politically for his part in organizing the Iron Front of the moderate left, which Zuckmayer also supported. Unfortunately his would-be Zeitstück *Phaea* about the film industry (where Reinhardt had just been trying his luck with United Artists in Hollywood) was a feeble pretext for Reinhardt's spectacular staging and for the acting of Heinrich George, Curt Bois, Kurt Gerron and the visiting Russian Michael Chekov. "A Pyrrhic victory for Max Reinhardt, "wrote Bernhard Diebold, "a defeat for the writer Unruh."[21]

As a result, all the outstanding new plays at the Deutsches Theater were directed by Hilpert, who had already proved himself to be the right man for the people's plays of Horváth and Zuckmayer. It was he who staged the premiere of *Elizabeth of England*, a historical play by Ferdinand Bruckner, on 1 November 1930, then went on to direct Horváth's *Tales from the Vienna Woods*

Brecht at the State Theatre, January 1932. His own production of Man equals
Man, with Peter Lorre as Galy Gay (left), the three soldiers—two of them on
stilts—right. Projections and a minimal set by Neher. Photo by Carl Koch.

and Zuckmayer's *Captain of Köpenick,* two of the best and most durable plays of
the genre. Like *Der fröhliche Weinberg,* Horváth's play conveys a great sense of
landscape and place—the Vienna outskirts and the lovely wooded hills behind them—and deals with a richly varied group of ordinary people on an
outing. Unlike Zuckmayer, however, the author consciously shows the ambiguities in their characters: the mixture of sentiment and cruelty, of geniality
and mutual contempt, of humor and nastiness which goes to make up the
country of Johann Strauss and Adolf Eichmann, all conveyed in economically
written dialogue touched with irony. Maybe his deflation of the operetta
image of Vienna was topically apt, and not unwelcome in the current state of
Berlin. But by all accounts *Tales from the Vienna Woods* was beautifully done by a
largely Austrian cast: the comedian Hans Moser, Frieda Richard, Paul Hör-
biger, and Lucie Höflich, along with Carola Neher and Peter Lorre from
outside Reinhardt's normal pool of actors. The sets were by Ernst Schütte, a
comparative newcomer to the Deutsches Theater who applied a conservative
eye to many of Hilpert's productions.

   The Captain of Köpenick is Zuckmayer's best play, even if historically it was
less of a turning point than *Der fröhliche Weinberg* had been. The theme was a
gift for him, in two senses of the word. First of all Kortner, talking about
possible subjects for a film, had told him of the Berlin shoemaker Wilhelm
Voigt, who in 1906 dressed up as a captain in the first Imperial Guards,

commandeered some soldiers, arrested the mayor and treasurer of Köpenick in the eastern suburbs, and went off with the municipal funds.[22] Secondly the inborn German reverence for the army and its uniforms had become all too topical, as had the cowardice of the civil authorities in the face of any show of force (though this was not to appear till later). Above all, the whole thing was a wonderful pretext for a cross-section of Berlin life under William II, ranging from the tramps and tarts of Voigt's wanderings to the Prussian officer visiting his tailor, and not forgetting representative figures from the deplorable middle: the Progressive Popular mayor, the socially ambitious tailor, and the rest. Zuckmayer, who had actually once seen Voigt exhibited at a fairground (after the Kaiser had pardoned him), thereupon read the old reports, saw the possibilities, and conceived the play in his head so vividly that Reinhardt, the "magical listener" to whom he outlined it at Leopoldskron in the summer of 1930,[23] agreed to produce it and asked for the script to be sent at once. In fact it took two months to write, then Hilpert cast its no fewer than 73 characters, with Werner Krauss as the flexible, resourceful, but also elderly and pathetic declassed craftsman. Given another realistic setting by Schütte, the production opened on 5 March 1931, some eight months before *Tales from the Vienna Woods;* it had 100 performances with Krauss in the part, then continued in the repertoire with the popular comedian Max Adalbert, who also played it on the screen. These two plays were then followed by Gerhardt Hauptmann's *Before Sunset,* very much a production of the old school, with the fifty-eight-year-old Reinhardt directing the sixty-nine-year-old author's story of an old man's love for a young girl.

All the same the new reactionary theatre was not entirely inactive, even though it had not been able to establish itself at the top level. Admittedly the vogue for war plays, coinciding with that for war novels from 1928 on, was an ambiguous factor; for whereas the naval dramas were imbued with a more or less revolutionary spirit (matching the attitude of the Kiel and Kronstadt sailors at the end of the war) the army plays, however disillusionedly pacifist their initial effect, could easily arouse nostalgic or militarist feelings. Perhaps this was not true of Sheriff's *Journey's End,* which Klein's German Arts Theatre gave as its first production on 29 August 1929 with Friedrich Kayssler as the colonel and Hilpert directing; but it did apply to *Douaumont* at the Volksbühne, to Gerhard Menzel's Expressionistic *Toboggan* at the Theater in der Königgrätzerstrasse (Barnowsky) at the end of 1928, and even to Graff and Hintze's *Endless Road (Die endlose Strasse)* at the Schillertheater early in 1932. Billinger's peasant plays had the same double-edged effect, and there was always the unambiguously nationalist appeal of any works dealing with German-speaking minorities and the frontier areas, notably Fred A. Angermeyer's *Fly, Red Eagle of the Tyrol,* which a group including Heinrich George and Agnes Straub performed at the Lessing-Theater.

But there was as yet no serious theatre devoted to such material, not even the National Theatre in Weimar, whose Intendant Franz Ulbrich had served throughout the Frick era; for Ulbrich seems at first only to have stepped up the ration of operettas and cut down on modern and non-German works. Certainly all attempts to found a Nazi or otherwise reactionary theatre in

Berlin quickly failed. In particular the National Socialist Volksbühne had ignominiously to give up the Wallner-Theater to Piscator in 1930 and move into the obscure Theater in der Klosterstrasse for its sporadic performances. Here and on its provincial tours it played such works as Gorch Fock's *Doggerbank;* a comedy by Dietrich Eckart (the first editor of the *Völkischer Beobachter,* to whose memory Hitler had dedicated *Mein Kampf*); and Goebbels's pseudo-Expressionist I-drama *The Wanderer,* a distant descendant of Sorge's *Beggar.* In mid-1931 it closed. As for the German National Theater at the Schiffbauerdamm, it managed to perform two works in its six weeks of life: Hans Kyser's *Es brennt an der Grenze (There's a Fire on the Frontier)* and Gerhard Menzel's muddled peasant drama *Bork* with the Sudeten German actor Fritz Kippel in the lead. A Kampfbundbühne of Rosenberg's Militant League again took the Wallner-Theater after Piscator had left, but had to close down after three weeks.

Ups and Downs of a Fatal Year

Even in the final year of the Republic's life, when the nationalists and the Nazis may have been able to do rather more damage, they were still nowhere near establishing a serious alternative theatre. Nationally, regionally, and locally, the popular vote during 1932 went overwhelmingly Hitler's way; moreover, he himself at last became acceptable, even attractive, to the Rhineland industrialists and to some of the aristocracy. It is true that he failed to win the presidency from Hindenburg in the April election, though interestingly some 1.3 million Communist votes appear to have switched to him on the second round. But in the Prussian Parliament at the end of that month the Nazis' representation went up from 9 seats to 162, making them bigger than the combined Left (not that the Left did combine), while in Oldenburg they for the first time gained an absolute majority. That same spring Hindenburg's Catholic chancellor Heinrich Brüning banned the paramilitary formations, including the SA, while an emergency decree of 27 March—promulgated doubtless with the presidential election in mind—forbade any public attempt to advocate civil disobedience or bring officials and religious bodies into disrepute, a provision which henceforward would restrict performances by agitprop groups.

With public opinion continuing to swing towards the Nazis (whose gains in the July Reichstag elections were even greater than in the landslide of September 1930), and unemployment still growing, Hindenburg and the army now decided to dispense with Brüning and deposed him in favor of their friend Franz von Papen at the beginning of June. This wholly untrustworthy figure—amateur rider, amateur officer and spy, ex-member of the Prussian Parliament—came in on a program of reducing social security, purging "art bolshevism," and bringing back Christianity to Germany. His real achievement, however, was to remove the ban on the SA ("wonderful human material," the ex–crown prince had called them) and depose the Socialist-led Prussian government. Though he had a certain pretext for this crucial act in that such a government no longer corresponded to the state of the parties, the effect was to remove the last major barrier to Hitler's rise to power, the strong and democratically led Berlin police; and undoubtedly his action was arbitrary and unconstitutional. Legality, however, was no longer the point: the fact was that the SPD cravenly abdicated before the merest show of force. If Wilhelm Voigt and a handful of soldiers had been enough to overcome the mayor of Köpenick, it now took even less to make the experienced Carl Severing abandon the Prussian Ministry of the Interior. This, alas, was neither a Berlin folk legend nor even a symbolic omen. It was a disastrous political fact.

If we take a quick look at the German theatre at this fatal juncture, we find Martin and Beer expecting to take over the Deutsches Theater, Legal about to leave the Staatstheater where Lindtberg had become a leading director, the Kroll Opera finished, the third Piscatorbühne out of business, the Volksbühne running normally enough under Hilpert, and the Theater am Schiffbauerdamm left without a policy and sometimes without a production. Thanks to Papen's coup the Prussian arts administration was losing its two outstanding officials: Carl Seelig, in charge of theatre; and Leo Kestenberg, in charge of music. At Dessau the new Nazi premier of Anhalt closed the Bauhaus and forbade the employment of Jews in the theatre; in Berlin a similar resolution was passed on 1 June by the new Prussian Parliament, though it was as yet disregarded in practice. In Frankfurt the city council removed Unruh's *Zero* from the repertoire, seemingly because of his association with the Iron Front; in Kassel the Prussian state theatres withdrew Robert Sherwood's *Waterloo Bridge* in response to Nazi agitation. Meanwhile the Communists had increasingly been brought to look on the Soviet Union as their temporary base. Not only had there been a number of productions of contemporary Soviet plays, from Tretiakov's *Roar China* in Frankfurt in October 1929 to plays by Bill-Belotzerkovski, Glebov, Kataev, and others in 1930–31, but there were also intensified exchanges of visits. The Meyerhold Theatre played in Berlin in April 1930, for instance, while the Group of Young Actors played in Moscow; Tretiakov toured Germany; Brecht, Wolf, and Jhering visited the USSR; Pudovkin filmed *The Deserter* in Hamburg; while Münzenberg and the IAH invited Piscator and his actors to make films at the Mezhrabpom (Russian acronym for IAH) Studios in Moscow. All this was overseen by the new international associations set up under the Comintern, of which the renamed International Association of Revolutionary Theatres (MORT) now extended its scope from the workers' groups proper to take in the whole left theatre, both amateur and professional. At the same time functionaries like Georg Lukács and Alfred Kurella had (it seems) been given the job of keeping the German Communist avant-garde close to the changing Soviet aesthetic line.

In January 1932 there were two historic events, one at each pole of the modern German theatre. The first was Brecht's last production before the Third Reich, a highly portable, didactic, agitational version of Gorky's 1905 Revolution story *The Mother*, which he had written in collaboration with Dudow and Eisler as a development of their work on *Die Massnahme*, and now staged using some of the Group of Young Actors and one or two amateurs alongside Helene Weigel (in the title part) and Ernst Busch. This was a tightly written, poetically and musically most powerful work, designed to use Russian experience (as Brecht understood it) as political training for a putative German revolution. Staged in the first place with Aufricht's support at the obscure Komödienhaus on the Schiffbauerdamm quayside, it toured the Berlin suburbs, playing in various halls and meeting places, even on one occasion dispensing with Neher's very simple canvas set in order to get around police regulations. It was also condensed into something more like a suite of songs for performance in Russian by Kolonne Links, who had been sent straight back to the USSR by Muenzenberg after their return early in 1931 and were now broadening their agitational style under the direction of the Soviet TRAM movement.

The second event occurred when, in the sharpest contrast, Ulbrich's National Theatre in Weimar staged the German premiere of *A Hundred Days*, a play about Napoleon written by Mussolini with the dramatist Giovacchino Forzano. Here, rather than in the various Nazi fiascos in Berlin, was the real prelude to the German Fascist theatre, for Hitler attended with the racist architect Paul Schulze-Naumburg in his train, while Emmy Sonnemann was in the not very distinguished cast: soon she would be Mrs. Hermann Goering. Also among the be-swastikaed audience were members of the Fascist Italian embassy and its Dresden consulate, as well as Nietzsche's sister, for whom Hitler brought a bouquet. According to the Nazi critic H. S. Ziegler in the *Völkischer Beobachter* the applause during the four-hour performance was a little tepid. But there was lengthy clapping at the end and cries of "Heil!"[24]

Despite the muzzling of the agitprop movement Wangenheim at the end of 1931 had launched his Truppe 1931, a collective of professional actors performing didactic scripts written by himself in a mixture of agitprop, speech chorus, and classic theatrical style; its members included the Japanese actor-director Koreya Senda. The last of its three productions, *That's Where the Dog is Buried*, actually opened five days after Hitler's appointment as chancellor on 30 January 1933. However, the autumn of 1932 belonged primarily to Gerhart Hauptmann, whose seventieth birthday fell on 15 November, prompting two notable revivals by Hilpert at the Volksbühne (*Die Ratten* [*The Rats*], with Käthe Dorsch in sets by Rochus Gliese) and by Jessner at the Staatstheater (*Gabriel Schillings Flucht* [*Gabriel Schilling's Flight*] with Krauss and Elisabeth Bergner). Yet even at this last moment the Berlin theatre could welcome a new left-wing writer in the shape of the Hungarian Julius Hay, a former student of stage design who had recently joined the KPD and begun writing plays, of which two had their premieres that December. Thus at the Deutsches Theater Martin directed the historical play *Gott, Kaiser und Bauer* (*God, Emperor and Peasant*) with Kortner, Wegener, Margarete Melzer, and Erwin Kalser (of whom the second had been waiting vainly in Russia for Piscator to start his film). At the Volksbühne three weeks earlier Hilpert staged *Das neue Paradies* (*The New Paradise*) with Anton Walbrook (still known as Adolf Wohlbrück). After that the Wagner jubilee began to loom up, and the Staatstheater mounted its great *Faust* production with Werner Krauss and Gustav Gründgens as Faust and Mephisto, the first part directed by Lothar Müthel on 2 December, the second by Gustav Lindemann a week before Hitler came to power. All this provided a

Contrasting productions of 1932. Above, Mussolini's Napoleon play *The Hundred Days* staged by Franz Ulbrich at the National Theatre, Weimar, before an audience of Nazi leaders and Fascist officials. Below, end of Brecht/Eisler's *The Mother* about the Russian Revolution in a portable production played in Berlin halls. Photos by Cologne University Theatre Museum and Akademie der Künste der DDR.

Last of the Left theatre. As Hitler came to power in January 1933 the Truppe 1931 was playing Wangenheim's *Wer ist der Dummste?* in Berlin. Photo by Cologne University Theatre Museum.

dignified theatrical link into the conservative monumentality of the Third Reich.

Brecht was left with two unproduced plays, his last works for the established theatre for the next five years: *Saint Joan of the Stockyards* and a *Measure for Measure* adaptation, which later became *The Roundheads and the Pointed Heads;* no management was prepared to risk them. Horváth's *Glaube Liebe Hoffnung (Faith, Love, Hope),* which was to have been staged by Hilpert at the Deutsches Theater was put off, as Reinhardt attempted in a last-minute maneuver to hand his theatre to the Volksbühne. Zuckmayer, who had just been dramatizing Hemingway's *Farewell to Arms,* became stranded on the pinnacle of his success, with revivals of three of his plays running in Berlin and a new play (*Der Schelm von Bergen* [*The Rogue of Bergen*]) awaiting completion for Hilpert to direct with Krauss, Dorsch, and a brilliant cast. Like Kessler three years earlier he could give a last look at a Berlin he no longer wished to work in, and sum up the loss now confronting them all: "Half our life remained there."[25]

PART III

Weimar and After

Actors of the Weimar theatre at its summit. Participants in the Staatstheater's memorial program for Albert Steinrück in 1929, grouped around its intendant Leopold Jessner. Including Max Pallenberg, Fritzi Massary, Tilla Durieux and Werner Krauss (all seated left). Heinrich George and Fritz Kortner (immediately behind Jessner). Elisabeth Bergner (seated to his right), Mady Christians, Carola Neher and Trudi Hesterberg (in armchair) and Tilly Wedekind (far right). Photo by Ullstein Bilderdienst.

8

The Continuity of Talent

Weimar's Four Great Innovators

In following the Republic and its theatre through so uncertain a moment of history I have had to single out the new developments in each of the main phases of the story. Thus we saw the short-lived upsurge of Expressionism at the end of the First World War, followed by the beginnings of epic theatre and the emergence of a new kind of popular realism leading to the people's plays of Fleisser and Horváth; then the socially critical Zeitstück (with or without the new documentary and technological element supplied by Piscator) and the simultaneous development of a modern opera and a radically different musical theatre; finally the political theatre of the last phase, with its rejection of the whole previous "apparatus." All these widely differing schools of theatre were shaped by the fluctuating adventures of the new German democracy, whose practical and spiritual implications for the arts I have tried to trace. At the same time, however, and linking even the most radical and the most conservative aspects of this whole cliff-hanging story, the individual makers of the Weimar theatre—the directors, designers, actors, technicians, and critics—remained for the most part active throughout those fourteen years, so that even after their ideas were no longer new and their contribution had become more or less taken for granted, they still exerted an influence and formed part of the rich Weimar mixture. In many cases these people changed less than the jagged outline of the peaks and summits of the period would suggest; they might become more or less fashionable, get better or worse notices from the critics, be more or less in demand professionally. But all the time they were there, and for the most part they applied their talents to giving the theatre whatever it might momentarily demand.

The major creative influences overlapped. Four decisive figures left their stamp not only on one or more generations of actors, but also on stage design and technique. It was they who established new ways of looking at the dramatic repertoire and the theatrical resources needed to realize it: prime movers with their own conceptions of theatre, expressed sometimes in essays and interviews but more often by the example of their practice and the force of their teaching. Among this quartet Jessner was the great innovator of the German Revolution, using the classics (especially Schiller and Shakespeare— in nine years he only directed five new plays) to point broadly democratic lessons, clarifying their plots and staging them with an austere but passionate and concentrated force. Halfway through his dominance of the Berlin scene Piscator arrived, to introduce a political and technological theatre of an entirely different kind, which not only helped to create a large pool of left-wing actors but established an approach to documentary theatre that remains suggestive even today. He in turn was joined and then overtaken by Brecht, the only playwright of the four, a man whose determination to control all aspects of theatre—language, narrative structure, acting, design, and music, not to mention the audience—led him to work out a consistent theory of theatre which became less and less compatible with the prevailing institutions. Finally but also primarily, underlying the three others, there was still Reinhardt, who even if he no longer led with respect to the visual, technical, and dramaturgical aspects of theatre, remained a masterly director of actors and a decisive influence far beyond his own commercial involvement. However his influence might dwindle throughout the period, he remained a presence and a standard by which the Weimar theatre's achievements were judged.

If Reinhardt was generally out of sympathy with the Expressionism of the first few postwar years, he was even less anxious to get involved with contemporary social problems, and to that extent he remained stuck in the past, particularly once the ambitious experiment of the Grosses Schauspielhaus proved impossible to sustain. The great imaginative leap forward which this had seemed in its first conception never entirely materialized: instead of leading to a new popular theatre (so Jhering suggested in an article of 1922) it became tangled in archaism, aestheticism, and commercial calculation. Only for the actors (and for Reinhardt himself as a director of crowds) did it represent a challenging extension of their range. Thereafter, while lieutenants like Felix Holländer went on trying to bring in new talents such as Engel, Neher, and Brecht, the Reinhardt theatres offered too little that was new to retain their interest. Formally conventional conversation plays like that masterpiece of Viennese comedy, Hofmannsthal's *Schwierige*, were no longer much appreciated in Berlin, while of the foreign imports of the stabilization period there was nothing to compare with the impact of Strindberg's work

Max Reinhardt arriving in
Chicago in December 1934
with his production of *A
Midsummer Night's Dream*.
Photo by "Dick" Whittington,
courtesy of the
Billy Rose Theatre
Collection, New York Public
Library (at Lincoln Center:
Astor, Lenox, and Tilden
Foundations).

before 1918. Of a total of 23,374 Reinhardt performances in the years 1914–1930 (so Alfred Muhr reckoned)[1] 2,727 were devoted to Shakespeare, 1,207 to Shaw, and 1,171 apiece to Wedekind and Hauptmann, followed in descending order by Goethe, Schiller, Büchner, Molière, and others. Much of this fell in the nine years when the Deutsches Theater was being run by Reinhardt's aides while he concentrated on his Austrian interests and his foreign tours, and as a result that theatre undoubtedly experienced a lowering of standards. For where previously Reinhardt had varied the casting of the leading parts in a given production as a means of maintaining the actors' and the audience's freshness of approach, his Berlin theatres now tended to operate the same star system as their commercial rivals. That is to say, the highly paid actor or actress with a reputation in the cinema would play a limited number of performances before handing the part over to a less expensive substitute. Sometimes this justified itself, as when Max Adalbert took over Werner Krauss's part in *Der Hauptmann von Köpenick*. But to the critics it was a continual cause for complaint.

Nonetheless Reinhardt's work with his actors left a lasting mark on the whole German-language theatre ranging from Nazi collaborators to the leaders of the agitprop Left. As Muhr put it, Reinhardt discovered actors; other directors collected them. And in the long list of those who passed through his hands "almost every second or third name was of world class. The rest were part of an unparalleled ensemble."[2] His particular gift, testified to by many of his former actors, was his watchful patience: his ability to listen and observe every detail of an audition or rehearsal, then see how the performer's individual interpretation and capacities could fit the director's overall conception of the play and the requirements of the ensemble. The necessary adjustments would be finely made, by suggestion rather than imposition; an actor himself, he could demonstrate almost in an undertone without appearing to take over the part. Thus Alexander Granach describes him dissecting a part into its component details and rehearsing them one by one with the actors, while Bernhard Reich, who came as an assistant director in 1920, sees an analogy with impressionist painting and the building up of a subtly varied picture by countless small touches. He was like a colleague rather than a headmaster, Rosa Bertens reported, but he could also react like a member of the audience. In such ways he proved exceptionally able to tend that delicate plant, the actor's confidence, and it is clear that many of his performers felt that they acted better and more fulfillingly for him than for anyone else. They felt secure in his choice of props and set, which were intended above all to serve the play in accordance with the actors' movements prescribed in his detailed Regiebuch. Given a great new space, however, like the Grosses Schauspielhaus or the cathedral square in Salzburg, he would not clutter or constrict it but would fill it by active, sweeping movements, whether of the individual or of the crowd, and a carefully orchestrated choral speech. His strength lay in his understanding of his performers' talents and the limits of time and space within which they had to be deployed. His weakness lay in his growing failure to understand unfamiliar types of play.

During the first half of the 1920s the outstanding director was more often thought to be Leopold Jessner, whose Intendantship turned the Staatstheater from a standing joke into a major European stage. As a director he, too, fought shy of new plays, though as an Intendant he took a favorable enough interest in them, traveling to Munich to see Brecht's *Edward II*, for instance, and giving Zuckmayer his chance in Berlin by letting Ludwig Berger stage *Kreuzweg*, the twenty-three-year-old author's first play. But he was clearly more in tune with the time than Reinhardt and more concerned with its issues. His aim was to give Germany a new start, and without claiming to be an Expressionist he applied the spirit and methods of this new movement not only to the staging of Wedekind (which had never really flourished in the chamber-music conditions favored by Reinhardt) but also to Shakespeare and Schiller. Here everything was a departure from Naturalism: the heightened tempo, the passionate actors, among whom Kortner was prominent; the largely abstract setting with its steps and platforms and symbolic colors recalling Appia's influence at Hellerau; the streamlining of the text to show the modern relevance of the story; the punctuation by drum rolls and rhythmic shouts; the use of spotlight beams to cut up the space. It all seemed a confirmation of the Expressionist theatre, focusing like it on Man, Der Mensch, rather than those oddly assorted individuals who go to make the concept up. So his work lacked the hedonism of Reinhardt's productions, the charm, the humor, the sense of fun. Nor was Jessner himself so easily likeable, with his bald head, his formal clothing, and stiff Gladstonian collar.

Leopold Jessner
photographed at his fiftieth
birthday party in March
1928. His wife is to the left
of him, his daughter to the
right. Photo by Cologne
University Theatre Museum.

Kortner ridiculed him as a typical long-standing member of the SPD, hard to pin down and reluctant to risk major conflicts; and indeed it appears to have been his record in the Genossenschaft deutscher Bühnenarbeiter (or German Equity) rather than any notable artistic promise that had led in the first place to his appointment. Nevertheless the Staatstheater for a time struck critics as the one really consistent theatre in Berlin, with its own recognizable hall-marks. By 1925 these were beginning to disappear in favor of a more varie-gated approach emphasizing the individuality of the characters, and this, along with the changes brought by the recruitment of Jürgen Fehling, turned it from a directors' theatre into a theatre of skillfully directed actors. In the process Jessner was subjected to a good deal of criticism for his overall policy, though his status as a director seems not to have been questioned.

The other two great pioneers of this period are nowadays more familiar, not least because both of them went back to work in Germany after Hitler's fall and continued active till past the middle of the century. Their achievements are appreciated right across the globe, their friends and disciples still alive enough to propagate them; hence we see them more fully than we do Jessner and Reinhardt; yet because we see them in a more modern perspective we do not always understand their impact at the time. Piscator, for instance, from 1925 on revolutionized the theatre's use of the new stage technology, which he

Erwin Piscator in the 1920s, around the time when he was setting up his own theatre.

handled at once extravagantly and with imagination, so as to bring life to now forgotten scripts. Yet because the cutoff point of his book *The Political Theatre* preceded his adoption of more economical methods we forget that the advanced stage apparatus of his first two companies was never essential to his idea as such. Politically he had been formed by the First World War and the pacifist, antimilitarist feelings which this bred in him and which he saw put into action by the Russian Revolution. His ideal was a modified Volksbühne, a people's theatre on the original Socialist lines as hardened by the war; and the essence of its politics was a combination of demonstration and argument, with the audience taking part, then going home heartened and convinced.

The actors' functions thus seemed somewhat secondary, even after Piscator's obsession with technology had been brought under control, and while they appreciated and indeed admired him it was because of his infectious enthusiasm and mastery of the whole complex montage, rather than on account of the detailed work which he did with them. He had in fact no distinctly new approach to acting, and although his Studio of 1927–28 set out to train young actors it seems to have served mainly to turn them into political human beings working with promising young directors: a good foundation for the collectives which followed his first two bankruptcies. His rehearsals would overrun until late in the night, and up to 1929 his productions depended on stars from Reinhardt's stable: Granach for *Hoppla, wir leben!*, Wegener for *Rasputin*, Pallenberg for *Schweik* (one of that actor's great performances), and Tilla Durieux for *Konjunktur*. Before that he had had Heinrich

Bertolt Brecht with two of his close collaborators in 1931–32: left, the composer Hanns Eisler; right, the film director Slatan Dudow.

George and other skilled Volksbühne actors at his disposal. For *The Merchant of Berlin* he brought over the Russian-Yiddish actor Paul Baratoff from New York.

Brecht in the 1920s was the odd man out, since he was not, like the others, in the first place an actor but a poetic genius with no inhibitions about telling the most eminent actors what they could do even if he had to interrupt the director to say so. Prompt from his arrival in Berlin in 1924 to air his views in the press about any literary or theatrical topic under the sun, he at first played the self-assertive enfant terrible from the provinces slightly too much for his politics, such as they were up to 1929, to be taken seriously. Yet all the time he was making productive friendships and alliances: an inner circle headed by Elisabeth Hauptmann—the so-called Brecht collective with which he researched, wrote, and revised his works—and an outer ring of talents at once complementary and comparable to his own: Erich Engel, Caspar Neher, Kurt Weill, Hanns Eisler. Among these was a strong nucleus of actors who he felt, on personal or technical grounds, were the right people to perform his plays: Homolka, Kortner, Granach, Lenya, Carola Neher (unrelated to Caspar) and, closer still to him, Lorre, Busch, and his own wife, Helene Weigel. Not all such players were prepared to conform to the distinctive principles of acting which he was working out as part of his theory of epic theatre, principles which at that time embraced a conscious shift from the emotional to the rational, an abandonment of empathy in favor of a more detached attitude to one's role, an externalization of psychological processes, and the dissection of the action into successive attitudes or "gests," all determined by an overriding concern with clarity and the understanding of the audience. Granach, for instance, played *Drums in the Night* with raucous outbursts of stored-up passion. Nonetheless, the principles themselves made Brecht seem fascinating, if at times rebarbative, to work with, and for many people in the theatre they remained his most challenging contribution. It was only a decade or more after leaving Germany that he started to modify them, since if anything they became strengthened by his contacts from 1930 on with untrained performers, who were that much likelier to accept them. So where Piscator found the final crisis years cramping, Brecht could see his theories becoming effective; moreover, the new forms of *Die Massnahme* and *The Mother* proved well adapted to the conditions of exile.

Directors for Unsettled Times

Such were the four innovators who from their different theatrical bases in Berlin drew the steadily extending boundaries of German theatre in these fourteen years. Within this territory the operation was backed up by countless directors, actors, designers, and technicians whose abilities were stimulated and engaged by the general sense of movement. So the north German Jürgen Fehling, who came to the Volksbühne as an actor and assistant director from the Vienna Volksbühne in 1918, began as an Expressionist in contrast to his Intendant, Friedrich Kayssler, and it was in this spirit that he staged Toller's *Masses and Man* on 29 September 1921 in predominantly black sets by Hans Strohbach—a prelude, he called it,

> to the poetry of world revolution, a stormy morning which may, in happier hours of daylight, be surpassed in lasting poetic value, but never in the passionate humanity from which it springs.[3]

Moving over to Jessner's Staatstheater in 1923, he again reacted against his new chief, whose special characteristic had been to simplify, heighten, and develop the dynamics of the text—editing Schiller's *William Tell*, for instance (according to Caspar Neher's recollection), down to some two hours by clever cuts.

> The subsequent production, on which I collaborated with Fehling, was the exact opposite. It lasted at least three hours, with each scene being developed realistically and at leisure. . . . Without doubt it was much the more thorough and artistic production, but it had nothing like as much sense of the overall shape.[4]

It was Fehling, then, who became the first true interpreter of the new popular realism of such supposedly Expressionist writers as Barlach and Else Lasker-Schüler: eccentricities of small-town life with mysterious, "magic" overtones such as demand individual rehearsal with the actors and a naturalistic set. This gift for staging a subtle and, in the superficial sense, undramatic play very remote from Jessner's sped-up simplifications came in part from a talent for comedy surprising in so depressive and seemingly prickly a character. Only *The Flood*, the least comic and most symbolic of Barlach's plays, slipped from his control: "German actors have forgotten how to play calmly," wrote Jhering[5] of Heinrich George's performance at Noah. Six years later, in 1931, the same director and actor gave the premiere of *Der Blaue Boll* in a production that the same critic could describe as "masterly."[6]

Of the other directors who set out as notable Expressionists, Karlheinz Martin appears to have had the longest career, starting with the historic production of *Die Wandlung*, which introduced Ernst Toller to Berlin, and ending well after the Second World War. From 1920 on he became Reinhardt's second director at the Grosses Schauspielhaus, when he staged Hasenclever's *Antigone*, Kaiser's *Europa*, and Toller's *Machine Wreckers*, though without ever successfully adapting their new Expressionist drama to its vast spaces. From there he moved to the private Renaissance-Theater and directed a notable space-stage setting of Wedekind's *Franziska* starring Tilla Durieux (which he brought from the Volkstheater in Vienna). Then in 1929 he took over the Volksbühne for three years, himself directing a number of the more interesting plays including Rehfisch's *Dreyfus Affair* and the revivals of *Der fröhliche Weinberg* and Kaiser's *Nebeneinander;* in the process he recruited some interesting actors from Brecht's circle, including Lorre, Lenya, and Busch. Yet there is nothing to suggest that Martin had any very marked personality as a director, and even before the end of Expressionism the critics were finding his work unexciting. Nor was this due simply to the skeptical climate of Berlin, for of the pioneering Expressionist directors in the provinces none was able to put his own distinctive stamp on any subsequent type of production, with the result that the originality of the early centers—such as the Frankfurt Schauspielhaus under Weichert, or the Munich Kammerspiele under Falckenberg—rather stagnated after 1923. Hartung at Darmstadt handed over his Intendantship to Ernst Legal, a man somewhat more in tune with the coming theatre, and moved to Cologne; from there he went to succeed Ferdinand Bruckner (then still known as Tagger) at the Berlin Renaissance-Theater. After three years in the capital without achieving any notable success there as a director he returned to Darmstadt to take over from Legal once more. Weichert, whom Zuckmayer found to be less bogged down in Expressionism, eventually moved to Berlin as a free-lance director of a number of reputable productions, but again without working his way into the first rank.

The outstanding figures of the post-Expressionist period were Erich Engel and Heinz Hilpert, with Berthold Viertel as an irregular visitor to the capital (disappearing in 1927 at Murnau's invitation to Hollywood, where his assistant was a cameraman called Fred Zinnemann). Hilpert, like Fehling, had been an acting pupil of Kayssler's and joined him at the Volksbühne at the end of the war. He was not so quick to break into direction, however, first becoming known through one-off productions for the Junge Bühne of early plays by Bronnen and Zuckmayer. Developing thereafter into a scrupulous naturalist, he came to direct the premieres of virtually all Zuckmayer's plays as well as Bruckner's *Criminals* and Horváth's *Tales from the Vienna Woods*, thereby succeeding Fehling as the chief interpreter of the new people's plays. He was the Deutsches Theater's last first-rate director before 1929, when he went over to replace Martin as artistic director of the Volksbühne for the Republic's last four years. Viertel, who had had both Hilpert and Aufricht as actors in his short-lived Die Truppe in 1923, was primarily a writer, a fine poet, and friend of the acerbic Karl Kraus. One of the most intelligent and widely read directors of the time, he, too, came from the Vienna Volksbühne and in three seasons after the end of the war directed a number of Expressionist productions in Dresden before Die Truppe's performance of *Nebeneinander* put an end to that movement. He still felt a certain nostalgia for Expressionism, however, directing two of Bronnen's plays for the Junge Bühne and writing as late as 1932 of

> that radical concern with a reborn idealism such as appears in its best manifestations. And if its elements—its apocalyptic vision of the world's end and its activist strivings for a purified humanity, a fraternal salvation of the world—prompted it to over-hasty solutions, at least they sprang from the problems of our age.[7]

The third man, Engel, was a far drier, more detached and analytical character, who came, like Martin and Kortner, from Hamburg at the end of the First World War to be the principal director at the Munich state theatres. There in the summer of 1922, he directed a production of Grabbe's nineteenth-century *Scherz, Satire, Ironie und tiefere Bedeutung (Joke, Satire, Irony, and Deeper Significance)*, which impressed Jhering as

> a masterpiece, fascinating in its precision. Fascinating in its variety. Without the slightest concession to outworn modes of expression, without any arbitrary distortion for mere experiment's sake.[8]

This led Reinhardt's emissaries to invite him to Berlin. He seems to have been the first of the new directors to arrive in the capital, and came uncluttered by Expressionist mannerisms, impressing Kortner with his intelligence and artistic insight. Zuckmayer, too, found him

> a splendid man: small, energetic with a well-shaped head like a late Roman sculpture. . . . His directorial style too seemed to reflect the hard, thrusting shapeliness of his head and the coolness of his thinking; it was never stiff or strained; indeed it was his achievement to loosen and supplant Expresssionist "formalism" by means of a new, fully thought-out realism.[9]

He was in fact very much the kind of director Brecht wished to be, and the two men's always productive if sometimes uneven relationship was cemented by their common respect for Caspar Neher, the designer who had helped to form Brecht's visual imagination from adolescence on. Not only did Engel direct virtually all those Brecht premieres which Brecht himself had not been able (or allowed) to direct, but some of his other productions with Neher (like their *Coriolanus* for the Deutsches Theater in February 1925) involved Brecht so closely that the latter came to look on them almost as his own. This implied no element of subordination: indeed, Engel's *sachlich* (or matter-of-fact) production of a condensed *Lulu* for Jessner in autumn 1926, with Kortner playing the same part as in Pabst's film with Louise Brooks three years later, began by showing the main characters as animals in a menagerie, a method which may well have influenced Brecht's prologues to *Puntila* and *Arturo Ui*. One way and

A star of theatre and cabaret: Trude Hesterberg as Mrs. Begbick in the 1931 Berlin production of *Rise and Fall of the City of Mahagonny* by Brecht and Weill. Photo by Zander & Labisch from the Cologne University Theatre Museum.

another Engel was much more in tune with Brecht's ideas than Piscator ever was—which may be why Brecht found him hard to write about detachedly.

Acting Styles and Stereotypes

The Weimar Republic is generally seen as a high point in the history of German and Austrian acting, and the films of the time still show us some astonishing performances, both individual and collective. Lorre in *M*, Kortner in *Pandora's Box*, Jannings in *The Last Laugh* and *The Blue Angel*, Bergner in *Der träumende Mund (The Dreaming Mouth)*, Krauss in *Geheimnisse einer Seele (Secrets of a Soul)*: these remain examples of great acting, and there are many others. The German public at the time, particular in Berlin during the "golden" middle of the period, was well aware of its luck in this respect and proud of its splendid corps of actors, whose individual qualities the great mass of theatregoers were happy to discuss and compare. All the same the records of the principal productions do give hints of a lack of variety: the corps of actors did form something of an "establishment," from which directors cast largely by type and by habit, and it was only in moments of crisis and regrouping (like the Revolution itself, the currency stabilization, and the crisis of 1929) that there was not a certain sameness to be felt. Repeatedly critics complained of the failure of directors to build an ensemble, while Brecht seems to have been unique in his demands for a radically new approach to acting. Most directors were content to accept the available talent, and although there were particular actors and directors who were at their best working with one another, the implications of this were not so marked as to make for sharp variations in performance. The result was a high standard rather than a climate of experiment; in fact the concepts of "experimental theatre" or "fringe" are not to be found in contemporary critical writing. Even Brecht, who called his published texts from 1929 on "Attempts," or *Versuche*, worked mainly through the established theatre, of which Helene Weigel, Busch, Lorre, and Carola Neher all formed part. Nor was he likely to turn down any sufficiently prominent actor who wanted to perform his work.

At the same time Brecht preferred the unusual and valued the freshness of such outsiders as Lenya, of cabaret artists like Hesterberg, Kate Kühl, Blandine Ebinger, and Rosa Valetti, above all, perhaps, of the great inventive clown Karl Valentin with his surreal south German dialect sketches—a unique artist with whom both Brecht and Engel worked on short films worthy to rank with those of Buster Keaton and other great Hollywood comics. If Brecht had been asked to name the outstanding actor of the age he would surely have said Chaplin.

Similarly Reinhardt was in his time a creative judge of actors, and if he strikes us now as a man of the establishment this is not so much because he accepted the Berlin corps of actors after 1918 as because he had so largely formed it in the first place. Pallenberg, for instance, had started as a comedian performing in obscure Viennese operetta theatres—"We all breathed a sigh of relief when he came to Reinhardt," wrote Tucholsky in 1917[10]—while in the Italo-Jugoslav-Jewish Alexander Moissi (originally recommended to him by Maximilian Harden in 1904) Reinhardt found a mysterious, uneasy actor of great passion and beauty whom he made into his theatre's principal (and highest-paid) star in defiance of those who could only see a "half-starved, wretchedly clothed actor-proletarian,"[11] rejected at first by his fellow actors, and only hear his unfamiliar foreign accent. Admittedly Reinhardt through his acting schools, first at the Deutsches Theater and then in the beautiful rococo theatre of Schönbrunn Palace in Vienna, was still able to train worthy successors to such players (in 1933 his young recruit Paula Wessely, for instance, was on the verge of her fame). But his most sensational discovery of the 1920s came from a very different world and did little to extend the art of acting. For Lady Diana Cooper, great beauty that she was, was restricted to touring performances of *The Miracle*, part of Reinhardt's worldwide achievement as a showman, but not exactly integral to the German theatre.

The seven-hundred-odd actors (both sexes) mentioned in Günther Rühle's invaluable *Theater der Republik* formed for the majority of directors and theatre managers a more than adequate resource, which they were happy to draw on, so that the most sought-after names crop up repeatedly in a wide variety of productions, as our appendices will show. At the base of their art and technique was the exact observation of detail practiced by the Meiningers

The flexible comedian. Max Pallenberg, star of Reinhardt's Deutsches Theater and Piscator's *Schweik,* photographed in 1928. Photo by Ullstein Bilderdienst.

half a century earlier, which Reinhardt had inherited from the Naturalist movement, then modified by his taste for improvised play and comic invention. From this mixture came the rich school of "Berlin realism," ranging from such solemn and dignified, even stiff performers as Kayssler, Bassermann, and Eduard von Winterstein, to actors of temperament and subtlety like Gertrud Eysoldt with her lively, thoughtful face and agile body, or the containedly powerful Paul Wegener. These particular people, characteristic products of the pre-1914 years, were from the start among the distinguished grandees of the Weimar theatre, but they were all more or less unsuited—and Bassermann by all accounts positively allergic—to the new Expressionist drama.

Jessner, therefore, in inaugurating his regime at the Staatstheater, sought out those other actors who, like Kortner, had deliberately chosen to swim against the mainstream or else, like Heinrich George, had remained outside it in the provincial theatres where Expressionism first reached the stage. This was not only because of the demands of the new movement but also due to what seemed to be Jessner's wish to break away entirely from anything that could be identified with the pre-1918 Empire. Thus even his classical productions demanded players capable of great outbursts of passion or fury and able to limit their physical expression to the most telling movement or gesture. Here, then, was a second ring of actors who often might be playing alongside

Lucie Höflich of the Deutsches Theater, here seen as Gretchen in Reinhardt's 1920 production of Goethe's *Faust*. Photo by Ullstein Bilderdienst.

the first. Finally, and cutting across both groups, there were the temperamentally left-wing, more or less politically aware actors who came to be associated with Piscator. Not that such groupings were all that exclusive. For none of the three were so rigid in their preferences that they would refuse to perform in a production that also drew on the others.

What gave the resulting casts their slight air of monotony was not the blurring of such major distinctions but what seems to have been an overriding demand on the part of audiences for specific types of actor—types that in some cases have gone on influencing the German theatre up to the present day. To a certain extent this kind of stereotyping is common to all Western theatre, if not beyond it, too: the soubrette, the character actor, the heavy father, and so on. So Germany had its madonna figures (like Else Helms and Helene Thimig, who successively married Reinhardt), its healthy blonde peasant girls (apt to be cast, like Lucie Höflich, as Gretchen in *Faust*), its handsome, relaxed, elegant men like Rudolf Forster and Adolf Wohlbrück. But there were, for instance, far fewer of this last category than in the French or Anglo-Saxon theatres, partly because the smooth conversation piece was felt to be at once boring and unserious: partly, as Viertel put it, because

> the people's favorites were character actors, not the handsome, well-proportioned *leading men*. It wasn't only critics who preferred the villain to the dreamboat. In German aesthetics madness counted as nobler than common sense.[12]

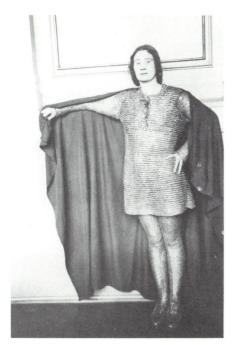

Two leading Berlin actors. Left: Agnes Straub as the queen in Brecht's *Edward II* as staged by Fehling at the Staatstheater in December 1924. Right, Paul Wegener in an unknown role. Photos by Cologne University Theatre Museum.

This was said à propos of Werner Krauss, whose tremendous range (embracing many of the great classical roles as well as that of Caligari in Wiene's film) puts him in a category of his own, overlapping Reinhardt and Expressionism; he could fulfill the requirements of both. But with the beginnings of Expressionist theatre in the First World War the neurotic, hysterical actor soon became essential: pain, emotion, the "outburst" (or *Ausbruch*), the cry or scream (as in Munch's seminal lithograph), such extremes had to characterize the anonymous sons and their mothers, the otherwise undefined ego-figures of writers like Sorge, Hasenclever and Toller, or the frenziedly seeking nonentities of Kaiser. From then on, the old imitative skills of social observation were of less use.

There were "establishment" actors, trained on Strindberg or Wedekind, who could go far to meet the new need: Krauss for one, also Wegener, Conrad Veidt, Eugen Klöpfer, and the young Alexander Granach. There was Pallenberg, from the musical comedy stage. But Expressionism also made the reputation of a number of new players, some of whom became specialists in the rolling eye movements, exclamatory cries, and angular gestures of hyper-intense performance. So Ernst Deutsch from Dresden became associated almost entirely with such parts, acting Sorge's poet in *Der Bettler*, Hasenclever's Son, and the Cashier in Robert Wiene's film of *From Morn to Midnight*. Agnes Straub started at the Grosses Schauspielhaus, then put all her power into Expressionist pieces like Stramm's *Kräfte* and Hasenclever's *Jenseits (Beyond)* to become "the first lady of Expressionism." Gerda Müller and Heinrich George brought their experience of such plays from Frankfurt to Berlin. Kortner, after bursting on to the republican scene with *Die Wandlung* in 1919, took his eruptive, domineering style of acting into the largely classical repertoire of Jessner's Staatstheater, whose Expressionist aspect he thenceforward helped to form. At the same time this spread of the new emotionalism to the classic stage linked rather less happily with the old vices of traditional German theatre: the shouting, the "will to power", the attempt to hypnotize the audience and force the character on it, against all of which Brecht's early notes and essays were directed. For overacting was not only an integral part of Expressionism but also a familiar aspect of old-fashioned theatre: the "empty, stupid declamation," the "bawling in lieu of song, braggadoccio in lieu of strength," which this precocious student had found and criticized in the Augsburg municipal theatre.[13]

Overlapping the general shift toward exaggeration and distortion was the special German affection for large, heavy, sometimes rather brutal-looking men, particularly if they were jovial drinkers. This category starts at the point where actors stop being described simply as masculine or manly (like Winterstein and Steinrück) and become *urwüchsig,* that untranslatable term meaning basic, earthy, with a touch of the primitive. Emil Jannings was one such, though during much of the 1920s he abandoned the theatre for film work; so were Homolka, Wegener, Friedrich Gnass and, above all, Heinrich George, the *Kraftnatur* (again untranslatable, with its implication of rudimentary strength), who acted in a wide range of plays from Piscator's Volksbühne productions to a blood-and-soil work at the Staatstheater called *Mensch, aus Erde gemacht,* or *Person Made of Earth.* Still more distinctively Nazi in spirit and physique was the new type of actor represented by the Bavarian Hans Albers, the musical comedy star who played the waiters in Bruckner's *Verbrecher* and Kaiser's *Zwei Krawatten:* "a true people's actor," Aufricht termed him.

> He went for the audience like a bull entering the ring. He would belch in a woman's face, and the audience would applaud his insolence; he would gulp, and they would dissolve in tears. He was the heartthrob of the time to come: big, blond, blue-eyed, with a walk like a beast of prey.[14]

"The blondest of the blond," said the dark-haired Kortner, who once again saw him as *urwüchsig.*[15] For the two men had a well-publicized fight during Piscator's production of Maxwell Anderson's *What Price Glory?* in March 1929, which ended with Kortner, the senior man, leaving the cast.

The last major newcomer to the republican stage was Gustav Gründgens, an elegant actor of slightly criminal parts who played a homosexual in *Verbrecher* alongside Albers. Tietjens, the State Opera Intendant who had admired his capacities as a director at the Kroll Opera, more or less imposed him on the Staatstheater as the Mephisto to perform opposite Werner Krauss in the two-part centenary *Faust* of winter 1932–33 and from then on he was identified with this role and ranked among the great actors. These were headed, in the view of profession and public alike, by Albert Bassermann,

The face of power. Heinrich George, here seen as Florian Geyer in Frankfurt in 1932, graduated from provincial Expressionism and Piscator's productions to leading roles in the theatre and cinema of the Third Reich. Photo by Ullstein Bilderdienst.

who held the Iffland Ring left for his successors by August Wilhelm Iffland, first Intendant of the Prussian Hof- (later Staats-) theater and greatest actor of Schiller's and Goethe's time. Alongside him stood Krauss, a wonderfully original and resourceful actor who was exceptional in not repeating himself, while Wegener and Moissi were also on the star level. As box office draws, however, no male actor except perhaps Albers could compare with the Austrian Elisabeth Bergner, reputedly the highest paid of them all. Bergner, who worked mainly for managements like Barnowsky's that would build productions round her, was a slight, boyish (*knabenhaft:* yet another term for a German stereotype) figure of exceptional dramatic power. "She could drive Macbeth to bloodshed," wrote Kortner, "act the inferno of Strindberg's women." At the same time

> You felt like freeing the childish creature from the menace besetting it, and shielding it in your lustful arms. Bergner was the child-bride incarnate, the wishful thoughts of old men. What is more, being half boy and half girl she offered all possible perspectives to the excessively loving Berlin public.[16]

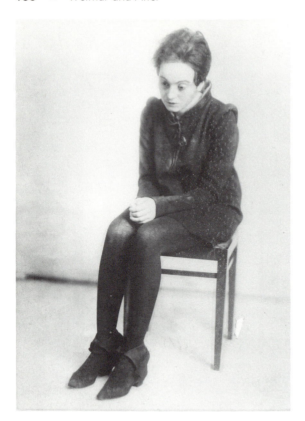

The greatest draw of the Weimar theatre: Elisabeth Bergner at the Deutsches Theater in 1924 as Reinhardt's *St. Joan*. Photo by Ullstein Bilderdienst.

Gifted with such contradictory qualities, a demanding businesswoman who at one time was in love with the Communist actor Hans Otto, she stood out head and shoulders from more conventional players such as Käthe Dorsch, Grete Mosheim, and the promising young Käthe Gold who played Gretchen alongside Krauss and Gründgens in the centenary *Faust*. These and other leading women of the Berlin stage are difficult to conjure up today except in terms of their beauty, charm or *Innigkeit* (inwardness), these being the qualities primarily in demand. Tilla Durieux, for instance, had a most striking, slightly oriental face, once painted by Renoir, but even Piscator gave her unrewarding parts; while Carola Neher, who had a great role waiting for her in Brecht's *Saint Joan of the Stockyards*, was never able to play it except on the radio, because at the end of the Republic no production of so fiercely Communist a work could be mounted.

Advances in Design and Theatre Music

If the standard of acting helped give the German theatre its preeminence in Western Europe after the First World War, an even more conspicuous factor, particularly for non-German speakers, was the quality of its design and staging. Here, the whole approach was different, for the masterpieces of stage design seen in France or Britain at that time were largely due to the Russian and Swedish ballets, who wanted a clear stage for the dances and could therefore commission the great modern artists to make what were in effect primarily blackcloths. With rare exceptions (such as Reinhardt at the beginning of his directorial career) the German theatre never turned to its country's leading painters—let alone the international masters of the modern movement—for the simple reason that in Germany and Austria stage design was not merely a respectable branch of "applied art" but a recognized profession, trained to work in the well-equipped and highly organized theatres of which Central Europe had so many. As a result it was not the leading Expressionist artists of the Brücke and Blauer Reiter groups who gave the new Expressionist theatre of 1916–1923 its distinctive face, but the regular designers of the theatres in question. Ludwig Sievert at the Frankfurt city theatres, August Babberger at Karlsruhe, Eduard Sturm at Düsseldorf, Friedrich Thiersch in Leipzig, Otto Reigbert in Munich—these, along with Robert Neppach for the Tribüne's *Die Wandlung* and Walter Reimann for the film of *Caligari,* were the artists who devised the jagged backgrounds, the toppling buildings, the deep chiaroscuros, and the crystalline vistas that characterized the Expressionist stage. Certainly they related it to the painters' movement, but the impetus came from within the theatre.

Different directors used their designers in different ways. Jessner appears to have had a clear idea of what he wanted, whether he was dealing with the Austrian designer Emil Pirchan or with César Klein, the ex-painter who taught stage design in the school of the Berlin Applied Arts Museum. Platforms and steps had to articulate the stylized action; no element of decoration was wanted aside from light and color; his stage had to be a largely abstract field for expressive speech and movement. Fehling at the same theatre got Rochus Gliese to provide evocative regional townscapes for the Barlach plays and *Die Wupper,* with plenty of detail. Reinhardt needed somebody who would think along the same lines as himself, visualize his concept of the play for him, and work with him on the most effective way of realizing it in terms of scene changes and the dimensions of the revolve. He found this in 1906 in the shape of Ernst Stern, who was able to design in many styles, frothy, serious, pseudorococo, even (for *Die Wupper* and the *Beggar*) Expressionist, and later did many of the big productions in the Grosses Schauspielhaus—though Poelzig himself designed the monumental *Oedipus* with which it opened. Once Reinhardt had left for Vienna, however, where Oskar Strnad was his preferred designer, Stern left to work mainly with Erik Charell, so that there was nothing like a distinct design policy at the Deutsches Theater until Hilpert began working regularly with Ernst Schütte in the late 1920s on such neoNaturalistic productions as *Verbrecher* and the Zuckmayer plays. Schütte had trained as a carpenter, worked for Ulbrich at Weimar, and was not a very interesting artist.

Piscator was even more demanding than Reinhardt, since he wanted an aesthetically and politically progressive designer who could realize his ambitious original ideas for the use of new stage technology. There were two men at the Volksbühne who appeared capable of doing this, but when he set up his own Piscatorbühne it was Traugott Müller, the more Constructivist in style, who went with him and Eduard Suhr who remained behind. Finally there was the exceptional case of Brecht, whose designer Caspar Neher was also his oldest and closest friend, with whom he had discussed his theatrical ideas from the very first. Engel, too, worked effectively and for preference with Neher, who produced some lovely designs for him. But for Brecht he was not merely the right designer but an important contributor to his whole aesthetic approach.

Unattached to any of these principal directors there were many other gifted designers, whether in the provinces or working free-lance in Berlin. Thus the Deutsches Theater briefly employed the photomonteur John Heartfield, who later designed the very striking setting for the Third Piscatorbühne's *Tai Yang erwacht*. Heartfield's friend George Grosz likewise designed the occasional production, not only *Schweik* and *Nebeneinander* but also the premiere of Kaiser's *Kanzlist Krehler (Clerk Krehler)* for the Kammerspiele in 1922. Together they made puppets for the Reinhardt cabaret Schall und Rauch. Lothar Schenck von Trapp and Hein Heckroth were outstanding among the provincial designers of the later 1920s, the former at Darmstadt with Legal and Carl Ebert, making use of interesting elements of montage and proto–pop art, while Heckroth at Essen was a protégé of Neher's who designed *The Green Table* and other works for the Folkwang Ballet under Kurt Jooss. There was also the whole orbit of the Kroll Opera from the beginning of the Klemperer era in autumn 1927 to its closure in July 1931. Here the chief figure was initially Edward Dülberg, an austere designer of formal Jessnertype sets whose efforts to modernize the presentation of the classics antagonized conservatives without really breaking new ground. Within eighteen months, however, his assistant Teo Otto was handling much of the work under the guidance of Klemperer's dramaturg Hans Curjel, and thanks to them a number of striking new designers were commissioned, including both Neher and Traugott Müller. The most startlingly original of these were Moholy-Nagy's sets for *Tales of Hoffmann*, which Legal directed in February 1929. Realized by Otto on the basis of the artist's very abstract geometrical projections, they posed less of a problem than the one commission (possibly the only one in any German theatre during the period) given to a foreign painter. This was when Giorgio de Chirico designed Krenek's *Life of Orestes*, providing a number of tiny pictures which had to be filled out by considerable use of Otto's imagination.[17]

The impact of Bauhaus design on the theatre is exemplified in the Kroll's case by Moholy's settings not only for *Tales of Hoffmann* but also for *Madame Butterfly* and Hindemith's *Hin und Zuruck,* along with Schlemmer's for Schönberg's *Die glückliche Hand (The Lucky Hand)*. It was somewhat muffled by the fact that the Bauhaus never had a true professional theatre department, only an experimental studio. Nonetheless Bauhaus artists had some influence both at the Kroll and in Piscator's scheme of things, to say nothing of such local effects as Kandinsky's sets for a Mussorgsky ballet at the Dessau theatre or Walter Dexel's largely abstract work for that at Jena. For Piscator not only demonstrated his wish to be identified with their school by getting Gropius and Breuer to design his Berlin flat (which was promptly featured in architectural publications and one of the glossy magazines) but brought in Moholy to provide the complex setting and film background for *The Merchant of Berlin* and supervise its working. In the "Totaltheater" project, too, which Gropius undertook for him (and which never got beyond a model exhibited in the old Nollendorf theatre foyer) he sponsored one of the most advanced pieces of theatre architecture in our century: a great two-thousand-seat auditorium with facilities for 360-degree Cinerama-style projection right round the walls and two eccentrically rotating blocks of seats which could be turned singly or together to make a complete arena, a thrust stage with revolve (as in the Grosses Schauspielhaus) or a proscenium stage capable of subdivision into three adjoining stages.[18] Even this, which clearly owes a good deal to Moholy's brilliant speculative thinking about the new electric technology, was in some respects superseded by Gropius's and Marcel Breuer's entries for the international competition for a "mass theatre" in Kharkhov in 1930—very nearly the last moment before the neoclassicists of the USSR and the architectural modernists of La Corbusier's CIAM decided to go their divergent ways. Both designs provided far better backstage facilities than the Totaltheater, with sliding stages and variable revolves, Breuer's auditorium being like a wedge thrust into the square working block.[19]

Traugott Müller was the right man to take the Piscatorbühne (in its first two versions) into this elevated sphere, for he indulged in comparable speculations, such as an outdoor arena for up to ten thousand people in the Ruhr with lighting towers like a football stadium. Moreover, he seems to have known the stage work of the Russian constructivists, and with Piscator's technical director Julius Richter he was able to harness the complicated new electric and mechanical aids envisaged by Piscator and apply them with spectacular results to his concept of a play. Some of these aids, like the treadmill, the simultaneous set, and the use of film were not so much new as new in relation to the serious theatre, though even so they presented many problems on account of their cumbersomeness and weight and their sometimes noisy operation. At the same time still further developments were going on in the area of sound reproduction and amplification, synthetic sound apparatus (such pioneering electronic instruments as the Theremin and the Ondes Martenot date from 1928), and wire or metal tape recording. But while Piscator's innovations began spreading to other German theatres, and doing so more and more widely as the relevant machines improved, after 1929 the reckless cost of his experiments stopped him from taking them any further. Müller moved over to the Staatstheater, where his work became a lot less exciting. Piscator himself, like Eisenstein after staging Tretiakov's *Gas Masks* in the Moscow gasworks, found that there was no further to go, and "fell into the cinema."

The most profoundly creative of all these designers, and also much the finest draftsman and colorist, was Neher, who seems, like Brecht and Engel, to have confined himself primarily to what could be done with the installations and equipment actually available. Even as a young man Brecht was a pragmatist who never went in for speculating about a perfectly planned and

Piscator's designer: Traugott Müller. A collaged design for the multiple set for the Piscatorbühne's opening production in September 1927: Ernst Toller's *Hoppla, wir leben!* The central projection screen shows the new German president—an ex-general. Photo by Cologne University Theatre Museum.

equipped theatre, but rather about a takeover of that cultural "apparatus," which seemed to have made the existing theatre more and more unapproachable and artistically reactionary. Similarly Neher's contribution was not only a pictorial vision midway between the pen drawings of Klee and those of George Grosz but also a wholly modern attitude to the selection and positioning of the objects and figures on the stage. This was not so much symbolic as at once narrative and economical, for the aim was to supply only those props or pieces of scenery that were essential to the action, and by these means and the grouping of the characters to express the "gests" (in the Brechtian sense) and the course of the story in a visually satisfying manner. The result was a form of selective realism akin to montage, in that it brought together disparate pieces of reality and sought to make their spatial relations beautiful, this beauty being expressed not only in exact placing but in color, texture, and the evidence of human labor. With *Mahagonny* he extended this approach by drawing satirical slides for projection so as to constitute the third element in a three-pronged attack on the audience in which words, music, and visuals would each tell the story in its own critical way. From this and the understanding with Weill that ensued, he went on to write several opera librettos, thus showing how well rooted his sometimes quite skeletal stage structures really were.

As for the musical element in the theatre of this time it benefited from

Brecht's designer: Caspar Neher. Designs for scene 1 of the Brecht-Weill opera *Rise and Fall of the City of Mahagonny* (1930 or 1931 production) (above), and a scene of the Brecht-Eisler *The Mother* (1932). Minimal settings with big projection screens and select realistic elements. Photos by Austrian National Library.

many specifically German factors. Reinhardt once again paved the way by the richness of his theatrical imagination as expressed in his Regiebücher, which noted the mood, duration, dynamics, and orchestration of each piece of incidental music required, together with the noise effects suggested by the text. Nobody before him, said his musical director Einer Nilson,[20] had paid so much attention to incidental music, its role in bridging gaps between scenes or dictating a scene's rhythm; its use of quotation, adaptation, and pastiche; and its placing of the musicians on or off stage, in costume or not. Reinhardt knew the value of punctuation, the tensing or heightening effect of a single organ note or drum roll. Jessner, it seems, concentrated mostly on developing similar sound effects, which like everything else in his theatre had to be kept simple and precise. Fehling worked with the left-wing composer Heinz Tiessen, described by Nicholas Slonimsky as "neo-Wagnerian." Piscator had a small orchestra under the direction of Edmund Meisel, composer of effective and widely used scores to accompany Eisenstein's films *Potemkin* and *October* as well as Ruttmann's *Berlin*. Kurt Weill (at Brecht's suggestion) and Hanns Eisler also wrote music for him, and from then on the film music and other utilitarian experiments conducted at the Neue Musik festivals had repercussions on the theatre. Jazz, and the influence of such cabaret composers as Friedrich Holländer and Spoliansky showed how its music could be clear and intelligible. Operetta with its syrupy happy endings became a target for parody, but it could sometimes be rescued and updated (as in Erich Korngold's revisions of Offenbach and Johann Strauss), and it taught some useful methods for adoption in such counter-plays as the Brecht-Weill *Threepenny Opera* and the Kaiser-Spoliansky *Zwei Krawatten*; thus actors, it was found, could sing a lot more articulately than tra ied singers, and often no more out of tune. Learning as they went, Weill set theatre texts by Kaiser, Feuchtwanger and Iwan Goll; Eisler, agitational texts by Weinert, Hermlin, and other political poets. Brecht, from devising or stealing his own tunes, arrived at the notion of "gestic" music, which he could hear brilliantly realized for him by Weill and Eisler, both strongly literate composers. Zuckmayer, who like Brecht and Klabund followed the Wedekind tradition of singing his own songs to the guitar, had the songs in his plays performed to popular tunes. Horváth, in his people's plays, followed suit. In such ways jazz, the Neue Musik and common popular melodies combined to prompt Eisler's redefinition of theatre music:

> *For the hitherto prevalent purpose:* atmospheric and contributing to illusion, no
>   independence.
> *For the new purpose:* independent element serving as musical commentary.[21]

A Contribution of Critics

It is difficult for us now to think ourselves back into the climate that bred this rapidly evolving modern theatre, which in terms of organization and technical resources outstripped even that of the Russians. Much of its progress—the

Schönberg's brother-in-law Alexander Zemlinsky, left, preparing his score for *Rise and Fall of the City of Mahagonny* at the Theater am Kurfürstendamm with Harald Paulsen the hero (1931). Photo by Ullstein Bilderdienst.

prodigal crop of new operas, for instance, the musical theatre of Brecht and Weill, the developments in staging, even the concept of political theatre—was part of the mainstream, not the work of an arcane "fringe" or "alternative" theatre as in the less purposeful western theatrical setup of today. This was due in the first place to the great shared experience of the war, the Revolution, and the disillusionment which followed, factors that bound together many of those interested in the arts and gave them the new illusion that the clock of cultural history could not be set back. But another important element was certainly the attention paid by the republican press to the arts and in particular to the theatre. Like the country itself, the German press was decentralized (as it is even now) so that some of the most acute theatre and film critics remained based in the provinces, like Bernhard Diebold and Siegfried Krakauer of the *Frankfurter Zeitung*. In Berlin alone, however, there were (so Arno Paul has reckoned) over a hundred daily or evening papers employing altogether fifty or more theatre critics, and these might write anything from one thousand to two thousand words on a single production.[22] They were widely read and discussed; influential papers like the right-center *Deutsche Allgemeine Zeitung* (with Paul Fechter as chief critic) or the Communist *Die Rote Fahne* (with "Durus," i.e. Alfred Kemény) might have small circulations by our own standards, but even the popular *Morgenpost* with a 1929 circulation of over six hundred thousand had a first-rate critic in Max Osborn. Within the theatre they were respected and even feared: Reinhardt, for instance, blamed them for the failure of the Grosses Schauspielhaus to live up to its aims, and they in turn at one time boycotted his theatres. Above all they took their readers and the theatre itself seriously, and they believed that what they wrote mattered. "Theatre criticism," said Kurt Pinthus in the *8-Uhr Blatt*, "is criticism of the times."[23]

So Siegfried Jacobsohn, whose analysis of the Reinhardt theatres before the war established him as one of the fairest and most farsighted of European critics, turned his theatre magazine *Die Schaubühne* in 1918 into *Die Weltbühne (The World Stage)*, a weekly of general topical comment, which with Tucholsky and Ossietzky as his lieutenants became the acutest and most independent-minded publication of the entire republican press, eventually earning Ossietzky a Nobel Peace Prize for its exposures of German militarism and class justice. Alfred Kerr, who covered the whole period, from *Die Wandlung* on, in his self-paradingly stylish reviews for *Der Tag*, took his Socialist convictions seriously enough first to support Piscator's initial ventures, then to accept the idea of a utilitarian theatre with political tasks. Emil Faktor, rated by Gerhard Rühle as one of the four best Berlin critics, became the editor of the *Berliner Börsen-Courier*, which he turned (not unlike its opposite numbers the *Financial Times* or the *Wall Street Journal*) into a remarkable cultural force, with himself, Herbert Jhering, and Oskar Bie writing the theatre and opera reviews, Oskar Loerke criticizing books, and many younger writers, including Brecht, contributing to the "Feuilleton," or arts magazine pages, on broad theatrical topics. There were also of course the conservatives, nationalists, and even budding Nazis, ranging from Paul Fechter, via the Hugenberg press's Franz Servaes (father of a Reinhardt actress) and Ludwig Sternaux, to the young Alfred Mühr, who joined the *Deutsche Zeitung* in 1924. But even these people were far from ignorant, for the main critics of every persuasion were well grounded in theatre history (in Germany long an accepted university subject) and/or had had practical experience as dramaturgs or theatre directors. They were not amateurs, and they knew what they were writing about.

Much the most impressive to reread today is the Hannoverian Jhering, who was no great stylist but shunned all posing and showing off, cared deeply for quality, and worked with astonishing persistence to establish a broad idea of socially relevant theatre based on the original principles of the Volksbühne. Like Kortner, Fehling, and Agnes Straub, he worked for the Vienna Volksbühne in the First World War, becoming its dramaturg in succession to Viertel and directing many plays. Starting work as a critic on his return to Berlin in 1918 at the age of thirty, he soon distinguished himself from his colleagues by discussing the real shifts of power, administrative structure, and artistic intention among the Berlin theatres as well as covering their individual productions. More than any other critic he would go far out of his way to report on whatever aroused his curiosity: the popular Berlin theatres of the Rotter brothers or of the Rose family, for instance, which other critics mocked and ignored; a provincial stage appearance by the film star Asta Nielsen; to say nothing of important premieres outside Berlin. Already he had had some contact with Expressionism, notably when the Vienna Volksbühne performed *From Morn to Midnight* with Pallenberg as the Cashier and the writer Egon Friedell as the Bank Manager, but he regarded that movement more as experiment than as fulfillment till he saw Kortner in Toller's *Die Wandlung* in 1919. Such an experience could not be repeated, and already *Masses and Man* in September 1921 struck him as a feeble echo of the earlier play. By then Jhering had been put on the advisory board of the Kleist Foundation, a body formed in 1911 to award prizes to promising and financially handicapped writers. Thereafter he became doubly concerned to see where the next original impulse was coming from. He unsuccessfully supported the little-known translator Paul Baudisch, then in 1922 discovered Bronnen, Barlach, and Brecht.

Jhering was a truly constructive critic, and he has a good claim to have affected the world's cultural history by giving that year's prize to Brecht for *Drums in the Night*, thus recommending the play to every German theatre and incidentally saving that writer from devoting himself to the cinema (as he was unsuccessfully beginning to do). In the process he influenced the careers of Engel and Neher, whom the Deutsches Theater promptly sent for to repeat the Grabbe production which he had found so good; and by this and his understanding of Barlach he helped bring about that shift to a firm but not unhumorous poetic matter-of-factness which is among the best aspects of the Weimar period. Perhaps he did not always avoid the strained judgments that come from publicly nailing one's critical flag to a particular mast. For even his continuing championship of Brecht was slightly touched, if not with prejudice, at any rate with predisposition, while in the case of Bronnen he took a very long while to see that his enthusiasm had been misplaced. Where Piscator was concerned, however, Jhering in the end maintained a fine balance, acknowledging his as the "one theatre that sets tasks, that forces you to adopt a position,"[24] yet continually putting a shrewd finger on its faults. His reviews of Zuckmayer, too, are models of intelligently qualified judgment which say a lot not only about that deceptively unpretentious writer but also by implication about the German theatergoer. Certainly he saw how open audiences were becoming to reactionary ideas from 1929 on and took pains on the one hand to encourage the emergent collectives and on the other to publicize the low level of the National Socialist Volksbühne (which a less conscientious critic might well have shunned). Yet when, like Piscator and Wolf, he visited Russia in the spring of 1931 he could maintain his critical coolness, commenting on the old-fashioned nature of Stanislavsky's historic productions, the basic inconsistencies in Meyerhold's *Last Decisive*, the Bolshoi's "terrible trashy ballet" (evidently Glière's *The Red Poppy*), and the general failure to develop a new dramaturgy for the new social themes.[25] Back in Germany he could still be seduced by great acting, such as he found in the Staatstheater's centenary *Faust* with Gründgens and Krauss, notably its second part (where he particularly praised Gustav Lindemann's direction and the playing of Hans Otto as the emperor). Commenting on the fact that virtually all that week's performances were sold out, he wrote that "it isn't the Berlin

A great actor carries on into the Third Reich. The ambiguous figure of Werner Krauss, star of Goebbels's anti-Semitic *Jew Süss* film, here photographed in the 1920s. Photo by Ullstein Bilderdienst.

audience but the Berlin directors that have let their theatre down. The trash has collapsed. This is the beginning of art."[26] This was a few days before the end of January 1933 and only eighteen months after he had given his considered verdict on the mounting crisis in an article called "Abbau des Geistes" (or, roughly, "Dismantling of the Intelligence"):

> A theatrical era is over: that of the irregular intellectual skirmishers. Another era is coming: that of brilliantly organised unintelligence. So the outsiders are the only hope. Set up theatres of outsiders![27]

When even the most perceptive critic becomes so divided in his attitude, something must be about to crack.

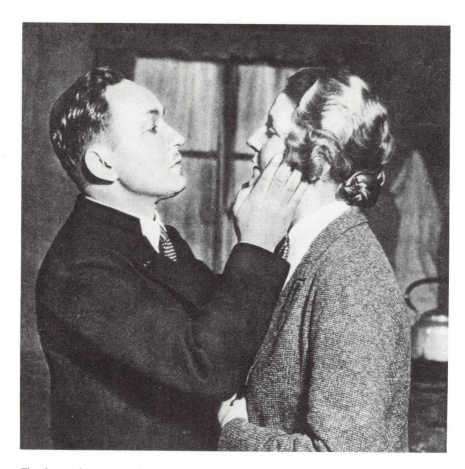

The Staatstheater celebrates Hitler's first birthday in power. Hanns Johst's Nazi play *Schlageter,* directed by Fritz Ulbrich, with Lothar Müthel (a new recruit to National Socialism) and Emmy Sonnemann (who soon afterwards married Hermann Goering). Photo by Cologne University Theatre Museum.

9

Parting of the Ways

Nazi Leaders Take the Limelight

With the explosive arrival of the Third Reich in the first half of 1933, the Weimar theatre finally flew apart, with effects that can be seen to this day. Germany had not exactly been governed by consensus even in its short interval of republican democracy, and naturally this was reflected in its entire culture, whose extraordinary progress in the Weimar years, however far it might seem to have penetrated the new society, was never secure. But from 1933 to 1945 the new rulers pursued a policy of deliberate division, with the idea of getting rid of all those elements—ranging from ordinary democratic legal and administrative checks at one end of the spectrum to the entire Jewish race at the other—that might prevent total unity along the lines of Hitler's *Mein Kampf.* In the process they destroyed the creative force of a theatre whose essence had been that it was *not* conformist, that it was repeatedly pushing out toward something new and not easily acceptable. All four of the great innovators discussed in the last chapter went into exile, Reinhardt and Jessner both dying before they could return, while many other theater people either chose to go or else were driven out. This left the second level of directors (that is to say the less radically creative ones) in so far as they were racially acceptable to the Nazis, also the major designers and technicians, a handful of non-Jewish critics, and the majority of the non-Jewish actors, including several of the most brilliant.

These people on the whole did not attempt to give the new Reich's theatre any distinctive character; they formed a kind of "inner emigration," which sought to maintain the standards of excellence attained under the Republic in the hope that they might be able to sit the new regime out. Many of the exiles at first held equally short-term views, thanks not least to the KPD's conviction that Hitler was a mere puppet of the real rulers, whom the working class would never support. It was only a minority who saw instantly, like Tucholsky (or, a little later, like Brecht) that "the working-class movement has suffered a decisive defeat."[1] But where the "inner emigrants" could deceive themselves and continue to be fully occupied and well paid, the exiles found few established theatres open to them, and these were for the most part sooner or later to become incorporated in the expanding Reich. By 1939 there was only one predominantly exile company left working on a scale comparable with that of a medium-sized German provincial theatre; this was the Zurich Schauspielhaus, whose role throughout the whole twelve years was exemplary. Otherwise the exiles had either to form themselves into small groups, operating often with amateurish equipment and on a cabaret scale, or else to change their style and their language and try to get accepted in the non-German theatre. At the end of it all there were not very many who either wished or were equipped to come back.

On 30 January when Adolf Hitler became nominal head of the new coalition government little of this could logically have been foretold. Encouraged by Papen, Hindenburg had refused to give Chancellor Schleicher the dissolution of Parliament for which he asked and withdrawn his objections to the political upstart whom he had hitherto treated as an Other Rank, a "lance-corporal from Bohemia." Though the newly acceptable Hitler had by then secured the support of the Rhine-Ruhr industrialists as well as one-third of the seats in the Reichstag, he was very much in the minority in his cabinet, in which Frick as minister of the interior was the only other Nazi. The expectation was that the more gentlemanly conservative element would be able to *einrahmen* him, or "box him in." But this is not what happened. For at the same time Papen as commissar for Prussia was letting the Nazis into the power vacuum created by his dismissal of the state government the previous summer. So the old party member Bernard Rust became his minister of education and (initially) culture, purging the Prussian Academy of such members as Kaiser and Unruh, appointing Hanns Johst and the Weimar Intendant Franz Ulbrich to take charge of the Berlin Staatstheater, and making SS Sturmbann-führer Hinkel a "state commissar" for theatre affairs within his department. Goering, as Prussian minister of the interior, had command of the Berlin police, and soon he would ease Papen out and annex his theatre responsibilities.

Already it was rumor[1] that some spectacular act of provocation was going to take place before the new Reichstag elections on 5 March, and whether or not Goering was personally involved (as historians for many years believed) he certainly seems to have orchestrated and conducted the course of events. For first he had the right-wing private armies—SA, SS, and Stahlhelm—appointed en bloc as auxiliary policemen, then as soon as the Reichstag went up in flames on the night of 27–28 February they swung into action; fifteen hundred Communists were said to have been arrested in Berlin that night and more than ten thousand altogether in the whole of Germany. The next day Hindenburg signed a decree suspending virtually every guarantee of individual rights. The KPD was banned, its leader Thälmann caught and put in one of the newly instituted concentration camps, Communist deputies were deprived of their immunity and Reichstag seats. Among those arrested was the Munich anarchist playwright and cabarettist Erich Mühsam, who was beaten and humiliated in the Sonnenburg camp, then murdered in the summer of 1934. Five days after the fire the elections brought the Nazis fifty-eight more seats, then on 21 March the Third Reich was solemnly proclaimed on the "Day of Potsdam," when exactly sixty-two years after the first Reichstag of the Hohenzollern Empire the first and only National Socialist Reichstag was inaugurated in the garrison church where Frederick the Great lay buried. A few days earlier Hindenburg had abolished the republican flag in favor of the old black-white-red colors and the new racist swastika symbol.

This was virtually the last time that the old-style nationalist Right was needed, for by the summer its parties had dissolved "voluntarily" in the National Socialist movement (the SPD by then having been made illegal and three thousand of its officials arrested). A year later Hindenburg died, to be succeeded by Hitler as *Führer,* or "Leader." The old man had already had his main presidential functions removed by the new Reichstag, which met again in the Kroll Opera two days after the Potsdam performance, its members now largely dressed up in Nazi uniforms, to pass Hitler's Empowering Law. This session, deeply humiliating for the 115 SPD members—5 had already been arrested—was presided over by Goering, who began by commemorating the birthday of Hitler's friend Dietrich Eckart with a short recitation almost worthy of Brecht's *Arturo Ui:* "My comrades," he called, "how often have you sung this song with us:

> Germany awake! Storm, storm, storm!
> Ring forth the bells this fateful dawn!
> Ring forth the men, old men and lads,
> Ring forth the sleepers from their beds!
> Ring forth the maidens from upstairs!
> Ring forth the mothers from their cares!
> Loudly thundering through the sky
> The knell of vengeance swift shall shake!
> Ring forth the dead from where they lie!
> Germany awake![2]

After standing in memory of this Nazi "poet-martyr" the *Kameraden* went on to give the chancellor power to enact decrees without reference to the president, never mind if they were or were not in accordance with the constitution. Hitler spoke twice, to every kind of applause except that of the SPD, and to concluding cries of "Heil!" In the process he had one or two things to say about the arts:

Besides sucking the political poison out of our public life the national government proposes to embark on a thorough moral cleansing of the body of our People. All our educational activity—theatre, film, literature, press, radio—will be treated as means to this end and esteemed accordingly. All must be applied to the conservation of those eternal values that are embedded in the essence of our Peoplehood; art will always be an expression and reflection of the wishfulness or reality of an age. The world of bourgeois introspection is on the way out. Heroism is passionately asserting its claim to shape and guide the Peoples' destinies in future. It is Art's task to be an expression of this decisive spirit of the time.

[*Loud agreement from the National Socialists.*]

Blood and race will once again become the source of artistic intuition.[3]

Less than a month later the Staatstheater celebrated Hitler's birthday with the first performance of Johst's play *Schlageter* about the Freikorps member and Nazi hero whom the French shot in 1923. It was directed by Frick's former Intendant Franz Ulbrich. Lothar Müthel played the lead, and Albert Bassermann, Maria Koppenhöfer and Emmy Sonnemann were in the cast. The author's dedication ran "For Adolf Hitler, in loving homage and inflexible loyalty."

The real pioneer of this conservative-racist culture was the editor of the *Völkischer Beobachter,* Dietrich Eckart's former aide Alfred Rosenberg, who had set up the Militant League, or KfdK, in 1929. And doubtless it was this league and its provincial offices, along with Rosenberg's collaborator Hans Hinkel in Berlin, which inspired the first purge of theatre Intendants in the early part of 1933. Thus twenty-three such changes were announced in March and thirteen more in April, covering most of the leading cities including Munich, though Otto Falckenberg in that city seems to have saved himself by agreeing to let the KfdK appoint its own dramaturg with a right to propose plays and veto both plays and appointments. In May Goebbels as the newly designated Reich Propaganda Minister told a meeting of theatre directors that there could be no internationalism in the arts, nor could a Jew ever be an interpreter of German *Volkstum,* or peoplehood (a favorite Nazi term). In June a ghettolike Jewish League of Culture was set up to perform to Jewish audiences only (non-Jewish spouses not being admitted); this was at first directed by Julius Bab and the former Städtische Oper Intendant Kurt Singer, later to die in the Theresienstadt extermination camp. (In 1939 they would be succeeded by the actor Fritz Wisten; then in 1941 the League's theatre was shut.) At the beginning of the next theatre season Goering and Goebbels announced what were to some extent meant to be mutually exclusive plans. The former as premier of Prussia proclaimed his cultural leadership (over that of Rust), set up a theatre commission under Hinkel, insisted that his state theatres come under no other authority but his own, and summoned their Intendants to hear that they must implement Hitler's "heroic doctrine of the value of blood, race and personality."[5] Goebbels for his part established a Theatre Chamber as part of his new Reich Chamber of Culture, of which all practitioners and critics of the arts had to be members, first proving that they and their spouses were of Aryan (or non-Jewish) descent. This was headed initially by the minor Staatstheater actor Otto Laubinger, a party member of one year's standing, with Werner

Nazification of Reinhardt's would-be mass theatre. The Grosses Schauspielhaus in 1935 as "Theatre of the People" for the German Labor Front. Photo by Ullstein Bilderdienst.

Krauss as his deputy.[6] All 248 theatres and 25,663 actors in the country were subjected to it. Its first act was to appoint a Reich Dramaturg called Rainer Schlösser, previously arts editor of the *Völkischer Beobachter,* with the job of vetting plays. Aided by the playwrights Möller and Gräff, his office was to ensure that "National Socialist cultural principles are applied in the German theatrical world."[7]

Gleichschaltung—or Uniformity—and the Problems of Survival

Much as they might hate "intellectuals," the trouble with the Nazi leaders was not that they were deliberately against the arts. On the contrary they poured money into them, nationalizing a further ten Berlin theatres, saving (and getting control of) the declining Volksbühne with a grant of 450,000 marks in April 1934, and turning the Grosses Schauspielhaus into a "Theatre of the People" where the classics would be performed for the ordinary comrade. "Every *Gauleiter,*" wrote Gründgens later, (i.e., each of the party's regional controllers, of whom Streicher in Thuringia was the most notorious),

> considered "his" theatre a prop to his self-importance. The previous number of theatres was almost doubled. Actors' incomes increased by leaps and bounds.

The invention of a "Strength through Joy" theatre provided jobs for a fresh flood of actors. Superficially and as far as the money went German actors had undoubtedly never had it so good as in the last years before the regime collapsed.[8]

It is still sometimes alleged that the jovial (and urwüchsig) Goering once said, "When I hear the word *culture* I reach for my revolver," but this is not only a misquotation but a misattribution of a line actually drawn from *Schlageter.* Nor was Adolf Hitler ever a housepainter (as Brecht, for one, used to claim) but a very amateurish and unsuccessful artist. "He loves artists," said Goebbels in 1938 to a meeting of theatre people in Vienna, "because he is an artist himself. Under his blessed guidance Germany is experiencing something like a new Renaissance age."[9]

Goebbels for his part had written *The Wanderer* and a latter-day Expressionist novel called *Michael;* there is also a draft for a debate on theatre between him and Piscator, though no evidence that it was ever held. Alfred Rosenberg trained as an architect in Riga and taught drawing at a school in Estonia. His aide-de-camp Thilo von Trotha believed that "the People's biological improvement should start with that moral institution the theatre"[10] and had a play, *Engelbrecht,* performed by the city theatre in Kiel. Wilhelm Kube, Gauleiter of the Kurmark (Brandenburg) and Grand Master of the Bismarck Order, wrote a play about the Ostrogoth king, *Totila,* which Hinkel vainly tried to impose on the Staatstheater; it was eventually done at Frankfurt an der Oder, in an undistinguished provincial theatre. In the 1940s, Kube became commissar for White Russia, where he was killed by a partisan bomb under his bed.

These people truly believed that the theatre was important, but as "artists" and upholders of the leadership principle they were also convinced that their judgment in cultural matters was bound to be right. In fact it was artistically third rate and permeated with crazed notions of Nordic blood, Wagnerian myth, and the Germanic backwoods of prehistory. The playwrights who rose to the surface of this witches' brew, like Friedrich Bethge, who joined the party in 1932 and crawled his way up via Hinkel and the SS to become chief dramaturg and acting Intendant in Frankfurt, had had little or no success with the Weimar critics and public. Only a handful of writers such as Billinger, E. G. Kolbenheyer perhaps, and the early Johst had made any kind of grade, along with the young and ambitious SS recruit E. W. Moeller, author of *Douaumont* and the anti-Semitic play *Rothschild siegt bei Waterloo (Rothschild the Victor of Waterloo).* Bronnen, already at odds with the party which he had supported, published nothing in the Nazi years apart from two prose works. Much the same situation can be seen in the cinema, where one of Hans Albers's films won the regime's National Prize for 1934: the more creative spirits had gone into exile, and for all the government money poured into it the Nazi cinema was uninspiring and of practically no artistic interest today.

There was one technically remarkable if politically horrifying exception to this: the monster National Socialist rituals filmed by Leni Riefenstahl. Reflecting perhaps her teacher Mary Wigman's view of 1934 (the year of the first of them, *Triumph of the Will*), that "individual fates are less important than the

10 October 1938. The Propaganda Minister's birthday is celebrated amid the relics of the Weimar Theater. Generalintendant Eugen Klöpfer offers congratulations on behalf of the creative artists of Germany, while Eugen Hadamovsky, the director of the German radio service, holds the microphone, and Heinrich George (center) looks on. Photo by Ullstein Bilderdienst.

whole great event . . . The call of the blood which has come to all of us has profound effects and touches the essential,"[11] this committed director seems to have had some influence on their actual staging. And this in turn relates closely to the one comparatively original element in the whole Nazi theatre, the pageantlike open-air performance called a *Thingspiel* or *Thing*-play, which was first seen at the Heidelberg Reich Festival in 1934.

The *Thing* form of mass theatre, the only theatre truly to express Hitler's mad ideology, is at first sight traceable back to earlier ideas of celebratory theatre, and particularly to the work of Appia and Jaques-Dalcroze at Hellerau (which is after all where the Wigman school originated). But it also has an oratoriolike aspect which links it, however contradictorily, with the Brechtian *Lehrstück*. Indeed it, too, aimed to be outside the traditional theatre, for *Thing*, as in old English, means a primitive place of judgment, and the works performed there had to be presented with the solemnity (as well as the political bias) of a Nazi court of law. So the dramatist Richard Euringer in the "*Thing*-play Theses" which he set out in the *Völkischer Beobachter* on 20 June and 3 July 1934 could write that:

> 3. . . . The *Thing*-play leads away from the theatrical arts to the site where judgement will take place. The play leads from the theatrical achievement away to the place of execution, for now matters are becoming serious. . . .

6. Without blood oath and incantation no *Thing;* without banishment no *Thing.* Entering the precincts the sworn hordes fall silent. Mutely they tread the place of judgement, for the soil is holy. . . .

8. No writer is being played, no play presented; rather it is the celebration of a feast. The State itself is at stake.[12]

There was, said the Propaganda Ministry, to be no division or curtain between stage and audience, no distinction of levels (cf. Gropius's Total-Theater), no separation of light and dark. Strict licensing rules were introduced by the Theatre Chamber, presumably because of the risk that an illegal agitprop group might slip in; even the term *Thing* must be restricted to authorized buildings. Laubinger of the Chamber opened the Heidelberg *Thingstätte,* or Thing-site, promising a target of four hundred such places, though only some twenty-five seem ever to have been built. Drawings and photographs show these with stepped-up stages à la Jessner and an arena not unlike the Ruhr project of Traugott Müller (who now became the Staatstheater's chief designer).[13] The former *Sturm* poet Kurt Heynicke wrote *The Road to the Reich,* the second script for Heidelberg—the first having been Euringer's—while another enthusiast was Anton Dietzenschmidt, the Sudeten German poet who had shared the Kleist Prize with Heynicke in 1920. Short-lived though it proved, the whole movement was strongly supported by the party aesthetician Wolf Braumüller, who regarded the annual Nuremberg Rally as "the Thing-concept made blood and spirit" and greeted the new twenty-thousand-seat open-air "Dietrich-Eckart Stage" in the woods outside Berlin as the Olympic Stadium's "spiritual sister."[14] This was inaugurated as part of the games celebrations on 2 August 1936 with a specially written work by Möller. Wigman and Harald Kreutzberg danced there; Laban, who had been commissioned to do the choreography, is said to have dropped out during rehearsal, and thereafter was exiled to a Bavarian village until he managed to escape to Britain. Riefensthal of course made the two Olympic films, using eurhythmics as an element in her pseudoheroic parade of Nordic health and strength.

To Goebbels all theatre was propaganda, and he did what he could to extend his ministry's area of operations. Thus he nationalized the Deutsches Theater, where Hilpert became the director in succession to the Neft/Achaz regime; restricted Goering's empire to the Berlin state theatre and opera; harnessed up the "Strength Through Joy" operation to other audience organizations; and in 1936 managed to merge Rosenberg's KfdK in the same body. Too many theatre directors, he complained to the Theatre Chamber's 1935 conference, were trying to avoid National Socialist themes by concentrating instead on classics and light entertainment. "That won't do for our time," he told them. On the contrary, it was their duty to promote the new ideology by methods like his own: "Is it demeaning Art if we align it with that noble art of People's Psychology which stepped forward to pull the Reich back from the abyss?"[15] Closer checks were instituted on the racial purity of actors and their wives. Werner Finck had his cabaret closed for showing "no positive approach to National Socialism," and was later expelled from the chamber altogether, i.e., denied the right to work. The same thing happened to Herbert Jhering, who had been denounced that June by the new Nazi Volksbühne director for

Laban's dance display for the Olympic Games of 1936. Collection of Lola Rogge.

"deliberate and systematic sabotage of National Socialist reconstruction"[16]—in other words unfavorable reviews—after which criticism other than conformist reporting was discouraged and, in the case of the visual arts, explicitly banned. Even the Thingspiel movement was halted for a mixture of reasons—including the banning of choral speaking, the fear of agitprop, and, it seems, the critical views of Hitler himself—so that its ambitious building program came to an abrupt end once the Olympics were over.

Such measures by the Propaganda Ministry made Goering's Staatstheater seem like a small haven of comparative freedom, and some of the best of the Weimar survivors now tended to gather there. This development can be dated from the beginning of 1934, when Goering, who had seen the thirty-four-year old Gründgens acting with Emmy Sonnemann, telephoned to tell him that he was to take over as artistic director, since Johst and Ulbrich had proved useless. Goering's artistic and literary standards were not exactly high; indeed the sight of some of his early love letters once led Tucholsky to exclaim:

> My god, it's pathetic. We all know what nonsense one writes to a woman one wants—but such a mélange of sales promoter, liftboy and racing motorist . . . I only recall one sentence: "Most evenings I sit at home by myself and think about life." With what results we all know. As for the poetic bits they smelt of candy flavouring and trouser seat. Depressing.[17]

It was Gründgens's readiness to please such a man that led Klaus Mann, his former brother-in-law and an uncompromising anti-Nazi, to write the novel *Mephisto* on which Istvan Szábo based his very brilliant film of 1981. For after taking four weeks to make up his mind, Gründgens began playing a hazardous game of diplomacy to keep his protector's favor. From then on he felt that he could secure Goering's intervention whenever needed (against the Theatre Chamber, against the Reich Dramaturg, against the *Völkischer Beobachter,* which found his *Hamlet* too un-Nordic, even once against the Gestapo itself) without losing his own independence. So he could apply his undoubted brilliance as an actor and skill as a director to rebuilding the Staatstheater's reputation on the new slippery footing.

His principal director there was Jürgen Fehling, a temperamental collaborator, some of whose productions seem to have been wholly alien to the Nazi aesthetic, while at the same time unlike anything prior to 1933; indeed they look forward to the theatre of West Germany in the 1950s. He also had the former actor Lothar Müthel, who had joined the party in May 1933 and would be promoted to run the Vienna Burgtheater after the Anschluss. As designers he had Rochus Gliese and Traugott Müller (who died of a stroke in 1949). His actors included Werner Krauss, Bassermann till he emigrated, Maria Koppenhöfer, Käthe Dorsch, Paul Bildt, Hermine Körner, Paul Wegener, Eugen Klöpfer, Walter Franck, Theo Lingen, Heinz Rühmann, and other well-known figures from Weimar times, as well as younger people like Elisabeth Flickenschild, Karlheinz Stroux, and Gustav Knuth, who were to be prominent after the Second World War. Not many of the actors were Nazis— between 5 percent and 10 percent according to Gründgens's estimates at different times—while a number had Jewish wives or mistresses whom he did much to protect. Nor was much concession made to Goebbels's call for more Nazi plays, for Gründgens claims to have put on only four or five of these in the ten years of his Intendantship, notably the Mussolini-Forzano *Hundred Days* (which Ulbrich again directed), and its successor *Cavour*—a production that gave great satisfaction to the government; likewise Hans Rehberg's *Great Kurfürst* (about Prussian history, directed by Fehling) and Johst's *Thomas Paine* (Fehling again). In addition there was the Schiller-Theater, which the Prussian administration was having modernized. From 1937 this was run as a city theatre by Heinrich George in apparent independence of Gründgens. His actors there included Agnes Straub, who later took over the Theater am Kurfürstendamm (renamed the Agnes-Straub-Theater), and the former Intendant Ernst Legal, whom Schlösser accepted as nonpolitical, having "the specific open-mindedness of an actor."[18] A genuine convert to the new ideology, George not only played in the Nazi Youth film *Hitlerjunge Quex* but also received open letters from both Hartung and Brecht about his failure to help the Communist actor and Equity official Hans Otto, who had been beaten to death in an SA barracks on 24 November 1933.

Georg Kaiser continued to live and work outside Berlin, though his works had been banned by Goebbels following the premiere of his musical play *Silver Lake* with Kurt Weill in February 1933. Rust expelled him from the Prussian Academy that May, even though he had signed the required declaration of allegiance to the Third Reich and gave no signs of opposition. His new play *Ossian Balvesen's Lottery Ticket,* for instance, was written in a conciliatory spirit and appears to have satisfied Gründgens's right-thinking dramaturg Alfred Muhr. Gründgens himself would not risk accepting it, however, and though Hilpert at the Deutsches Theater was slightly bolder, it was finally forbidden him by the Reich dramaturg. Hilpert's position in the new order of things was that he had been called in by the Theater Chamber to take over the Deutsches Theater once Goebbels began subsidizing it in 1934, and from then on all his significant decisions had to be cleared with the Propaganda Ministry. One of his first ambitions on returning to Reinhardt's old house had been to stage the postponed premiere of Horváth's *Glaube Liebe Hoffnung*, and with this in view Horváth himself sought to assure the new authorities that he was by no means to be identified with people like Piscator and Brecht but had left Hungary in 1919 as an anti-Communist refugee:

> I have categorically refused to do anything by speech or writing against Germany and her government . . . Not only have I refused to sign any protests but I have actually stated in public that I will not work for the émigré press, and have nothing whatever to do with it . . . I would be greatly hurt if I were not allowed to help to the best of my powers in Germany's reconstruction.[19]

This appeal was turned down by the ministry, as was Hilpert's request to make Engel his *Oberspielleiter*, or director of productions; though Engel and Neher were conceded one production per season, usually a Shakespeare play. Apart from agreeing not to victimize Hilpert's staff designer Ernst Schütte, whose former wife was Jewish, the authorities were reluctant to make him any concessions, partly perhaps because he found difficulty in filling his two theatres (to which the Theater in der Josefstadt became added after the occupation of Austria). Finally in 1944 he was accused of making anti-Nazi remarks in a railway carriage to the eminent surgeon Sauerbruch (e.g., saying that he had "only known decent Jews"—this on the evidence of a Dr. Mahlo, a dutiful civil servant who had been eavesdropping).[20] Thereupon he was called up for war work in the Telefunken factory.

Meanwhile the declining Volksbühne was taken over in a somewhat similar way. First it was put under a stupid-looking aristocratic SA Sturmführer called Solms, who had been badgering Hinkel for a job; then it was bailed out by the government when Solms in two years ran up a record deficit of 1.4 million marks. Following this, the rump of the old board under its last chairman Curt Baake appointed the SA's "cultural director" Franz Moraller to be the new *Vereinsführer*, or leader of the association, then he in turn induced the board to resign as a body, leaving the way clear for the old combined "Volksbühne E.V." to be dissolved and the Propaganda Ministry to take its theatres over. For a while the ministry tried to make Fehling the new Intendant, but Goebbels appears to have taken against him and appointed Eugen Klöpfer instead to run a competent but broadly conformist program with such actors as Kayssler, Legal, Renée Stobrawa, and the young Werner Hinz. As director of productions he had Richard Weichert, the former Frankfurt Intendant, though Lucie Höflich also directed a certain number of plays; while in 1941 they were reinforced by Karl Heinz Martin, who seems till then to have had no regular work. Among the designers used were César Klein, Eduard Suhr, and the new "Reich Stage Designer" Benno von Arent, whose primary task however was the staging of party rallies and other showpiece occasions under the Führer's supervision.

Last Bastions of an Anti-Nazi Theatre

For those who could not or did not wish to be incorporated in the cultural apparatus of the new Reich the exodus had two, or in some cases three, main phases. Initially the rest of the German-speaking world was open to the exiles so long as they could get the necessary residence and work permits: that is to say Austria, Switzerland, the German-speaking parts of Czechoslovakia, and the Volga Republic, together with other scattered enclaves in the USSR. All these except the last had their established German-language theatres, some of which (like the Vienna Burgtheater) had a long history and, at times, a high reputation. These were, however, just the places most threatened by Hitler's expansionist policy, and in 1938 and 1939 the National Socialist armies moved first into Austria, where they were hysterically greeted by a largely Nazi population—see Kortner's memoirs for a vivid comparison of the attitude of the Viennese with that of the Berliners five years earlier—and then into the frontier areas of Czechoslovakia, followed by Prague itself. For many of the exiles this meant a second emigration, virtually coinciding with a smaller and less publicized exodus from the USSR as Stalin's great purge got under way and foreign communities there came under automatic suspicion. In many cases this time the émigrés went overseas, mostly to the Americas, though some went as far as Shanghai, Australia (the jazz band Weintraub's Syncopators) or New Zealand (the poet Karl Wolfskehl). For those who remained, the war which engulfed Europe between 1939 and 1941 hemmed them into a few small countries (Britain, Ireland, Sweden, Switzerland) or forced them yet again to move.

Early in 1933 Reinhardt finally cut his ties with Berlin, which had been getting gradually looser ever since the establishment of the Republic and the failure of the Grosses Schauspielhaus to fulfill its aims. He had been rehearsing the Calderon/Hofmannsthal *Das grosse Welttheater* at the Deutsches Theater when the Reichstag went up in flames less than a kilometer away. Accordingly he left on 8 March as soon as the play opened. In June he wrote to tell Rust that he was now convinced that this theatre could no longer exist without subsidy, and accordingly was making it over to the German state.[21] He got no answer. But he still had his Austrian interests—the festival at Salzburg and his neighboring Schloss Leopoldskron, likewise the beautiful Theater in der Josefstadt in Vienna, which he had been running with some of the same actors and much the same repertoire as the Deutsches Theater. It seems, however, that the latter's tour of the United States in winter 1927–28 (when all losses were guaranteed by the banker Otto Kahn) had already turned his mind toward that country. Thus in 1932 he agreed to stage a "dramatic-musical" festival for the Los Angeles Olympics, and although this never materialized he did open the new California Festival in 1934 with an open-air production of *A Midsummer Night's Dream* staged in the Hollywood Bowl and repeated in some fifteen other cities. Meanwhile he gave the management of the Theater in der Josefstadt first to the young actor-director Otto Preminger, then from 1935–38 to the popular novelist and dramatist Ernst Lothar, author of "Little Friend," the story whose filming by Viertel is the theme of Isherwood's *Prater Violet*. In such hands the Josefstadt's repertoire was not exactly creative, much of it consisting of Broadway, West End, or boulevard successes of a comfortably banal kind. Though there was still highly polished acting to be seen under Reinhardt's auspices, whether in Salzburg or in Vienna, he himself was mostly concerned with the same old productions: *Everyman*, *Faust*, the *Dream*, *Fledermaus*, and *La Belle Hélène*. As he told his Salzburg neighbor Zuckmayer (a fellow exile from Germany), 'You can feel the taste of mortality on your tongue."[22]

Like his other neighbor Horváth, who would be killed somewhat astonishingly, in a Paris thunderstorm shortly after leaving Austria, Zuckmayer continued living in the lovely Salzburg countryside until the Anschluss with Nazi Germany in 1938, stubbornly continuing to write plays. But new plays by the Berlin exiles were generally not performed in conservative Austria, and in February 1934 the Clerical party and the homegrown Fascists, somewhat like Papen a year and a half earlier, launched an attack on the Socialist party and the Vienna municipality. Though in contrast with the German Left these offered armed resistance, after a week's fighting in and around the great housing estates (and a number of hangings) socialism and parliamentary government were alike broken, the refugee Julius Hay being among those jailed. From then on the country was not particularly welcoming to the anti-Nazi Germans, while anti-Semitism was already strongly in evidence, though as yet not in violent form. Kortner, himself of Austrian birth, moved on to England; Erich Ziegel, who had a Jewish wife, gave up the search for an Austrian theatre and actually returned to Hamburg. Admittedly Kaiser's *Ossian Balvesen's Lottery Ticket* was eventually staged by the Burgtheater on 26 November 1936, but Bruckner, another Austrian by birth, found that his subtle and independent-minded play *Die Rassen (Race)* could not be performed either in Vienna or in Prague. To our shame it was banned in England too.

In Prague the argument adduced for such decisions was that the Neues Deutsches Theater (which had once had so creditable a record as a pioneer of Expressionism) must not handicap any of its actors who might wish to take jobs in Germany. The fact, however, seems to have been that some of those actors were pro-Nazi or at least on good terms with the German embassy. Admittedly it took on a number of exiles, but these were mostly of Czech nationality, like Ernst Deutsch, Friedrich Richter, and the director Julius Gellner; Friedrich Valk was already there, and there were also many distinguished guest performers. Carl Meinhard went to Brünn as an actor, Paul Barnay from Breslau took over the theatre at Reichenberg (Liberec) in the Sudetenland, while Rudolf Zeisel in Mährisch Ostrau (Moravská Ostrava) ran perhaps the most enterprising of the German-language theatres. Of Horváth's new plays *Der jüngste Tag (The Day of Judgement)* had its premiere there on 11 December 1937, while *Figaro Gets Divorced* and *A Village Without Men* were first performed at the Neues Deutsches Theater on 2 April and 24 September respectively. What most differentiated Czechoslovakia from Austria as a place of refuge, however, was not its lack of Nazis—for in fact the German minority, the so-called Sudetens in the frontier areas, were aggressive and well supported by the Nazis in Germany—so much as Prague's role as headquarters of the exiled SPD and a main communications centre for the illegal KPD. This attracted not only important sectors of the exiled press and publishing business but also such elements of the alternative theatre as Maxim Vallentin and others from "The Red Megaphone," the young Erwin Geschonneck and the Piscator actor Fritz Erpenbeck with his wife Hedda Zinner. It was she who in 1933 founded "Studio 34," one of the first of the political cabaret groups that were to become common throughout the emigration.

The great stronghold of the exiled theatre throughout the twelve years of the Reich was Switzerland, despite the unwelcoming attitude of the federal police, who arranged with the German government to have all Jewish passports marked with the letter *J*. Admittedly the municipal theatres in Bern and Basel were likewise prepared to yield to German and nationalist pressure (the Germans, for instance, threatening to withhold their opera singers without whose guest appearances the Swiss-German operas could not have functioned), so that the fiercely anti-Nazi Gustav Hartung was first denied his promised Intendantship of the former, then lost his post as artistic director of the latter in 1939. Nonetheless they gave employment, however briefly, to Carl Ebert, Alwin Kronacher from Frankfurt, and Fritz Jessner, while in Zurich the private and unsubsidized thousand-seat Schauspielhaus was able to resist all concessions and compromises and become the world's outstanding anti-Fascist theatre thanks partly to its repertoire, which included historic premieres of such exiled dramatists as Wolf, Kaiser, Bruckner, Zuckmayer, and Brecht, and partly to the attitude and talents of its predominantly exiled company.

This previously quite undistinguished theatre was owned and managed by a wine merchant, Ferdinand Rieser, who had married Franz Werfel's sister Marianne. In 1933 he appointed as his dramaturg Kurt Hirschfeld, recently dismissed from the Darmstadt Landestheater along with Hartung; and thereafter he appears to have followed Hirschfeld's advice and judgment, which he backed to the hilt against all comers, including the Swiss and German authorities. On the other hand it must be said that he paid low wages, allocated Teo Otto his designer 150 francs per play to spend on sets, insisted on a weekly repertory and each season expected it to include one of his wife's plays. Repeatedly, however, he allowed his company to persuade him that topicality and great art, classic or modern, can pay. Behind an inflexibly commercial facade, he remains one of the German-language theatre's unthanked heroes.

Apart from Hartung, who directed some important premieres in the 1933–34 season (including Hermann Broch's anti-Nazi play *Denn sie wissen nicht, was sie tun* [*For they know not what they do*]) the company was relatively young, only the directors Leopold Lindtberg and the actors Steckel, Kalser and Ginsberg being at all widely known for their work with Piscator in Berlin, while Therese Giehse and Kurt Horwitz came from the Munich Kammerspiele, and Wolfgang Heinz and Teo Otto had been dismissed from the Staatstheater on the day of the Reichstag fire. Karl Paryla had been at Breslau under Barnay, as had his brother Emil Stöhr; Wolfgang Langhoff came straight from spending a year in concentration camps after having worked at the Düsseldorf Schauspielhaus and simultaneously with Friedrich Richter and Hermann Greid in the Rhineland collective Truppe im Westen. Politically the Zurich company thus covered a broad front, and its repertoire was a correspondingly wide one. Bruckner's *Die Rassen,* which established the theatre's reputation that same season in front of a distinguished exile audience headed by Thomas Mann, gives a moving account of the impact of the Nazi ideology on a small group of students; coming only nine months after the Fire it was a shock and a revelation to the Zurich public. Wolf's *Professor Mannheim* a year later (better known by the name of its Soviet film version, *Professor Mamlock*) was *Die Rassen's* openly Communist counterpart, and correspondingly even more controversial. Staged by Lindtberg, with Horwitz as the professor, Langhoff as the young Communist, and Heinz Greif (of Wangenheim's Truppe 1931) as the Nazi doctor, it was the most successful of all the company's productions, though today its dialogue and characterization seem cliché-ridden by comparison with *Die Rassen.* There were also some remarkable Shakespeare productions (on a week's rehearsal apiece) including Hartung's *Richard III* with Bassermann playing Richard, while among the other new plays prior to 1938 were Zuckmayer's *Schelm von Bergen* (which Julius Bab thought his best play),[23] Lasker-Schüler's *Arthur Aronymus,* and Horváth's rather slight *Hin und Her (Hither and Thither)* directed aganst Europe's frontier police.

So far the nationalist and anti-Semitic opposition inside Switzerland had only been able to score one point, when it managed to make Rieser curtail a summer visit by E. F. Burian's Prague company with his version of *The Threepenny Opera.* It had been more successful in shutting up Erika Mann's satirical cabaret *The Peppermill,* which moved from Munich early in 1933 and set up shop in a Zurich hotel; here Giehse and Robert Trösch (a Swiss member of Truppe 1931) mocked the Nazis until they were banned. With Mathilde Dannegger of the equivalent Swiss cabaret Cornichon both these performers were also acting with the Schauspielhaus company. Following the Austrian Anschluss in 1938, however, Rieser was persuaded by the Swiss government to resign his management and rent the theatre to a new board headed by the former Basel Intendant (and Appia enthusiast) Oskar Wälterlin, who had been directing in Frankfurt but now proved as resolute as Rieser, if less demanding of the actors. Under him company and policy alike remained virtually unchanged, and during the war years they gave first productions not only to three of Brecht's big exile plays—*Mother Courage, Galileo,* and *The Good Person of Szechwan*—but also to two of Georg Kaiser's new pacifist works, *Zweimal Amphitryon* and *Der Soldat Tanaka (Twice Amphitryon* and *The Soldier Tanaka)* the latter being one his finest plays. Two other Kaiser premieres were given by the Basel Stadttheater, and altogether in this last phase of his life this often underrated dramatist was extraordinarily productive. Since leaving Germany hurriedly in 1938, when he thought that his scurrilous rhymes about the Nazi leaders were about to get him into trouble, he had been an illegal resident with friends in Switzerland, never (it seems) visiting the theatre, yet writing twelve plays mainly on war themes up to the time of his death in 1945. There was also a big Lehrstück-like work written by another illegal entrant, Hans Sahl, for the Swiss "worker-singers" with music by the Hungarian Tibor Kasicz. This was *Jemand* or *Somebody*—as against Reinhardt's *Jedermann* or *Everybody*—a form of cantata based on Frans Masereel's woodcut series *The Passion of a Man*. Performed in June 1938 to an audience of between five and six thousand in a temporary hall, this had Heinrich Gretter of the Schauspielhaus as an evangelist-like announcer. "Then the leader gave the order for the execution," he said before the last scene, "and they shot Somebody, and with him twelve comrades to his right and left."[24]

Stalin, Hollywood, and War

Piscator, after finishing his film in Russia, moved away from practical direction into high-level planning and administration, He had already in 1932 been elected to the Presidium and Secretariat of MORT—the new acronym for the International Association of Workers' Theatres set up three years before in Moscow—and now in November 1934 a further broadening of that organization led to his appointment as president. Originally the association had been confined to workers' theatre proper, which in Weimar Germany meant above all the agitprop groups; but belatedly it was extended to the "revolutionary theatres" of its changed title, in other words not just to amateurs but to such left-wing professional collectives as the Junge Volksbühne, Burian's D34, and the American Theater Union. With the Comintern's new secretary Georgi Dimitroff pushing the Communist movement toward the Popular Front policy formulated at its Seventh Congress in 1935, Piscator hoped finally to unite the whole anti-Nazi theatre, from the French surrealists to the last relics of agitprop, around MORT's bulletin *The International Theatre* and other publications—to include a broad new review edited by his deputy Bernhard Reich. Simultaneously he was trying to set up a professional German-language theatre in the USSR which would be on a level with the Zurich Schauspielhaus and make use of Steckel, Heinz, Teo Otto and others of its members. This started as a scheme for reinforcing Kolonne Links, which since its return to Russia in the autumn of 1931 had been performing to groups of German workers in Soviet industry. First Wangenheim and his wife Inge arrived to take it over, bringing in a number of new members such as Greif and Curt Trepte of their own Truppe 1931 and the costume designer Sylta Busse; in addition they hoped to recruit Granach from Warsaw, Geschonneck from Prague, and Carola Neher, who had married a Soviet-German engineer and was as yet unemployed. On 25 February 1934 the reinforced company gave a preliminary program in the Moscow Foreign Workers' Club with two short anti-Nazi plays by Wangenheim; later they added a staged version of Brecht's "Ballad of the Reichstag Fire" (to the "Mac the Knife" tune). They hoped to get a permanent theatre at the start of the following year.

When this proved impossible, Wangenheim abandoned the project in order to work on *Kämpfer* (*Borzhy,* or *Fighters*), a film about Dimitroff and the KPD resistance to Hitler in which Granach played Dimitroff, and Busch, Lotte

Loebinger, Giref, and Erpenbeck all had parts. The Resistance hero was played by Bruno Schmidtsdorf of Kolonne Links. Accordingly Piscator sent for Maxim Vallentin in Prague to take over what remained of the company, which now became a traveling theatre for the Dnjepropetrovsk region, the Deutsches Gebietstheater Dnjepropetrowsk. Strengthened in the course of 1935 by the arrival of Richter and his wife Amy Frank from Prague, along with Hermann Greid, who had been with them in the Truppe im Westen, and Gerhard Hinze, one of the last to see Hans Otto alive, the Deutsches Gebietstheater began work that summer and continued for about a year, mainly under Mischket Liebermann's management. Thereafter it became swallowed in Piscator's slightly improbable scheme for a major exiled theatre at Engels, the capital of the then Volga German Republic and its population of about 650,000 Germans whose settlement (and dialect) dated back to Catherine the Great's time. For this enterprise he had tried to recruit Granach, Busch, and Carola Neher, as well as the Zurich group, to work with himself and Reich as directors and Brecht (he hoped) as dramaturg. Impracticable anyway in view of the accommodation problems and (it seems) the local feelings, the whole operation including MORT itself and Piscator's closest Comintern supporters was torpedoed by the wave of "vigilance"—i.e., denunciations and spy mania—that followed Stalin's first great show trial of "rightists" in August 1936.

Piscator, who was in Paris with a whole sheaf of plans relating to the transfer of MORT headquarters to that city, was warned by Wilhelm Pieck not to come back; his invitations to Engels were not taken up; the Deutsche Gebietstheater was dissolved. There were also many arrests. They included those of Granach (allowed to leave the country on Feuchtwanger's intervention), and Carola Neher and her husband, neither of whom survived. Vallentin was able to get himself and some of his actors "rehabilitated"; Hans Drach was detained till the Russians handed him to the Gestapo in 1940; Trepte, Hinze and the Richters were expelled from the country; Reich and his wife Asya Lacis were arrested and sent to camps, while of the earlier Engels exiles Karl Weidner disappeared for good, and the conductor Hans David (formerly of the Düsseldorf Schauspielhaus) was in due course handed over to the Gestapo and gassed at Maidanek. Kolonne Links was briefly revived in 1937, then demolished. Helmut Damerius spent fifteen years in camps. Bruno Schmidtsdorf, Karl Oefelein, and Kurt Arendt were never heard of again.

The most hopeful place in the summer of 1936 appeared to be France. That was the year when the Popular Front policy looked like succeeding, and the Spanish Civil War gave its supporters everywhere a cause for which to fight. This had many implications for the exiled theatre, ranging from the blooming of the French cinema to the various grand schemes which kept Piscator fruitlessly occupied till his departure for America at the end of 1938. Aufricht organized a French-language production of *The Threepenny Opera* for the Paris International Exhibition of 1937; it included Yvette Guilbert as Mme. Peachum. The same year Brecht wrote his Spanish Civil War one-acter, *Señora Carrar's Rifles,* for Dudow to direct with Helene Weigel and the cabaret group Die Laterne, which had been formed in winter 1933–34 out of the Paris

Helene Weigel as "The Jewish Wife," in the Paris émigré production of Brecht's *Fear and Misery of the Third Reich,* 1938, his only topical play, consisting of a sequence of separate realistic scenes.

remnant of Truppe 1931 when the Wangenheims went to Moscow. This was followed on 21 May 1938 by the same group's performance, again with Dudow and Weigel, of eight scenes from Brecht's new cycle *Fear and Misery of the Third Reich,* a unique work that was at once economical and adjustable to the needs of an impoverished theatre; both plays were staged in hired halls. Meanwhile Brecht himself was based in Scandinavia, where he wrote some of his finest plays and poems, several major theoretical essays, and the related *Messingkauf Dialogues* without immediate access to any theatre, though there was a none-too-successful Danish production of the play *The Roundheads and the Pointed Heads,* which he had failed to get accepted in Zurich or Moscow. He was also marginally involved with the Swedish amateur theatre, as were Trepte and Greid on their return from the USSR.

Elsewhere Jessner had begun in 1933 to tour the Low Countries with a small exiled company performing Schiller's *Kabale und Liebe (Intrigues and Love)* and Sudermann's *Heimat (Home).* This broke up at the end of the year, when Jessner refused to consider any less uncommercial program. There was a move to give him a permanent post with the Hebrew-speaking Habima theatre in Tel Aviv, where he directed *Wilhelm Tell* and *The Merchant of Venice* in the 1934–35 season, but his reception there was unenthusiastic. As for England, where he also went, the German-language theatre there was confined to the émigré clubs, though Ernst Toller and his plays aroused some public interest. There was, however, always a place on Shaftesbury Avenue for skilled actors capable of mastering the language and contributing discreetly to a polished ensemble in the Reinhardt tradition. Thus whereas Kortner and Lorre could only be used in films (*Abdul the Damned* for the one; *The Man Who Knew Too Much* for the other) such players as Conrad Veidt, Lucie Mannheim, Oskar Homolka, Friedrich Valk, Lilli Palmer, and Adolf Wohlbrück (Anton Walbrook) became established in London's somewhat depressing commercial theatre of the 1930s. Above all, Elisabeth Bergner made an instant hit in C. B. Cochran's production of Margaret Kennedy's *Escape Me Never*, and from the royal family down much of England took her to its heart.

Three years after the failure of the Popular Front, when the French and British governments at last decided that the expansion of the Third Reich must be halted, half the functioning outposts of the real German theatre had been lost; and with the outbreak of war that was soon reduced to Zurich and Basel, plus a few small cells in Britain, Sweden, and the USSR. Though Britain is generally reckoned to have been the country most welcoming to the anti-Nazi exiles, particularly after the fall of Austria and Czechoslovakia and the Soviet purges, it was now at war with Germany and for at least two years remained in a dangerously exposed position, so that any émigré in his or her senses must be hoping to get to the United States if not already there. Certainly this applied alike to Reinhardt, Jessner, Brecht, and Piscator, all of whom had reached that ultimate haven by August 1941, the first three settling in the Los Angeles area, where Jessner became president of the Jewish Club and worked as a script reader for MGM and Walter Wanger. Hollywood rather than New York was the great attraction for them, and this was not simply because of the money to be earned, nor even the presence of such Olympians as the Mann brothers, the Werfels, Döblin, and Feuchtwanger among the writers, or Stravinsky and Schönberg among the musicians, but also because of the long-standing connections between the modern German theatre and the American motion picture industry. These had perhaps originated with Carl Laemmle, the elderly head of Universal, and under the Republic had already pulled in Lubitsch, Dieterle, Stroheim, Murnau, Ludwig Berger, the Viertels, Wilder, Pommer, Siodmak, and Zinnemann, to cite only the main producers and directors. These in turn attracted lesser directors (Detlev Sierck, for instance, who came to prominence under the Nazis before emigrating as Douglas Sirk) as well as musicians like Toch, Holländer, Korngold, and Wachsmann (Waxman), and a long list of actors ranging from Jannings and Dietrich at the one end to such friends of the Brechts as Lorre, Kortner, Homolka and Curt Bois at the other. It was easy for anybody arriving after 1937 to find a familiar circle, and generally it could be felt that German organization, acting, and stage technology were closer to the requirements of the Hollywood cinema than to the demands and practices of the New York stage.

Whether those requirements went any further was another matter, and the art, the passion, the committedness of the best German theatre were generally much less needed, particularly when coupled with the financial extravagance to which both Reinhardt and Piscator had become accustomed at the peak of their fame. Thus up to 1933 Reinhardt's visits to the United States had been highly successful, since even when they lost money (as the 1927–28 tour had done) there had been somebody to pick up the bill. Subsequently, however, the economic slump had come; his backer Otto Kahn had died; and an originally warm welcome always looks different as soon as a visitor hints at staying for good. Two particularly costly ventures helped to change the picture for Reinhardt. First there was the staging of the great Jewish pageant *The Eternal Road* (text by Werfel, music by Weill) for which he got Norman Bel Geddes largely to rebuild the little-used Manhattan Opera House; this project initiated at the end of 1933 only materialized on 7 January 1937 and achieved (so Reinhardt's friend Rudolph Kommer was to remind him) "the greatest theatrical deficit of all time."[25] Secondly there was the film version of *A Midsummer Night's Dream,* which he made for Dieterle at Warner Brothers in 1935, with James Cagney as Bottom and Mickey Rooney as Puck; for it too, while one of the best Shakespeare films ever made, failed to recoup its investment, with the result that the planned series of six other classic films which he was supposed to make was canceled. If it is true that "nothing succeeds like success," it is also very evident that in the United States nothing fails like failure, and unhappily both these enterprises were fresh in American commercial memory when Reinhardt finally left Austria for Hollywood in October 1937. As a result, neither his film plans nor his desire to build an arts theatre in New York found the necessary support, and even the school which he started in 1938 under the name Hollywood Workshop for Stage, Screen and Film collapsed two years later. He had met the "rough side" of Hollywood, said Zuckmayer[26] (who himself soon found the place unbearable and retired to farm in Vermont); those film tycoons who were once only too anxious to be invited to Leopoldskron now stopped coming to his productions at the school. Kortner, himself unwanted by the casting directors because of his overemotional acting, reported Reinhardt and Helene Thimig in their villa living in "slightly damaged splendid isolation." Later, in New York, where he was to die in 1943, "Only his eyes continued to speak, when his hands lost the power to write what his paralysed tongue could no longer say."[27]

On 25 May 1939 Jessner made yet another attempt to establish himself when he directed *Wilhelm Tell* in the El Capitan Theatre in Los Angeles with a large cast including Deutsch and Granach and music by Ernst Toch. But neither Jessner nor Reinhardt seems to have realized how unexportable the great German classics can be, and from then on, says Kortner, he declined.[28] Leo Reuss (now Lionel Royce) organized a solitary performance at the Wilshire Ebell Theatre in the same city to celebrate Jessner's sixty-fifth birthday (6 March 1943, with the Kortners, Deutsch, Granach, and Helene Weigel all taking part). Piscator, by contrast, still only forty-five at that time, was not even given the chance to show what he could do and how much money he could spend, for he never went to Hollywood, and the great *War and Peace* project for which he had come to America was almost immediately called off by its backer, Gilbert Miller. Nor did he manage to get more than a single Broadway production to direct, this being Irving Kaye Davis's *Last Stop* in 1944—evidently an unhappy experience. Schemes apart, his activity was focused almost entirely on the school which he started in 1940 as the Dramatic Workshop of the New School, the New York adult education college which did so much to absorb the exiles from Europe. Here he worked with such colleagues as the playwrights Ferdinand Bruckner and Hans Rehfisch, the actor Herbert Berghof, and, from the music department, Hanns Eisler; it was thanks to him, moreover, that Brecht in Scandinavia was sent the teaching invitation which got his family their visas for the United States. But although the Dramatic Workshop, both within the New School and later outside it, helped train some outstanding American actors and had a recognizable influence on the young Tennessee Williams, the progressive left wing of American theatre had changed too much since the mid-1930s, and it no longer felt quite the old respect for either Piscator or Brecht. Thus the Federal Theatre Project, with its Living Newspapers, was killed in June 1939; the Theater Union (which had staged *The Sailors of Cattaro* and *Mother*) was already dead; while the Group Theatre disintegrated as its leading actors and writers were sucked away by Hollywood. As a result, Brecht could spend his six years in Santa Monica (with the occasional visit to New York) largely isolated from American theatre people. All but one of his commissions—including the writing of *Schweik in the Second World War* and *The Caucasian Chalk Circle,* the adaptation of *The Duchess of Malfi,* and the American version of *The Good Person of Szechwan*—came from within the exiled community. The exception was the new English-language version of *Galileo,* which he made with Charles Laughton. It was also the only one of his projects to reach the Broadway stage, where it ran briefly in 1947 after he himself had returned to Europe.

The Divided Republic Lives On

During the twelve years of its existence much was done both inside and outside Hitler's manic Reich to conserve and even propagate the achievements of the Weimar theatre. Inside Germany it was at least possible to keep the apparatus in being so long as its physical fabric could withstand the air raids (as that of the Staatstheater, the Volksbühne's theatre on the Bülowplatz and many other theatre buildings throughout the country could not). The actors, too, were in some ways well placed to exercise their art, though the banning of all critical judgments (as against straight reporting) in November 1936 removed one of their sharper incentives. (Jhering by then had been forbidden to write for the press at all.) But in 1935 when Moissi died in Vienna, Bassermann, the then holder of the Iffland Ring, took it off and laid it on the dead man's coffin, as if to indicate that no actor in the Nazi theatre was worthy to wear it.[29]

Nearly twenty years later the Burgtheater revived the award and gave it to Werner Krauss, who, in Kortner's words, had "underwritten Hitler's anti-Semitism with his own, by putting his great artistry at the disposal of that monster's craze for extermination."[30] The preservation of standards, then—if such people actually achieved it—could not be taken purely at its face value; nor is posterity likely to forget the use made of the Harlan/Krauss *Jew Süss* film, which was shown by Himmler's orders to all police and SS men, and according to a report of 1943[31] had a great success with audiences in the former Baltic states, actually rivaling such hits as Willi Forst's *Operette* and the 1931 Wilder-Preminger film *Die grosse Liebe.* In 1951, too, Hilpert set down his directorial credo in an eleven-line sentence of the utmost vagueness, suggesting that the important thing was to

> transmit our whole life substance and all our inner and outer experience as concentratedly and intensively as possible by our work as directors, in order that chaos, confusion and impotence can be overcome so that the form and dimension of an art exposed at all times, and on all sides to accident and disintegration can be transmitted in their purity to a new time now emerging. . .[32]

—and thereby (in effect) to give Youth a chance to do better. Compare what Brecht said on revisiting Germany for the first time in August 1948 and seeing a production by Hilpert in Konstanz: "This is where we need to start again from scratch."[33]

The exiles on the other hand were generally deprived of the apparatus and sometimes of the German language, and even in such a miraculous enclave as the Zurich Schauspielhaus they were reduced to minimal rehearsals and often worked off their feet. They also ran great personal risks at the hands not only of the conquering Nazis but even more fatally of the Russians, in whom many of them had put their faith. Thus they had little chance to refine their art or make formal or technical experiments; the rare attempts to evolve a form for the special conditions of the times were, like Brecht's *Fear and Misery* sequence, so unobtrusive as to have remained almost unnoticed. It was unfortunate, too, that those who stayed in the USSR after the demise of MORT and all it stood for allowed themselves to become indoctrinated with a Stanislavskian Naturalism dating back to the end of the nineteenth century, a style by no means aesthetically incompatible with that followed in Nazi Germany. And yet despite such handicaps, and despite the stifling commercialism of the English-language theatre at that time, the exiles managed to preserve the essence of the Weimar theatre, that is to say its spirit. This was most evident perhaps in the work of the playwrights, much of which was of the highest order and a marvelous reflection of the times through which they somehow managed to live. Nothing in the Nazi theatre can compare with it, for the search for a National Socialist drama never turned up a single work which even the most convinced party member could wholeheartedly admire. It was a great relief, so Gründgens recorded[34] saying to Goebbels in their inaugural discussion on 9 April 1934, to find that within his own four walls the Propaganda Minister, too, believed that there was no such thing as Nazi art.

What the National Socialist experience did to the Weimar theatre was to split it, with effects that have been felt ever since. For both its inner and its outer members were on the defensive: the one group against the Gestapo and increasingly against its own conscience and the thought of what the exiles would say to it when they returned, the other against isolation, poverty, internment, deportation, and the "Final Solution." Both had their victims, as exemplified not only in the dead already listed but in the internment of Wolf by the French, the suicides of Toller and Hasenclever, the trial for high treason of Ernst Busch on the one side; and the postwar internment or imprisonment of Gründgens, Harlan, and Heinrich George (who died in Germany in a Russian camp) on the other. Both sides suffered from decline of talent, seen most conspicuously perhaps in the case of Piscator, who never again reached his former heights after completing his one film, *The Revolt of the Fishermen*, in 1934. Both provided important survivors who could carry the living tradition of Weimar into the postwar German theatre, where younger generations have been delighted and fascinated to learn from it. But while the one group moved back into the old apparatus as if resuming a familiar routine with nothing more than a bit of updating and a dab or two of whitewash, the others returned with something of that extraordinary force that allowed Helene Weigel in *Mother Courage* to conquer the Berlin stage after not acting at all during more than nine years. This contrast was not just due to one side having "won" the war while the other "lost," for not many of the exiles had actually taken part in the war, while the real victors, the occupying armies of 1945, were largely unconscious of their significance. One thing, however, was unique to the exiles, and that was a corpus of new German plays ranging from *Die Rassen, Galileo,* and *Der Soldat Tanaka* through *Jacobowsky and the Colonel* and *The Devil's General* to the new Swiss plays of Max Frisch and Friedrich Dürrenmatt, which the Zurich exiles so largely helped to inspire. The imagination, and the power to put life into the theatre, were all on their side.

It is instructive to see what happened when Brecht and his old friend Caspar Neher met again in the autumn of 1947. For more than sixteen years they had (to judge from their surviving letters and notebooks) not even communicated, doubtless because both realized that Brecht would have been a dangerous man to know for anybody working in the Third Reich. Yet they had been the closest of collaborators up to 1933, and certainly Brecht's most radical productions of the Weimar era would have been inconceivable without Neher's participation; in fact his visual contribution was an integral part of Brechtian epic theatre as we now understand it. In a typically pragmatic way Brecht wrote from America to propose that they meet in Zurich to pick up the threads, and Neher unquestioningly arranged to leave Hamburg, where he had been working for Alfred Nöller, the Nazi-appointed opera Intendant, and join Wälterlin and Teo Otto at the Schauspielhaus.

It is generally agreed that Neher had not compromised politically or even ideologically during the Nazi years. He worked with the more reputable directors—Engel, Wälterlin, Felsenstein, Schuh, Hilpert—and although he designed the occasional play by such approved playwrights as Bethge and Möller he managed to concentrate his efforts mainly on opera and the major classics. Technically he had made considerable advances since Brecht last saw him, learning on the one hand how to delegate work to assistants and on the other how to design for a modern theatre in the style of the Galli-Bibienas and other classical artists. Nevertheless the great originality of his pre-1933 stage and costume designs had vanished, and much of the life had gone from his

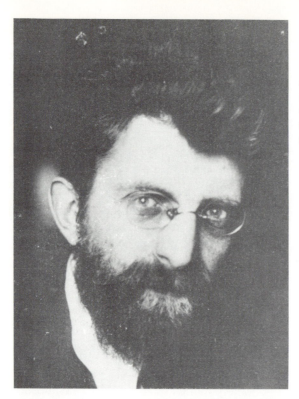

Some Victims of the Third Reich.

(a) Erich Mühsam, an anarchist poet and cabaret performer, was beaten to death in 1933 in Oranienburg concentration camp.

(b) Hans Otto, Staatstheater actor and Communist union organiser, was beaten to death in a Berlin SA barracks in 1933.

(c) Kurt Singer, Intendant of the Städtische Oper in 1931 and subsequently one of the leaders of the segregated Jewish League of Culture. Killed in the Terezin extermination camp in 1944.

(d) Franz-Jacob Spira, Berlin actor, was killed in the Ruona concentration camp in occupied Yugoslavia in 1943. Photos (a) and (d) by Thomas Willett, (b) and (c) by Ullstein Bilderdienst.

drawings. He had kept going despite some initial difficulties, and at least within the field of opera had acquired what proved to be an international reputation. But at a perceptible cost.

Brecht for his part had suffered the obvious drawbacks of exile: amputation from the German theatre, linguistic isolation, and lack of orthodox publishing outlets, to say nothing of such matters as loss of citizenship, money worries, and the overhanging threat from the Nazis. He, too, changed his manner of working in that his plays seemed to become more timeless, their casts much bigger. This was because from 1938 on he was writing for the desk drawer, without the old production pressures; here again a certain tension and tautness had gone out of his work. But once he and his friend met there was no question who had the most to give. Brecht needed Neher partly as a trustworthy guide to what had been going on in the German theatre during his absence, but primarily as the inspired designer who could still understand, complement, and realize his own theatrical ideas. For Neher, however, the returning playwright was clearly a lot more: he was like a dose of oxygen, something that had to be breathed deeply after the terrible atmosphere of the Third Reich, and the impact on his own work was startling.

For a while the reunion was stimulating to them both, in a way that promised well for their collaboration in the new Berliner Ensemble; and their joint productions—first of *Antigone* in Switzerland, then of Lenz's *Tutor*—were high points of the postwar theatre. Then the years of divergence began to tell. Neher was not prepared to ignore the calls of the opera houses and the revived Salzburg Festival, thereby forcing Brecht at times to use other designers. Brecht for his part began making outward concessions to the official cultural policy of the Soviet sector and occupation zone where his new company was based, something that for Neher was uncomfortably reminiscent of his experience of the Theatre Chamber. By 1952 their collaboration was effectively at an end. On top of this of course came the larger difficulties imposed by the cold war, but for us the lesson is already evident. Whatever the respective achievements of the two wings of Germany's divided theatre in the 1930s these could hardly stand much chance of coming productively together if even such old partners could not manage to combine their talents for more than a handful of plays. The damage done in 1933 could at best be got over. It could not be shrugged off.

10

Weimar in Retrospect

A Question of Angles

Vividly as the theatre of the Weimar Republic may strike us today, we cannot survey it as if it had only just ended. Perhaps in the 1930s this would have been possible, at least to those who thought that Hitler represented nothing more than a continuation of the class war by other means; though it never seems to have been done either by German critics or by outside observers, with the sole exception of the French critic René Lauret. Today the position has altered: we have acquired the necessary distance on the one hand and a new sense of relevance on the other. But between our own time and those last months of the Weimar theatre—months that saw such productions as *The Mother*, the Mussolini/Forzano *Hundred Days*, and the two parts of the centenary *Faust* in a disorientated Staatstheater—now lies the uniformed corpse of the Third Reich as it expired in the rubble of Berlin. Neither inside nor outside the rival (if mutually complementary) Germanies of today can this rotting barrier be ignored, for in the theatre as in other respects Hitler's Reich was at once the fulfillment of certain trends in the short-lived Weimar democracy and a cause of the present divisions and unresolved ambiguities in German culture. To show this is one of the objects of the immediately preceding chapter, with its attempt to give some idea of the conflicting directions which the active survivors of that theatre then took.

But if all alike must bear in mind the aftermath as well as the actual Weimar theatre of 1918–33 there were nonetheless bound to be conflicting angles of approach. Within Germany, once the dictatorship had fallen and the urgent problem of reassimilating the forbidden works and methods been tackled, the interest of critics and academics began to move on to the Nazi period and the problem of continuity. If the 1950s and 1960s were a period of rediscovery, first of the Expressionist movement and then of Neue Sachlichkeit and the militantly "proletarian" art that followed, much was done in the 1970s to reevaluate the theatre of the Third Reich and to identify some of its roots in the nationalist, historicist, and blood-and-soil dramas which were so largely ignored under the Republic. This new perspective certainly had its ambiguities, for it revived the image of a theatre of "excellence" pursued by a disinterested band of inner emigrants under the aegis of Reich Marshal Goering—something that Brecht for one had thought artistically most questionable—and certainly it must have been a relief to those artists and arts administrators who had prospered under Hitler. At the same time it did allow more critical spirits to try to demystify Nazi ideology and Nazi aesthetics by showing how far these depended on underlying factors, some at least of which have by no means been eradicated since the end of the Reich.

The danger here of course is that those psychopathological elements that distinguished German national socialism, not only from more conservative reactionary movements but even to some extent from other brands of fascism, will get overlooked. Some may find comfort in this, since swallowing a mad ideology seems a shade more discreditable (to artists and intellectuals at least) than being manipulated by wicked but intelligent capitalist wirepullers. But it risks repeating the errors of the Weimar Marxists, who saw the Nazis as mere hirelings of the old German ruling class—the view expressed at the beginning (though not the end) of Brecht's *Arturo Ui*—and accordingly underestimated not only their competence but their profound popular appeal and the nature of the ingrained opposition to them, which largely transcended classes, not least in other countries.

From the point of view of the non-German (and specifically the English-language) theatre the focus is once again different. For in coming up against the Weimar theatre, with all its unfamiliar features, most of us have to take stock of the German theatre for the first time, and much that seems remarkable about it is not specific to the Weimar years but part of a much longer tradition. This the German student of the subject almost takes for granted, for it is built into the nature of that theatre, part of the conditions within which it functions. For us, however, it is to a great extent what caused the extraordinary phenomenon on which Iwan Goll commented in *l'Esprit Nouveau* at the very outset of the Republic—the head start that the German theatre enjoyed over all others. Long unrecognized by the outsider, the relevant factors are now clear enough to anyone who comes in contact with them: the decentralization; the high level of state and municipal subsidy; the admirable public commitment to theatre, music, and opera; the importance given to criticism; the virtually unquestioned assumption that the arts are part, not of "leisure" but of *Bildung:* in other words the intangible equipment of a well-ordered life. All these emerge from German history, where the aristocracy, the rise of a new middle-class élite in the late nineteenth century, and the aspirations of the Socialist workers combined in their various ways to bring about a favorable climate for the performing arts. And with these less tangible factors went also the advanced technical equipment which came to distinguish the German theatre, the natural contribution of the growing electrical and engineering industries.

Other aspects are perhaps less easily grasped, though they too arise from the special nature of that country. Thus in some respects the arts there are remarkably homogeneous, so that it was not for nothing that Wagner could set himself the objective of the *Gesamtkunstwerk,* or "total work of art." German writers to this day spill over into the visual arts and vice-versa, as did Barlach, Kandinsky, Else Lasker-Schüler, and Schwitters; chamber music is part of social and family life; the Wedekind tradition of ballad singing (as practiced by Brecht and Zuckmayer) still goes on. There is nothing especially dilettantish about this, for it seems consistent with a high degree of professionalism; thus Neher might codirect plays with Brecht and write libretti for Weill and Wagner-Régeny, but as a designer he was a full-time professional with a recognized place in the theatrical structure; and similarly the technical director and the dramaturg occupied acknowledged slots in the German system, whereas our own arrangements were (and often still are) more haphazard. At the same time it does seem to be conducive to a breaking of barriers not only between but also within the arts. In particular the Weimar period was remarkable for its freedom from those distinctions between "high" and "low" culture that used so to bedevil the arts in England and to some extent in other countries too.

Serious writers from Wedekind on were not ashamed to write for the cabaret, nor highbrow composers to use the new conventions of jazz, and as a result not only were their works more accessible to popular audiences but new forms might result, as happened most conspicuously with the 'music theatre' pieces emerging from Hindemith's Neue Musik festivals and the circle around Weill and Brecht. For much the same reasons too there was less of an isolating wall between the so-called avant-garde and the rest of the cultural world, and the ghettolike groupings and coteries of modernism elsewhere were lost in those broad movements which for most of the period operated across a wide spectrum of the arts and within the existing "apparatus," or establishment. Only during the final years of sharp political polarization did men like Walter Benjamin begin to see the bourgeois apparatus as a distorting factor (rather as Marshall McLuhan was later to see the medium as determining the message) and call for its capture or replacement. Up till then the new aesthetics, the new technologies and the new audience appeared to be mutually compatible, with no need for a plethora of isms or any paranoid pretense of an "underground."

Images and Their Significance

Though such matters are basic, they are seldom what alerted us to the Weimar theatre in the first place. Look back at our own theatre's concern with it—or perhaps at your own first encounter—and you will be struck by the impact which it appears to have made. This came, for most of us, not through actual performance (though there are films and records of that period which give an idea what such performance might have been like) but from books and photographs and word of mouth, backed up by some of the implications of productions in the post-1945 theatre. Such impressions may be thought very superficial, but then superficial impressions are what the theatre uses in order to achieve its deeper effects. Often they are strong ones, a matter of powerful images or unfamiliar angles and rhythms: Barlach's drawings for his own plays, for instance, Moholy-Nagy's setting for *Tales of Hoffmann*, Peter Lorre's "human fighting machine" in *Man Equals Man*, Falckenberg's first Expressionist production of *Drums in the Night*, the skulls and barbed wire in Toller's first play, the tightly condensed dialogue of Sternheim and Kaiser: all this can even now be very striking.

That said, it is evident that acting, in the fullest sense, is not a particularly significant part of the Weimar heritage as it has reached us: makeup, stylized attitude, and gestures, yes, but not the voice or the interpretation of the part. This is partly because of the difficulty of conveying what is distinctive about an actor's performance as opposed to his appearance, but partly, too, perhaps because there is such a range of excellent actors in our own theatres today. Acting collectives are not now unusual, while left-wing convictions have become such a commonplace in our green rooms as to be something of a joke outside the theatre. What seems much more remarkable, then, is a particular tradition of actors' singing: that clearly audible, often rather informal, consonantal, nonsingerly delivery which characterizes Lenya or Ernst Busch far more sharply than does any aspect of their acting. Even Brecht's most radical ideas about the actor, his empathy or alienation, are less relevant in our theatre than in their original context. For those vocal excesses, that heightened emotion, that assault on the audience which used to characterize the bad old German theatre against which he reacted, are a lot rarer in the English-speaking world.

For us, then, the main achievements of the Weimar theatre lie in the areas of direction and design, though there is also a good deal that is stimulating about its plays, even if these cannot always be taken over as they stand. Certainly Reinhardt, Piscator, and Brecht have proved to be its most inspiring influences—Jessner much less so, Brecht perhaps doubly in his unique capacity of playwright and director with a comprehensive view of the theatre. What Brecht in particular has taught us with regard to the actor has been to avoid obvious typecasting and an undue emphasis on physical beauty, though it would be wrong to attribute this lesson to the Weimar theatre as a whole. Reinhardt for instance would vary his casting within wide limits, but this was partly for the sake of the actors themselves and to allow for their outside engagements; and if we look back over the list of productions it is difficult to avoid the impression that the same hard core of actors kept reappearing in play after play—an impression reinforced by the memories of those who saw them and keep referring to "der" Kortner, "die" Bergner, and so on, "der" and "die" being the definite article, suggesting the kind of old-fashioned theatre where the play changes but the players do not. Grouping and movement of those actors, however, is a very different matter—Reinhardt's handling of crowds, Jessner's dramatic use of bodies in carefully articulated space, Brecht's silent-film concept of telling the story by means of their relative positions—and repeatedly we get the example, from such directors, of a clear overall view of the play, put across by a concentration of every available means: lighting, color, the spatial organization of the set, the actors' moves and gestures, the incidental sounds (musical or not); reinforced over the years by such new devices as amplification and the use of film, all as a moving framework for the actor.

It was in short a directors' theatre, even more than it was an authors', for it could make its impact (as Piscator so largely managed to do) without first-class scripts and often even without particularly outstanding performers. What it could not dispense with, however, was the finely tuned, organized, well-equipped apparatus of the theatre itself which could put all those means at the director's disposal and allow the "theatrical theatre" to be practiced on the highest level. This was not a fringe or a shoestring operation; the avant-garde was no handicapped minority but right at the center of things. Schlemmer at the Bauhaus, for instance, would have been more than welcome in the established theatre, and the Bauhaus itself in any case became increasingly engaged with social and industrial tasks; it was no ivory tower. This flexibility and continual extension of resources was what made the German theatre so uniquely able to reflect the changing moods of that eventful time, from the Expressionism and Utopian Activism of the First World War up to the intense political commitments of its last critical years.

In this book we have dealt with Expressionism largely as a culmination of previous influences and innovations, both literary and technical, but the impact made by its appearance on the public (uncensored) stage at the end of the war was sudden and extraordinary, and it retains this power wherever the same passions and anxieties are felt in our own time—as they were for instance in the American Beat movement and the European student upheavals of 1968, and still are in some of the liberation movements of the Third World. Dada, though its spirit remains active even now, was always more marginal, yet here, too, something of the prewar Munich theatre permeated the Cabaret Voltaire under Hugo Ball, while in Berlin there was a strong Dada element at first in the postwar Schall und Rauch, though Goll's farces and Zuckmayer's iconoclastic version of *The Eunuch* were about the only plays to result. But it was primarily Expressionism that gave the German theatre its tremendous appeal to certain English, Irish, and American theatre people back in the 1920s: Eugene O'Neill, Elmer Rice, Denis Johnson, Ashley Dukes, the Gate Theatre director Peter Godfrey, the designer Robert Edmond Jones, followed later by W. H. Auden and his friends and by J. B. Priestley. Ben Hecht, too, was a friendly spectator of some of the Berlin Dada manifestations.

The greater sobriety which prevailed after the 1923 stabilization has not perhaps offered us quite so many compelling models. At least the new naturalism of Barlach and the people's plays that followed, while in some ways congenial to our theatre (though not with respect to the size of their casts), has never seemed all that novel to it, and much the same is true of the play of the times, for we too have had plays on topical themes, and topical themes by definition are likely to date. But Piscator's concept of documentary theatre, with its use of factual material conveyed in the form of film and still projections, and its oscillation between performance and lecturing, was revived in the 1960s (not least by himself, with his staging of the new plays of Hochhuth and Peter Weiss), and has done a good deal to extend our theatre's range and resources, not to mention its sense of spectacle. Brecht's epic theatre too remains exemplary, with its freedom in handling time and place, its use of songs, its dramaturgical shortcuts and its direct addressing of the audience, while its montagelike structure exemplifies that new condensed, selected, and recomposed realism which was also to be found in photomontage and in the great Russian films of the period.

The same principle is brilliantly exemplified in Caspar Neher's settings, with their selection and exact placing of those disparate elements that are essential for the play and for the actor's movements, and it finds its most extreme realization in the opera *Mahagonny,* where the text itself is largely a collage of poems, while both the designer's projected drawings and the composer's musical numbers act as independent contributions according to Brecht's new doctrine of "separation of the elements." This, while ostensibly in contradiction of Wagner's completely fused "total work of art," depends equally on the absence of aesthetic barriers between media, for those separate elements—words/action, "visuals," and music—are made to drive toward a common goal even while remaining distinct in the perceptions of the audience. Here the writer/director was not claiming to dictate the music or the visual images, but rather calling for a montage on the highest level, where three like-minded collaborators would do the selecting and the sticking together, with a single result in view.

Such collective creativity inspired and informed that new approach to the staging of opera which could be seen in the work of Klemperer's team at the Kroll-Oper, of Carl Ebert at the Städtische Oper, and in some of the great provincial opera houses like those at Leipzig and Frankfurt. Though this was nothing like as fundamental as what was going on in the area centering on Brecht and Hindemith, for thirty years or more after the end of the Republic it remained far in advance of anything achieved elsewhere. The musicians' virtually monopolistic position was abandoned, and the nonmusical aspects of the performance brought into much closer conformity with the standards prevailing in the rest of the theatre: setting, acting, the performers' costumes and looks, the intelligible communication of the story, the avoidance of needless improbabilities. It is doubtful if any present-day opera house has yet gone further, nor has our "music theatre" movement devised new forms as truly radical as those which were being developed in Germany around the same time.

This latter movement started after the Second World War from much the same foundations as that of the 1920s, that is to say from Stravinsky's *Soldier's Tale* and Schönberg's *Pierrot Lunaire,* but it has remained too remote from the mainstream theatre to live up to elementary standards of theatrical quality and dramatic interest. As a result the special forms pioneered by Hindemith and Brecht still seem exemplary—a challenge to our own time to devise a wholly new type of musical stage work outside the conventional concert and opera apparatus. Prominent among them were the didactic Lehrstück and such variants as the radio cantata, the school opera, and the mini-opera, all of which have retained a certain freshness even some sixty years later, because they were the successful result of a kind of sociomusical experimental activity that has never yet been resumed. Of course agitprop, too, remains of considerable interest for theatrical as well as merely political reasons—a combination of clear theme, minimal overheads, and direct contact with a nontheatrical audience. But the principal creative talents involved (like Friedrich Wolf, Eisler, and Béla Balázs) did not include Brecht, and the surviving texts are unimpressive—particularly now that such an audience is better reached by television or video. They are suggestive today mainly as exercises: stimulating models for the social engagement of the actor and singer.

The Price of Upheaval

If we compare the significance to us of the Weimar theatre with that of the French theatre of the interwar years, say, we cannot but see that much of what seems special and interesting about the former is due not merely to previous history but to the particular social and political currents of that time. The major movements themselves relate to the main politicoeconomic phases so much more closely than in most other countries: thus Expressionism dominates the theatre of the immediate postwar years; Neue Sachlichkeit and the realist revival begin with the stabilization; light entertainment and the opera boom are the accompaniments of prosperity; theatre of the times appears with the start of the economic crisis; the political theatre with the growing polarization. Historical periods that appear on the surface so clear-cut and compact always have a particular appeal to the observer, and in this case all the more so because the fifteen years of the Weimar Republic took a great nation through every level of collective experience from defeat and revolution via near-anarchy and repression, boom and slump, utopia and mass unemployment to the acceptance of an inhuman, militarist, racist regime such as no civilized country had yet known. Much of the world's history in this century is, as it were, compressed between the two extremes of the Weimar experience, extending from Einstein's physics at one end to Himmler's extermination camps at the other, and in so far as this was reflected in the German theatre it is bound to appear relevant and instructive to our own.

More clearly than elsewhere the main roots of a modern theatre lie exposed here. And so, if the reader is interested, do the experiences of the individuals who were most closely involved. For the great tensions and uncertainties of those years, the manic hopes and sometimes suicidal despair, appear not only in the extroverted passions of the Expressionist drama or cinema but much more directly in the biographies, memoirs, letters, and diaries of such men as Toller, Plievier, Franz Jung, Grosz, Aufricht, Zuckmayer, Brecht (in his poems too), and Kortner. Here one learns of the price which the sensitive and creative individual had to pay for living in so intensely exciting a time. Not many of them were able to see it through—with all its accompanying features of exile, humiliation, possible arrest, political disillusionment, and so on—without losing the impetus which it had once given them. Few, too, could give artistic expression to what they endured after 1933 any better than could those "inner emigrants" like Kästner and Neher who sat it out in Nazi Germany in the hope of one day being free to find their old touch. But together they provide us with a vivid and often moving picture of what it was like to be part of a theatre so closely bound up with such times. It was not enviable, and the reader may well feel that he would have put up no better a resistance to Hitler than they, if as good.

Let us then profit from their errors of judgment as well as from their theatre achievements and hope that we can make positive use of the latter without ever having to go through the tensions and tragedies by which they were often propelled. At least we have the advantage today of being unable to think about Weimar Germany without also reflecting on the Nazi-dominated New Order to whose triumph it so nearly led. Being wise after the event is not always so easy as is popularly supposed. But we should try to learn from the interplay between the best and the worst of their experience.

PART IV

Basic Details of the Weimar Theatre and Its Aftermath

Note on the Appendices

The appendices that follow are meant to substantiate the story outlined above. The first of them gives some idea of the richness and geographical extent of the German theatrical establishment as it existed during the Weimar period, along with some indications of what happened to it afterward, first under the Nazis and then, more recently, in our own time. The concentration here is on those theatres which for one reason or another, seemed most significant between 1918 and 1932, and the changing teams that ran them, particularly around the end of the 1920s. They tended to center in Berlin, which accordingly is separately dealt with, but they were not confined to Germany, and the divided history of the German-language theatre under Hitler's Third Reich shows how important the Swiss, Czech, and Austrian theatres could be. The two maps provided should convey the basis for this, though of course they cannot deal with the small émigré groups overseas.

Appendices 2 to 4 are concerned with the works performed in such theatres and with the principal people responsible. They are prefaced by a list of nearly two hundred actors (of both sexes) with the abbreviations by which they are referred to. Then come first a chronology of the more important or characteristic theatre productions with the names or abbreviations of those involved in them, followed by similar lists of filmed or recorded performances from which something of the distinctive quality of the German theatre of the period can be absorbed. Theatrically significant opera productions are included in the main list, though without detailing the singers. The same abbreviations for the actors are used in all three lists.

This information is not as complete and exact as might be wished, and although it has been taken from what seem to be reliable sources it has not been possible to do more than a limited amount of checking. In particular certain limitations affecting the dates given need to be understood and allowed for. Generally the dates of premieres and other important performances will be right, though sometimes there were previews or closed performances that make the exact day debatable. In Appendix 1, the theatre list, the dates are a good deal more ambiguous, owing partly to the difference between the calendar year and the theatre season (generally from the start of September to the end of May) and partly to gaps in our information. If a person is cited as occupying a particular post as Intendant or designer—say, in 1931—all that can be taken for granted is that he will have held it at some point during that year. He may already have been doing the job for some years, or have continued after the dates given; in other words the date given is just an indicator, a benchmark in the longer career of the person on the one hand and of the theatre on the other.

In Appendix 2, which is the main chronology, political or parallel events have not been included. This is due to the author's wish to make the list of productions as full as possible, since nothing quite of this kind is accessible elsewhere, whereas general comparative chronologies are: for instance in *Art and Politics in the Weimar Period*, alternatively known as *The New Sobriety*. It is of course essential to see all the information given here in the light of larger historical events.

Appendix 1
The Main German-language Theatres

This list of over 180 theatres includes virtually all those mentioned in this book, along with the names of those fulfilling the main artistic functions in them at their times of greatest significance. The asterisk (*) is used to mark the break that occurred in 1933 or (for Austria) 1938. The most important cities and theatres (not necessarily the biggest by any means) are picked out in bold type. Approximate capacity, in terms of places rather than seats, is given, as are proscenium widths of the bigger houses. For abbreviations see p. 255.

It is divided as follows:

The Berlin Theatres
1. State and other Public Theatres
2. Principal Independent Managements and Collectives
3. Berlin Private Theatres

Provincial and Other German-language Theatres

Generally it attempts to give a picture of the German theatrical establishment, its organization and distribution, particularly toward the end of the 1920s. Since these were being modified all the time, as theatres were closed (mostly for economic reasons) or grouped together under a common administration, whether public or private, there has been some simplification, particularly of the more obscure structural changes.

217

Intendant is the term for the artistic and administrative head of a public theatre or (in the case of a *General-Intendant*) group of theatres. *Director* is used for the head and/or artistic director of a private theatre or theatrical management: whoever appears to have been the leading figure in deciding its policy. Lesser directors, or *stage directors*, are the most interesting of the directors otherwise responsible for its productions, whether or not their position was a regular one. Similarly with conductors and designers, who may or may not have had long-term contracts or been on the staff. The actual balance of influence within the theatre hierarchy will have differed from one outfit to another.

No attempt has been made to include the revue, variety, and operetta stage, or to deal with theatreless companies other than those Berlin managements included under "Principal Independent Managements and Collectives." The agitprop groups in particular are a large area which has to be treated as outside the establishment. But important elements of the artistic and political avant-garde were inside it.

The Berlin Theatres

1. State and Other Public Theatres

Staatstheater (Schauspielhaus). 1,000 pl. Prosc. width 11 m ST Am Gendarmenmarkt, W. 8.

Intendants: Leopold Jessner 1919, Ernst Legal (acting) 1931–32. * F. Ulbrich 1933, G. Gründgens 1934–44 (deputies A. Patry, A. Muhr).

Main directors: Reinhold Bruck 1920, Ludwig Berger, Jürgen Fehling 1922–44.
Dramaturgs incl. Heinz Lipmann, Eckart v. Naso * Naso and A. Muhr.
Designers incl. Emil Pirchan 1919, César Klein, Caspar Neher 1926, Teo Otto 1930, Rochus Gliese * Gliese and T. Müller.

Was originally the Prussian Royal Theatre, taken over in 1919 by the Socialist-led Prussian *Land* administration. Demolished by bombing 1944 and still not rebuilt.

Schiller-Theater 1,400 pl. Prosc. with 10 m SchT Charlottenburg, Grolmanstrasse 70–72.

Was a municipal theatre for Charlottenburg till that city was incorporated in Berlin, and thereafter a second house for the ST from 1923 to 1932. Under the Nazis it was briefly used by the "Prussian Theatre of Youth" before its rebuilding in 1937–38, then once again a municipal theatre with Heinrich George as Intendant and Ernst Legal as chief director.

State Opera 1,800 pl. Prosc. width 13.5 m

Intendant: Max von Schillings 1919, Heinz Tietjen 1926–44. (From 1931 Tietjen was

SO
Unter den Linden, C2.

General-Intendant, with authority also
over the ST.)
Director * W. Furtwängler 1934, C. Krauss
1935, R. Heger 1937.
Conductors incl. Leo Blech to 1923 and from
1926 to 1937, Erich Kleiber 1923–35, Georg
Szell 1924, Fritz Zweig 1931.
Designer: Panos Aravantinos (to end 1930).

Major rebuilding from 1926 to 1928, when performances had to be held in the KrO.
Damaged by bombing in WW II, it was reconstructed in the mid-1950s, after an interim
period under Ernst Legal's Intendantship (1945–52) with performances in the
Admiralspalast. It is now the State Opera of the GDR.

Kroll Opera   2,000 pl.
Prosc. width 12.5 m
KrO
Platz der Republik.

Intendant: Ernst Legal 1928

Conductor and artistic director: Otto
Klemperer 1927. Assistants: Alexander v.
Zemlinsky 1927, Fritz Zweig 1927.
Dramaturg: Hans Curjel 1927 (deputy
director 1930).
Head designer: Ewald Dülberg 1927–30, Teo
Otto 1931.

Originally a winter garden built by Joseph Kroll in 1844, this former royal theatre was
made over to the Volksbühne, who reconstructed it as a house where the State Opera
would put on performances for VB members. From 1924, when this had been
completed, the KrO was in effect run by the SO, who soon decided that it needed its
own company. This opened under Klemperer in 1927, but with the economic crisis of
1929 and the ensuing successes of the right-wing parties the Prussian Assembly forced it
to close in the summer of 1931. The Reichstag met there after the Fire, but otherwise it
was not subsequently used.

Städtische Oper (City Opera)   2,300 pl.
Prosc. width 13 m
StdO
Bismarckstrasse 34–37.

Intendant: Heinz Tietjen 1925–30 and 1949–
54, Kurt Singer (acting) 1931, Carl Ebert
1931–33 * W. Rode.
Conductor: Bruno Walter 1925–29. Assistant:
Fritz Stiedry 1928–33 * E. Jochum 1933, A.
Rothe.
Assistant artistic director: Rudolf Bing 1931–
33.

Opened as the Deutsches Opernhaus in 1912, it, too, at first belonged to the old
Charlottenburg municipality, then was transferred on the latter's incorporation in Berlin.
It opened under the new regime in 1925. In 1933 it resumed its old name and is now the
Deutsche Oper in West Berlin.

Volksbühne am Bülowplatz   2,000 pl.
Prosc. width 11.5 m
VB
Bülowplatz C25.

Artistic director: Max Reinhardt 1918,
Friedrich Kayssler 1919, Fritz Holl 1923,
Heinrich Neft 1928, Karlheinz Martin
1929, Heinz Hilpert 1932 * Solms 1934,
Klöpfer 1936–44.
Directors incl. Jürgen Fehling and Hilpert
1919–22, Erwin Piscator 1924–27, H. D.

Kenter 1930, H. Hinrich and K. H. Stroux
1931 * Kenter 1936–40, D. Sierck,
R. Weichert 1935–40.
Dramaturgs incl. Günther Stark 1930.
Designers incl. Oskar Schlemmer, Eduard
Suhr, Traugott Müller, Caspar Neher 1929,
Nina Tokumbet * J. Fenneker 1934, B. v.
Arent 1936–40.

Built by Oskar Kaufmann and opened 1914 by the Verband der freien Volksbühnen as
their own theatre, though they continued to make block bookings for members at other
houses. It was bankrupted in 1933 by the Berlin municipality and then taken over by the
Propaganda Ministry. Damaged in the Second World War, it was reopened in 1953 by
the East German VB. The Bülowplatz, renamed Horst-Wesselplatz by the Nazis, is now
the Rosa-Luxemburg-Platz.

2. Principal Independent Managements and Collectives

Reinhardt-Bühnen

Overall director: Max Reinhardt to 1933 *
Hilpert 1934–44.

Administrator: Edmund Reinhardt to 1929.

Included at different times the DT, DT KS, Kom, GS, the Schall und Rauch cabaret, and
the Vienna TidJ. Other theatres (e.g., the LT) might be rented for specific productions.
In 1933 Reinhardt left Germany and made his theatres over to the state, which put them
under the Propaganda Ministry, renaming the GS the Theater des Volkes. After 1945 the
DT, KS, and GS were taken over by the East German administration, the last-named
becoming the Friedrichstadt-Palais. It has now been demolished.

Meinhard and Bernauer

Directors: Carl Meinhard and Rudolf
Bernauer.

Dramaturg: Schanzer.
Designers incl. Rochus Gliese, Hermann
Krehan, and Benno von Arent.

Their main theatre prior to 1925 was the TidK. In addition they managed the BT, the
KomH, and the TamN (later associated with Piscator). Thereafter they virtually
abandoned management apart from the odd musical, till in 1935 they took back the TidK
and the KomH for one last year, with Max Ophüls as principal stage director.

Barnowsky

Director: Victor Barnowsky. Deputy: Ludwig
Körner.

Dramaturgs: Arthur Eloesser till 1920, Julius
Berstl, Lutz Weltmann, Fritz Walter 1931.
Designers incl. Carl Rachlis, César Klein,
Hermann Krehan, Erich Ernst Stern.
Other directors incl. Ralph Arthur Roberts,
Erich Engel, H. D. Kenter.

Barnowsky succeeded Brahm at the LT in 1913, managed it till 1924, but gave it up to the Rotter brothers. He then took over the TidK from Meinhard/Bernauer, along with the Tribüne and KomH. In 1931, having lost the Tribüne, he yielded the other two to the Rotters. Later he emigrated to the United States.

The Rotters

Directors: Alfred and Fritz Rotter, Fritz Friedemann-Frederich.

Dramaturgs and occasional directors incl. Georg Altmann, Robert Pirk, Oskar Kanehl, John Gottowt.

The Rotters were regarded as the black sheep of the Weimar theatre, with their preference for staging lucrative musicals and operettas of low quality. By 1922 they controlled the ResT and Reinhardt's old KT, then added the CenT and Trianon T, followed in 1924 by the LT. A number of provincial theatres also fell into their hands, notably in Breslau, Stettin and Dresden. The crisis of 1929–30 first lured them into further takeovers, then drove them into bankruptcy, and they became a particular target of the Nazis. Fleeing the country in spring 1933, Alfred committed suicide in Liechtenstein.

Saltenburg-Konzern

Director: Heinz Saltenburg. Deputies: Robert Klein to 1925, Rudolf Eger 1931.

Dramaturg: Otto Zarek.
Other directors incl. Emil Lind, Martin Zickel.
Designers incl. Ernst Stern, César Klein.

Formerly a producer of operettas, Saltenburg took over the LS in 1921, the DKT in 1925, and the TamS till 1927. That year he took the LT, followed later by the WT, BT, and TdesW. He was managing the LT in 1930–31.

Robert-Bühnen

Director: Eugen Robert.

Dramaturgs incl. Emil Geyer, Ernst Stahl-Nachbaur, Arthur Rabenalt.
Consultant designer: Eduard Suhr.

Managed the ResT 1920, the TamK (opened October 1921), and the Tribüne 1929–32.

Hellmer

Director: Arthur Hellmer.

Designer: Carl Zuckermandel.
Other directors incl. Berthold Viertel, Gustav Hartung.

Hellmer's main theatre was the Neues Theater in Frankfurt (q.v.), but in 1925–26 he was also managing the LT, KT, and TrianonT.

Aufricht-Produktion

Director: Ernst-Josef Aufricht. Deputy: Heinrich Fischer.

Dramaturgs: Robert Vambéry, Emil Hesse-
Burri.
Other directors incl. Erich Engel, Berthold
Viertel, Hans Hinrich.
Consultant designers: Caspar Neher, Eduard
Suhr.
Musical director: Theo Mackeben.

Managed TamS 1928–31. Subsequently rented TamK 1931–32, LS 1932. Aufricht
emigrated to France in 1933 and subsequently to New York. He returned to Berlin after
1945.

Piscatorbühnen   Director PB 1 and 2: Erwin Piscator 1927–29.
     PB   PB 3 was a collective 1930–31.

                                         Administrator: Otto Katz 1927–29.
                                         Principal dramaturgs: Felix Gasbarra, Leo
                                              Lania 1927. Others incl. Bertolt Brecht
                                              1927, F. Erpenbeck 1929, Franz Jung 1930.
                                         Designers incl. Traugott Müller 1927–30,
                                              László Moholy-Nágy, George Grosz, John
                                              Heartfield, Wolfgang Böttcher (PB3 only).
                                         Music incl. Edmund Meisel, Kurt Weill,
                                              Hanns Eisler.
                                         Film: Alex Strasser; Curt Oertel.

Leased TamN 1927–29, LT 1928 and 1930, WT 1930–31. Dissolved 1931 after Piscator had
moved to the USSR. Though later he emigrated to the U.S., returning to West Germany
in 1951, he never tried to reestablish the Piscatorbühne.

Gruppe junger Schauspieler   Collective 1929–31.
     GjS
                                         Administration: R. Bernt, W. Pledath.
                                         Directors: Hans Deppe, Wolfgang Böttcher.
                                         Dramaturg: Kurt Werther

An actors' collective formed after the failure of the first PB. It played in the ThaliaT, the
LT, and other available theatres during the economic crisis.

3. Berlin Private Theatres

This includes those used by the above managements. It is not an exhaustive listing, since it omits disused or mainly inactive theatres, along
with some which were mainly used as cinemas. The most important
houses are given in bold type. Proscenium widths are quoted only for
those then ranked among the 74 largest theatres in the country (excluding
variety theatres etc.).

Admiralspalast 2–3,000 pl.   Director: Leo Bachuschek 1925, Hermann
     AdP   Haller till 1931, Aufricht 1932–33 * Robert
     Friedrichstrasse 101.   Liedemit.

Used for revues, musicals, and ice shows. Rebuilt 1930. Closed 1934–36. In 1938–39 W. Felsenstein was operetta director under W. Hochtritt's direction. After 1945 it housed the State Opera while the latter's building on Unter den Linden was reconstructed.

Apollo-Theater   1,350 pl.   Director: James Klein in 1920s.

Berliner Theater   1,450 pl.   Meinhard/Bernauer to 1925.
   BT
   Charlottenstrasse 90–92, SW 68.   Directors thereafter: Maximilian Sladek 1926,
                                             Robert Klein 1929, Joachim von Ostau
                                             1930 * Gollong, Seifert 1933–34.
                                           Dramaturgs: Otto Zarek, Emil Lind.
                                           Directors incl. Hilpert 1930, Lothar Körner
                                             1931.
                                           Designers incl. Rochus Gliese, E. E. Stern.

   Was closed during 1931–32 season.

Casino-Theater   700 pl.   Owner/director Hans Berg.
   CasT
   Lothringerstrasse 37,N 54.

   Used for variety 1933–34.

Central-Theater   1,000 pl.   Owned 1920 by Metropol-T. Director: Emil
   CenT   Berisch. Rotters 1925. Various lessees
   Kommandantenstrasse 57, S 14.   1931–34.
   or Alte Jakobstrasse 30–32, SW 68.   Artistic director: Martin Zickel 1920, Erwin
                                             Piscator 1922.
                                           Design consultant: Edward Suhr 1922.

   Built 1906, was Eden T till its reconstruction in 1920. Also known as Zentral-T, T in der Alten Jakobstrasse, and T in der Stadt. Housed Piscator and Rehfisch's short-lived Proletarische Volksbühne. Was closed from 1934.

Deutsches Theater   1,000 pl.   Owned by Reinhardt till 1933. * Reich theatre
   Prosc. width 8.5 m   1934–45.
   DT
   Schumannstrasse 12–13a.   Artistic directors: Felix Holländer 1920–23,
                                             Karl Rosen 1923, A. J. Licho 1925, Robert
                                             Klein 1926–29, Carl Achaz and Heinrich
                                             Neft 1933 * Hilpert 1934–44.
                                           Dramaturgs incl: Arthur Kahane, Felix
                                             Holländer, Heinz Herald * W. Drews
                                           Stage directors incl. Erich Engel 1924,
                                             Alexander Granowsky, Heinz Hilpert
                                             1926–29 * Engel 1935, G. Haenel 1938.
                                           Principal designers: Ernst Stern to 1920,
                                             Hermann Krehan, Caspar Neher 1924–26,
                                             Ernst Schütte 1926 to 1940s.
                                           Musical directors: Einar Nilson, Erich
                                             Korngold * E. Mausz.

Kammerspiele   300 pl.
DT KS
Schumannstrasse 14.

The Deutsches Theater was built by the playwright Adolf L'Arronge and leased by him in 1894 to Otto Brahm. Reinhardt and his brother Edmund took it over in 1906, and within a year had added the Kammerspiele by converting the adjoining dance hall. After the First World War the two theatres became somewhat peripheral to Reinhardt's other interests, but they remained his property until he made them over to the nation in 1933. Following the Nazi interlude they were reopened as the principal East Berlin theatre, headed first by Gustav von Wangenheim, then after 1946 by Wolfgang Langhoff, under whose regime they were also used by Brecht's Berliner Ensemble from 1949–53.

Deutsches Künstler-Theater   1,050 pl.   Barnowsky management 1915–24, Saltenburg
DKT   1925, Robert Klein 1929–30, Robert 1930–
Nürnbergerstrasse 70/71, W. 50.   31, Barnowsky 1931–32 * Leased to H.
                                                       Wölffer 1934. Annexed to ST 1936.

                                                       Stage directors incl. Emil Lind, Reinhold
                                                       Bruck, Gustav Hartung 1926.

Built in 1911 by Hildebrandt and Nikolaus and converted in 1913 by Oskar Kaufmann for a collective of actors who left the LT after Brahm's death. This included Gerhart Hauptmann, who directed the opening production. Barnowsky took over after two years, again linking the theatre to the LT. Under the Nazis it became the KH of the ST under Gründgens in 1935–36.

Grosses Schauspielhaus   3,000 pl.   Owned by National-Theater AG (formed by
Prosc. width 13 m   the Reinhardts) to 1931, Rotter brothers
GS   1932 * Kraft durch Freude 1934.
Am Zirkus 1 (Karlstrasse).
                                                Directors: Maximilian Sladek 1923, Karl
                                                   Rosen 1926, * W. Brügmann 1934–37, O.
                                                   Maurenbrecher.
                                                Artistic Directors: Max Reinhardt and
                                                   Karlheinz Martin 1919–24, Erik Charell
                                                   1925–31, Heinz Herald 1931–32.
                                                Principal designer: Ernst Stern 1919–31.

Converted by Hans Poelzig from former Schumann Circus building and opened in 1919. Closed during 1933–34, then renamed Theater des Volkes. Damaged by bombing 1944. Reopened 1945 as Friedrichstadt-Palais, an East Berlin variety and operetta theatre. Being demolished 1985.

Goethe-Bühnen (see Theater in der Klosterstrasse).

Grosse Volksoper (see Theater des Westens).

Hebbel-Theater (see Theater in der Königgrätzerstrasse).

Intimes Theater   320 pl.
  Bülowstrasse 6.

Opened under Anton Herrnfeld's direction in 1921.

Kleines Schauspielhaus
  Charlottenburg, Fasanenstrasse 1

Opened by Maximilian Sladek in the Hochschule für Musik for the first production of
Schnitzler's *Reigen (La Ronde)* in 1920. Not known to have functioned subsequently.

Kleines Theater   400 pl.   Directors: Georg Altmann c.1920, A. and F.
  KT   Rotter 1924, Kurt Hellmer 1926, Fritz
  Unter den Linden 44.   Friedemann-Frederich 1929.

Originally opened as Reinhardt's Schall und Rauch cabaret in 1901, this became his KT
the following year, where he staged *Salomé* and *The Lower Depths*. It seems to have been
closed at some point in 1931–32, then for two seasons was used for guest performances.
Under the Nazis it was renamed Theater unter den Linden, then again closed in 1938.

Komische Oper   1,200 pl.   Directors: Gustav Charlé 1919, James Klein
  Friedrichstrasse 104–104a, NW 7.   1921, Martin Zickel 1929 * E. Wenck 1933,
                                       K. K. Strickrodt 1934, H. Horak 1938.

Reconstructed 1915 and 1929. Used for musicals and operettas. Walter Felsenstein's East
Berlin opera of the same name opened in December 1947 in the former Metropol-T.

Komödie   500 pl.   Owner: Emil Heinicke AG. Lessees: Max
  Kom.   Reinhardt 1925 * W. Hoffmann-Harnisch
  Kurfürstendamm 206, W 15.   1934, H. Wölffer 1935–40.

Built by Oskar Kaufmann for intimate comedy and a West End audience and opened on
1 November 1924. This, rather than the DT, was at first Reinhardt's counterpart to the
Vienna TidJ. It was shut in 1932–33, subsequently separating entirely from the DT.

Komödienhaus   750 pl.   Under Meinhard/Bernauer management to
  Kom H   1924 and in 1932–33, Barnowsky 1925–31.
  Am Schiffbauerdamm 25.

After 1933 came under a number of different managements.

Lessingtheater   1,140 pl.   Management: Barnowsky to 1924, A. and F.
  Prosc. width 9.7 m   Rotter 1925, Hellmer 1926, Saltenburg
  LT   1927 and 1930–31, A. and F. Rotter 1932–
  Friedrich-Karl-Ufer 1, NW 40.   33 * R. Handwerk.

Had been Otto Brahm's theatre after he lost the DT to Reinhardt. From 1925 on, had a
somewhat patchy career, being rented often by such companies as the DT, the GjS, and
the first and third PBs. Now destroyed.

Lustspielhaus   600 pl.
  LS
  Friedrichstrasse 236, SW 48.

Direction: Saltenburg 1924, Martin Zickel 1929, Curt Goetz 1930, A. and F. Rotter 1931–33 * E. Pabst 1937.

Known after 1933 as Theater in der Friedrichstrasse. Closed 1933–37.

Metropol-Theater   1,800 pl.
  MetT
  Behrensstrasse 55–57, W 8.

Direction: Fritz Friedemann-Frederich, Rotter brothers 1930, * W. Tholen 1933, H. Hentschke 1938.

Formerly Theater unter den Linden. Used for operettas. Renovated 1928. Taken over as the East Berlin Komische Oper after 1945.

Nelson-Theater (See Theater der Komiker).

Neues Operettenhaus, Neues Theater (See Theater am Schiffbauerdamm).

Neues Theater am Zoo   800 pl.

Directors: Gustav Charlé 1924, A. Gerusch.

Opened in 1921 for operettas. Closed from 1933.

Neues Volkstheater
  NVT

Opened in 1920 as a second theatre for the VB, which gave it up in summer 1922.

Ostend-Theater (see Rose-Theater).

Renaissance-Theatre   620 pl.
  RenT
  Charlottenburg, Hardenbergstr. 6.

Directors: Theodor Tagger (Ferdinand Bruckner) 1922, Gustav Hartung 1927, Robert Klein 1930 * A. Bernau 1934–40. Other directors incl. Ludwig Berger, Karlheinz Martin, Heinz Hilpert.

Enlarged in 1927. Closed for the 1932–33 season.

Residenz-Theater   700 pl.
  ResT
  Blumenstrasse 9, 0 27.

Director: Eugen Robert 1920, Felix Meinhard 1925, Martin Zickel 1926?

Reconstructed 1929–30, but thereafter appears not to have been used as a theatre.

Rose-Theater   1,100 pl.
  Grosse Frankfurterstr. 132, 0 17.

Directors: Bernard Rose 1920, Emma Rose 1930, * H and P. Rose 1935.

Popular theatre in Berlin East End.

Schiller-Theater Ost (See Wallner-Theater).

Schlosspark-Theater   470 pl.
  Schloss-Strasse 48, Steglitz.

Directors: Paul Henckels and Hans Lebede
  1921, S. von Lutz 1929, Hans Junkermann
  1932.

Opened 12 March 1921, renamed Schauspielhaus Steglitz in 1932. Closed from 1934, but
survived World War II to become a West Berlin theatre directed by Boleslav Barlog.

Thalia-Theater   1,100 pl.
  Dresdenerstrasse 72–73, S 14.

Directors: Jean Kren, Karl Platen 1924, Kurt
  Berendt 1929.

Was formerly the Adolf-Ernst-Theater. Did some productions for the VB between 1926–
1929. Closed during 1932–33; thereafter taken by the Stettin Singers but closed from
1936.

Theater am Hermannplatz   2,200 pl.
  Urbanstrasse 72–76, S 59.

Director: Hans-Otto Fricke 1933.

Built in 1928, closed 1934–35.

Theater am Kurfürstendamm   800 pl.
  TamK
  Kurfürstendamm 208–9, W 15.

Direction: Robert-Bühnen 1921, Reinhardt
  1931 * Van der Straaten and Hochtritt
  1933, A. Straub.

Stage directors incl. Wolfgang Hoffmann-
  Harnisch, Robert Pirk.

A West End theatre, opened October 1921 and rebuilt by Oskar Kaufmann in 1930. From
1931 to 1933 was a second theatre for the DT. From 1935–39 it was the Agnes-Straub-
Theater, under the direction of the actress; Liebeneiner, Harlan, and Günter Weisenborn
were among her stage directors. It survived the Second World War, to open in
September 1949 as the theatre of the West Berlin VB, where first O. F. Schuh and then
Erwin Piscator were artistic directors.

Theater am Nollendorfplatz   1,100 pl.
  Prosc. width 10 m
  TaN
  Nollendorfplatz 5, W 30.

Direction: Hermann Haller 1920, Meinhard/
  Bernauer 1924, first Piscatorbühne 1927,
  Reinhold Bruck 1928, Ludwig Klopfer (for
  second PB) 1929, A. and F. Rotter 1930,
  Saltenburg 1932 * W. Jenkuhn 1933, Solms
  1936, H. Paulsen 1938.

Used mainly for operetta, musicals, etc., except between 1927–29. Was closed during
1930–31. Taken over in 1935 by the Nazi Kulturgemeinde and linked to the VB. Is now a
cinema.

Theater am Schiffbauerdamm   890 pl.
  TaS
  Am Schiffbauerdamm 4a.

Direction: Saltenburg 1925, Aufricht 1928–31,
  Wolf Leutheiser 1932.

Built in 1880s, became Neues Theater under Reinhardt, then Neues Operetten-Theater. Came under various managements under the Nazis and was renovated in 1936. Survived Second World War to become part of E. Berlin VB under Fritz Wisten, then in 1953 was allocated to Brecht's Berliner Ensemble. Now called T. Am Bertolt Brecht-Platz.

Theater der Komiker 1,000 pl. TderK Kurfürstendamm 156, W 15.	Director: Rudolf Nelson, Kurt Robitschek 1928.

Started as the 300-place Nelson-Theater, which was enlarged and reopened as the TderK on 19 September 1928. Closed 1933, reopened 1938–39 with W. Schaefers as lessee.

Theater des Westens 1,700 pl. TdW Charlottenburg 2, Kantstrasse 9–12.	Direction: Beese and Bieber, Otto W. Lange 1922, Carl Richter 1925, A. and F. Rotter 1929, Saltenburg 1930.

Rented by Lange for the Grosse Volksoper, which he had launched in 1919, and which collapsed in 1924. Normally used for operetta, musicals etc. Taken over 1935 to be a Volksoper again with E. Orthmann as Intendant.

Theater im Palmenhaus
TiP
Kurfürstendamm 193–94.

Was closed 1929–30.

Theater in der Alten Jakobsstrasse (See Central-T).

Theater in der Behrensstrasse 580 pl. Behrensstrasse 53–54, W 8.	Director: Ralph Arthur Roberts 1929–40. Designer: Benno von Arent.

Opened 17 September 1928. Used for matinees by The English Players and for light comedies. Adjoining the Komische Oper. Note the continuity of direction.

Theater in der Friedrichstrasse (See Lustspielhaus).

Theater in der Klosterstrasse 780 pl. TidKlo Klosterstrasse 43, C 2.	Director: R. Pirk 1925, Franz Sondinger 1929.

Was built in 1924 and closed from 1933 on. Used by the NS VB in 1930.

Theater in der Königgrätzerstrasse 750 pl. TidK Königgrätzerstrasse 57–58, SW 11.	Direction: Meinhard/Bernauer 1911–24, Barnowsky 1925 * Legal/Raeck 1934, Ingolf/Kuntze 1936.

This street became renamed Stresemannstrasse c. 1930, which the Nazis changed after 1933 to Saarlandstrasse. The theatre's name changed accordingly. In 1936 it became linked to the VB, then after the Second World War the name was altered by Karlheinz Martin, its then director, to the much earlier Hebbel-Theater.

Theater in der Kommandantenstrasse. (See Central-Theater.)

Theater in der Lützowstrasse   800 pl.   Director: Max Samst.
   Lützowstrasse 111–12, W 35.

   In the Kammermusikhaus. Opened on 4 September 1925; had closed by 1930.

Theater in der Saarlandstrasse or Stresemannstrasse (See TidKöniggrätzerstrasse).

Theater in der Stadt (See Central-Theater).

Trianon-Theater   550 pl.   Direction: Emil Lessing 1918, Alfred Rotter
   Georgenstrasse 9, NW 7.   1919, Hellmer 1925, Leo Walter Stein
                                                     1929.

   Was renovated and reopened on 30 August 1929. Closed apparently within a year.

Die Tribüne   300 pl.   Director: F. Mellinger 1919, Eugen Robert
   Tr   1929–33.
   Berliner Strasse 31, Charlottenburg.   Designers incl. Robert Neppach 1919,
                                                     Edward Suhr 1929.

   The Tribüne closed in 1935, reopened briefly, then in 1937 became the ST acting school.

Walhalla-Theater   1,750 pl.   Direction: Bernhard Rose 1919, Max Samst
   WhT   1929 * G. Schenck 1934.
   Weinbergstrasse 18–20, N 54.

   Mainly an operetta house. Shut during 1931–32 season, and again from 1935.

Wallner-Theater   1,200 pl.   Direction: Saltenburg 1919, Maximilian
   WT   Sladek 1920, NS-Volksbühne 1929, Third
   Wallnerstrasse 35, 0 27.   Piscatorbühne 1930–31, Alfred Probeck
                                                     1931–32, G. Manzel

   Originally a Schillertheater-Ost under the same management as the Schiller-Theater proper. Was closed in 1933.

Provincial and Other German-Language Theatres

Listed by town (with approximate population in 1930). Abbreviations follow the same principles as before—i.e., generally S for state, Std for city, T for

theatre, O for opera, G for big (Gross), K for small (Klein), H for Haus, LT for
Landestheater (Regional Theatre), KS for Kammerspiele, etc. Usually the
biggest theatre in any city was used for opera. Once again, the list is not
exhaustive; bold type is used for the most important houses; and proscenium
widths are given only for the biggest of them, variety and operetta theatres
excluded.

Aachen 154,000	Stadttheater 1,100 pl.	Chief conductor * H. v. Karajan, 1934–40.
Augsburg 170,000	Stadttheater 1,300 pl. Prosc. width 12.5 m	
Barmen (see Wuppertal).		
Baden-Baden 30,000	Städtische Schauspiele (Land and City subsidy): (a) Grosse Bühne (Kurhaus) 1,200 pl. (b) Kammerspiele 300 pl. (c) Kleines Theater 750 pl.	Intendant: H. Grussendorf 1930. Musical Director: Ernst Mehlich
Basel 155,000	**Stadttheater** 1,130 pl. (City subsidy)	Director: Leo Melitz sen. 1918, Ernst Lert 1919, Otto Henning 1925. Artistic director: Oskar Wälterlin 1925, Egon Neudegg 1932–40. Stage directors incl. Gustav Hartung 1937–40, Alfred Braun 1937, Kurt Horwitz 1938. Conductor: Felix Weingartner 1934–38. Designer: Cajo Kühnly, Hugo Schmitt 1934–36, André Perrotet 1936–40.
Bern 113,000	(a) **Stadttheater** 1,100 pl.	Director: A. Kehm 1919, K. L. Peppler 1925, Hans Kaufmann 1926, 1932, Karl Lustig-Prenn 1931, 1933, Hans Zimmermann 1934–37, Eugen Keller 1937. Stage directors incl. F. Jessner 1937, W. Brügmann 1939, Sigfrit Steiner 1939.

(b) Kammerspiele
(c) Schänzlitheater   1,000 pl.   Opened 9 November 1933.

Bochum Opened end 1925.	Stadttheater 1,000 pl.	Intendant * Saladin Schmitt 1935–40.

Braunschweig
  150,000
	(a) Landestheater 1,600 pl.
	     Prosc. width 11.5 m
		Intendant: Julius Frh. von
		  Wangenheim 1918, Hans
		  Kaufmann 1925, Thur
		  Himmighoffen 1930 * O.
		  Walleck 1933, A. Schum
		  1934–40.

	(b) Kammerspiele 340 pl. (c) Neues Operetten-Theater	

(c) was opened on 1 January 1929 and had 1,100 places.

Bremen
  305,000
	(a) **Stadttheater** 1,700 pl.
	     Prosc. width 10.7 m
		Intendant: Julius Otto 1925,
		  Willy Becker 1930 * C. Gerdes
		  1934–40.
		Director and dramaturg: Walter
		  Dworkowski 1919.

	(b) Schauspielhaus 800 pl.	Direction: J. Wiegand and E.
		  Ichon 1925–40.
		Chief directors incl. Detlef Sierck
		  1925.

Other theatres included the Thalia- (or Deutsches) Theater and the 2,000-seat Tivoli operetta theatre (municipal). (a), used for opera and plays, was owned by the state of Bremen.

Breslau
  600,000
	(a) **Stadttheater** 1,300 pl.
	     prosc. width 10.7 m
	     (Opera, subsidized by Lower
	     Silesia and city.)
		Intendant: H. Tietjen 1924, J.
		  Turnau 1925, G. Hartmann
		  1929 * M.Berg-Ehlert 1933.
		Producers incl. Felix Klee 1929.
		Designers incl. Oskar
		  Schlemmer 1929, J. Hahlo
		  1930.

	(b) Vereinigte Theater:	Intendant: R. Gerter 1918, Paul Barnay 1924.

	Lobe-Theater 1,100 pl.
	Thalia-Theater 1,350 pl.
		Directors incl. Hans von
		  Wolzogen, Leo Mittler 1924,
		  Renato Mordo 1925, Max
		  Ophüls 1929.

Also an operetta theatre, the Schauspielhaus, seating 1,700, and a 550-seat Kammerspiele, which was opened in 1932 by the Deutsche Bühne e.V., a nationalist organization. In 1933 the KS director W. Bäuerle replaced Barnay at the privately owned Lobe-T, which now came under the Nazi-appointed opera Intendant Berg-Ehlert. The

Thalia-T was owned by the Breslau VB and renamed Gerhart-Hauptmann Theater in 1930. By 1937 it had closed.

Breslau became incorporated in Poland after the Second World War and is now called Wrocław. Among the eminent actors to have passed through Barnay's theatres were Giehse, Käthe Gold, Lederer, Lorre, Carola Neher, and Karl Paryla.

Brno (Czechoslovakia) 221,000	(a) Stadttheater 1,300 pl.	Director: Rudolf Beer 1918, Franz and Georg Hoellering 1921, Julius Herzka, Hans Demetz 1926, Felix Knüpfer 1932, Leopold Kramer 1933–38 * A. Modes 1939.
	(b) Deutsches Schauspielhaus 620 pl. (c) Deutsches Haus (operetta) 720 pl.	

These three theatres became grouped together as Vereinigte Deutsche Theater.

Chemnitz
350,000
	(a) Städtische Oper 1,300 pl.
	  Prosc. width 10.5 m
	(b) Städtisches Schauspielhaus 1,030 pl.
	  Prosc. width 9.5 m	

Now a leading industrial center in the GDR, Chemnitz has been renamed Karl Marx-Stadt.

Cologne (See Köln).

Danzig 240,000	Städtisches Theater 1,100 pl. Prosc. width 9.5 m

Now incorporated in Poland as Gdańsk.

Darmstadt 90,000	**Hessisches Landestheater** Grosses Haus 1,370 pl. Prosc. width 12.4 m	Intendant: Adolf Kraetzer 1918, Gustav Hartung 1921–24 and 1931–33, Ernst Legal 1924, Carl Ebert 1927–31 * R.Prasch 1933, F. Everth 1934. Conductors: Josef Rosenstock 1925, Karl Böhm 1927, Hans Schmidt-Isserstedt 1931–33.
	Kleines Haus 812 pl.	Dramaturgs: Peter Suhrkamp, H. D. Kenter and Arthur Rabenalt 1922, Jakob Geis 1924, Paul Kornfeld 1927, Carl Werckshagen 1929, Kurt Hirschfeld 1931–33. Designers: Lothar Schenck von Trapp 1924–33, Arthur Pohl 1924–27, Wilhelm Reinking 1927–34.

Directors incl. Günther Haenel
and Renato Mordo 1928–32.

Dessau 70,000	Friedrich-Theater 1,200 pl. Prosc. width 10 m	
Dortmund 536,000	(a) Städtisches Theater 1,200 pl. Prosc. width 11 m (b) Burgwall-Theater 1,400 pl.	

Dresden
630,000

(a) Sächsische Staatstheater:

Oper 1,800 pl.
Prosc. width 13 m

Schauspielhaus 1,300 pl.
Prosc. width 11.5 m

General-Intendant: Graf v.
Seebach 1918, Alfred Reucker
1922–33 *P. Adolph 1933.
Generalmusikdirektor: Fritz
Busch 1922–33 * K. Böhm.
Theatre director: Georg Kiesau
1929–33.
Stage directors incl. Berthold
Viertel 1918, Lothar Mehnert
1922–27, Josef Gielen 1929–
36.
Dramaturg: Karl Wolff 1923–33 *
W. Nufer 1933–34.
Designer: Adolf Mahnke.

(b) **Albert-Theater** 1,300pl.
(private)

Director: Paul Willi 1918,
Hermine Körner 1925, Hans
Fischer 1926, H. W. Philipp
1927, Wolf Leutheiser 1930,
Paul Medenwald 1931, R. Pirk
1932 * H. W. Philipp 1933, P.
Rainer 1934.
Stage directors incl. Leo Mittler
1922–23, Paul Verhoeven
1925–30.
Dramaturg: Hans von Wild 1922–
24.

Dresden had several other theatres, including two operetta houses, the private Thalia-
Theater and Fritz Fischer's Die Komödie, a 700-seat private theatre built in 1926. In 1933
the Nazis replaced Reucker and Busch by P. Adolph and Karl Böhm. R. Schroeder
became director of the Schauspielhaus with Gielen under him and Wilfred Nufer (an SS
member) as his dramaturg. The (hitherto private) Albert-Theater was municipalized and
in 1935 was renamed Theater des Volkes. Since 1945 the Intendants of the Dresden State
theatres have included Karl von Appen and Martin Hellberg.

Düsseldorf
454,000

(a) Städtische Theater:

Intendant: Ludwig
Zimmermann 1918, Willy
Becker 1922, Heinz Hille
1925, W. B. Iltz 1927–37, * O.
Krauss 1938.

Opernhaus 1,400 pl.
Prosc. width 10 m.

Kleines Haus 910 pl.

Conductors incl: Georg Szell 1922–24, Rudolf Schwarz 1927–28, Jascha Horenstein 1928–33 * H. Balzer.
Dramaturgs incl. Kurt Heynicke 1927–28, Rudolf Frank 1928–29, H. J. Weitz 1929–34 * A. Schneider 1934.
Stage directors incl. A. Pohl 1927, Leopold Lindtberg, Wolfgang Langhoff and Felix Klee 1932 * Hannes Küpper 1933–37.
Designers incl. G. Hacker and T. Schlonski 1921–28, H. Jürgens 1930–35.

(b) **Schauspielhaus** 1,000 pl.
Prosc. width 9.2 m

Directors: Louise Dumont/ Gustav Lindemann to 1933.
Deputies: Paul Henckels 1918, Felix Emmel 1924.
Dramaturg: Kurt Heynicke 1924–26.
Music director: Hans Curjel 1924–26.
Designers inc. Knut Strom 1918, Eduard Sturm 1922.
Stage directors incl. Berthold Viertel 1924–25.

Louise Dumont died in May 1932. The following year Lindemann, her husband, left the theatre, which was then added to the city theatres under Iltz, who was left in his post as Intendant till 1937. In all other respects the Nazis appear to have made fewer changes in Düsseldorf than in most other major theatre centers.

Erfurt
148,000

Städtisches Theater 1050 pl.

Intendant: H. Maisch 1930, Paul Legband 1931–33 * Hptm a. D. Krause 1934.

Essen
643,000

Städtische Bühnen:

Intendant: Willy Becker 1918, Stanislaus Fuchs 1922–32 * A. Noller 1933.

Opernhaus 800 pl.
Prosc. width 7.5 m

Opera director: Ferdinand Drost 1922, Felix Wolfes 1924–27, Rudolf Schulz-Dornburg 1927–32, Ewald Lengstorff 1932–33.

Schauspielhaus 630 pl.
Prosc. width 9 m

Theatre director: Ferdinand Sebrecht 1926 and 1929–31, Martin Kerb 1927–28, Alfred Noller 1931–33.

Dramaturg: Rudolf Düsing 1923,
Hannes Küpper 1927–33 * C.
Werckshagen 1933.
Designers: Hein Heckroth 1926–
33, Caspar Neher 1927–31 *
Rochus Gliese 1933.

There was a major reconstruction of both theatres in summer 1927.

Frankfurt-am-Main   (a) Vereinigte Städtische   General Intendant: Carl Zeiss
550,000   Theater: 1918–20 * H. Meissner 1933,
                                                           deputy H. Bethge.

                        Opernhaus   1750 pl.   Conductors: Gustav Brecher, L.
                            Prosc. width 12m   Rottenberg 1918–28, Wilhelm
                                                           Steinberg 1930.
                                                        Opera director: Clemens Krauss
                                                           1924–29, Josef Turnau 1929–
                                                           33.
                                                        Producers: Lothar Wallerstein,
                                                           Herbert Graf * O. Wälterlin
                                                           1933, W. Felsenstein 1934, G.
                                                           Rennert 1936.

                        Schauspielhaus 1200 pl.   Theatre Intendant: Richard
                            Prosc. width 11 m   Weichert 1922, Alwin
                        Kammerspiele   310 pl   Kronacher 1929.
                                                        Stage directors incl. Walter
                                                           Brügmann 1918, Gustav
                                                           Hartung 1918–22, Heinz
                                                           Hilpert 1926, F. P. Buch 1929,
                                                           Jakob Geis 1932–34.
                                                        Designers incl. F. K. Delavilla
                                                           1918, Ludwig Sievert 1922–
                                                           37, Heinz Hamann 1931 * C.
                                                           Neher 1934.
                                                        Dramaturgs: Hermann Bürger
                                                           1922–30, F. P. Buch 1924–33,
                                                           Arthur Sakheim 1927–31,
                                                           Jakob Geis 1932.

                        (b) **Neues Theater** 800 pl. Directors: Arthur Hellmer 1918–
                                                           35, Max Reimann 1918–c. 22.
                                                        Stage directors: Clemens Wrede,
                                                           Otto Wallburg, Max Ophüls
                                                           1927–28, Hans von Wild 1928,
                                                           Renato Mordo 1929–33.
                                                        Design consultant: Julius Hahlo
                                                           1918.

There was also a VB branch called the Künstlertheater and another private theatre, the Intimes Theater. In 1933 Josef Turnau went into exile and Hans Meissner took over the opera as General-Intendant, with the playwright Hans Bethge—who also became the Nazi Gau Kulturwart—as his deputy. The city took over the Neues Theater in 1935 and renamed it the Kleines Haus. Among the actors who had played in the company there were Graetz, Klöpfer, Lingen, and Wallburg, while former SH members included Fritta Brod, Mary Dietrich, Ebert, Johanna Hofer, Constanze Menz, Gerda Müller, Odemar, Leontine Sagan, and Renée Stobrawa.

Freiburg im Breisgau 90,000	Stadttheater 1,200 pl. Prosc. width 11m	
Gera 83,000	Reuss'sches Theater 1100 pl. Prosc. width 9m	Intendant: Walter Bruno Iltz 1925. Director of productions: Paul Medenwaldt 1919, Karl Rosen 1929–34.

A survival from pre-1918 Germany. This was a private theatre run by the hereditary princes of Reuss.

Giessen 35,000	Stadttheater 850 pl.	Director: Hermann Steingoetter (from 1903), Rolf Prasch 1930–33 * H. König.

Gladbach-Rheydt
200,000
	(a) Stadttheater 1100 pl.
	    Kammerspiele 500 pl.
	(b) Rheydt Schauspielhaus
	    400 pl.	

Görlitz 95,000	Stadttheater 1,000 pl.	Intendant: W. O. Stahl 1930–32 * P. Hoenselaers 1933. Dramaturg: Hans Doerry.
Gotha	Landestheater 988 pl. Prosc. width 8.6 m	Intendant: Rolf Roennecke to 1930, Curt Strickrodt 1932–33.

Linked 1930 with Altenburg Stadttheater (1,100 seats) under the Weimar Intendant Franz Ulbrich.

Hagen 150,000	Stadttheater 950 pl.	
Halberstadt 50,000	Stadttheater 900 pl.	

Halle an der Saale
203,000
	(a) Stadttheater 1,200 pl.
	    Prosc. width 9.5 m
	(b) Thalia-Theater 850 pl.
	
	(c) Mitteldeutsches
	    Landestheater
		
		Directors: Leopold Sachse 1919,
		W. Dietrich 1925–34.
		Directors: Ernst Rescha and
		Hermann Lange.

(c) was a traveling theatre which formed part of the VB organization. Halle also had a 2,600-seat operetta theatre and the Modernes Theater (or Kammerspiele) seating 400.

Hamburg 1 million	(a) **Stadttheater** (opera) 1,800 pl. Prosc. width 12.6 m.	Intendant: Leopold Sachse 1922–33 * H. K. Strohm. Musical director: Egon Pollak, Karl Böhm 1931–33, * E. Jochum 1934. Deputy: H. Schmidt-Isserstedt 1935. Producers incl. O. F. Schuh 1932–40. Designers: Bernd Steiner 1922 * G. Richter 1933, W. Reinking 1934, C. Neher 1941.
	(b) Vereinigte Schauspielbühnen:	Generaldirektor: Hermann Röbbeling 1928–32.
	Deutsches Schauspielhaus 1,850 pl. Prosc. width 11m	Directors: Paul Eger and Ernst Koehne 1919, Karl Wüstenhagen 1932–40. Stage directors incl. Arnold Marlé 1924, Erich Ziegel 1926–28, Hans Wengraf, Adolf Winds, Günter Haenel 1932–38. Designers incl. H. Groninger 1924, H. Daniel 1927, G. Buchholz 1930–32.
	Thalia-Theater 1,300 pl.	Director: Hermann Röbbeling 1919–28.
	(c) **Kammerspiele** (private)	Directors Erich Ziegel 1920, and Miriam Horwitz 1926. Stage directors incl. Fritz Jessner, Ernst Matray, Gustav Gründgens 1924–28, Hans Schalla 1929–30. Dramaturg: Erich Engel before 1919, Arthur Sakheim. Designer: Johannes Schroeder 1926–34.

There were several other theatres in Hamburg and the neighbouring Altona, whose Stadttheater was linked to that at Hamburg. After the Nazis came to power the latter became the State Theatre under the General-Intendant H. K. Strohm. The Kammerspiele moved from its 330-seat theatre in 1932 and took the Thalia-T (hitherto linked to the DSH), but closed in 1934–35, after which the Ziegels moved to the ST in Berlin. Among the actors who had been through their theatre were Kortner, Anni Mewes, Hubert von Meyerinck, Werner Hinz, Friedrich Gnass, and Wolfgang Heinz. Meanwhile the old theatre became the Kleines Schauspielhaus under Friedrich Lobe, whose actors included Albin Skoda and Annemarie Hase.

Hannover
450,000

Städtische Bühnen:

	Intendant or director: Willy Grunwalt 1923, Arthur Pfahl 1928–34.
Opernhaus 1,700 pl. Prosc. width 11.5 m	Music director: Rudolf Krasselt 1925–38. Ballet mistress: Yvonne Georgi 1928–36.
Schauspielhaus (formerly Schauburg) 1,000 pl. Prosc. width 9 m	Director: Rolf Roennecke 1923–27, Georg Altmann 1928–33 * A. Pape 1934. Dramaturg: Johann Frerking 1924–27. Design consultant: Heinz Porep 1923, Kurt Söhnlein 1929–38.

Deutsches Theater   830 pl. (rented to private lessees and closed in 1933–34).

Heidelberg
80,000

Stadttheater   820 pl.

Heilbronn
46,000

Stadttheater   900 pl.

Jena
48,000

Stadttheater   900 pl.

Karlsruhe
150,000

Badisches Landestheater   1500 pl.

General-Intendant: August Bassermann 1919, Robert Volkner 1923, Hans Waag 1927 * T. Himmighoffen 1933.
Generalmusikdirektor: Josef Krips 1927 and Rudolf Schwarz 1928 * J. Keilberth 1935.
Dramaturg: Otto Kienscher 1923–34.
Stage directors incl. Felix Baumbach 1926, H. E. Mützenbecher 1930.
Designers: Emil Burkhard 1923, Torsten Hecht 1928 * H. Zircher 1934.

Kassel
175,000

Staatliches Theater   1,400 pl.
Prosc. width 10m

Intendant: Paul Bekker 1925–27, Max Berg-Ehlert, Edgar Klitsch 1933 * W. Holthoff v. Fassmann 1934, F. Ulbrich 1936.

Conductors: Robert Laugs 1930 *
R. Heger 1936.
Stage directors: Walter Sieg, Fritz
Berend, F. Siems, Jakob Geis
1930.
Designers incl. Ludwig Schenk
von Trapp 1931–32.
Theatre conductor: Maurice
d'Abravanel 1930.

Kleines Theater   380 pl.

Directors incl. Rudolf
Scheurmann, Otto Clemm,
Hans von Wild.
Designer: Helmut Schubert 1930.

The Kassel, like the Wiesbaden state theatres, came under the Prussian Land
government.

Kiel
215,000

Vereinigte Städtische Theater:

General-Intendant: Georg
Hartmann 1925–32 * E.
Martin 1934, H. Schulz-
Dornburg 1936.
Designer: F. X. Scherl 1930–38.
Dramaturg: Erich Munk 1930–32
* H. Hartwig 1934.

Stadttheater   1,050 pl.
    Prosc. opening 10.4 m
Schauspielhaus   670 pl.

Koblenz
60,000

Stadttheater   640 pl.

Director: Ludwig Meinicke 1910,
Richard Jost 1930, Bruno
Schoenfeld 1931 * H. Press
1933.

Köln
733,000

Städtische Bühnen:

General-Intendant: Fritz
Rémond 1925, Max
Hofmüller 1930–33 * A.
Spring 1934.

Oper   1,800 pl
    Prosc. width 12.75 m

Generalmusikdirektor: Eugen
Szenkar 1925–33 * F. Zaun
1934.
Conductors incl. Otto Klemperer
1917–24, Wilhelm Steinberg.
Producer: W. Felsenstein 1933.

Schauspielhaus   1300 pl.
    Prosc. width 10.5 m

Intendant: Gustav Hartung 1925,
Ernst Hardt 1926, Theo
Modes 1930, Franz Holl 1931–
33 * F. Everth 1934.
Stage directors incl. Hans
Rodenberg 1930 * R.

Dornseiff 1934–36, A. Godard
1936–39.

Among other Cologne theatres were the 2,000-seat Reichshallen operetta theatre (which survived into the Third Reich) and a privately owned Deutsches Theater, which had ceased operating by 1925.

Königsberg
300,000
	(a) Stadttheater (opera)
	1,400 pl.
		Intendant: Josef Geissel 1925,
		  Hans Schüler 1930–33.
		Music director: Werner Ludwig
		  1930.
		Designers incl. K. Jacobs, P.
		  Freund.

	(b) Neues Schauspielhaus
	900 pl.
		Director or Intendant: Leopold
		  Jessner 1918, Richard
		  Rosenheim 1925 * K.
		  Hoffmann 1934.
		Artistic director: Fritz Jessner
		  1925–33.
		Dramaturgs incl. Julius Bab 1918,
		  Martin Borrmann 1930–33.
		Designers incl. Friedrich
		  Kalbfuss 1930–33 * E. Loeffler
		  1935, E. Suhr 1938.

Königsberg, the capital of East Prussia, was cut off from the rest of Germany after the First World War and incorporated in the Soviet Union after the second. It is now called Kaliningrad.

Konstanz 35,000	Stadttheater 600 pl.	

Linked with smaller theatres at Winterthur and Schaffhausen.

Krefeld 160,000	Stadttheater 1,000 pl.	

Leipzig
690,000
	(a) Städtische Theater:	Intendant: W. A. Meyer-Waldeck
		  1918, Guido Barthol 1923–32 *
		  H. Schüler 1934–37

	Neues Theater
	(opera) 1,600 pl.
	Prosc. width 11 m
		Director: Otto Lohse to 1923,
		  Gustav Brecher (music) and
		  Walter Brügmann
		  (production) 1924–33 * F.
		  Köppen 1933, H. Schüler
		  1934–36.
		Dance: Emma Grondona 1923,
		  Erna Abendroth 1924–28,
		  Harald Kreutzberg 1929 *
		  Erna Abendroth 1933.

Designers: Alex Baranowsky
1924, Paul Thiersch 1925 * K.
Jacobs 1934.

Altes Theater 1,050 pl.
Prosc. width 13.4 m

Director: Alwin Kronacher 1918–
29, Detlev Sierck 1929–35.
Dramaturgs: Paul Prina 1919–31,
G. Scherler, and M. Gero
1932–33 * F. Zürner 1934–39.
Stage directors incl. Hans Zeise-
Gott and Erich Schönlank
1928–32.
Head of acting school: Adolf
Winds 1923, Detlev Sierck.

(b) **Schauspielhaus**
(private)   950 pl.

Owners and directors: E. E.
Schwabach, Kurt Wolff and
Fritz Viehweg (director till
1929), Otto Werther (director
1931–35).
Dramaturg: Hans Rothe 1923.
Design consultant: Franz Nitsche
1923–35.

(c) Komödienhaus (Battenberg-T
to 1929–30)   700 pl.

Directors: Paul Baumgartner
1923–28, H. Nietan and F.
Kranz 1929–31.

The Schauspielhaus was taken over by the city in 1938, by which time the
Komödienhaus had already closed. Now complemented by a Kammerspiele, the former
still exists. A new opera house was completed and opened in 1960.

Lübeck
130,000

Stadttheater   1,050 pl.
Prosc. width 9.5 m
Kammerspiele 320 pl.

Magdeburg
300,000

Stadttheater   1,200 pl.
Prosc. width 8.6 m
Zentral-Theater (private) 2,000
pl.

Mährisch Ostrau
(Moravská Ostrava)
(Czechoslovakia)
160,000

Deutsches Theater

Director: Rudolf Zeisel 1919–35.
Dramaturgs and stage directors:
Georg Hoellering and Carl
Pfann 1923, Kurt Wonger
1926–28, Karl Stransky 1928.

Also performing in Teschen and two other DTs.

Mainz
110,500

Stadttheater   1,460 pl.
Prosc. width 11.5 m

Intendant: Hans Islaub 1914–27,
Edgar Klitsch 1928–32 * P.
Trede 1933.

Musical director: Albert Gorter
1924, Paul Breisach 1926–30.
Music staff incl. Paul Dessau
1924, H. F. Redlich 1926–29.
Stage directors incl. Wolfgang
Hoffmann-Harnisch 1924,
Paul Peters 1925, Theodor
Bögel 1929, A. Springer 1930.

Mannheim 260,000	**Nationaltheater** (city-subsidized) 1,300 pl. Prosc. width 9.6 m	Intendant: Carl Hagemann 1919, Adolf Kraetzer 1923, Francesco Sioli 1925–30, Herbert Maisch 1931–33 * K. Scheffelmeister 1935.

Conductors and musical
directors: Wilhelm
Furtwängler 1915–21, Erich
Kleiber to 1923, Richard Lert
1925–28, Erich Orthmann
1930, Josef Rosenstock 1931–
32.
Directors incl. Richard Weichert
1919, H. D. Kenter, R.
Meyer-Walden and Hermann
Wlach 1926–29, Richard
Dornseiff 1930–33.
Dramaturg: Eugen Felber 1923–
25, Erich Dürr 1926–33.
Design consultants: Heinz Grete
1926–29, Eduard 1931–33.

Meiningen 20,000	Landestheater 885 pl. (Thuringia)	Intendant: Otto Osmar 1919, Franz Ulbrich 1923–24, Franz Nachbaur 1925–27, Willi Loehr 1928–35. Designer: Ernst Schütte 1923–24.

This was the former grand-ducal theatre, home of The Meininger in the late nineteenth
century.

Münster 117,000	Stadttheater 800 pl.	Lessee: Alfred Bernau to 1932.

In 1932 this was taken back under city management, with Fritz Berend as Intendant, and
renamed the Theater der Stadt. Following the Nazi takeover it was renovated in the
summer of 1933.

Munich 715,000	(a) Bayerische Staatstheater	General Intendant: Frh. von und zu Franckenstein 1919, Carl Zeiss 1923–24, Franckenstein 1925–34 * O. Walleck 1935.

Technical director: Adolf
Linnebach to 1940.
Head of design: Leo Pasetti to
1937.

Nationaltheater 1,900 pl.
Prosc. width 12.5 m
Residenz-Theater 640 pl.
Prosc. width 10 m
Prinzregenten-Theater
1,200 pl.
Prosc. width 13 m

General-Musikdirektor: Bruno
Walter 1919, Hans
Knappertsbusch 1925–36, * C.
Krauss 1937–40.
Other conductors incl. Robert
Heger 1923, Karl Böhm 1926.
Director of plays: Albert
Steinrück 1919, Carl Zeiss
1923–24, Alfons Pape 1925–
32, Richard Weichert 1933 * F.
Förster-Burggraf 1934–38, H.
Schweikart 1938, A. Golling
1939–40.
Dramaturgs: Gerhard Gutherz
1919–40, Jakob Geis 1924, E.
L. Stahl 1930–36.
Other directors incl. Erich Engel
1924, Richard Weichert 1931–
32.

(b) **Schauspielhaus**
(private) 727 pl.

Director: Hermine Körner 1919–
25, Ernst Bach 1926, deputy
Richard Revy.
Dramaturg: Alfred Noller 1923–
24.
Designer: E. E. Stern 1923–26.
Other directors incl. Max
Bruckner-Rüggeberg, Rudolf
Forster-Larrinaga 1929.

(c) **Kammerspiele** 525 pl.

Directors: Otto Falckenberg
1919–40 and Benno Bing
1919–25. Deputies incl.
Rudolf Frank 1925, Julius
Gellner 1930.
Dramaturgs incl. Otto Zarek
1923–25, Bertolt Brecht 1923–
24, Otto Zoff 1926, Heinrich
Fischer 1927–28 and 1932 * B.
Wellenkamp 1935, R.
Badenhausen 1936.
Other directors incl. B. Reich
1924, Hans Schweikart 1923–
31, Robert Forster-Larrinaga

and Julius Gellner 1924–32, Richard Revy 1928–35, Kurt Horwitz, Wolfgang Liebeneiner, and Max Ophüls, all 1932, Jakob Geis and Paul Verhoeven 1936.
Designers: Otto Reigbert 1923–38, Caspar Neher (consultant) 1924 * E. Preetorius (consultant) 1933, E. Sturm 1939–40.

(d) Schaubühne 250 pl.

Director: Friedrich Mellinger. Other directors incl. Hans Zeise-Gott.

(e) Theater am Gärtnerplatz (private). 1,050 pl.

Director: Hans Warnecke 1919–30 * P. Wolz and O. Reimann 1933.

In 1926 the Vereinigte Münchner Bühnen were organized under Ernst Bach, comprising the KS, the SH, and the 1,200-seat Munich Volkstheater. Thereafter the KS played in the SH. Among other Munich theatres were the Lustspielhaus (or Münchner Operettenbühne) and the Münchner Theater.

Nordhausen
35,000

Stadttheater 620 pl.

Director: Julius Heydecker 1917, Heinz Huber 1925.

Nuremberg
500,000

(a) Stadttheater:

General Intendant: Johannes Maurach 1926–34. Directors incl. Gustav Landauer 1918, Rudolf Klein-Rogge, Friedrich Neubauer, Hans Hübner 1925–34, E. L. Schön 1925–33.

Neues StdT am Ring 1,500 pl.
  Prosc, width 12.3 m
Altes StdT am Lorenzplatz
  750 pl.
  Prosc. width 9.5 m

(b) Kammerspiele 450 pl.

Director of productions: Oskar Walleck 1926.

In 1930 the KS, under the new title of Intimes Theater, was directed by Hans Merck. In 1933 Julius Klinkowström was director and the theatre closed.

Oberhausen
192,000

Stadttheater 800 pl.

Intendant: Ernst Hellbach-Kühn 1930–31.
Conductor: Wilhelm Brückner-Ruggeberg 1930–31.

Linked with Duisburg before 1930.

Oldenburg 55,000	Landestheater 1,000 pl. Prosc. width 10 m	Intendant: Richard Gsell 1925, Hellmuth Goetze 1929–32, Rolf Roeneke 1932–33.
Osnabrück 100,000	Stadttheater 800 pl. Prosc. width 9 m	Intendant: Erich Pabst 1929–32, Fritz Berend 1932–33 * W. Storz 1933.
Prague	**Deutsches Landestheater** 1,600 pl.	Director: Leopold Kramer 1919–27. Head of opera: Alexander von Zemlinsky 1919–26. Dramaturg: Hans Demetz 1919–26.
	Neues Deutsches Theater 1,900 pl. Prosc. width 13 m Kleine Bühne 400 pl.	Intendant: Leonard Kaiser 1930. Director: Robert Volkner 1928–32, Paul Eger 1933–37. Conductors incl. Wilhelm Steinberg 1927–29, Georg Szell 1930–37, Fritz Zweig 1935–37. Dramaturgs: Karl Johs 1928, H. Fischer 1929–30, Hans Brunow 1932, C. Werckshagen 1932, Hans Burger 1933. Stage directors incl. Oskar Fritz Schuh 1932 (opera), Julius Gellner 1934–37, Renato Mordo 1935–37 (opera and dramaturg). Designers: Emil Pirchan 1933–36, Emil Schultes 1936–37.

In 1918 Prague had a German-speaking population of some 300,000, but this declined when Czechoslovakia became independent. The DLT then lost its theatre, which was the old Austrian Royal theatre built in 1783, and handed on its name to the NDT. A number of refugee anti-Nazi actors found employment there in the mid-1930s: notably Friedrich Valk, Arnold Marlé, and Friedrich and Emmy Richter. Jane Tilden, Richard Romanowsky, and Walter Taub were others who played there. When the Nazis occupied the country in March 1939 the Czech-language Ständetheater became the Deutsches Schauspielhaus under Oskar Walleck.

Regensburg 80,000	Stadttheater 1,040 pl.	Intendant; Herbert Reusse 1929–33 * M. Linnbrunner.
Rostock 80,000	Stadttheater 1,080 pl. Kammerspiele 600 pl.	Intendant: Ernst Immisch 1929–34. Conductor: Hans Schmidt-Isserstedt 1929–31.

Saarbrücken 130,000	Stadttheater 800 pl.	Intendant: Georg Pauly 1931–33 * H. Huber 1934.
Schwerin 48,000	Landestheater 1,000 pl. Prosc. width 10.5 m	Director: Fritz Felsing 1919–33 * F. Mechelenburg.
Stettin 268,000	(a) Stadttheater 1,000 pl.	Director: Arthur Illing 1919 (since 1906). Intendant: Otto Ockert 1925–30, Hans Meissner 1930–33 * F. Siems 1933–34.
	(b) Bellevue-Theater (private) 1,200 pl.	Owned by the Rotter brothers 1929.
Stuttgart 370,000	(a) **Württembergisches Landestheater:**	Intendant: Albert Kehm 1923–33 * O. Krauss 1934–37, G. Deharde 1938–40.
	Grosses Haus 1,400 pl. Prosc. width 11.5 m	Music directors and conductors: Max von Schillings 1918, Carl Leonhardt 1923–36, Hans Swarowsky 1928–31, Franz Konwitschny 1930–33 * R. Krauss 1937.
	Kleines Haus 800 pl. Prosc. width 8m.	Stage directors incl. Viktor Stephany 1919, Franz Holl 1923, Wolfgang Hoffmann-Harnisch 1924–26, Friedrich Brandenburg 1927–33 * K. H. Böhm 1934–36, R. Dornseiff 1937–40. Dramaturgs: Wilhelm von Scholz 1919, Manfred Schneider 1924, Curt Elwenspoek 1925–30, Walter Schaefer 1931–34 * H. Tessmer 1935, H. Müller-Eschhorn, 1936–40, E. A. Winds 1937. Designer: Felix Ciossek 1919–39.
	(b) Schauspielhaus 750 pl.	Director and owner: Claudius Kraushaar 1923–36.
	(c) Residenz-Theater 900 p.	Directors: Theodor Brandt and Ferdinand Skuhra 1919.

The Res-T had closed before the end of the 1920s. In 1925 Kraushaar took over the Wilhelma Theater (operettas), forming the short-lived Vereinigte Theater. The second of these closed c. 1929, while the SH, after being leased for a year to the Land (now state) theatres in 1934, was taken over by the city.

Ulm 75,000	Stadttheater 810 pl.	Intendant: Erwin Dieterich 1929–34. Conductors incl. Herbert von Karajan 1929–34.
Vienna 2 million	(a) Bundestheater (Federal theatres)	Director-General: Frh. von Andrian zu Werburg 1919, committee 1920–26, Franz Schneiderhan 1927–30 * F. Plattner 1939.
	Burgtheater 1,500 pl. Prosc. width 12 m BurgT	Directors: A committee (with Max Devrient and Hermann Bahr) 1919; Albert Heine 1920–21, Anton Wildgans 1922 and 1931, Max Paulsen 1923, Franz Herterich 1924–30, Hermann Röbbeling 1932–38 * U. Bettac 1938, L. Müthel 1939. Dramaturgs: Josef Ratislav and Erhard Buschbeck 1918–40. Stage directors incl. Max Ophüls 1926, Hans Brahm 1926–30, Heinz Hilpert 1930, Josef Gielen 1937 * K. H. Stroux 1939. Designers incl. K. A. Wilke 1922, Remigius Geyling 1923–40.
	Akademietheater	
	Staatsoper 2,500 pl. Prosc. width 13 m SO	Director: Hans Gregor 1919, Richard Strauss 1920–25, Franz Schalk 1920–27, Clemens Krauss 1929, Felix Weingartner 1935, Erwin Kerber 1936–40. Other conductors incl. Karl Alwin and Robert Heger 1926–30, Josef Krips 1935. Producer: Lothar Wallerstein 1930–38 Designers: Hans Pühringer 1919, Alfred Roller 1920–30, Robert Kautzky 1935–40.
	(b) **Deutsches Volkstheater** 1,900 pl. DVT	Director: Carl Wallner 1918, Alfred Bernau 1919–24, Rudolf Beer 1925–32, Rolf Jahn 1933–38 Dramaturgs: Paul Czinner and Bernhard Reich 1919, Herbert Furreg 1931.

Stage directors incl. Heinrich
Schnitzler 1934–37, Emil
Geyer 1936.

The DVT was taken over by the Nazi Labor Front in 1938 and put under W. B. Iltz as
Intendant, with G. v. Manker as designer.

    (c) **Kammerspiele** 500 pl.

Director: Alfred Bernau 1918.
Then attached to DVT from
1919 and to Ren-Bühne 1922.
Later under Franz Wenzler,
Rudolf Beer 1932, Aurel
Novotny 1933, Erich Ziegel
1934–36.
Conductor: Frank Fox 1931.
Dramaturg: Paul Czinner 1918.

    (d) Komödie

Director: Rolf Jahn 1930–32,
Hans Demetz 1933, Konrad
Dwerton 1934.

    (e) Modernes Theater

Directors: Siegfried Geyer 1925,
R. Blum 1926, Ludwig Körner
1927. Closed by 1930.

    (f) **Raimund-Theater**
        1,500 pl.

Director: W. Karczag 1918–21,
Rudolf Beer 1922–32, Rolf
Jahn 1933, Stefan Hock and
Paul Barnay 1934–35 * W.
Seidl 1938–40. Deputy:
Karlheinz Martin 1926.
Dramaturgs: Franz Theodor
Czokor 1922–26, Lutz
Weltmann 1925.
Stage directors: Rudolf Zeisel
1923–24, Renato Mordo 1924,
Ferdinand Exl 1930–31.

    (g) Renaissance-Bühne 630 pl.

Direction: Alfred Bernau, Harry
Walden 1920–21, Siegfried
Geyer 1922, E. Robert 1922–
24, Friedrich Feher 1925, Josef
Jarno 1926–31. Then closed.

    (i) **Theater in der**
        Josefstadt 750 pl.
        TidJ

Direction: Josef Jarno 1918,
deputy Rudolf Beer; Max
Reinhardt 1924; deputies
Stefan Hock 1924, Emil Geyer
1926–33, Otto Preminger
1933–35, Ernst Lothar 1935–
38 * Heinz Hilpert 1938–44.
Dramaturg: Paul Kalbeck 1924 *
A. Ibach 1938.
Music director: Bernhard
Paumgartner 1924.
Designers: Oskar Strnad 1924,
Oskar Laske, Otto

Niedermoser, Alfred Roller,
Hans Kautzky * E. Schütte.

(k) **Neue Wiener Bühne**
800 pl.
NWB

Director: Emil Geyer 1918–22,
Siegfried Geyer 1923–25.
Closed by 1930.

(l) Volksoper   1,900 pl.

Directors: R. R. Mader 1920,
Felix Weingartner 1922–24,
August Markowsky 1924,
Fritz Stiedry 1925, Leo Blech
1926 * A. Baumann 1939

Closed in 1930, reopened, then taken over by the city in 1938.

(m) Theater an der Wien
1,360 pl.

Directors: Wilhelm Karczag
1918–24, Hubert Marischka-
Karczag 1924–34, Arthur
Hellmer 1936–38. Then shut.

(n) Stadttheater

Under same management as the
above, from 1930 on.

(o) Volksbühne   1,000 pl.

Directors: Arthur Rundt and
Hans Ziegler 1919.
Dramaturg: Herbert Jhering
1919. Closed in the 1920s.

(n) Carl-Theater (former
Leopoldstädter-T)   1,200 pl.

Director: Alfred Bernau 1925–26.
Closed 1934.

There were anything up to a dozen other Vienna theatres of lesser significance,
including for a while a Neues Operettentheater owned by the Austrian Socialist party.

Weimar
50,500

(a) **Deutsches National-
Theater**   1,120 pl.
Prosc. width 11 m

Intendant: Carl von Schirach
1918–19, Ernst Hardt 1920–
24, Franz Ulbrich 1925–33 * E.
Nobbe 1934–36, H. S. Ziegler
1936–40.
Dramaturg: Karl Stang 1920,
Friedrich Sebrecht 1924 * H.
S. Ziegler 1934–36.
Stage directors: Waldemar
Jürgens 1918–20, Helmuth
Ebbs 1930–31, Sebrecht 1932,
Richard Crodel 1932–33 *
H.S. Ziegler 1934–36.
Designer: Fritz Lewy 1922–24,
Ernst Schütte 1925, Alf Björn
1926–33 * R. Stahl 1936–40.

Kammerspiele   740 pl.

(b) Residenz-Theater   600 pl.

Owner and director: Siegfried
Deutsch 1920–26. Closed by
1930.

From 1922 Weimar also serviced the Jena StdT. After 1934 Hans Severus Ziegler (stage director) was also Generalkommissar for all the Thuringian theatres.

Wiesbaden 135,000	**Staatstheater:**	Intendant: Kurt von Mützenbecher 1919, Carl Hagemann 1920–27, Paul Bekker 1927–32 * M. Berg-Elert 1933, C. v. Schirach 1934–40. Conductor: Otto Klemperer 1924–27, Karl Rankl 1932 * K. Elmendorff 1933–36, K. Fischer 1936. Designer * L. Schenck v. Trapp 1934–40.
	Grosses Haus 1,400 pl. Prosc. width 12 m	
	Kleines Haus 750 pl.	Director of plays: Ernst Legal 1920, Wolff von Gordon 1925–32 * F. Sebrecht 1933–40. Design consultants: Lothar Schenck von Trapp 1921, G. T. Buchholz 1927, Gustav Singer 1931–33.

Until summer 1932 these were Prussian state theatres, owned by the city but under the ultimate direction of Berlin. They next came under the Nassau Land government, then after 1933 under the Propaganda Ministry. The KH was the former Residenz-Theater, which from 1922 was rented from its private owners; previously it had been an operetta theatre directed by its owner, Norbert Kapferer. In 1935 it resumed its own name and became independent of the opera.

Wuppertal	Barmen Stadttheater 1,200 pl. and Elberfeld Stadttheater 1,100 pl. Prosc. width 9 m	Intendant: Arthur von Gerlach 1919, Otto Maurenbrecher 1930–32 * G. Stark 1934–40. Directors incl. Paul Legband 1925, Max Ophüls.

Wuppertal, the valley of the river Wupper, comprises the adjacent towns of Barmen and Elberfeld.

Zurich 210,000	**Stadttheater** 1,200 pl. Prosc. width 12 m	Director: Alfred Reucker 1919, Paul Trede 1925–32, Karl Schmidt-Bloss 1933–40. Stage directors: Josef Dannegger, Richard Revy 1919. Music staff incl. Philipp Jarnach. Dramaturg: Paul Apel 1919. Designer: Roman Clemens 1933–40.
	Schauspielhaus	Direction: Stadttheater 1919, Ferdinand Rieser 1926, Oskar Wälterlin 1938

Dramaturgs: H. Jarno 1930,
Franz Mirow 1931, Kurt
Hirschfeld 1933–45, Felix
Gasbarra 1934–35, Edgar
Pauly, 1935–37.
Stage directors: Cäsar von Arx,
Hans Peppler 1926, Herbert
Waniek 1930–33, Gustav
Hartung 1933–34, Leopold
Lindtberg 1933–45, Leonard
Steckel 1933–45, Carl Ebert
1935–36.
Designer: Wilhelm Heller 1930,
Heinz Porep 1930–33, Teo
Otto 1933–45.

Corso-Theater

Directors: Max Steiner-Kaiser,
Hans Curjel.
Designer: Wolfgang Roth.

The Schauspielhaus was rebuilt in 1926, and when it reopened that autumn the
Stadttheater went over exclusively to opera and—from 1930—operetta.

Appendix 2
Thirty Years of German-language Theatre

List of Actors and Abbreviations

ad	Max Adalbert (1874–1933)	ch	Mikhail Chekhov (1891–1955)
al	Hans Albers (1892–1960)	cl	Erik Charell (1895–1977)
as	Raoul Aslan (1890–1958)		
au	Ernst Josef Aufricht (1898–1971)	d	Ernst Deutsch (1890–1969)
		da	Josef Dannegger
b	Albert Bassermann (1867–1952)	dc	Bruno Decarli (1877–1950)
ba	Roma Bahn (1897–1975)	dg	Wilhelm Diegelmann (1861–1934)
bd	Fritta Brod	dh1	Mary Dietrich
be	Rosa Bertens (1860–1934)	dh2	Marlene Dietrich (1902 or 1904–)
bf	Paul Baratoff (1878–1952)	di	William Dieterle (1893–)
bg	Elisabeth Bergner (1897–1986)	do	Käthe Dorsch (1889–1957)
bh	Herbert Berghof (1909–)	dp	Hans Deppe (1897–1969)
bi	Sybille Binder (1898–1962)	dr	Berta Drews (1905–)
bie	Gerhard Bienert (1898–)	du	Louise Dumont (1862–1932)
bk	Maria Becker (1920–)	dv	Lil Dagover (1894–)
bn	Wolf von Beneckendorff (1891–1960)	dx	Tilla Durieux (1880–1917)
bo	Curt Bois (1901–)		
br	Felix Bressart (1892–1949)	eb	Carl Ebert (1887–)
bs	Ewald Balser (1898–)	ec	Else Eckersberg
bt	Paul Bildt (1885–1957)	ed	Anton Edthofer (1883–)
bu	Ernst Busch (1900–)	ei	Maria Eis (1896–1954)

er	Blandine Ebinger (?1914–)
es	Peter Esser (?d. 1970)
et	Karl Etlinger (1882–1946)
ey	Gertrud Eysoldt (1870–1955)
ez	Camilla Eibenschütz
f	Rudolf Forster (1884–1968)
fa	Erwin Faber (1891–)
fh	Albert Florath (1888–1957)
fi	Werner Fink (1902–)
fk	Walter Franck (1896–1961)
fl	Elisabeth Flickenschildt (1905–1977)
fll	Egon Friedell (1878–1938)
fn	Maria Fein (1900–1965)
fo	Willy Forst (1903–)
fs	Adolf Fischer
g	Heinrich George (1893–1946)
gb	Ernst Ginsberg (1904–1964)
gd	Hermann Greid (1892–)
ge	Kurt Gerron (d. 1944)
gf	Heinz Greif (1907–1946)
gg	Gustav Gründgens (1899–1965)
gie	Therese Giehse (1898–1975)
gn	Friedrich Gnass (1892–1958)
go	Käthe Gold (1907–)
gö	Curt Goetz (1888–1960)
gr	Alexander Granach (1890–1945)
gt	Max Gülstorff (1882–1947)
gü	Paul Günther (1887–)
gw	Fritz Genschow (1905–)
gz	Paul Graetz (1890–1937)
ha	Paul Hartmann (1889–)
hd	Günther Hadank (1892–)
he	Trude Hesterberg (1897–1967)
hf	Johanna Hofer
hk	Paul Henckels (1885–1967)
hl	Veit Harlan (1899–1966)
hm	Oskar Homolka (1901–)
hn	Max Hansen (1897–)
hö	Lucie Höflich (1883–1956)
hp	Heinz Hilpert (1890–1967)
hr	Albert Hoerrmann (1899–)
hs	Else Heims (1878–1958)
hu	Ludwig Hartau
hw	Kurt Horwitz (1897–1974)
hwm	Miriam Horwitz (1898–)
hy	Brigitte Horney (1911–)
hz	Wolfgang Heinz (1900–)
j	Emil Jannings (1894–1950)
k	Werner Krauss (1884–1959)
ka	Erwin Kalser (1883–1958)
kä	Helmut Käutner (1908–)
kb	Hilde Körber (1906–1969)

ki	Franziska Kinz (1897–)
kk	Arthur Kraussneck (1856–1941)
kl	Eugen Klöpfer (1886–1950)
kn	Gustav Knuth (1901–)
ko	Fritz Kortner (1892–1970)
kö	Hermine Körner (1878–1960)
kör	Lothar Körner
kp	Maria Koppenhöfer (1901–1948)
kr	Rudolf Klein-Rogge (1888–1955)
ks	Oskar Karlweis (1894–1956)
ku	Margarete Kupfer (1885–1953)
kü	Kate Kühl
kw	Victor de Kowa (1904–1973)
ky	Friedrich Kayssler (1874–1945)
la	Wolfgang Langhoff (1901–1966)
lb	Hans Leibelt (1885–1974)
lg	Ernst Legal (1881–1955)
li	Theo Lingen (1903–)
lj	Lotte Lenya (1900–)
lk	Maria Leiko
ln	Margo Lion
lo	Peter Lorre (1904–1964)
lö	Lotte Loebinger (1905–)
lr	Franz Lederer (1906–)
ls	Theodor Loos (d. 1954)
lsn	Lina Lossen (1878–1949)
lu	Ernst Lubitsch (1892–1947)
lz	Elisabeth Lennartz
m	Gerda Müller (1894–1951)
ma	Lucie Mannheim (1899–1976)
me	Erika Mann (1905–1969)
mi	Bernhard Minetti (1905–)
mn	Eleonore von Mendelssohn (1900–1951)
mo	Grete Mosheim (1905–)
moi	Alexander Moissi (1879–1935)
mr	Margarete Melzer
ms	Hans Moser (1880–1964)
mü	Lothar Müthel (1896–1965)
mw	Annie Mewes (c. 1896–)
mz	Constanze Menz (1905–)
ne	Carola Neher (1905–1942)
nm	Elisabeth Neumann
od	Fritz Odemar (1858–1926)
ok	Maria Orska (?1893–1930)
os	Marianne Oswald
ot	Hans Otto (1900–1933)
p	Max Pallenberg (1877–1934)
pa	Albert Patry
pi	Lupu Pick (1886–1931)
pn	Harald Paulsen (1895–1954)
po	Erich Ponto (1884–1957)

py	Karl Paryla (1905–)	th4	Hans Thimig (1900–)
		tr	Curt Trepte (1902–)
qf	Willi Quadflieg (1914–)	tw	Hans Heinrich von Twardowski (1898–1958)
ra	Luise Rainer (1912–)		
re	Leo Reuss	ul	Luise Ullrich (1911–)
ri	Frieda Richard (1873–1946)		
ro	Hans Rodenberg (1895–1978)	v	Conrad Veidt (1892?–1943)
rü	Heinz Rühmann (1902–)	va	Rosa Valetti
		ve	Albert Venohr
s	Agnes Straub (1890–1941)	vk	Fritz (Frederick) Valk (d. 1956)
sa	Lyda Salmonova (1889–1968)	vl	Hermann Vallentin
sch	Heinrich Schnitzler (1902–)	vy	Toni van Eyck (1913–1969)
se	Dagny Servaes		
sk	Rudolf Schildkraut (1862–1930)		
sm	Oskar Sima	w	Paul Wegener (1874–1948)
sp	Steffi Spira (1908–)	wa	Elsa Wagner (1881–1975)
spc	Camilla Spira (1906–)	wb	Otto Wallburg
sr	Albert Steinrück (1872–1927)	we	Otto Wernicke (1893–1965)
ss	Hermann Speelmans	wg	Helene Weigel (1900–1971)
st	Leonard Steckel (1901–1971)	wh	Gustav von Wangenheim (1895–)
sv	Renée Stobrawa	wk	Pamela Wedekind
sw	Hans Schweikart (1895–1975)	wm	Hans Wassmann
sz	Reinhold Schünzel (1888–1954)	wn	Eduard von Winterstein (1871–1961)
		wo	Adolf Wohlbrück (Anton Walbrook) (1900–1967)
ta	Walter Taub	wu	Gustav Waldau (1871–1956)
te	Johanna Terwin	wy	Paula Wessely (1908–)
th1	Helene Thimig (1889–1974)		
th2	Hugo Thimig (1854–1944)		
th3	Hermann Thimig (1890–)	zi	Erich Ziegel (1876–1950)

Chronology: Noteworthy Productions and Performances from 1916 to 1945

This list begins with what is generally regarded as the starting point of Expressionism in the German theatre: the production of Hasenclever's *Der Sohn* in wartime Prague, then still part of Austria-Hungary. It coincided with the apex of Max Reinhardt's influence, when he was directing not only the Berlin Deutsches Theater and its Kammerspiele but also the Volksbühne's new theatre, and at the same time planning his mass theatre the Grosses Schauspielhaus, which would open three years later. He, too, was about to flirt briefly with the new movement, which largely inspired his Junges Deutschland series of performances; but then to lose interest in it.

The thirty years that followed took the theatre of the Weimar Republic as we now see it (though the actual limits of that republic were 1919–33) right through the Nazi period up to the end of the Second World War. This overspill is necessary both to trace the effects of the division which took place in that theatre after Hitler's accession to power—one half of it struggling to persist against all odds through his consequent *Gleichschaltung*, or realignment of the arts and media—while the other carried on under the constraints of exile, and also to mark the beginnings of a reunion after mid-1945. It may be interesting to keep an eye on the names of those who first began the restoration which followed—Karlheinz Martin; Herbert Jhering the critic; Friedrich Wolf and others returning from Soviet exile; a nucleus from Zurich, followed a little later by Brecht, Piscator, and Zuckmayer from further West; also Schuh, Gielen, the designer Caspar Neher, and others involved in the revival of opera. Still others, like the actors Kayssler, Granach, and (in an internment camp) Heinrich George, were reaching the end of their lives. This, then, is not just a calendar but the story of a generation.

Abbreviations used are: ad. = adaptation; chor. = choreography; des. = designer; dir. = director; mus. = music composed by; trans. or trs. = translation. The initials used for theatres follow some general principles: T = Theater, G = gross (large), K = Klein (small), A = Alt (old), N = Neu (new), H = Haus, SH = Schauspielhaus, ST = Staatstheater, LT = Landestheater (regional theatre), StdT = Stadttheater (municipal theatre), O = opera house, KS = Kammerspiele (chamber theatre). For details, and for the exceptions, see the list of theatres in Appendix 1. If no place name is given, then the theatre concerned is in Berlin. A number of theatres changed their name during this period, but will generally be referred to by their best-known name, or the name which they bore around 1930.

Play titles, but not those of ephemeral revues or of most musicals, are given in bold type on the occasion of their German-language premiere (which normally was also their world premiere). German premieres of translated plays are not so treated, though where they were significant this is noted. Their titles are normally given in English; occasionally, however, in their language of origin, if this is likely to be more familiar or less ambiguous.

For the abbreviation of actors' names see pp. 252–254. The sign > introduces those known to have been in a particular production.

Date		Author(s)	Title—Theatre—Director, designer etc.—Actors
1916			
September	30	Hasenclever	**Der Sohn** Prague DLT.
October	7	Gorky	*The Lower Depths* VB, dir. Vallentin/Winterstein. > bt, ey, v, wm, wn. 41 perfs.
	8	Hasenclever	*Der Sohn* Dresden, Albert-Th., dir. Licho. >d.
	13	Lenz	*Die Soldaten* DT, dir. Reinhardt, des. Stern.> dg, ez, j, k, kö, mü, te, th3, wa, wn. 16 perfs.
	20	Strindberg	*The Ghost Sonata* DT KS, dir. Reinhardt, des Knina.> ba, dc, ey, ha, w, wa. 98 perfs.
	?	Wedekind	**Hidalla** Königsberg NSH, dir. Jessner.
November	18	Wildgans	**Liebe** Vienna DVT.
	19	Franckenstein/Wiesenthal	**Die Biene** (mime) Darmstadt LT.
December	15	Büchner	*Dantons Tod* DT, dir. Reinhardt, des. Stern. > da, do, fn, gt, k, v, wa. 62 perfs.
	17	Schickele	**Hans im Schnakenloch** Frankfurt, NT, dir. Hellmer.> gz, lk.
	23	Feuchtwanger	**Warren Hastings, Gouverneur von Indien** Munich SH.

1917

January	20	Shaw	*John Bull's Other Island* (trs. Trebitsch) LT.
	29	Kaiser	**Die Bürger von Calais** Frankfurt, NT, dir. Hellmer. > gz, kl
	30	Wilde	*A Florentine Tragedy* Stuttgart LT, mus. Zemlinsky.
February	19	H. Mann	**Madame Legros** Munich KS.
	?	Kaiser	**Kindermord** LT.
March	5	Feuchtwanger	**Der König und die Tänzerin** (after Kalidasa) Munich KS, des. Pasetti.
	6	Kaiser	**Die Sorina** LT.
	30	Schickele	*Hans im Schnakenloch* KT, dir. Altmann. > bt, pi.
April	28	Kaiser	**Von Morgens bis Mitternachts** Munich KS, dir. Falckenberg, des. Pasetti. > ka, m.
May	12	Busoni	**Turandot** Zurich, SdtT.
		Bartók	**Der Holzgeschnitzte Prinz** (ballet). Budapest Opera.
	26	Feuchtwanger	**Pierrots Herrentraum** (mime) Munich SH, mus. Hartmann-Trepka.
	31	Kaiser	**Die Versuchung** Hamburg, Thalia-T.
June	3	Kokoschka	**Hiob, Der brennende Dornbusch** and *Mörder, Hoffnung der Frauen* Dresden, Albert-T, dir. George. > d, g.
	12	Pfitzner	**Palestrina** Munich, Prinz-Regenten-T.

Start of 1917–18 Theatre Season

September	9	Sternheim	**Perleberg** Frankfurt SH, dir. Hartung.
	14	Przybyszewski	*Schnee* Munich SH.
	15	Essig	**Die Glückskuh** Leipzig, AT.
	25	Tolstoy	*The Living Corpse* DT, dir. Reinhardt, des. Knina. > bt, dy, hö, lk, moi, te, waa, wn. 109 perfs.
	28	S. Giedion	**Arbeit** Vienna VB.
October	13	Rilke	**Das tägliche Leben** Vienna KS.
		Feuchtwanger	**Jew Süss** Munich SH.
	14	Kaiser	*Von Morgens bis Mitternachts* Vienna, Neue Wiener Bühne, dir. Gottowt.
	17	Carl Hauptmann	**Winterballade**
	23	Kaiser	**Der Zentaur** (later renamed **Konstantin Strobel**) Frankfurt SH, dir. Hartung.
	27	Kaiser	**Die Koralle** (a)Frankfurt NT, dir. Hellmer. > gz, kl. (b) Munich KS, dir. Falckenberg, des. Pasetti. > ka.
November	2	Johst	**Der Einsame** Düsseldorf SH, dir. Lindemann.
	9	Chekhov	*The Cherry Orchard* Munich KS (German premiere).
		Schiller	*Don Carlos* DT, dir. Reinhardt, des. Stern. > dc, fe, ha, hs, k, moi, w.
	10	Dehmel	**Die Menschenfreunde** LT.
	14	Schnitzler	**Fink und Fliederbusch** Vienna DVT.
	24	Fontana	**Marc** Vienna, Neue Wiener Bühne.
December	8	Kornfeld	**Die Verführung** Frankfurt SH, dir. Hartung. > hf.
	15	Hasenclever	**Antigone** (Awarded Kleist Prize 1917. Banned after premiere).
		Essig	**Der Herr vom Wald** ST.
	23	Sorge	**Der Bettler** DT, dir. Reinhardt, des. Stern. > d, dc, ey, j, th1, v, w. Awarded Kleist Prize 1912. Four perfs. in "Das junge Deutschland" series.

| | 26 | Sorge | *Metanreite* Munich KS. |
| | 27 | Kaiser | *Von Morgens bis Mitternachts* Vienna, VB. > p. |

1918

January	17	Kaiser	*Die Koralle* DT KS, dir. Holländer, des. Knina. > d, ec, k, w. 21 perfs.
	18	Hasenclever	*Der Sohn* Mannheim NT, dir. Weichert, des. Sievert. > od.
	25	Kleist	*Die Hermannschlacht* VB, dir. Reinhardt, des Stern. > d, k, v, wa, 19 perfs.
	26	Kaiser	*Rektor Kleist* Königsberg, NSH.
February	8	Feuchtwanger	*Vasantasena* (after Sudraka), Munich KS, dir. Falckenberg, des. Pasetti > bi, fa, mw
	10	R. Goering	*Seeschlacht* Dresden SH, dir. Lewinger, des. Linnebach (Single closed performance).
	16	Janáček	*Jenufa* Vienna State Opera.
	18		First Dada evening, J. B. Neumann gallery, Berlin.
	20	Strindberg	*Der schwarze Handschuh* DT KS, dir. Hermine Körner, des. Stern. > ey, gt, k, kö, lk, te, wa. 7 perfs.
	23	Hauptmann	*Hanneles Himmelfahrt* VB, dir. Reinhardt, des. Stern. > gt, j, ku, lk, moi, th1. 43 perfs.
	27	S. Zweig	*Jeremias* Zurich, StdT.
March	1	Zoff	*Kerker und Erlösung* Munich KS.
	3	Goering	*Seeschlacht* DT, dir. Reinhardt, des. Stern. > j, k, thi, v, w. ln 'Das Junge Deutschland' series, 1 perf.
	10	Max Brod	*Die Höhe des Gefühls* Dresden SH.
	18	Kaiser	*Von Morgens bis Mitternachts* Frankfurt NT. > kl.
	23	Kaiser	*Frauenopfer* Düsseldorf SH.
	24	Hasenclever	*Der Sohn* DT KS, dir. Holländer, des. Stern. > d, hs, k, th3, w. ln 'Das junge Deutschland' series. 3 perfs.
	30	Johst	*Der Einsame.* Munich KS, dir. Falckenberg. > ka
April	9	Strindberg	*Easter* Hamburg, Thalia-T, dir. Karlheinz Martin.
	11	Kokoschka	*Hiob, der brennende Dornbusch; Mörder, Hoffnung der Frauen.* Frankfurt NT, dir. Heinrich George. > g, m.
	25	Schreker	*Die Gezeichneten* Frankfurt O.
May	8	Franz Schmidt	*Notre Dame* Berlin SO
June	8	Essig	*Die Glückskuh* Munich KS, dir. Falckenberg, des. Pasetti, > fa.
	9	Werfel	*Besuch aus dem Elysium* DT, dir. Herald, des. Stern. Das junge Deutschland series. > le, v.
	16	Unruh	*Ein Geschlecht* Frankfurt SH, dir. Hartung, des. Babberger. > bt, eb, m.
July	26	Andreiev	*Du sollst nicht töten* (trs. A. Scholz) Munich SH.
August	1	Erik Charell	*Die Dame ohne Herz* (ballet) LT.

Start of 1918–19 Season

September	4	Immermann	*Merlin* VB, dir. Berger, des. Dülberg, mus. Tiessen. > di, die1, ho, ky, wm.
	9	Johst	*Der Einsame* KT. > bt, pi.
	14	Shakespeare	*Measure for Measure* VB, dir. Berger, des. Dülberg. > ho, ky, wm.
	21	Giedion	*Arbeit* KS, dir. Gregori, des. Stern. > ku, th3. 4 perfs.
	29	Wedekind	*Frühlings Erwachen* KS, dir. Reinhardt, des. Stern. > d, ku, wa, wn. 220 perfs.

October	10	Sternheim	*Perleberg* Munich KS, dir. P. Marx.
	15	Stramm	*Sancta Susanna* Sturm-Bühne, dir. Schreyer.
	21	Kaiser	**Juana; Friedrich und Anna; Claudius** (one-acters) Frankfurt NT.
	25	Goering	**Der Erste** DT KS, dir. v. Busse, des. Stern. > ey, th3, w. 6 perfs.
November	2	Curt Goetz	**Nachtbeleuchtung** ("three grotesque pieces") DKT.
	16	Kaiser	**Brand im Opernhaus** Hamburg KS, dir. Ziegel. > hw, ko.
	22	Hasenclever	*Der Sohn* DT KS, dir. v. Busse, des. Stern. > d, gz, hs, k, w. 44 perfs.
	26	Kaiser	*Brand im Opernhaus* KS, dir. Kaiser, des. Stern. > dc, gü, te. 6 perfs.
	28	Kaiser	**Gas 1** (a) Frankfurt NT, dir. Hellmer, des. Neppach. (b) Düsseldorf SH, dir. Lindemann, des. Ström. > du, es.
December	13	Tolstoy	*Und das Licht schien in der Finsternis* DT, dir. Reinhardt, des. Stern. > bt, d, dy, hö, kö, moi. 79 perfs.
	20	Wedekind	*Die Büchse der Pandora* KS dir. Carl Heine, des. Stern. > ey, j, kö, ku. 151 perfs.
		Grabbe	*Hannibal* Munich NT.
	25	S. Zweig	**Legende eines Lebens** Hamburg, DSH.
	29	Unruh	*Ein Geschlecht* DT, dir. Herald, des. Stern and Jaeckel. > az, bt, ha, lk. 8 perfs. 'Das junge Deutschland' series.

1919

January	8	Schiller	*Wilhelm Tell* VB, dir. Kayssler, des. Dülberg.
	23	Sternheim	**1913** Frankfurt SH, dir. Hartung, des. Delavilla. > g.
	25	ditto	**Tabula Rasa** KT, dir. Altmann. > pi.
	31	Kaiser	*Von Morgens bis Mitternachts* DT, dir. Holländer, des. Stern. > gä, gz, hz, ku, p, wa. 5 perfs.
February	1	Sudermann	*Das höhere Leben* ResT.
	7	Johst	**Der junge Mensch, ein ekstatisches Szenarium** Munich KS.
	8	Wildgans	**Dies Irae** (1) Vienna, BurgT. (2) Halle a.d. Saale StdT.
	20	Hasenclever	*Antigone* Frankfurt SH, dir. Weichert. > eb, g, m. First regular performance since Dresden ban.
	25	Kaiser	*Gas 1* VB. dir. Legband, des. K. J. Hirsch
	27	Shakespeare	*As You Like It* DT, dir. Reinhardt, des. Stern. > d, dy, gz, moi, te, th1, th3, wm. 67 perfs.
March	12	Yeats, Synge, Lady Gregory (three Irish one-acters) Frankfurt SH.	
	16	Wedekind	**Felix und Galathea** Hamburg KS.
	18	Humperdinck	**Gaudeamus** (Comic opera, text by L. Misch) Darmstadt LT.
	20	Barlach	**Der arme Vetter** Hamburg KS, dir. Ziegel. (The first of Barlach's plays to be staged.)
	23	Unruh	*Ein Geschlecht* Hamburg, Thalia-T, dir. Martin. (With ba.)
	27	R. Faesi	**Die Fassade** Zurich SH. (And in Frankfurt SH April 4.)
April	2	Crommelynck	**Der Maskenschnitzer** Munich KS, dir. Falckenberg.
	5	Beer-Hofmann	**Jaakobs Traum** Vienna, Burg-T.
	27	Lasker-Schüler	**Die Wupper** DT, dir. Herald, des. Stern, mus. Holländer. > gü, gz, th3, wa. In 'Das junge Deutschland' series. 6 perfs.
May	10	Mechtilde Lichnowsky	**Der Kinderfreund** DT KS.

	25	Kokoschka	*Job, The Burning Bush* DT, dir. Kokoschka, des. Stern. > d, fe, gü, gz, kö. In 'Das junge Deutschland' series. 1 perf.
	27	Kaiser	*Gas 1* Königsberg, NSH, dir. Jessner.
June	7	Shaw	*Catherine the Great* Frankfurt SH.
	28	H. Lautensack	**Die Pfarrhauskomödie** Munich SH.
August	7	Joyce	*Exiles (Verbannte)* Munich SH.
	14	Hardekopf	**Der Abend** Berlin, Phantastisches T (T am Lietzensee).

Start of 1919–20 Season

September	1	Wedekind	**Herakles** Munich, Prinz-Regenten T.
	5	Sternheim (after Diderot)	*Die Marquise von Arcis* Frankfurt SH.
	12	Hasenclever	**Der Retter** and **Die Entscheidung** Tribüne, dir. Martin.
	19	Unruh	*Ein Geschlecht* Vienna, Burg-T.
	27	Kaiser	*Die Bürger von Calais* VB, dir. Legband.
	30	Toller	**Die Wandlung** Tribüne, dir. Martin, des. Neppach. > ko.
October	9	Wolf	**Das bist du** Dresden SH.
	10	Shakespeare	*Cymbeline* DT, dir. Berger, des. Stern. > az, do, ha, kö, sw, th1, th3, w, wm, wn. 14 perfs.
	11	Strauss/ Hofmannsthal	**Die Frau ohne Schatten** Vienna SO.
		Ernst Weiss	**Tanja** Prague DT.
	21	Klabund	**Hannibals Brautfahrt** ("farce for serious persons"). Basel StdT.
	29	A. Zweig	**Die Sendung Semaels** Frankfurt.
November	7	Beer-Hofmann	*Jaakobs Traum* DT, dir. Reinhardt, des. Stern. > d, fe, ha, hs, moi, sw. 59 perfs.
	9	Kaiser	*Gas 1* Munich SH. > di1, gr, mü.
	14	Hermann-Neisse	**Albine und August** DT KS, dir. Martin.
	20	Goering	**Scapa Flow** Jena StdT.
	22	Barlach	**Der tote Tag** Leipzig SH, dir. Fr. Märker.
		H. Mann	**Brabach** Munich, Res-T.
		Zoff	*Der Schneesturm* Frankfurt SH.
	29	Aeschylus	**The Oresteia** GS, dir. Reinhardt, des. Stern, mus. Nilson > fn, hs, ku, moi, s. 73 perfs.
December	5	Kaiser	**Hölle, Weg, Erde** Frankfurt NT, dir. Hellmer, des. Delavilla.
	8	W. Mehring	*Einfach Klassisch* dir. Hecker, des. Grosz, mus. F. Holländer > eb, wm. Opening of revived Schall und Rauch cabaret in basement of GS.
	6	H. E. Jacob	**Beaumarchais und Sonnenfels** Bochum StdT.
	9	Strindberg	*Advent* DT KS, dir. Berger, des. Stern, mus. Tiessen. > be, ey, w, wa, wä.
	12	Schiller	*Wilhelm Tell* ST, dir. Jessner, des. Pirchan. > ko, b, wn.
	14	Kranz	**Freiheit** Proletarian T (in Philharmonie), dir. Martin.
	23	Hamsun	*Spiel des Lebens* Dresden SH.
1920			
January	10	Julius Maria Becker	*Das letzte Gericht* Darmstadt LT.
	17	Shakespeare	*Hamlet* GS, dir. Reinhardt, des. Stern, mus. Tiessen. > gt, k, moi, s, th1, th3, w. 73 perfs.

	20	Kaiser	*Hölle, Weg, Erde* LT, dir. Barnowsky, des. Klein. > dx, kl, ls.
	25	A. Zweig	*Die Sendung Semaels* DT, dir. Herald, des. Stern. > d. gü, gz, j, swe, wa. 29 perfs.
	28	Kaiser	**Der gerettete Alkibiades** Munich Res-T.
		Toller	*Die Wandlung* Stuttgart DT, dir. Skuhra, des. Baumeister.
	?	Kaiser	*Gas 1* Hamburg KS, dir. Engel.
February	9	Nestroy/Tucholsky	*Judith und Holofernes* GS, dir. Reinhardt, des. Stern. > gz, p. 2 perfs.
	14	Rolland	*Danton* (trans. L. von Jacobi and W. Herzog) GS, dir. Reinhardt, des. Stern. > be, d, k, w, wä. 6 perfs.
	26	C. Goetz	**Menagerie** (four one-acters) DKT.
	27	Balázs	*Tödliche Jugend* Vienna, Neue Wiener Bühne.
	?	Kaiser	*Gas 1* Dresden, dir. Viertel.
	27	Sorge	*Der Bettler* Munich KS, dir. Zoff. > ka.
March	4	Hauptmann	**Gabriel Schillings Flucht** DT KS, dir. Holländer, des. Stern. > as, be, s, se, th1. 27 perfs.
	12	Wedekind	*Der Marquis von Keith* ST, dir. Jessner, des. Pirchan. > dx, ko, mü.
		Brust	**Der ewige Mensch** Halberstadt StdT.
	19	Kranz	*Freiheit* Stuttgart DT, dir. Skuhra, des. Baumeister. > lsn.
	25	Schnitzler	*Die Schwestern* Vienna Burg-T.
	28	Hauptmann	**Der weisse Heiland** GS, dir. Martin, des. Stern. > j, moi, sw, wä. (Martin's first GS production). 53 perfs.
April	1	Johst	*Der junge Mensch* Tribüne.
	8	Kornfeld	*Die Verführung* Hamburg KS, dir. Engel, des. Schroeder.
	9	Sternheim	*1913* KSH, dir. Altmann. > b.
	11	Wildgans	**In Ewigkeit, Amen** Brünn, DT.
	13	Goethe	*Stella* DT KS, dir. Reinhardt, des. Stern. > as, ku, s, th1.
	18	Hasenclever	*Antigone* GS, dir. Martin, des. Martin, mus. Pringsheim. > be, ey, j. 1 perf.
		Strauss/Hofmannsthal	*Die Frau ohne Schatten* Berlin SO.
	21	Kornfeld	**Himmel und Hölle** DT, dir. Berger, des. Bamberger. > gü, k, s, wa. 3 perfs. in series 'Das junge Deutschland.'
	23	Evreinov	*Die Kulissen der Seele* (trs. Czokor) Vienna, Ren-T.
		Shaw	*The Dark Lady of the Sonnets* Vienna, Ren-T.
May	7	Klabund	**Die Nachtwandler** Hanover SH.
	15	Hasenclever	**Die Menschen** Prague DLT KS.
	22	Johst	**Der König** Dresden SH, dir. Wiecke, des. Poelzig/ Linnebach.
		Rubiner	**Die Gewaltlosen** NVT.
	28	Shakespeare	*Julius Caesar* GS, dir. Reinhardt, des. Stern, mus. Pringsheim. > az, di, hs, k, j, moi, s. 70 perfs.
June	3	Unruh	**Platz** Frankfurt SH, dir. Hartung, des. Babberger. > bd, eb, g, m. Hartung's last production before move to Darmstadt.
	11	Aristophanes	*Lysistrata* GS, dir. Reinhardt, des. Stern, mus. Holländer. > az, ec, gt, gz, hs, j.
	19	Shakespeare	*A Midsummer Night's Dream* Munich KS. > bg, bi. 55 perfs.

Start of 1920–21 Season

August	28	Dumas/Edschmid	*Kean* DT, dir. Hartung, des Pillartz/Pinner. > b, dp, gz, sw, wä.
	29	Zarek	*Kaiser Karl V* DT, dir. Herald. Last production of 'Das Junge Deutschland.' One perf.
September	4	Shakespeare	*Romeo and Juliet* DT, dir. Reinhardt. > az, di, dv, ku, moi, pn, te.
	18	Hofmannsthal	*Jedermann* GS, dir. Reinhardt, des. Stern/Roller > di, dg, ey, g, k, moi, ro, te.
October	2	Heynicke	*Der Kreis* ("play about the senses"), Frankfurt NT.
	9	Johst	*Der König* Munich KS, dir. Falckenberg, des. Reigbert. > ka.
	14	Wittfogel	*Der Krüppel* Proletarian T, dir. Piscator, des. Heartfield. (Played in various Berlin venues with two other short plays.)
	22	Goethe	*Urfaust* DT, dir. Reinhardt. > d, di, gz, ha, s, th1, th3. (First production of Holländer's management.)
	28	Hasenclever	*Jenseits* Dresden SH, dir. Viertel.
	31	Lothar Schmidt	*Fox-trott* (three short plays) Duisburg StdT.
November	5	Shakespeare	*Richard III* ST, dir. Jessner, des. Pirchan. > be, f, hf, ko, mü, wn.
		Kaiser	*Europa* GS, dir. Martin, des. Kainer, mus. W. R. Heymann. > ba, g, moi, thi3. 8 perfs.
	12	Rehfisch	*Chauffeur Martin* Mannheim NT.
	15	Toller	*Masse-Mensch* Nuremberg, StdT, dir. Neubauer. (Five closed perfs. for union members.)
	16	Shaw	*Heartbreak House* (trs. Trebitsch) Vienna, Burg-T.
	20	Rehfisch	*Der Chauffeur Martin* DT, dir. and des. Martin. > kl, ro, v, wa.
December	1	Claudel	*L'Echange* (trs. J. Heyner) Basel StdT.
	4	Korngold	*Die tote Stadt* (a) Cologne Opera. (b) Hamburg StdT.
	5	Sinclair	*Prinz Hagen* Prolet. T, dir. Piscator, des. Moholy-Nágy.
	7	Feuchtwanger	*Der Amerikaner* Munich KS, dir. Falckenberg, des. Reigbert. > bi.
	10	Zuckmayer	*Kreuzweg* ST, dir. Berger, des. Bamberger. > dc, hf.
	16	T. Tagger	*Annette* (From cycle '1920 oder Die Komödie vom Untergang der Welt'). Vienna, DVT KS.
	22	Shaw	*Caesar and Cleopatra* DT, dir. Wendhausen, des. Grosz and Heartfield. > di, ec, ey, gt, k, kö.
	23	Schnitzler	*Reigen* (*La Ronde*) KSH, dir. Reusch, des Stern. > edt, gö. Banned; released 3 January; trial held in June.)
		Tagger	*Harry* Halle a.d. Saale.
1921			
January	5	Hauptmann	*Florian Geyer* GS, dir. Martin, des. Martin/Hahlo. > di, kl, wä.
	8	Griese	*Die Stadt* Schwerin, LT.
	12	Wildgans	*Kain* Rostock StdT.
	18	Wolf	*Der Unbedingte* Stettin StdT.
	28	Dietzenschmidt	*Die Sankt Jakobsfahrt* Schwerin LT.
	31	Kaiser	*Die jüdische Witwe* (a) Meiningen LT. (b) Nordhausen StdT.
February	2	Kokoschka	*Orpheus und Eurydike* Frankfurt SH.

	3	Hasenclever	*Jenseits* Munich KS, dir. Viertel.
	4	Strauss/Kessler/ Hofmannsthal	***Josefslegende*** (ballet) Berlin SO.
	8	Brust	***Die Schlacht der Heilande*** Halberstadt SdtT.
	13	Sternheim	***Herr von Steingalt*** Darmstadt LT.
	17	Sternheim	***Der entfesselte Zeitgenosse*** Darmstadt LT, dir. Hartung.
	19	Schiller	*Die Jungfrau von Orleans* GS, dir. Martin, des. B. Taut, mus. Pringsheim > di, ha, k, s, sw.
	24	Hasenclever	*Jenseits* DT KS, dir. Grossmann, des. Hahlo. > di, s.
	26	ditto	ditto Frankfurt SH, dir. Weichert, des. Sievert. > eb, m.
		Shaw	*Captain Brassbound's Conversion* VB, dir. Fehling. > hp, ky.
March	4	Czokor	***Die rote Strasse*** Brünn (Brno) DSH.
		Tagore	*Der König der dunklen Kammer* (trs. G. Landauer/H. Lachmann) DT KS, dir. Reich, des. Heartfield. > di, kl, wä. 31 perfs.
	8	Kranz	*Freiheit* Vienna DVT.
	11	v. Wangenheim	***Der Mann Fjodor*** NVT Berlin.
	12	Shakespeare	*The Merchant of Venice* GS, dir. Reinhardt, des. Beugen, mus. Humperdinck > di, g, gt, gz, k, kö, s, sw, te, th3.
	22	Unruh	***Prinz Louis Ferdinand*** Darmstadt LT, dir. Hartung, des. Pilartz. > g.
	23	Barlach	***Die echten Sedemunds*** Hamburg KS, dir. Ziegel, des. Schroeder. > bn, hwm, mw.
	24	Molnar	*Der Schwan* Vienna, Burg-T.
	30	Péladan	*Semiramis* (trs. Schering) Munich SH.
April	1	Barlach	*Die echten Sedemunds* ST, dir. Jessner. > f, fh, ko, lg, mü.
	5	Büchner	*Woyzeck* DT, dir. Reinhardt, des. Heartfield/Dvorsky. > di, dy, kl. 9 perfs.
	12	Stramm	***Kräfte*** DT KS, dir. Reinhardt, des. Dvorsky/Haas-Heye. > hl, kl, s, th1.
	14	Kaiser	*Von Morgens bis Mitternachts* LT, dir. Barnowsky, des. Klein. > gr.
	15	Haller/Künnecke/ Rideamus	***Der Vetter aus Dingsda*** TamN.
	19	Shakespeare	*A Midsummer Night's Dream* GS, dir. Reinhardt, des. Meid > di, dg, ey, ha, k, mw, th1, th3.
	21		Closure of the Proletarian Theatre by Berlin police.
May	2	Shaw	*Misalliance* DT KS, dir. Reich, des. Heartfield. > edt, gt, pa, sw.
	6	Schiller	*Fiesco* ST, dir. Jessner. > d, f, ko, lg.
	14	Wassermann/Wellesz	***Die Prinzessin Girnara*** Hanover Opera.
		Stramm	***Erwachen*** and ***Haidebraut*** Dresden SH.
	15	Schnitzler	***Casanova in Spa*** Königsberg NSH.
June	4	Kokoschka/Blei/ Hindemith	*Mörder, Hoffnung der Frauen, Das Nusch-Nuschi.* Stuttgart LT.
	5	Johst	*Stroh* ("peasant comedy")
	17	F. C. Weiskopf	***Föhn*** Bad Harzburg, Kurtheater.
	20	Hauptmann	*Die Weber* GS, dir. Martin, cost. K. Richter. > di, k, sw, wä. 75 perfs.
July	27	Kornfeld	*Die Verführung* Munich KS, dir. Engel.

Start of 1921–22 Season

September	7	Goethe	*Götz von Berlichingen* GS, dir. Martin, des. H. Bengen. > as, di, gü, kl, sw.
	15		Wilde Bühne opens in basement of T des Westens.
	19	Hebbel	*Herodes und Mariamne* DT, dir. Falckenberg, des. Reigbert. > di, k, s. 13 perfs.
	26	Schiller	*Die Räuber* GS, dir. Martin, des. K. Richter. > di, dg, ha, ka. 51 perfs.
	29	Toller	*Masse-Mensch* VB, dir. Fehling, des. Strohbach, mus. Tiessen. > dh1, hp)
October	10		Opening of T am K, Berlin.
	19	Unruh	*Louis Ferdinand, Prinz von Preussen* DT, dir. Hartung, des. Pilartz. > di, dg, gü, ha, k, th1, wä. 61 perfs.
November	7	Hofmannsthal	**Der Schwierige** Munich Res-T, dir. Stieler. > bg, ks, we, wu.
	11	Shakespeare	*Othello* ST, dir. Jessner, des. Pirchan. > f, hf, ko, sr, wa.
	17	Rolland	*Le Temps viendra* Cen-T, dir. Piscator, des. Schmalhausen. > hk.
	28		Stanislavsky and the Moscow Art Theatre open in Berlin.
	30	Hofmannsthal	*Der Schwierige* DT, KS, dir. Reich, des. Rachlis. > edt, gt, mw, th1, th2, th3. 9 perfs.
		C. Hauptmann	**Musik** (a) Leipzig AT. (b) Dortmund StdT.
December	13	Strindberg	*The Dream Play* DT, dir. Reinhardt, des. Dworsky, mus. Nilson > k, kl, th1, th3. 35 perfs.
	17	Büchner	*Dantons Tod* GS, dir. Reinhardt/Held, des. Dworsky, mus. Wladigeroff. > dc, di, ha, k, kö. 49 perfs.
December	31	Offenbach	*Orpheus in the Underworld* GS, dir. Reinhardt, des. Rée. > dg, kp, p. 45 perfs.

1922			
January	6	Schnitzler	*Anatol* DT KS, dir. Schmith, des. Heartfield. > ed, th3. 70 perfs.
	12	Kornfeld	*Himmel und Hölle* Frankfurt SH, dir. Weichert, des. Sievert. > bd, eb, m, od.
February	2		Rolf de Maré's Swedish Ballet opens at GS (Till 13 Feb.)
	5	Jahnn	**Die Krönung Richards III** Leipzig SH, dir. Rothe.
	13	Schiller	*Don Carlos* ST, dir. Jessner, des. Strnad. > d, dc, hf, mü.
	14	Kaiser	**Kanzlist Krehler** DT KS, dir. Herald, des. Grosz/Heartfield. > gz, kf.
	20	Rolland	*Die Wölfe* (trs. Herzog) DT, dir. Viertel, des. Dworsky/Heartfield. > di, k, kl, wä. 13 perfs.
March	10	Hauptmann	*Die Ratten* VB, dir. Fehling, des. Strohbach. > dh1, hp, ky, ma.
		L. Berger	*Genofeva* ST
	11	Hebbel	*Judith* DT, dir. Viertel, des. Schütte. > dp, g.
	15	Feuchtwanger after Calderon	**Der Frauenverkaüfer,** Munich KS, dir. R. Frank, des. Reigbert. > b, kp
April	22	Bronnen	**Vatermord** Frankfurt SH, dir. Hoffmann-Harnisch, des. Sievert. > m, wg.
	29	Brust	*Der singende Fisch* DT, dir. Reich. > ba, di, wa. 1 perf.
May	5	Grabbe	*Napoleon oder die hundert Tage* ST, dir. Jessner, des. Klein. > f, hu, hz, mü, re, wa.
	9	Nestroy	*Einen Jux will er sich machen* Neues Operetten-T, dir. Ettlinger, des. Heartfield. > ed, et.

	14	Hauptmann	*Die versunkene Glocke* GS, dir. Martin, des. Bengen. > ba, di, ha, kl.
		Bronnen	*Vatermord* JB in DT, dir. Viertel, des. Dworsky. > bg, gr, hp, s, tw.
June	30	Toller	**Die Maschinenstürmer** GS, dir. Martin, des. Heartfield and Dworsky, mus. Pringsheim. > di, gä, gr, wä.
July	5	Grabbe	*Scherz, Satire, Ironie und tiefere Bedeutung* Munich KT, dir. Engel. > fa, we.
August	6	Toller	*Bilder aus der grossen französischen Revolution* (Pageant for Leipzig trade union festival)

Start of 1922–23 Season

September	7	Strindberg	*The Father* DT, dir. Holländer, des. Knina. > gt, kl, s, wä.
	14	Shakespeare	*King Richard II* DT, dir. Viertel, des. Pillartz. > bg, de, dg, ey, g, gr, moi, ro.
	22	Brecht	**Trommeln in der Nacht** Munich KS, dir. Falckenberg, des. Reigbert. > fa, hw, kp, lb. Kleist Prize for 1922.
October	2	Shakespeare	*The Taming of the Shrew* GS, dir. Schmith/Reinhardt, des. Pilartz. > bg, dg, dh1, gz, kl, kö.
	18	Lessing	*Miss Sarah Sampson* Ren-T, dir. Berger.
November	8	Strindberg	*Luther* GS, dir. Révy, des. Pilartz. > di, gü, k, sv, wä
	10	Shakespeare	*Macbeth* ST, dir. Jessner, des. W. Reimann. > eb, f, ko, m, mü)
	13	O. Straus	*Die törichte Jungfrau* GS, dir. Schmith/Feld, des. Pilartz. > dg, kö, th3, wm.
	14	Shakespeare	*King Richard II* DT, dir. Viertel. > bg, g, moi.
	27		Start of Berlin actors' strike.
	18	Weill	**Zaubernacht** Tamk, dir. F. L. Hörth, cond. Weill. > lj.
December	20	Brecht	*Trommeln in der Nacht* DT, dir. Falckenberg, des. Pilartz, > er, g, gü, gz, kü. 4 perfs.

1923

January	24	Maugham	*The Circle* DT KS, dir. Reich, des. Pilartz. > bg, dh1, gt, te.
February	1	Kleist	*Kätchen von Heilbronn* ST, dir. Fehling, des. Neher. > eb, lg, m, ma.
	22	Strindberg	*Miss Julie* DT KS, dir. Reich, des. Dworsky. > bg, g, sv.
	23	Meyer-Förster	*Alt-Heidelberg* DT, dir. Gülstorff, des. Dworsky. > di, gt, gz, k, mo.
March	18	Ernst Weiss	**Olympia** JB in Ren-T, dir. Martin, mus. Pringsheim. > g, s, tw.
April	7		Tairov and the Kamerny Theatre from Moscow in Berlin till c. 20 Apr. (with *Andrienne Lecouvreur*, *Giroflé-Giroflà*, *Phèdre*, *Princess Brambilla*, and *Salomé*)
	13	Goethe	*Faust, Part 1* ST, dir. Jessner, des. Klein, > bt, eb, kl, m, wa.
	20	Shakespeare	*King Lear* GS, dir. Reich, des. Poelzig. > di, ey, fe, g, k, sv.
	24	Ibsen	*John Gabriel Borkman* ST, dir. Viertel. > ko.
	25	Shakespeare	*As You Like It* LT, dir. Barnowsky, > bg.
May	2	Kornfeld	*Die Verführung* DT KS. dir. Révy, des. Krehan. > gr, gü, kö, kü, sv.

	9	Brecht	*Im Dickicht* Munich Res-T, dir. Engel, des. Neher. > fa, kp, we.
	23	Barlach	*Der arme Vetter* ST, dir. Fehling, des. Rochus Gliese. > g, hf, ka, lg, wa.
	24	Barlach	*Der tote Tag* NVT, dir. Paul Günther, des. Dahl. > az, s, st.
July	16	Schiller	*Die Räuber* Schauspielertheater in Cen-T, dir. Martin.
August	16		Opening of Bauhaus Week in Weimar and Jena.

Start of 1923–24 Season

August	24	Jahnn	***Pastor Ephraim Magnus*** (ad. by Brecht/Bronnen) 'Das Theater' in the Schwechtensaal, dir. Bronnen. Disowned by Jahnn.
September	1	Lessing	*Nathan der Weise* Sch-T Marked the Schiller-T's opening as part of the ST.
September	14	Millöcker	*Der Bettelstudent* GS, dir. J. Brandt, des. Krehan. Start of Sladek management of GS.
	18	Shakespeare	*The Merchant of Venice* 'Die Truppe' ? in LSH, dir. Viertel. > ko.
		Shaw	*Pygmalion* DT, dir. Schwannecke, des. Krehan. > do, ey, gt, k, kü.
	19	Toller	***Der deutsche Hinkemann*** Leipzig AT, dir. Wiecke. > dc.
	23	Essig	***Überteufel*** JB in ST, dir. Jessner. > di, f, kl, m, ma, s, tw.
October	6	Hamsun	*Vom Teufel geholt* "Die Truppe", dir. Viertel.
	9	O'Neill	*Anna Christie* DT, dir. Wendhausen, dir. Krehan. > do, gt. 2 perfs.
	19	Ibsen	*An Enemy of the People* SchT, dir. Jessner. > fl, kl, wa.
November	2	Marlowe	*Edward II* 'Schauspielertheater' dir. and ad. Martin. > bg, d, g.
	3	Kaiser	***Nebeneinander*** 'Die Truppe' in LSH, dir. Viertel, des. Grosz. > au, f, sa, st, wä.
	20	J. Strauss	*The Gypsy Baron* GS, dir. Brandt, des. Krehan.
	24	Dario Nicodemi	*Tageszeiten der Liebe* DT, dir. Forster-Larrinaga, des. Krehan.
December	2	Musil	***Vincenz, oder die Freundin bedeutender Männer*** 'Die Truppe' in LSH, dir. Viertel, des. Singer/Dicker. > bi, f, st, wä.
	8	Brecht	***Baal*** Leipzig AT, dir. Kronacher, des. Thiersch. > kö.
	22	Grabbe	*Scherz, Satire, Ironie* DT, dir. Engel, des. Krehan. > gt, gü, ko, mw.
	29	Shakespeare	*Twelfth Night* LT, dir. Barnowsky. > bg.
	31	Goetz	*Ingeborg* DT KS, dir. Goetz, des. Krehan. > ku.

1924			
January	8	O'Neill	*The Emperor Jones* 'Die Truppe' in LSH, dir. Viertel, des. Kiesler. > hm, hp, wä.
	17	Toller	*Hinkemann* Dresden SH, dir. Wiecke. > dc. Withdrawn after one performance.
February	1	Sternheim	*Der Nebbich* DT KS, dir. Sternheim, des. Thea Sternheim. > fe, gz, sv.
	15	Suppé	*Boccaccio* GS, dir. F. Gross, des. Krehan. > do, wm.

	29	Büchner	*Dantons Tod* DT, dir. Engel, des. ?Strnad. > fe, hf, ko, ku.
	?	Barlach	*Der tote Tag* Munich KS, dir. Falckenberg. > kp, sw.
March	6	Wedekind	*Der Liebestrank* 'Die Truppe' in LSH, dir. Hilpert.
	11	Kornfeld	*Palme oder der Gekränkte* DT KS, dir. Schwannecke, des. Krehan. > et, gt, mw.
	19	Brecht	**Leben Eduards des Zweiten** (after Marlowe) Munich KS, dir. Brecht, des. Neher. > fa, hm, kp, sw.
	25	K. Kraus	*Traumtheater, Traumstück* 'Die Truppe' in LSH, dir. Viertel.
	27	Kaiser	**Kolportage** LT, dir. Lind, des. Krehan. > hs, kr.
April	1	Goldoni	*The Servant of Two Masters* Vienna TidJ, dir. Reinhardt, des. Laske. > bi, da, ha, se, th1, th2, th3, wu. Inaugurating Reinhardt's management of TiJ. 61 perfs.
	6	Bronnen	**Anarchie in Sillian** JB in DT, dir. Hilpert. > ei, fk, ki, tw. Later transferred to Ren-T.
	8	Hebbel	*Die Nibelungen* ST, dir. Fehling, des. Pirchan. > be, eb, g, gr, lg, re, s, wa.
	16	Hofmannstahl	*Der Schwierige* Vienna, TiJ, dir. Reinhardt, des. Strnad. > ec, fll, th1, wu.
	19	Toller	*Hinkemann* Res-T, dir. Lind, des. Klein. > g.
	25	Wedekind	*König Nicolo* Sch-T, dir. Jessner, des. Pirchan. > fk, gr, lg, ma, w, wa.
May	26	Paquet	**Fahnen** VB, dir. Piscator, des. Suhr. > ha, st.
June	23	O'Neill	*Anna Christie* TiJ, dir. Kalbeck, des. Niedermoser. > di, fe, hm.

Start of 1924–25 Season

September	6	Lissauer	**Yorck** Kiel SH.
	7	Kranz	**Fussel** Mannheim NT.
	9	Freksa	*Sumurûn* (revival of prewar mime) DT, dir. E. Matray, des. Stern, mus. V. Holländer. > bi, fk, mü.
	27	Barlach	**Die Sündflut** Stuttgart LT, dir. Hoffmann-Harnisch, des. after Barlach.
	30	Ernst Fischer	**Das Schwert des Attila** Vienna, Burg-T.
October	1	Goetz	*Die tote Tante und andere Begebenheiten* DT, dir. Goetz, des. Krehan and Dworsky (100 perfs.)
	3	Brust	**Tolkening** (*Die Wölfe, Die Würmer, Der Phönix*). Markowitz Mus. Dram. T.
	10–11	Schiller	*Wallenstein* ST, dir. Jessner, des. Klein. > eb, gr, gü, ha, k, re, s, vk.
	13	Goll	**Methusalem oder Der ewige Bürger** 'Dramatisches Theater,' dir. Neubauer.
	14	Schoenberg	**Die glückliche Hand** Vienna, Volksoper.
		Shaw	*Saint Joan* DT, dir. Reinhardt, des. Strnad. > bg, bt, f, fk, ha, mü. 168 perfs.
		Galsworthy	*Loyalty,* trs. Schalitt (a) Frankfurt NT (b) Leipzig SH.
	23	Shelley	*The Cenci* (trs. A. Wolfenstein) Frankfurt SH.
		Hindemith/Krell	**Der Dämon** (mime) Duisburg StdT.
	26	Krenek	**Zwingburg** ('scenic cantata') Berlin SO.
	29	Brecht	*Im Dickicht* DT, dir. Engel, des. Neher. > bt, fk, ki, ko, m, mü.
	30	O'Neill	*The Hairy Ape* Cologne SH.

	31	Vischer	*Chaplin* (Tragigroteske) Lübeck StdT.
November	1	Goldoni	*The Servant of Two Masters* Kom, dir. Reinhardt, des. Krehan/Laske. > bi, fll, ha, se, th1, th2, th3, wu. Inaugurating Reinhardt's new Berlin theatre. (Cf. TidJ 1 Apr 1924.)
		R. Strauss	*Intermezzo* Dresden SH.
	11	Schanzer/Welisch/ Nelson	*Harem auf Reisen* (revue) Nelson-T.
	26	Molière	*Le Malade imaginaire* Kom, dir. Reinhardt, des. Kaufmann/Krehan. > bi, bt, di, ec, fll, p, sp.
	28	Bronnen	*Katalaunische Schlacht* Frankfurt SH, dir. Weichert, des. Neher. > bd, od.
	29	Strindberg	*Gustav III* (trs. Schering) Stuttgart LT KH. German premiere.
December	1		Kurt Robitschek opens his 'Kabarett der Komiker' in Berlin.
	4	Brecht	*Leben Eduards des Zweiten* (after Marlowe) ST, dir. Fehling, des. Gliese.> fa, gü, k, re, s, vk.
	9	Melchior Vischer	*Der Teemeister* (Japanese legend). Leipzig StdT.
	13	Kornfeld	*Sakuntala* (after Kalidasa) Cologne SH.
	18	Sternheim	*1913* DT KS, dir. Sternheim. > sr.
	19	Wedekind	*Franziska* Vienna DVT, dir. and des. Martin.> dx.
	21 {	O'Neill	*Moon of the Caribees* and
	{	Brust	*Südseespiel* VB, dir. Piscator, des. Malik, mus. Zeller.
	23	Milne	*The Dover Road* (trs. H. Richter)
	30	Pirandello	*Six Characters in Search of an Author.* Kom, dir. Reinhardt, des. Krehan. > bt, dg, ho, ki, ku, p.
	31	Brandon Thomas	*Charley's Aunt* ST, dir. Jessner, des. Klein, mus. H. Hirsch. > fl, k.

1925

January	3	Klabund	*Der Kreidekreis* (ad. from the Chinese). Frankfurt SH, dir. Weichert, des. Sievert. > bd.
	9	Zoff	*Maria Orlowa* Hamburg DSH.
	15	Pirandello	*Die Wollust der Ehrlichkeit* (a) Darmstadt LT (b) Frankfurt NT.
	16	Burri	*Amerikanische Jugend* Hanover, Schauburg.
	17	Schanzer/Welisch/ Straus	*Riquette* DKT.
	19	Goetz	*Der Lampenschirm* DT KS, des. Dworsky. > bie, gö.
	25	Pirandello	*Der Mann, das Tier und die Tugend* Breslau, Lobe-T.
	29	Toller	*Der entfesselte Wotan* Prague NDT KB, dir. K. Demetz. (World premiere in Bolshoi, Moscow 16 November 1924).
	31	Rehfisch	*Wer weint um Juckenack?* VB, dir. Piscator. > g, m.
February	3	Kaiser	*From Morn to Midnight.* Sch-T
	13	Kleist	*Der Prinz von Homburg* ST, dir. Berger, des. Bamberger. > ha, k.
	15	Zuckmayer	*Pankraz erwacht* JB at DT, dir. Hilpert, des. Strohbach. > f, fk, gr, m, st.
	27	Shakespeare	*Coriolanus* DT in LT, dir. Engel, des. Neher. > fk, ko, s.
March	10	Dumas	*Camille* (ad. Bruckner). DT, dir. Reich, des. Krehan/Ilse Fehling. > bg, gü, mü.
	11	Milne	*The Romantic Age* Ren-T.
	14	R. Leonhard	*Segel am Horizont* VB, dir. Piscator, des. T. Müller. > hk, m, ve, wä, wh.

	25	Pirandello	*Henry IV* Hamburg, Thalia-T.
		Pirandello	*Die lebende Maske* ditto.
	28	Okonkowski/	*1000 süsse Beinchen* (revue) Metropol.
		Steinberg/Bromme	
April	2	Wedekind	*Franziska* TidK, dir. Martin. > dx. The Vienna production of 19 Dec.
		Bartók/Balázs	*Duke Bluebeard's Castle* Weimar NT
	7	Galsworthy	*Urwald* (trs. Schalitt) Hamburg Thalia-T.
	16	Johst	**Die fröhliche Stadt** Düsseldorf SH KH.
	24	Pirandello	*Die Wollust der Anständigkeit* DT KS, dir. R. Gerner, des. Dworsky. > kl.
May	13	Shakespeare	*Hamlet* VB, dir. Günther, des. Schlemmer. > az, wä.
	16	Bronnen	**Rheinische Rebellen** ST, dir. Jessner, des. Pirchan. > m, s, sr, wa.
	19	Romains	*Dr. Knock* DT, dir. Engel, des. Neher. > kl, ku, wg.
	21	Busoni	**Doktor Faustus** Dresden SO.
	26	Werfel	*Juarez und Maximilian* Vienna TidJ, dir. Reinhardt.
June	2	Jooss	*Die Brautfahrt* (ballet) Münster StdT.
	7	Bronnen	**Die Excesse** JB in LT, dir. Hilpert. > ba, bo, fk, ha, m, st, tw, wä. Transfer to TidK in Feb. 1926.
	20	Max Halbe	*Jugend* ST, dir. Fehling. > hl, ma, st.
July	12	Gasbarra (et al.)	*Trotz alledem* (Communist historical pageant) GS, dir. Piscator, des. Heartfield, mus. Meisel.
	?	E. E. Kisch	**Die gestohlene Stadt** Stuttgart SH.

Start of 1925–26 Season

September	1	Shakespeare	*As You Like It* TidK, dir. Barnowsky. > bg, ko.
	4	Kaiser	**Margarine** Kom-H.
	13	Hauptmann	**Veland** Hamburg DSH.
	18	Pirandello	*Das Leben, das ich dir gab* (trs. H. Jacob) Frankfurt SH.
	19	Pirandello	*Spiel der Parteien* (trs. E. Hecht) Mannheim NT.
	21	Shaw	*Back to Methusaleh* (trs. Trebitsch) parts 1 and 2 Tribüne, dir. Kerb. > di, ho, gö.
	22	Pirandello	*Der Mann, das Tier und die Tugend* DT KS, dir. Henckels, des. Schütte. > bt, gt, hm.
	25	Galsworthy	*Loyalties* (trs. Schalitt) Kom, dir. Reinhardt, des. Dworsky. > d, ec, gö, ha, kl, th1, wh.
	?	Charell/Benatzky	*Für Dich* (musical). GS, dir. Charell, des. Stern.
October	2	Zerlett/Rebner/	*Confetti* (revue) Nelson-T.
		Nelson	
	12		Three-day visit to Berlin by Teatro d'Arte di Roma with *Sei personaggi, Enrico IV*, and *Il piacere dell' onestà* by Pirandello.
	13	O'Neill	*Desire under the Elms* LT, dir. Viertel, des. T. Müller. > m, mü, w.
	17	Grabbe	*Hannibal* ST, dir. Jessner, des. Sebba. > eb, fa, k, s, vk.
	19	Pirandello	*Jeder nach seiner Art* (trs. Zoff) Darmstadt LT.
	20	Klabund	*Der Kreidekreis* DT, dir. Reinhardt, des. Neher/Pritzel. > bg, bt, fk, kl, kp, th4.
	21 {	E. Schulhoff/J. Benes	**Ogelala** and
	{	W. Grosz	**Sganarell** Dessau, Friedrich-T.
	22	Lernet-Holenia	**Dr. Demetrius** Leipzig AT.
	24	Wedekind	*Frühlings Erwachen* KS, des. Walser. > de, mo, ro, sp, wa.

		Maugham/Colton/ Randolph	*Rain* TamK, dir. Reinhardt, des. Schütte. > do, hm, hö, kl.
	29	Max Mell	*Das Apostelspiel* DT KS, dir. Reinhardt, des. Dworsky. > gö, hm, th1, th4.
November	7	Kaiser	*Die jüdische Witwe* TamS, dir. Martin, des. Schön. > ec, hm, st.
	12	Heynicke	**Das Meer** Lübeck StdT.
		Kaiser	**Der mutige Seefahrer** Dresden SH.
	14	Klabund	**Der Teufelspakt** (a) Hamburg KS. (b) Hanover Schauburg.
	26	Shaw	*Back to Methusaleh,* parts 3–5 (trs. Trebitsch) TidK, dir. Barnowsky, des. Klein. > ba, bd, dx, f, gö, ko, ls, tw.
	28	Shaw	*You Never Can Tell* DT, dir. Engel, des. Neher. > mo, mü.
December	5	Zech	**Erde** Königsberg NSH.
	13	Bronnen	**Die Geburt der Jugend** JB in LT, dir. Neubauer. > ha, sp, tw, wä.
	14	Alban Berg	**Wozzeck** Berlin SO, cond. Kleiber.
	22	Zuckmayer	**Der fröhliche Weinberg** TamS, dir. Bruck, des. Von Arent.
	23	ditto	ditto Frankfurt SH, dir. Hilpert. > mz, od.
	25	Galsworthy	*Sensation* (trs. Schalitt) Hamburg DSH.

1926

January	8	Aristophanes	*Lysistrata* DT, dir. Engel, des. Neher. > bo, ec, mo, mw, ro, sp, st.
	14	Rebner/Zerlett/ Nelson	*Nacht der Nächte* (revue) TamK, dir. Martin. > ad, pa.
	15	Döblin	**Lusitania** Darmstadt LT KH.
	16	Euripides	*The Bacchae* (ad. Viertel) Mannheim NT, mus. Toch.
	24	H. Kasack	**Die Schwester** Heilbronn StdT.
	28	O. Dymow	*Die letzte Geliebte* DT KS, dir. Licho, des. Schütte. > ey, fe, kl, mo.
	29	Bronnen	**Ostpolzug** ST, dir. Jessner, des. Herlth/Röhring. > ko.
		Werfel	*Juarez und Maximilian* DT, dir. Reinhardt, des. Schütte, mus. Wladigeroff. > bi, bt, d, ha, hk, hm, kp.
	30	Lehár	**Paganini** (operetta). DKT.
February	14	Brecht	*Lebenslauf des Mannes Baal* (revision of *Baal*) JB in DT, dir. Brecht/Homolka, des. Neher. > bi, bt, ge, hm, tw, wg.
	19	Fried. Holländer	*Laterna Magica* (revue) Ren-T.
	20	Rehfisch	**Duell am Lido** ST, dir. Jessner, des. Pirchan. > dh2, f, ko, ma.
	21	Paquet	**Sturmflut** VB, dir. Piscator, des. Suhr. > g, gr, ka, re.
	23	Toller	*Der entfesselte Wotan* Tribüne, dir. Fehling, des. Krehan. > et, ge, lsn, sv, tw.
	27	Goll	**Der Stall des Augias** Kassel KT.
March	4	Lunacharsky	*Don Quixote Liberated* VB, dir. Holl.
	5	Maugham	*Home and Beauty* (trs. M. Zoff) Kom, dir. Reinhardt, des. Kainer, mus. Spoliansky. > bo, gö, gt, ro.
	12	Schiffer/Strasser/ Gray	*Die fleissige Leserin* (revue) Ren-T. > ln.
	19	Raynal	*Le Tombeau sous l'Arc de Triomphe* KT, dir. Viertel. (Moved to TaS).

	22	K. Mann	*Anja und Esther* LT, dir. Fisch. > ha, os, vy.
	23	Hasenclever	**Mord** DT, dir. Engel, des. Neher. > bt, kl, kp, st.
	26	Hebbel	*Herodes und Mariamne* ST, dir. Jessner, des. Müller, mus. B. Goldschmidt. > fa, fh, ko, va, wg.
	27	Vischer	*Fussballspieler und Indianer* Darmstadt LT, dir. Löwenberg, des. Schenck von Trapp.
		Weill/Kaiser	**Der Protagonist** Dresden Opera.
April	3	Pirandello	*Die Nackten kleiden* DT KS, dir. Hoffmann-Harnisch, des. Schütte. > gt, hk, ok, sp.
	10	Wolfenstein	**Sturm auf den Tod** (one act) Mannheim NT.
	15	Kaiser	**Zweimal Oliver** Dresden SH, Düsseldorf SH and other theatres.
	21	Klabund	**Brennende Erde** Frankfurt SH.
	22	Essig	**Des Kaisers Soldaten** Dresden Albert-T.
	24	Coward	*Hay Fever* DT KS, dir. Engel, des. Schütte. > bt, gt, sp, va.
	25	Fleisser	**Fegefeuer in Ingolstadt** JB in DT, dir. Bildt, des. Müller. > fa, fk, kp, re, tw, wä, wg.
May	4	Jahnn	**Medea** (adaptation) ST, dir. Fehling, des. Gliese. > fa, ha, s, vk. Taken off after protests.
	15	O'Neill	*The Emperor Jones* TiJ, dir Balázs, des. Kunz. > hm. 3 perfs.
	21	Zech	**Das trunkene Schiff** VB, dir. Piscator, des. Grosz, mus. Zeller. > az, st.
	28	Rehfisch	*Nickel und die 36 Gerechten* Sch-T, dir. Florath. > f, ma, s.
June	1	Tony Impekoven/ Hans Reimann	*Das Ekel* DT, dir. Kuhnert, des. Dworsky. > ad. 92 perfs.
	14	Pirandello	*Alles zum guten* Koblenz StdT.

Start of 1926–27 Season

September	1	Charell/Darewski	*Von Mund zu Mund* (revue) GS.
	2	Shaw	*Androcles and the Lion* DT, dir. Engel, des. Schütte. > gö, hm, va. 29 perfs.
	3	Bourdet	*Die Gefangene* DT KS, dir. Reinhardt, des. Dworsky. > d, dv, ls, mo, th1.
	4	Klabund	**Cromwell** LT.
		Kleist	*Amphitryon* ST, dir. Jessner, des. Pirchan. > eb, fl, pt, wa.
	11	Schiller	*Die Räuber* ST, dir. Piscator, des. Müller, mus. Meisel. > bt, eb, fh, ha.
		Schanzer/Welisch/ Nelson	*Es geht schon besser* (revue) TamK.
	21	Sternheim	**Die Schule von Uznach** *oder Die Neue Sachlichkeit* Hamburg DSH, Mannheim NT and Cologne SH.
	25	Brecht	**Mann ist Mann** (a) Darmstadt LT, dir. Geis, des. Neher. > lg. (b) Düsseldorf SH KH, dir. Munch. (With bs).
October	1	Langer	*Periferie* (trs. Otto Pick) DT, dir. Reinhardt, des. Strnad. > gt, hm, ki, th3.
	3	Eulenburg	*Die beste Polizei* (after Schiller) ST.
	9	Prokofieff	*The Love of the Three Oranges* Berlin SO in Kr-O.
	13	Barlach	**Der Blaue Boll** Stuttgart LT KH.
	15	Lenz	*Die Soldaten* Sch-T, dir. Fehling, des. Klein. > fa, ma, pa, wa.

	17	Bruckner	***Krankheit der Jugend*** Hamburg KS, dir. M. Horwitz.
	20	Claudel	*Le Pain dur* Oldenburg LT.
	22	Wedekind	*Lulu* (both plays) ST, dir. Engel, des. Neher. > bt, ha, hö, ko, m, wä.
	26	W. Goetz	*Neidhardt von Gneisenau* DT, dir. Hilpert, des. Neppach. > gt, hm, k, wn. 119 perfs.
	27	Rehfisch	***Razzia*** Halle a.d. Saale StdT.
	28	Gantillon	*Maya* (trs. R. Blum) DT KS.
	30	Werfel	***Paulus unter den Juden*** Simultaneous premieres in Bonn, Breslau, Cologne, Düsseldorf (SH) and Munich (PR-T).
		Wedekind	***Bismarck*** Weimar NT.
November	4	Marischka/ Granich- staudten/Straus	***Die Königin*** (operetta) DKT.
	6	Kornfeld	***Kilian oder die gelbe Rose*** Frankfurt SH, dir. Weichert.
		Ben Jonson (ad. S. Zweig)	*Volpone* Vienna, Burg-T.
	9	Hindemith	***Cardillac*** Dresden Opera.
	10	Gorky	*The Lower Depths* VB, dir. Piscator, des. Suhr. > g, gr, ka, lk, s.
	20	Hauptmann	***Dorothea Angermann*** Vienna TiJ, dir. Reinhardt. (With hk, hm, ky).
	27	Bartók/Lengyel	*The Miraculous Mandarin* Cologne O.
		Krenek/Kokoschka	***Orpheus und Eurydike*** Kassel ST.
		Heynicke	***Kampf um Preussen*** Hanover SH and Leipzig SH.
December	3	Shakespeare	*Hamlet* ST, dir. Jessner, des. Neher, mus. Meisel. > bt, er, hl, ko, kp, w
	4	Galsworthy	*Escape* (trs. Schalitt) Frankfurt NT.
	11 ⎰	Brecht	***Die Hochzeit*** (one-acter) and
	⎱	Lernet-Holenia	***Ollapotrida*** (ditto) Frankfurt SH, dir. M. Vischer.
	13	Jahnn	*Die Krönung Richards des Dritten* JB in TamS, dir. Kerb. > ba, bi, fk.
	18	J. Arendt/O. Brock/ P. Strasser	*Oh, USA* (revue) KT.
	21	Chekhov	*The Three Sisters* ST, dir. Fehling, > hö, lsn, m, ma. First German production.
	31	Achard	*Voulez-vous jouer avec moâ?* Düsseldorf SH.
1927			
January	12	Hasenclever	***Ein besserer Herr*** Frankfurt SH, dir. Weichert, des. Sievert. > od.
	13	Honegger/Morax	*Judith* Cologne O.
	15	B. v. Brentano	***Geld*** Darmstadt LT KH.
	21	H. Mann	***Das gastliche Haus*** Munich KS, dir. Piscator, des. Reigbert.
	29	Unruh	***Bonaparte*** Breslau, Lobe-T.
February	1	Lunacharsky	*The Bear's Wedding* (trs. Götz and Nestriepke) Stettin SdtT.
	4	Rehfisch	*Razzia* Sch-T, dir. Martin, des. Pirchan. > bt, gz, ky, m.
	10	Krenek	***Jonny spielt auf*** Leipzig NT.
		Lania	***Friedenskonferenz*** Krefeld Sdt-T.
	12	Kennedy	*The Constant Nymph* TidK, dir. Barnowsky. > bg, ho.
	15	Unruh	*Bonaparte* DT, dir. Hartung, des. Schütte. > ey, f, hm, k.

	16	Langhoff	*Knockout* Wiesbaden ST KH.
		Lehár	*Der Zarewitsch* DKT.
	22	A. Neumann	*Der Patriot* LT, dir. Martin, des. Neher, mus. Pringsheim. > fk, ki, ko, w.
		Galsworthy	*Der Erste und der Letzte* (trs. Meyerfeld) Lübeck KS.
	27	Kornfeld	*Kilian oder die gelbe Rose* ST, dir. Engel, des. Pirchan. > fa, fh, wä.
March	2	Weill/Goll	*Royal Palace* and *Der neue Orpheus* SO, dir. Hörth, cond. Kleiber, des. Aravantinos.
	18	Hasenclever	*Ein besserer Herr* ST. > bt, hl, wa.
	23	Welk	*Gewitter über Gotland* VB, dir. Piscator, des. Müller. > g, gr, ka, st, ve.
	25	Shaw	*The Doctor's Dilemma* DT, dir. Engel, des. Neher. > d, hm, k, ls, ri.
	30	Johst	*Thomas Paine* Bremen SdtT and other theatres.
April	1	Wolf	*Der Mann im Dunkel* Essen SdtT.
	7	Schiffer/Holländer	*Was Sie wollen* Kom, dir. Fried. Holländer, des. Erich E. Stern. > do, ln.
	9	Maugham	*Caesar's Wife* (trs. M. Zoff) Hamburg Thalia-T.
	14	Arno Holz	*Ignorabimus* Düsseldorf SH.
	16	Rehfisch	*Skandal in Amerika* DKT, dir. Martin. > f.
	28	Wolf	*Kolonne Hund* Hamburg DSH, dir. Werther, des. Daniel.
May	2	K. Mann	*Revue zu Vieren* DT KS, dir. Gründgens, des. Thea Sternheim > dc, gg, wk.
	6	Hauptmann	*Florian Geyer* ST, dir. Jessner, des. Neher. > fk, fl.
	17	Sternheim	*Der Snob* Kom, dir. Ralph Roberts, des. E. E. Stern. 65 perfs.
	27	Wallace	*The Ringer* (trs. R. Matthias) DT, dir. Hilpert, des. Schütte. > hm, kö, sr, ss. 97 perfs.
	28	Kaiser	*Papiermühle* DT KS, dir. Viertel, des. Pohl. > mo, mü, rü, wb. 34 perfs.
June	11	Shakespeare	*Measure for Measure* ST, dir. Fehling.
	17	Claudel	*L'ôtage* Mannheim NT.
July	17	Brecht/Weill	*Mahagonny* (Songspiel) Baden-Baden Festival, dir. Brügmann, des Neher, cond. Mehlich > lj.
	21	Fried. Holländer	*Das bist du* (revue) TamK.

Start of 1927–28 Season

September	2	Haller/Rideamus/ Wolff	*Wann und wo?* AdP, mus. Kollo, des. Kainer. (Revue with Tiller Girls.)
		Pirandello	*Henry the Fourth* ST dir. Martin, des. Neher, mus. Pringsheim. > d, Kl, w.
	3	Toller	*Hoppla, wir leben!* First PB in TamN, dir. Piscator. des. Müller, mus. Meisel. > bt, bu, gr, gz, sm, sv. c.60 perfs.
		Shaw	*Widower's Houses* Kom, dir. Forster-Larringa, des. E. E. Stern. > gt, mo, sr, ss.
	13	Shakespeare	*Troilus and Cressida* DT, dir. Hilpert, des. Pohl. > er, ey, fa, hm, mü, ri, wn.
	21	Sternheim	*Die Schule von Uznach* TidK, dir. Hartung, des. Klein. > br, lz, wk.
	22	F. Joachimson	*Fünf von der Jazzband* ST.

October	1	Robitschek/ Hansen/ Spoliansky	*Du holdes Kind vom Rhein* (revue) TdKomiker.
		James Klein	*Alles nackt* (revue) Kom. O.
	2	Brust	**Cordatus** Königsberg NSH.
	3	Krenek	*Jonny spielt auf* Std O, dir. Martin, des. Vergo/Von Arent.
	7	Galsworthy	*Justice* DKT, dir. Martin. > d, gö.
	14	Zuckmayer	**Schinderhannes** LT, dir, Bruck, des. Max Liebermann. > do, kl.
		Johst	**Der Ausländer** Hamburg, Thalia-T.
	15	Lasker-Schüler	*Die Wupper* ST, dir. Fehling, des. Neher. > fh, hd, hö, ma, mü, va.
	18	Hauptmann	*Dorothea Angermann* DT, dir. Reinhardt, des. Dworsky. > ey, hk, hm, k, ky, ri, th1. 80 perfs.
	27	Strindberg	*Gustav III* TidK, dir. Barnowsky, mus. Weill, cond. W. Goehr.
	28	Gantillon	*Maya* DT KS, dir. and des. G. Baty. > ec, er, fa, ks, ls, ri, ss.
		Maugham	*The Constant Wife (Die beständige Gattin*, trs. R. Blum). Vienna TidJ.
	31	Feuchtwanger	**Die Petroleuminseln** Hamburg DSH.
November	10	Paquet	**William Penn** Frankfurt SH.
		A. Tolstoy/ Shchegolev	*Rasputin* 1stPB in TamN, dir. Piscator, des. Müller. > dx, edt, ka, w.
	12	Brecht	*Lebenslauf des Mannes Baal* Kassel ST KH.
		Feuchtwanger	**Kalkutta 4 Mai** Krefeld StdT and Königsberg NSH.
	17	Shakespeare	*The Merchant of Venice* ST, dir. Fehling, des. Klein. > bg, bt, hz, ko, mü, pa, vk.
	19	Beethoven	*Fidelio* Kr-O, dir. and cond. Klemperer, des. Dülberg. First production of K's regime at the Kroll-Opera.
	25	Coward	*Die Ehe von Welt* (trs. Kommer) Kom, dir. Forster- Larrinaga, des. Schütte, mus. Spoliansky. > er, mo.
	28	Wolfenstein	**Bäume in den Himmel** Oberhausen SdtT.
December	2	Dymov/Spoliansky	*Bronx Express* DT KS, dir. Hilpert, des. Schütte. > bo, de, fa, ks, sr. 45 perfs.
	10	Brecht	*Im Dickicht der Städte* (revised version) Darmstadt LT KH, dir. Ebert.
	14	Büchner	*Woyzeck* Sch-T, dir. Fehling, des. Krehan. > fh, fk, ma, pa, wa, wä.
		Toller	*Hinkemann* VB, dir. Toller, des. Suhr. > g, gn, sp, wg.
	23	Lernet-Holenia	**Erotik** Breslau Lobe-T and Frankfurt SH.
	25	Holländer/Seeler	*Bei uns um die Gedächtniskirche rum* (revue) TamK.

1928

January			Reinstitution of Generalintendanz (or unified direction) for Prussian theatres.
	4	Brecht	*Mann ist Mann* VB, dir. Engel, des. Neher, mus. Meisel. > g, gn, lb, wg.
	6	Ibsen	*Peer Gynt* (trs. C. Morgenstern) DT, dir. Viertel, des. Strnad. > eb, fa, hf, k, ri. 28 perfs.
	8	F. Jung	**Heimweh** Piscator Studio, dir. Steckel, des. Heartfield, mus. Eisler. > bie, sv, st.
	11	Honegger/Cocteau	*Antigone* Essen Opera.
	17	Maugham	*The Constant Wife* (trs. M. Zoff) DT KS, dir. Forster- Larrinaga, des. Schütte. > be, gt, ls. 152 perfs.
	21	Lissauer	**Yorck** Cologne SH.

	22	Schoenberg	*Erwartung* Wiesbaden ST.
	23	Hašek/Brod/ Reimann	*Schweik* (ad. Gasbarra, Brecht, Piscator, et al.) 1stPB in TaN, dir. Piscator, des. Grosz. > da, edt, p, sm.
	27	Kaiser	*Der Präsident* Frankfurt SH.
	28	Rehfisch	*Der Frauenarzt* Frankfurt NT
February	3	Duvernois/ Birabeau	*Marcel Fradelin* (trs. B. Frank) Kom, dir. Forster- Larrinaga, des. E. E. Stern. > hm, k, mo. 82 perfs.
	4	Hauptmann	*Die Weber* ST, dir. Jessner, des. Neppach, mus. Schmidt-Günther. > hl, gö, kp, lb, mü, vk, wa.
		Hofmannsthal	*Der Turm* Munich PRT, dir. Stieler.
	14	Menzel	*Toboggan* Dresden ST, dir. Gielen. > po. Shared Kleist Prize for 1927.
	15	Wolfenstein	*Celestina* Frankfurt SH.
	18	B. Frank	*12,000* DT, dir. Hilpert, des. Schütte. > k, sr. 54 perfs.
	18	Weill/Kaiser	*Der Zar lässt sich photographieren* Leipzig NT, dir. Brügmann, cond. Brecher.
	25	Stravinsky/Cocteau	*Oedipus Rex* KrO, dir. and cond. Klemperer, des. Dülberg. First stage prod.
March	1	U. Sinclair	*Singing Jailbirds* Piscator-Studio, dir. Lönner, mus. Meisel > bie, gr, ka, sv.
		Wedekind	*Sonnenspektrum* TamK, dir. Martin, mus. Holländer. > er.
	13	Kaiser	*Oktobertag* Hamburg KS, dir. Gründgens. > gg.
		Unruh	*Louis Ferdinand, Prinz von Preussen* ST, dir. Jessner, des. Neppach. > f, fl, hk, ma, wä.
	27	Fleisser	*Pioniere in Ingolstadt* Dresden, Kom, dir. Mordo.
April	1	Robitschek/ Morgan/Kollo	*Die grosse Kaiserin* TdKomiker.
	5	Kalmán	*Die Herzogin von Chicago* Vienna, TadWien.
	10	Lania	*Konjunktur* 1stPB in LT, dir. Piscator, des. Müller, mus. Weill. > dx, st.
	13	Shaw	*Pygmalion* DT, dir. Mittler, des. Dworsky. > ey, gt, k, ne, sr. 55 perfs.
	19	E. W. Möller	*Aufbruch in Kärnten* Elberfeld Std-T.
	20	Milhaud/Hoppenot	*Die verlassene Ariadne* Wiesbaden ST KH.
	21	Barlach	*Der Findling* Königsberg NSH.
	25	Bronnen	*Katalaunische Schlacht* ST, dir. Hilpert, des. Müller. > fk, mü, vk.
	26	Bruckner	*Krankheit der Jugend* Ren-T, dir. Hartung. > kb.
	29	Mühsam	*Judas* Piscator-Studio, dir. Lindtberg.
	30	Stramm	*Das Opfer* Gotha LT.
May	6	Heynicke	*Wer gewinnt Liselotte?* Darmstadt LT.
		Krenek	*Der Diktator, Das geheime Königreich,* *Schwergewicht* (three short operas) Wiesbaden ST.
	10	E. G. Kolbenheyer	*Heroische Leidenschaften* Düsseldorf SH.
	15	Schiffer/Spoliansky	*Es liegt in der Luft* (revue) Kom., dir. Forster- Larrinaga, des. Trier/Pirchan. > dh2, ks, ln.
	19	Toller	*Die Rache des verhöhnten Liebhabers* Braunschweig LT.
June	6	Strauss/ Hofmannsthal	*Die Ägyptische Helene* Dresden O.
	9	Watters/Hopkins	*Artisten* (ad. Dymov) DT, dir. Reinhardt, des. Schütte, mus. Heymann. > gü, mo, ms, se.
	12	Feuchtwanger	*Die Petroleuminseln* ST, dir. Fehling, des. Neher, mus. Weill.
	19	Schiffer/Goehr	*Ein Stück Malheur* KomH.

	28	Dietzenschmidt	*Hinterhauslegende* Sch-T, dir. Hoffmann-Harnisch, des. Pirchan. (With kp, wä).
July	11	Fried. Holländer	*Es kommt jeder dran* (revue) DKT.
August	14	W. Goldbaum	*Zürich 1914* Bad Kreuznach Kur-T.
	21	Haller/Schiffer	*Schön und Schick* (revue) Admiralspalast.

Start of 1928–29 Season

August	30	Kaiser	*Oktobertag* DT KS, dir. Forster-Larrinaga, des. Schütte. > hm, sr. 42 perfs.
	31	Brecht/Weill	*Die Dreigroschenoper* TaS, dir. Engel, des. Neher. > ba, bu, ge, lj, pn, po, va.
September	1	J. Strauss	*Casanova* (ad. Schanzer/Welisch, Benatzky) GS.
		Robitschek/ Morgan/ Kollo	*Killy macht Karriere* Tder Komiker.
	8	Kaiser	*Gas 1* Sch-T, dir. Jessner, des. Pirchan. > fk, gr, ha, kp, lb, mü, wa.
	12	Shaw	*Misalliance* Kom., dir. Hilpert, des. E. E. Stern. > hs, od, rü, sm, wb.
	15	Unger	*Der rote General* TidK, dir. Engel, des. Neher. > br, ko, wh.
	20	Dreiser	*The Hand of the Potter* (trs. P. Eger). Ren-T.
	26	E. Fischer	*Lenin* Vienna, Carl-T.
October	4	Lehár	*Frederike* (operetta). Metropol-T.
	7	Strauss/Hofmannsthal	*Die Ägyptische Helene* Berlin SO.
	11	Stravinsky/Ramuz	*L'Histoire du Soldat* Kr-O, dir. Geis, des. Müller.
	12	Goethe	*Egmont* ST, dir. Jessner, des. Neher. > f, fk, gr, ku, mü, sv.
		Hasenclever	*Ehen werden im Himmel geschlossen* DT KS, dir. Forster-Larrinaga, des. E. E. Stern. > k, ls, mo, ne, th3. 98 perfs.
	16	Weisenborn	*U-Boot S4* VB, dir. Reuss, des. Suhr, film Oertel/ Lania, mus. Zeller. > g, gb, kw, s.
	20	Bulgakov	*The White Guard* (trs. K. Rosenberg). Breslau, Lobe-T.
	21	C. Morgenstern	*Egon und Emilie* (one-acter) Mannheim NT, mus. Toch.
	22	H. Mann	*Bibi, Jugend 1928* TiPH, mus. Nelson.
	23	Bruckner	*Die Verbrecher* DT, dir. Hilpert, des. Gliese/Ulmer. > al, fa, fe, gg, hö. 114 perfs.
	24	Johst	*Komödie am Klavier* Düsseldorf SdtT KH.
	25	Shakespeare	*Romeo and Juliet* BT, dir. Reinhardt, des. Schütte, mus. Nilson. > bg, dg, lr, wh, wn. 52 perfs.
	27	O'Neill	*The Great God Brown* (trs. K. Maril) Cologne SH.
November	2	Rehfisch	*Der Frauenarzt* TidK, dir. Barnowsky, des. Krehan. > f, gz.
	22	R. Sherwood	*Hannibal ante Portas* (trs. F. Angermayer) Bremen SH.
	24	Kaiser	*Die Lederköpfe* Frankfurt NT.
	26	Molnár	*Olympia* Kom., dir. Forster-Larrinaga, des. Dworsky. > d, wb. 106 perfs.
		Claudel	*Le Père humilié* (trs. A. Joseph) Dresden SH.
	28	Feuchtwanger	*Die Petroleuminseln* ST, dir. Fehling, des. Neher, mus. Weill. > bt, fk, fl, kl, kp, lj, mü, pa.
December	2	Lampel	*Revolte im Erziehunghaus* GJS in Th-T, dir. Deppe, des. Böttcher. > bie, gw, sv.

		Krenek	*Schwergewicht oder Die Ehre der Nation* Kr-O, dir. Legal, cond. Klemperer, des. Strnad. (And the other two one-acters premiered in May 1928.)
	16	M. Ophüls	***Fips und Stips auf der Weltreise*** Breslau, Lobe-T, mus. H. Krieg.
		Menzel	*Toboggan* TidK, dir. Barnowsky, des. Müller. > ba, br, f.
		Robitschek/ F. Günther	*Der selige Theophil* TdKomiker.
	21	Zuckmayer	***Katharina Knie*** LT, dir. Martin. > b, bu, gw, lz, od.
		Nelson/Landry/Rillot	*Weisst du was?—wir heiraten!* (operetta) NTamZ.
	31	Lernet-Holenia	***Parforce*** Düsseldorf SH.

1929

January	3	Schiffer/Spoliansky	*Es liegt in der Luft* Vienna TidJ, dir. Reinhardt. From Kom.
	4	Sophocles	*Oedipus* (condensed by H. Lipmann). ST, dir. Jessner, des. Poelzig. > fk, gr, hl, ko, lj, mn, mü, wg.
	5	Cocteau	*Orphée* (Trs. Hardekopf/Fischer). TamS studio, dir. Gründgens.
		Wagner	*The Flying Dutchman* Kr-O, dir. Fehling, des. Dülberg, cond. Klemperer.
	26	Wolfenstein	***Die Nacht vor dem Beil***
February	2	Toller/Hasenclever/ Kesten	***Bourgeois bleibt Bourgeois*** (after Molière) LT, dir. Granowsky.
	12	Offenbach	*Tales of Hoffmann* Kr-O, dir. Legal, cond. Zemlinsky, des. Moholy-Nágy.
	14	Janáček/Čapek/Brod	*The Makropoulos Affair* Frankfurt StdO.
	15	L. Frank	*Karl und Anna* ST. > do, g, hm, ma.
		Shakespeare	*The Merry Wives of Windsor* DT, dir. Hilpert, des. R. Gliese. > fa, fe, gg, hö, hs, k, rü, st, wn. 64 perfs.
	16	E. W. Möller	***Douaumont*** Dresden Kom. and Essen SH.
	20	Lampel	***Die Verschwörer*** Trianon-Th.
March	5	Lampel	***Giftgas über Berlin*** GjS in TamS. > bie, gw, sv, ve. (Closed performance. Play then banned.)
	13	L. Frank	*Die Ursache* DT KS, dir. Hans Deppe, des. Schütte. > d, er, ey, gö, ri. 32 perfs.
	14	Kalkowska	***Josef*** Dortmund StdT.
	15	Maugham	*Wann kommst du wieder?* DT KS, dir. Gründgens, des. E. E. Stern. > mo, wb. 49 perfs.
	20	Anderson/Stallings	*What Price Glory?* (Rivalen, trs. Zuckmayer) TidK, dir. Piscator, des. Neher. > al, br, bu, ko, ss.
	21	Shaw	*Arms and the Man* BT, dir. Kalser, des. Schütte. > gt, ma, th3, v.
	30	Fleisser	***Pioniere in Ingolstadt*** TamS, dir. Geis, des. Neher. > hr, kb, lj, lo, mr.
April	5	Lonsdale	*Aristocrats* (trs. Sil-Vara) Vienna, Kom.
	12	Wagner-Régeny	***Moritat, Moschopoulos, Sganarelle*** (Three short operas) Essen StdO, des. Neher.
	13	Max Brand	***Maschinist Hopkins*** Duisburg, StdT.
	20	Werfel	*Paulus unter den Juden* DT, dir. Martin, des. Schütte, mus. Pringsheim. > d, de, fa, ge, ky, ls, st, tw, wn. 29 perfs.
	22	Mühsam	***Sacco und Vanzetti*** November-Studio in TidStadt, dir. Lindtberg, > bu, gn.
	30	Anderson	*Outside Lookin' In* (*Zaungäste*, trs. Rita Matthias and L. Keneth) SchT. > bt, hl, wä.

		A. Zweig	*Die Umkehr* Frankfurt NT.
May	1	Robitschek/Stransky	*Moderne Backfische* ("Travestie") TderKomiker.
	3	Shakespeare	*King John* ST, dir. Jessner, des. Neher. > f, fk, fl, gr, hz, mü, wg.
		Wallace	*Der Mann, der seinen Namen änderte* (trs. Rothe) Kom., dir. Hilpert, des. E. E. Stern. > hm, mo. 60 perfs.
	5	Wellenkamp	*Der Frisör von Rosslangen* SchT, dir. Fehling, des. R. Gliese. > fl, wä.
		Karl Kraus	*Die Unüberwindlichen* Dresden, Studio deutscher Schauspieler, dir. Verhoeven. (Third act banned.)
	7	Maugham	*Die heilige Flamme* (trs. M. Zoff). Ren.T.
June	5	Lernet-Holenia	*Tumult* Munich, Res.T.
	8	Hindemith/Schiffer	*Neues vom Tage* Kr-O, dir. Legal, des. T. Müller.
		J. Strauss	*Die Fledermaus* (revised Schiffer/Rössler/Korngold) DT, dir. Reinhardt, des. Kainer. > da, ks, ms, th3, wb. 136 perfs, plus 81 at TamN.
	11	Hecht/MacArthur	*The Front Page* (trs. R. Lothar). BT, dir. Hilpert, des. Schütte. > f, ge, st, wa.
	16–17	Diaghilev Ballet visits Berlin with *Le Fils prodigue, Le Chat, Le Chant du Rossignal*, and the Polovtsian dances from *Prince Igor*.	
July	15	Death of Hofmannsthal.	
	19	Death of Edmund Reinhardt.	
	28	Brecht/Hindemith	*Lehrstück* (*Badener Lehrstück vom Einverständnis*) Baden-Baden festival, dir. Brecht, cond. Dressel.

Start of 1929–30 Season

August	29	R. C. Sheriff	*Journey's End* DKT, dir. Hilpert, des. R. Gliese. > ky.
	31	Géraldy/Spitzer	*Die Unwiderstehliche.* DT KS, dir. Gründgens, des. R. Gliese. > gg, mo, mw, pa, r. 73 perfs.
		Büchner	*Dantons Tod.* VB, dir. Martin, des. Suhr, mus. Eisler. > fk, lj, lo, mr.
		Schanzer/Welisch/Benatzky	*Die drei Musketiere* GS. (Musical).
September	3	E. Hauptmann/Brecht/Weill	*Happy End* TamS, dir. Engel/Brecht, des. Neher. > ge, hm, li, lo, ne, wg.
	4	Schickele	*Hans im Schnakenloch* ST.
	5	Kaiser/Spoliansky	*Zwei Krawatten* TidCharlottenstrs. > al.
		O. Straus	*Marietta* (operetta) Met-T.
	6	F. Wolf	*Cyankali* GjS in LT, dir. Hinrich, des. Böttcher. > bie, fs, sv.
		W. Mehring	*Der Kaufmann von Berlin* Second PB at TamN, dir. Piscator, des. Moholy-Nágy, mus. Eisler. > ka, st, sz.
	16	Kaiser	*Kolportage* Kom., dir. Engel, des. Schütte, mus. W. Goehr. > dp, fo, gt, le, wb, wn. 53 perfs.
	25	Strindberg	*Der Befreier* (trs. Schering) Gotha LT.
	27	Cocteau/Milhaud	*Le Pauvre matelot* Kr-O, dir. Gründgens, des. Neher. (With Ravel, *L'Heure espagnole* and Ibert, *Angelique*).
	28	Max Halbe	*Präsidentenwahl* Oldenburg LT.
October	1	Duschinsky	*Stempelbrüder* Ren.T. > g.
	5	Kleist	*Michael Kohlhaas* (ad. Bronnen). Frankfurt a.d. Oder, StdT.
		Carl Credë	*§218* Leipzig Kom.H. (see 23 Nov.).

	10	Shaw	*The Apple Cart* (*Der Kaiser von Amerika*, trs. Trebitsch) DT, dir. Reinhardt, des. Schütte. < fll, ge, gt, k, ln, th1, tw. Over 200 perfs.
	11	Angermayer	*Flieg, roter Adler von Tirol* Bremen SH.
	12	Sternheim	*Die Königin* Görlitz StdT.
	13	Horváth	*Sladek oder der schwarze Reichswehrmann* Aktuelles Th. im LT, dir. Erich Fisch.
	14	Wedekind	*Spring Awakening* VB, dir. Martin, des. Neher. >fk, gb, lj, lo.
	19	Kaiser	*Hellseherei* Oldenburg LT.
		Pagnol	*Marius* (ad. Bruno Frank) Breslau, Lobe-T.
	27	Hanns Minnich	*Schlafstelle* Novemberstudio in TamS.
	30	Lampel	*Pennäler* TamS, dir. Hinrich, des. Böttcher. > gb.
November	1	Essig	*Des Kaisers Soldaten* Sch-T, dir. Fehling, des. R. Gliese. > hl, kp, lk, wa.
	2	Lissauer	*Luther und Thomas Münzer* Stuttgart LT KH.
		V. Kirschon	Roter Rost (trs. H. Reisiger) Leipzig SH.
	3	Schiller	*Don Carlos*, ST, dir. Jessner, des. Klein. > bi, ko, mn, mü
	4	O'Neill	*Strange Interlude* (*Seltsames Zwischenspiel*) DKT, dir. Hilpert. > bg, f, fa, hö, ls.
	6	Balázs/Tetzner	*Hans Urian geht nach Brot* GjS in LT.
	9	Tretiakov	*Roar China* (*Brülle China*, trs. Lania) Frankfurt SH, dir. Buch.
	11	Milhaud	*Salade* and *La Création du monde* SO.
		Hamsun	*Vom Teufel geholt* DT, dir. Reinhardt, des. Neher. > hm, hö, kl, mo. 77 perfs.
	19	Kolbenheyer	*Die Brücke* Düsseldorf SH.
	23	Credé	*§218* Mannheim, Piscator-Kollektiv, dir. Piscator, des. Roth. Touring production.
	24	Hofmannsthal	*Der Tor und der Tod* Weimar NT.
		Herzog/Rehfisch	*Die Affäre Dreyfus* VB, dir. Kenter, des. Suhr. > fk, gb, hk, hw, mr, st.
	28	Barlach	*Die gute Zeit* Gera, Reuss'sches T.
December	5	Stramm	*Die Bauern* Oldenburg LT.
	7	C. Goetz	*Der Lügner und die Nonne* Hamburg Thalia-T.
	12	Ungar	*Die Gartenlaube* TaS, dir. Engel, des. Neher. > kb, po, sm.
	16	Brust	*Das Nachthorn* Coburg LT.
	23	Guitry	*Désiré* DT KS, dir. Mittler, des. Schütte. > bo, mw, ri, wb. 31 perfs.
	26	Schiffer/Holländer	*Ich tanze um die Welt mit dir* (musical). Darmstadt LT.
	31	Reyher	*Don't Bet on Fights* (*Harte Bandagen*, trs. E. Hauptmann). ST, dir. Jessner. > bt, gr, kn, lb, lj, mü.
Also in 1929:		Claudel	*Partage de midi* Darmstadt LT, dir. Ebert, des. Schenck von Trapp. > m, mi, va.
		Kalkowska	*Josef* GjS in LT, dir. Deppe, des. Tokumbet. > gb.

1930

January	12	Verdi	*Simone Boccanegra* (ad. Werfel) Vienna SO.
	15	Kraus	*Die letzte Nacht* (from Die letzten Tage der Menschheit). TamS Studio, dir. Reuss, des. Tokumbet, mus. Eisler.
	16	Baum	*Menschen im Hotel* (*Grand Hotel*). TamN, dir. Gründgens, des. Schütte, mus. Goehr. > bi, ks. 69 perfs.
	18	Zuckmayer	*Kakadu Kakada* (for children). Ren-T, dir. Hartung.

	E. W. Möller	*Kalifornische Tragödie* Erfurt SdtT.
19	Finkelburg	*Amnestie* VB, dir. Stark, des. Tokumbet.
	Krenek	*Leben des Orest* (opera) Leipzig NT.
24	Rice	*Street Scene* (trs. H. Reisiger). BT.
27	Sternheim	*Der Kandidat* DT KS dir. Hinrich, des. Grosz. > dp, fn, fo, gü, lo, w, wb. 41 perfs.
	K. Mann	*Gegenüber von China* Bochum StdT.
28	Stravinsky	*Apollon Musagète* Königsberg O.
29	Dietzenschmidt	*Der Verräter Gottes* Ulm StdT.
30	Bronnen	*Reparationen* Mannheim NT.
February 1	Schönberg	*Von heute auf Morgen* Frankfurt O.
8	Hasenclever	*Napoleon greift ein* Frankfurt NT.
16	Goering	*Die Südpolexpedition des Kapitans Scott* ST, dir. Jessner, des. Neher. > bt, fk, hl, lsn, mü.
22	A. Glebov	*Raketenflugzeug* (trs. J. Gotz) Erfurt SdtT.
March 4	Krenek	*Leben des Orest* Kr-O, dir. Legal, cond. Klemperer, des. Chirico.
7	Haller/Wolff/Kollo	*Der doppelte Bräutigam* (revue) TamS.
8	Hans Rehberg	*Cecil Rhodes* Bochum StdT.
9	Czokor	*Die Gesellschaft der Menschenrechte* VB dir. Rodenberg, des. Suhr.
	Brecht/Weill	*Aufstieg und Fall der Stadt Mahagonny* Leipzig NT, dir. Brügmann, cond. Brecher, des. Neher.
10	Bruckner	*Kreatur* Kom., dir. Reinhardt, des. Strnad. > f, hö, th1.
18	Shakespeare	*Love's Labours Lost* ST, dir. Fehling, des. Gliese. > bt, fh, gr, hl, lei, wä.
	F. Ziege	*Herr Rechtsanwalt verteidigt sich* TamS.
23	Balázs/Grosz	*Achtung, Aufnahme!!* Frankfurt Opera.
	Grossmann	*Die beiden Adler* VB, dir. Grossmann, des. Gliese. > bu, fk.
31	Michael Gold	*Das Lied von Hoboken* (ad. Weisenborn) VB, mus. W. Grosz.
	A. Zweig	*The Case of Sergeant Grischa* TamN, dir. Granowsky, des. T. Müller, cos. Grosz. > gb, gn, ky, th3. 50 perfs.
April 1	Impekoven/Mathern	*Die neue Sachlichkeit* (farce) Frankfurt SH.
3	Credé	*§218* PB in WT, dir. Piscator. (Start of third PB in Berlin.)
4		Meyerhold's theatre from Moscow starts a guest season at the TidK.
14	Feuchtwanger	*Wird Hill amnestiert?* ST, dir. Jessner, des. Schütte. > fh, lb, ma, wä.
May 2	Shaw	*Soll man heiraten?* Kom., dir. Martin, des. Schütte. > gg, gt, lz, mw, rü, wa, wb. 44 perfs.
5	Claudel/Milhaud	*Christophe Colomb* SO, des. Aravantinos.
10	Herzog	*Krach um Leutnant Blumenthal* Leipzig KT.
13	Unruh	*Phaea* DT, dir. Reinhardt, des. Schütte, mus. Holländer. > bo, ch, g, mo, pn. 110 perfs.
14	Coward	*Tratsch* (trs. Berstl) TamS.
24	Wagner-Régeny	*Esau und Jakob* (scenic cantata). Gera Reuss'sches T.
25	Antheil	*Transatlantic* Frankfurt Opera, dir. Graf, cond. Steinberg, des. Sievert.
28	Lernet-Holenia	*Die Attraktion* Kassel ST.
31	Pirandello	*Tonight We Improvise* LT, dir. Hartung. > lz, pi.
June 3	Strindberg	*Gustav Adolf* ST, dir. Jessner, des. Neher. > bt, f, fh, gr, hl.
7	Schönberg	*Erwartung* (1) and *Die glückliche Hand* (2). Kr-O, dir. Rabenalt, des. Otto (1) and Schlemmer (2).

	14	Herzog	*Krach um Leutnant Blumenthal.* Spielgemeinschaft Berliner Schauspieler at TamS.

14   Herzog   *Krach um Leutnant Blumenthal.* Spielgemeinschaft
Berliner Schauspieler at TamS.

15   Joachimson/   *Wie werde ich reich und glücklich?* Kom.
Spoliansky

23   Brecht/Weill   ***Der Jasager*** (school opera) Zentralinstitut für
Erziehung, dir. Brecht/Weill.

Start of 1930–31 Season

August   29   B. Frank   ***Sturm im Wasserglas***   Dresden SH.

31   Toller   ***Feuer aus den Kesseln***   TamS, dir. Hinrich, des.
Neher. > hr, po, ss.

Plievier   ***Des Kaisers Kulis*** PB in LT, dir. Piscator, des. T.
Müller.

September   1   G. W. Müller   ***1914*** DT, dir. Gründgens, des. Schütte, mus. M.
Bensussan. > hk, wn. 19 perfs.

16   Sternheim   *Bürger Schippel*   ST, dir. Bildt, des. Otto. > fh, gr, kb,
mü, wä.

20   Hauptmann   *Die Weber*   VB, dir. Martin, des. Neher. > bu, li, mr, ss,
st.

30   G. Menzel   ***Bork*** Breslau, Lobe-T and Hamburg DSH.

October   4   Lania   ***Gott, König und Vaterland***   Frankfurt NT.

7   Kornfeld   ***Jud Süss***   TamS, dir. Jessner, des. Neher. > d, gb, kb,
li, lj, mn, po, we.

10   Rehfisch   ***Brest-Litovsk***   TdW.

Lehár   ***Das Land des Lächelns***   Met-T, dir. Frederich, des.
Bornemann/Schott.

11   V. Kataev   *Squaring the Circle* (trs. R. Hoffmann/D. Umanskij)
Leipzig SH.

18   Goethe   *Götz von Berlichingen*   ST, dir. Legal. > bn, g, gr, kp, mi.

J. Deval   *Etienne* (trs. Blei) Tribüne.

Chlumberg   ***Wunder um Verdun*** Leipzig SH.

24   Wagner-Régeny   ***La Sainte courtisane***   Dessau, Friedrich-T.

25   E. W. Möller   ***Panamaskandal***   Frankfurt NT, des. Neher.

November   1   Bruckner   ***Elisabeth von England*** DT in LT, dir. Hilpert, des.
Schütte. > gg, gt, k, s, wi, wn. 122 perfs.

6   Giraudoux   *Siegfried* (trs. H. Feist) Hamburg KS and Osnabrück
StdT.

8   Müller/Gilbert/   *White Horse Inn* (musical) GS, dir. Charell. > hn, sp, wb.
Benatzky   416 perfs.

Wolf   ***Die Matrosen von Cattaro*** VB, dir. Stark, des.
Tokumbet. > bh, bu, ss.

11   Hugo   ***Lord Spleen*** Dresden Opera.
Königsgarten/
M. Lothar

12   Lampel   ***Wir sind Kameraden*** TamS.

Cocteau/K. Mann   *Geschwister* (from *Les Enfants terribles*) Munich KS in SH.

19   Graf/Hintze   ***Die endlose Strasse***   Aachen StdT, dir. Schroeder.

Ottwalt   ***Jeden Tag vier*** PB in WT, dir. Neubauer. > lö, tr, ve.

26   J. M. Becker   ***Die Nacht der Könige***   Mainz StdT.

28   Bill-Belotserkovski   ***Mond von links*** PB in WT, dir. Kerb, des. Böttcher,
mus. Goehr.

29   Döblin   ***Die Ehe***   Munich KS in SH.

December   2   Karl Th. Bluth   *Nacht überm Kreml* Sch-T.

6   Werfel   ***Das Reich Gottes in Böhmen*** Vienna, Burg-T.

		Barlach	*Der blaue Boll* ST, dir. Fehling, des. Gliese. > g, hl, lb, mr.
	7	Brecht/Weill	*Der Jasager* Kr-O.
	10	Brecht/Eisler	*Die Massnahme* GS, dir. Dudow, des. Roth, cond. Rankl. > bu, gr, wg.
		Rathaus	*Fremde Erde* SO.
	12	Hindemith/Schiffer	*Hin und Zurück* Kr-O, dir. Curjel, cond. Klemperer, des. Moholy-Nágy. (With three other short operas.)
		Brust	*Schmoff* Gera, Reuss'sches T.
	13	Kataev	*The Embezzlers* (ad. Polgar) VB, dir. Martin, des. Neher. (With p).
	20	Maugham	*The Breadwinner* (trs. M. Zoff) Ren.T.
	23	Schiller	*Die Jungfrau von Orleans* ST, dir. Jessner, des. Neher. > fk, fl, gr, hz, kp, mi, mü.

1931

January	6	Molnár	*Liliom* (ad. Polgar) VB, dir. Martin, des. Neher, mus. Mackeben. > al, bh, dr, st.
	7	O'Casey	*The Plough and the Stars* (trs. Erich Glass) Osnabrück.
	15	Wolf	*Tai Yang erwacht* PB in WT, dir. Piscator, des. Heartfield. > gb, mz.
		Giraudoux	*Amphitryon 38* (trs. H. Feist) TidK. > bg, d, ot
	23	Emil Ludwig	*Versailles* Bremen SH.
	31	E. G. Kolbenheyer	*Jagt ihn—ein Mensch!* (a) Düsseldorf SH. (b) Baden-Baden StdT.
February	6	Brecht	*Mann ist Mann* ST, dir. Brecht/Legal, des. Neher, mus. Weill. > bt, gr, hz, li, lo, re, wg. 6 perfs.
	14	Schnitzler	*Der Gang zum Weiher* Vienna Burg-T.
	16	Weisenborn	*S.O.S.* Coburg LT.
	17	Glebov	*Inga (Frau in Front)* PB in WT, des. Böttcher. > ka, lö, ve.
	23	Puccini	*Madame Butterfly* Kr-O, dir. Curjel, cond. Zemlinsky, des. Moholy-Nágy.
	25	Paul Schurek	*Wozu der Lärm?* Flensburg StdT.
March	5	Zuckmayer	*Der Hauptmann von Köpenick* DT, dir. Hilpert, des. Schütte. > dp, gt, k, wn. 149 perfs.
		Galsworthy	*Feuer* (trs. Schalit) Vienna Ak-T.
	9	Czokor	*Die Gesellschaft der Menschenrechte* VB, dir. Rodenberg, des. Suhr. > gb, hw, ss.
	12	C. von Arx	*Spionage* Zurich StdT.
	18	Gräff	*Der einsame Tat* Gera Reuss'sches T.
	20	Horváth	*Italienische Nacht* TamS, dir. F. von Mendelssohn. > was. Aufricht's last production at the TamS.
	21	Hasenclever	*Kommt ein Vogel geflogen* Kom., dir. Hartung, des. Rachlis. > d, mo, mw. 18 perfs.
		O. Zoff	*Die weissen Handschuhe* Stuttgart SH.
	27	Kraus/Offenbach	*Périchole* Kr-O, dir. Hinrich, cond. F. Zweig, des. Otto.
April	11	Schiffer/Spoliansky	*Alles Schwindel* TamK, dir. Gründgens, des. Reinking. > li.
	17	Döblin	*Die Ehe* VB, dir. Martin, des. Neher. > bu, dr, ss.
		Lessing	*Emilia Galotti* ST, dir. Jessner, des. Otto. > kp, ky, ot, wä.
	19	R. Billinger	*Rosse* Munich Res-T.
	23	Herzog	*Panama* Hamburg DSH.
	30	Bois/Hansen	*Dienst am Kunden* (farce) Kom.
May	5	Klaiser	*König Hahnrei* ST, dir. Fehling, des. Gliese. > g, kö, mi, mt, mü.

	29	Janáček	*From the House of the Dead* Kr-O, dir. Curjel, cond. F. Zweig, des. Neher.
June	7	Shaw	*Heartbreak House* ST, dir. Jessner, des. Otto. > fh, lb, wy.
	9	Rehberg	*Cecil Rhodes* ST. > fk.
		Hecht/MacArthur	*The Front Page* TidJ. 23 perfs.
	15	Offenbach	*La Belle Hélène* TamK, dir. Reinhardt, des. Schütte/ Czettel, cond. Korngold. > fll, li, ms, wb.
	26	W. Harlan	*Das Nürnbergische Ei* ST, dir. Jessner, des. Pirchan. > ls.
July	31	Closure of the Kroll-Oper.

Start of 1931–32 Season

September	1	Hemingway/ Zuckmayer	*A Farewell to Arms* DT, dir. Hilpert, des. Schütte. > do, dp, wn. 20 perfs.
		Verdi	*Macbeth* StdO, dir. Ebert, cond. Stiedry, des. Neher.
	3	B. Frank	**Nina** Dresden SH.
	11	Lampel	**Vaterland** Mannheim NT.
	16	Kaiser	*Nebeneinander* VB, dir. Martin, des. Gliese. > bu, lo, ul.
	18	Reimann/Spoerl	**Der beschleunigte Personenzug** (farce) TaN.
	25	D. Ogden Stewart	*Rückkehr* (trs. Grete Szereny) Kom, dir. Gründgens, des. Schütte. > do, thi4. 32 perfs.
		Lernet-Holenia	**Kapriolen** Munich SH.
	30	R. A. Stemmle	**Kampf um Kitsch** VB, dir. Martin, des. Tokumbet, mus. A. Gray.
October	1	Paul Osborn	*Ich weiss etwas, was du nicht weisst* (trs. L. Hirschfeld) TidK.
	10	Billinger	**Rauhnacht** Munich SH, dir. Falckenberg, des. Reigbert (after Kubin). > bs, gi.
	16	Kästner/Nick	**Leben in dieser Zeit** Leipzig AT.
	17	Toller/Kesten	**Wunder in Amerika** Mannheim NT, dir. Dornsaft.
	20	C. von Arx	**Vogel, friss oder stirb** Zurich SH.
		R. Sherwood	*Waterloo Bridge* (trs. Heinrich Kranz) Tribüne.
	21	Death of Arthur Schnitzler, aged 69.
	22	Lissauer	**Aufruhr des Goldes** Cologne SH.
	27/29	Schiller	*Wallenstein* (in two parts) ST, dir. Jessner, des. Klein. > fk, g, ho, k, m.
	29	Gilbricht	**Die Grossstadt mit einem Einwohner** Erfurt KS.
November	2	Horváth	**Geschichten aus dem Wienerwald** DT, dir. Hilpert, des. Schütte. > dg, hö, lo, ms, ne, ri. 37 perfs.
	5	Ilse Langner	**Die Heilige aus USA** TaK, dir. Berger, des. Bamberger, mus. Toch. > dp, fll, hy, s, ss, wa.
	7	Kyser	*Es brennt an der Grenze* Deutsches NT in TamS, dir. Bernt Hofmann, des. Von Arent.
	10	Fred Neumeyer	**Die Herde sucht** Sch-T, dir. Fehling, des. Gliese, mus. Goldschmidt. > bt, hl, kp, lb, mi, wä.
	14	Kolbenheyer	**Das Gesetz in Dir** Dresden SH, Munich Res. T, Weimar NT, Baden-Baden SH. Quadruple première.
	20	(collective)	*Wir sind ja sooo zufrieden* (revue) JVB in Bach-Saal, des. Pillartz and Roth, mus. Eisler/Lewy/Schmidt/Weill. > bi, bu, lj, wg.
	27	Offenbach	*Tales of Hoffmann* (arr. Friedell/Sassmann, Blech) GS, dir. Reinhardt, des. Strnad, cond. Blech, chor. Nijinska/ Dolin. > dg, gz, th3, wm. Ran till 18 April.

December	2	O. Wälterlin	*Papst Gregor VII* Basel StdT.
	17	Billinger	*Rauhnacht* ST, dir. Fehling, des. Gliese. (With k, kp, mü, pa, ul).
	20	Max Mell	*Sieben gegen Theben* Meiningen LT.
	21	Brecht/Weill	*Aufstieg und Fall der Stadt Mahagonny* TamK, dir. Brecht/Neher, des. Neher, cond. Zemlinsky. > he, hr, lj, pn, 42 perfs.
		Wolf	*Die Jungens von Mons* BT, dir. Weichert. > bh, s.
	22	Wangenheim	*Die Mausefälle* Truppe 1932 in KT, dir. Wangenheim, des. Lex-Nerlinger. > sp, tr, wh.
	30	Jones	*The Geisha* (ad. Schiffer) SO.
Also in 1931		Bethge	*Reims* TdesW, dir. Von Möllendorf. (With lk.)
		Kolbenheyer	*Jagt ihn, ein Mensch* Munich Res. T, dir. Ulmer, des. Linnebach. (With we.)

1932

January	14	Emil Ludwig	*Das Bildnis* Frankfurt NT.
	17	Brecht/Eisler	*Die Mutter* KomH, dir. Burri, des. Neher. > bi, bu, fs, hr, li, ve, wg.
	19	Shakespeare	*Othello* ST, dir. Jessner, des. Fenneker. > g, k, kp, lz, mi, ot.
	22	Jakob Wassermann	*Lukardis* Heilbronn StdT.
	27	Bruckner	*Timon* DT, dir. Hilpert, des. Strnad (With hm, hy, ky, m, od, sm.)
	28	Eulenberg	*Thomas Münzer* Hannover SH.
	30	Mussolini/Forzano	*100 Days* Weimar NT, dir. Ulbrich.
February	16	Hauptmann	*Vor Sonnenuntergang* DT, dir. Reinhardt, des. Schütte, > gt, hk, k, kp, mn, sm, th1, wn. 85 perfs.
	23	Graff/Hintze	*Die endlose Strasse* SchT. > fk, gw.
March	5	C. Goetz/Benatzky	*Zirkus Aimée* (operetta) Basel StdT.
	10	Neher/Weill	*Die Bürgschaft* StdO, dir. Ebert, cond. Stiedry, des. Neher.
	12	Paquet	*Stinchen von der Krone* Mainz StdT.
	17	Paul Beyer	*Düsseldorfer Passion* Arnstadt LT. (Deutsches National-Festspiel for KfdK).
	26	Goethe	*Egmont* ST, dir. Fehling, des. Gliese, cond. Klemperer. > f, gw, hl, kp, lb, mü, wa, wä.
	29	Schnitzler	(posthumous fragments) Vienna DVT.
April	2	Schurek	*Kamrad Kasper* VB, dir. Stark. > bu, dr, gb.
	11	Brecht	(*Saint Joan of the Stockyards* Broadcast Berlin Radio, dir. Alfred Braun. > bt, gn, ko, ne, wg. Only performance till 1959.)
	16	Dreiser	*An American Tragedy* Vienna DVT.
	19	Offenbach	*La Belle Hélène* (ad. Friedell/Sassmann/Korngold) GS, dir. Reinhardt, des. Schütte/Czettel, cond. Korngold, chor. Massine. > gz. 43 perfs. Transfer from TaK (see 15 June 1931).
	26	Brecht/Weill	*Aufstieg und Fall der Stadt Mahagonny* Vienna Raimund-T, dir. Heinsheimer.
	29	Schiller	*Die Räuber* SchT, dir. Jessner, des. Neher. > fk, fl, gr, hl, mi, ot.
May	6	Wedekind	*Der Liebestrank* ST, dir. Fehling, des. Gliese. > bt, g, kp, ma, wä.
	8	Unruh	*Zero* Frankfurt SH, dir. Buch, des. Neher.
	13	Impekoven/ Reimann/Gilbert	*Der Stänker* (farce) TamN.

	30	Eisler	*Tempo der Zeit* (radio cantata) Darmstadt LT KH.
		Plievier	***Haifische*** TidK, dir. Lindtberg. > ss, sv.
June	7	Max Halbe	***Ginoveva*** Munich Res.T.
	?	Holberg	*Jeppe vom Berge* ST, dir. Lindtberg, des. T. Müller.

Start of 1932–33 Season

August	end	Osip Dymow	*Europa A. G.* Kom., dir. Gottfried Reinhardt.
September	1	Chlumberg	*Miracle at Verdun* DT, dir. Martin, des. Schütte. > bh, bi, ey, hr, ka, ls, wn. 17 perfs.
	2	Credé	***Aertzte im Kampf*** Rose-T.
	23	Lehár	***Der Fürst der Berge*** (operetta) TamN.
October	7	Billinger	*Das Verlöbnis* Schultes-Truppe in DT KS, dir. Joseph, des. Padua.
	8	Schiller	*Wilhelm Tell* ST, dir. Fehling, des. Neher. > bt, fh, fk, gr, hl, hz, k, kp, mi, mn, ot, wä.
	14	Julius Hay	***Sigismund*** Breslau Lobe-T.
	18	Wangenheim	***Da liegt der Hund begraben*** TamS, dir. Wangenheim, des. Lex-Nerlinger, mus. Wolpe.
	22	Romberg	*The Student Prince* GS.
	25	Anna Gmeyner	***Automatenbufett*** Hamburg Thalia-T KS.
	28	Hauptmann	*Gabriel Schillings Flucht* ST, dir. Jessner, des. Schütte. > bg, k, lb.
	29	Schreker	***Der Schmied von Gent*** StdO, dir. Zindler, des. Neher, cond. Breisach.
	30	Toller	***Die blinde Göttin*** Vienna Raimund-T, dir. Fehling, des. Frey. > ma, sw.
November	5	Hartmann Frhr. v. Richthofen	***Hardenberg*** Hanover SH.
	9	Vaszary	***Ich habe einen Engel geheiratet*** Prague NDT.
	18	Horváth	***Kasimir und Karoline*** Leipzig SH, dir. Von Mendelssohn, des. Neher, mus. Bürger. > eb, ul. Transfer to Berlin Kom.H a week later.
	25	J. M. Becker	***Ludwig II*** Kiel StdT.
	26	Griese	***Mensch, aus Erde gemacht*** Stuttgart LT.
December	1	Molnár	*Harmonie* DT, dir. Reinhardt. > p.
	2	Goethe	*Faust, Part 1* ST, dir. Müthel, des. Zweigenthal. > gd, gg, k. Centenary production.
	3	Hay	***Das neue Paradies*** VB, dir. Hilpert, des. Gliese. > wo.
	7	Böddinghaus	***Kampfstaffel 303*** Coburg LT.
	22	W. Gilbricht	***Oliver Cromwells Sendung*** VB, dir. Hilpert, des. Neher. > kl.
		Schiffer/ Joachimson/ Spoliansky	*Das Haus dazwischen* (revue) Kom.H.
	23	Hay	***Gott, Kaiser und Bauer*** DT, dir. Martin, des. Schütte, mus. M. Lothar. > dg, hr, ka, ko, mz, w. 8 perfs.
		Decsey/Holm/ Marischka/ Kreisler	***Sissy*** (musical) Vienna TadWien.
	26	S. Graeff	***Die vier Musketiere*** Altona StdT.
	30	Herczeg/Klein/ Schiffer/ Spoliansky	*100 Meter Glück* (musical) Met-T.
	31	C. Goetz	***Dr med. Hiob Prätorius*** Stuttgart LT KH.

1933

January	4	Haller/Rideamus/ Kollo	*Die Männer sind mal so* (revue) Sch-T.
	9	K. Otten	***Die Expedition nach San Domingo*** Altona StdT.
	10	Ringelnatz	*Die Flasche (und mit ihr reisen)* DT KS. 7 perfs.
	14	P. J. Cremers	***Die Marneschlacht*** Mannheim NT.
	18	B. T. Withahn	***Ostmark*** Regensburg StdT.
	22	Goethe	*Faust, Part 2* ST, dir. Lindemann, des. Otto. > gg, k. Second part of centenary production.
	23	P. Rieschel	***Infanterist Buttermilch, der Vater der Kompagnie*** (army farce) Bremen, Thalia-T.
	24	Zuckmayer	*Schinderhannes* VB, dir. Hilpert, des. Neher. > sp.
	25	Billinger	***Lob des Landes*** Leipzig AT.
February	4	Wangenheim	***Wer ist der Dümmste?*** (ad. from Wittfogel) dir. Wangenheim, des. Otto, mus. Wolpe.
	11	Billinger	***Der Rossknecht*** Düsseldorf StdT KH, mus. Zillig.
	12	Wagner	*Tannhäuser* SO, dir. Fehling, des. Strnad, cond. Klemperer.
	18	Kaiser/Weill	***Silbersee*** Leipzig AT, dir. Sierck, des. Neher, cond. Brecher. Simultaneous premieres at Erfurt and Magdeburg.
	21	E. Castonier	***Sardinenfischer*** VB. > ra.
	22	H. Graedener	***Sickingen*** Gera, Reuss'sches T.
	25	Bruckner	***Die Marquise von O*** Erfurt StdT.
March	1	Billinger	***Rosse*** ST, dir. Jessner, des. Karl Roll. > fk, gr.
		Calderon/ Hofmannsthal	*Das grosse Welttheater* DT, dir. Reinhardt, des. Strnad, mus. Lothar and Nilsson. > dg, kl, kö, thl, wn. Reinhardt's last production in Germany. 31 perfs.
	5	Alsberg	*Konflikt* Prague NDT, dir. Martiin. > b, dx.
	11		Suicide of Hans Warnecke (from third floor of Munich Justizpalast).
	14	Weisenborn/Huelsenbeck	***Warum lacht Frau Balsam?*** DKT.
	26	H. Heiseler	***Der junge Parzival*** Wuppertal/Barmen StdT.
	29	M. Ziese	***Siebenstein*** ST, dir. Fehling, des. Gliese. > fh, fk, gw, hl, kb, kp, mi, mü.
April	4	Kurt Kluge	***Ewiges Volk*** DT, mus. Peterka.
	5		Suicide of Alfred Rotter in Vaduz.
	11	Kyser	***Schicksal um York*** Leipzig AT.
	12	Karl Leyst	***Gneisenau und Napoleon*** Potsdam SH.
	16	Angermayer	*König Ludwig II von Bayern* Prague NDT. > d.
	20	Johst	***Schlageter*** ST, dir. Ulbrich, des. von Arent. > b, kp, lb, mü. Hitler's birthday. Emmy Sonnemann's first appearance in Berlin.
	24		Suicide of Arthur Illing in a train.
July	15	K. Sommerer	***Horst Wessel*** Wiesbaden ST KH.

From this point till May 1945 the left-hand column will represent the anti-Nazi theatre outside Germany. Theatres will be transferred to the right-hand column as they come under Nazi rule: Vienna in May 1938, Prague in March 1939, Paris in June 1940, Zurich (fortunately) never.

Start of 1933–34 Season

1 Jul. R. Strauss/Hofmannsthal *Arabella* Dresden O.

22 Aug. F. Weigel *SA-Mann Altenberg*
          Zwickau, Neue Kulturbühne.

23 Sep. Griese *Mensch, aus Erde gemacht* ST,
          dir. Fehling, des. T. Müller > bt,

30 Sep. Zuckmayer *Kakadu Kakada* Vienna
          TidJ, dir, Kalbeck, des. Horner. 7
          perfs.
          Stolz **Zwei Herzen im**
          Dreiviertel-takt (operetta).
          Zurich StdT.

          g, kp, ky, mi.

1 Oct. Blunck **Erntedank** Ulm StdT.

2 Oct. A. Armstrong *Ten-Minute Alibi* (trs.
         Glass) Vienna TdKom.

11 Oct. Paul Ernst **York** Kiel StdT.

12 Oct. Strauss/Hofmannsthal *Arabella* SO.

15 Oct. Hauptmann **Die goldene Harfe**
          Munich KS.
          Max Petzold **Yorck** Elbing StdT.

28 Oct. Paul Gurk **Kaiser Heinrich VI**
          Erfurt DVT.

7 Nov. Baumbauer **Brand im Haus** (a
         separatist play) Kaiserslautern LT

9 Nov. Hilker **Der braune Soldat**
         Frankfurt a.d. Oder StdT.

10 Nov. Duschinsky **Makart** Vienna TidJ.

10 Nov. Schiller *Maria Stuart* VB, dir. Hilpert,
         des. Schütte. > do, m)

11 Nov. Ian Hay *Hier bin ich, hier bleib ich* (trs.
         Berstl) Munich KS in SH.

18 Nov. E. Ortner **Jud Süss** Breslau, Lobe-T.

21 Nov. Osswald-Bayer **Der Sturmtrupp**
         Gotha LT for KfdK.

23 Nov. J. Deval *Tovarisch* Vienna TidJ.

25 Nov. Schiller-Theater closes.

27 Nov. Schreyvogel *Tod in Genf* VB, dir.
         Kerb, des. Neher.

30 Nov. Bruckner **Die Rassen** Zurich SH,
         dir. Hartung, des. Otto. > bi, gb.

3 Dec. Rehberg **Johannes Kepler**
         Wuppertal/Elberfeld.

5 Dec. Billinger **Stille Gäste** Leipzig AT.

20 Dec. Dietrich Eckart **Ein x-beliebiger**
         Mensch. Augsburg StdT.

21 Dec. Johst *Propheten.* ST, dir. Fehling, des.
         T. Müller, mus. von Borck. > fh,
         fk, g, hl, hö, kp, ky, lsn, mi, mü.

25 Dec. Welleminski/Künnecke *Tanzende*
         Flammen (operetta) TdW.

1934

6 Jan. C. von Arx **Der Verrat von**
         Novara Zurich SH.

20 Jan. Lehár **Giudetta** Vienna SO.

16 Jan. Klabund/Zemlinsky **Der**
         Kreidekreis Stettin StdT.

23 Jan. Kyser **Rembrandt vor Gericht** DT.

4 Feb. Schiller *William Tell* K. Schouwburg,
         The Hague, dir. Jessner/van der
         Lugt.

15 Feb. Mussolini/Forzano *100 Days* ST. >
         gg, k.

16 Feb. Jerome/Mackeben *Lady Fanny*
         (operetta) DKT.

21 Feb. Cocteau *La Voix humaine* Vienna
TidJ, dir. Reinhardt. > th1.

16 Mar. Broch **Denn sie wissen nicht, was
sie tun** Zurich SH, dir. Hartung.

28 Mar. Rehfisch **Semmelweiss** Vienna
DVT.

10 Apr. Goetz **Benjamin im Fegefeuer**
Tilsit, Grenzlandtheater.

20 Apr. Meyer-Förster *Alt-Heidelberg* Vienna
TidJ, dir. Preminger, des.
Niedermoser. > edt, py, wy.

10 May Shaw *A Village Wooing* Zurich SH

3 Aug. Verneuil/Blum/Benatzky *Die
Prinzessin auf der Leiter* Vienna
TidJ, dir. Kalbeck, des. Dworsky.
> br, ks. 37 perfs.

4 Mar. Dietrich Eckart **Ein Kerl, der
spekuliert** (comedy) Leipzig AT.

8 Mar. Graeff: *Die Heimkehr des Matthias
Bruck* ST.

9 Apr. Dietrich Eckart **Der Erbgraf**
Eisenach StdT.

13 Apr. Blunck **Land in der Dämmerung**
ST, dir Fehling, des. Neher. > bt,
fh, fk, ky, mi.

24 Apr. Molière/Blümner. *Die Wunderkur*
Stettin SdtT.

5 May M. Jelusich *Cromwell* Bochum StdT.

17 May Carl Hauptmann *Musik* ST, dir.
Fehling, des. Neher, mus.
Tiessen. > g, kp, mi.

30 May Hans Schwarz **Rebell in England**
ST.

28 Jul. Euringer **Deutsche Passion 1933**
Heidelberg Festival. (Thing-play).

Start of 1934–35 Season

4 Sep. Ortner *Meier Helmbrecht*

5 Oct. E. W. Möller **Rothschild siegt bei
Waterloo** Aachen StdT.

6 Oct. S. Graeff **Hier sind Gemsen**
Leipzig AT.

8 Oct. Shakespeare *Twelfth Night,* dir.
Sierck, des. Fenneker. > fi.

11 Oct. Swerling/Edward G. Robinson
Kiebitze Vienna KS.

13 Oct. Kaufman/Ferber *Dinner at 8* (trs.
Kommer) Vienna DVT.

15 Oct. Duschinsky **Anny** Mährisch-Ostrau
(Moravská Ostrava) DT.

13 Oct. Kolbenheyer **Gregor und Heinrich**
Dresden SH.

20 Oct. Griese **Die Schafschur** Düsseldorf
SH.

3 Nov. Stolz *Grüezi* (revue) Zurich StdT.

8 Nov. Wolf **Professor Mannheim**
(Mamlock) Zurich SH, dir.
Lindtberg, des. Otto. > bn, gf,
ka, la, st).

9 Nov. Kingsley *Men in White* Vienna TidJ,
dir. Preminger, des.
Niedermoser. > py, ra. 110 perfs.

1 Dec. Gorky *The Lower Depths* Zurich SH, dir. Lindtberg.

13 Dec. Horváth **Hin und her** Zurich SH, dir. Hartung, des. Otto. > hw, hz, ka, st.

1935

2 Feb. Zuckmayer **Der Schelm von Bergen** Zurich SH, dir. Hartung. > st.

10 Feb. Kaiser **Adrienne Ambrosat** Vienna TidJ, dir. Preminger, des. Strnad. > bh, d, py, wy). 20 perfs.

5 Apr. Zech **Nur ein Judenweib** Buenos Aires, Th. Ombu.

6 Apr. Schiller *Maria Stuart* Zurich SH, dir. Hartung.

18 Apr. Benatzky **Der König mit dem Regenschirm** (operetta) Vienna TidJ, dir. Preminger, des. Niedermoser. > ks, py, wb. 104 perfs.

28 Nov. F. G. Jünger **Der verkleidete Theseus** Frankfurt SH.

30 Nov. Rehberg **Der grosse Kurfürst** ST, dir. Fehling, des. Gliese. > fh, fk, gd, kl, kö, kp, lb, mi.

5 Dec. Buch **Vertrag um Karakat** Bremen SH.

6 Dec. L. E. Huxley *Jenny Comes Across* (*Grossreinemachen*, trs. Merck) Kom.

20 Dec. Hodge *The Wind and the Rain* (ad. Sierck) DT KS.

5 Jan. J. M. Becker **Nacht ohne Morgen** Nürnberg StdBühnen.

21 Jan. Kolbenheyer *Heroische Leidenschaften* ST. > k, ky, mü.

23 Jan. Wolfgang Böttcher **Hochzeit an der Pauke** TamS, mus. Schmidt-Boelicke.

30 Jan. Bethge **Hungermarsch der Veteranen** Augsburg StdT.

1 Feb. Kaj Munk *Im Anfang war das Wort* Schwerin, StdT.

20 Feb. Neher/Wagner-Régeny **Der Günstling** Dresden SO, dir. Gielen, cond. Böhm, des. Neher.

23 Mar. Kranz **Zwei Sonnen über uns** Frankfurt SH.
Max Mell *Spiel von den deutschen Ahnen* Dresden SH.

26 Mar. Erich Gower **Herr über England** Guben StdT.

30 Mar. Shaw *The Simpleton of the Unexpected Isles* (*Land der Überraschungen*, trs. Trebitsch) Leipzig SH.

6 Apr. Nedbal/Stein *Polenblut* Frankfurt Opera, dir. Felsenstein, des. Neher.

10 Apr. Rehberg **Friedrich I** Leipzig AT.

13 Apr. Gilbricht **Michael Kohlhaas** DT.

7 May Lipp. *Der Pfingstorgel. Eine Moritat aus dem Gauboden* Frankfurt SH, dir. Felsenstein, des. Neher.

21 May Kästner *Das lebenslängliche Kind*
(from his novel *Three Men in the Snow*) Zurich SH.

11 May L. Lenz/R. A. Roberts *Meine Tochter—deine Tochter* TidBehr.

12 May Egk *Zaubergeige*. Frankfurt SO, des. Neher.

8 Jun. Agnes Miegel **Die Schlacht von Rudau** Königsberg Opera.

20 Jul. Heynicke **Der Weg ins Reich** (Thing play) Heidelberg Thingstätte, mus. Blumensaat.

18 Aug. K. Fischer **Ewiges Volk** (Weihespiel) Hannover.

Start of 1935–36 Season

24 Sep. Bethge *Marsch der Veteranen*, VB, dir. Solms, des. T. Müller, > gw.

23 Oct. Möller **Bauern** Sibiu, DLT for Rumania.

27 Oct. Laban/Zillig **Gaukelei** ("dance ballad") Düsseldorf Opera.

30 Oct. Rombach **Ein Mann an der Wende** DT, mus. H. Steinkopf.

12 Nov. Graeff **Anna und Adalbert** Bremen SH.

Billinger **Die Hexen von Passau** Augsburg StdT.

16 Nov. Johst *Thomas Paine* ST dir. Fehling, des. Müller, mus. Lothar. > fh, gg, kl, mi, mü, wä.

18 Nov. H. Gobsch **Unstern über Russland** Braunschweig LT.

19 Nov. Hauptmann **Hamlet in Wittenberg** Leipzig AT.

Giono *Das Salz der Erde* Frankfurt NT.

25 Dec. Schurek **Die blaue Tulpe** Hamburg SH.

31 Dec. Künnecke/Stoll/Roemmer: *Die grosse Sünderin* (operetta) SO.

Also in the course of 1935:
Horváth **Mit dem Kopf durch die Wand** Vienna.
Shaw *Caesar and Cleopatra* Prague NDT. > vk.
Wolf **Floridsdorf** Moscow, Suchlinov factory club (in Russian).

1936

17 Jan. Hebbel *Maria Magdalena* VB, dir. Weichert, des. Müller. > w.

31 Jan. Lipscombe and Minney *Clive of India* (trs. E. Schoeller) Altona StdT.

6 Feb. Tolstoy/Shchegolev *Rasputin* Zurich
SH, dir. Steckel, des. Otto

10 Feb. Molière *Tartuffe* (trs. Blümner) VB,
dir. Lucie Höflich, des. v. Arent.
> li.

15 Feb. Steguweit **Der Nachbar zur
Linken** Mannheim NT.

12 Mar. Liliane Wied **Wanderkönigin
Christine von Schweden**
TamK, dir. Stahl-Nachbaur, des.
Neher. > s.

24 Mar. Menzel **Scharnhorst** Hamburg SH.

7 Apr. Dodie Smith *Call It a Day* Vienna,
TidJ, dir. Kalbeck, des. L. Haas.
> edt, th4. 63 perfs.

19 Apr. Rehberg **Friedrich Wilhelm I** ST,
dir. Fehling, des. Gliese, mus.
Lothar. > bt, fh, fk, kl, lsn, mi,
pa, wä)

30 Apr. Reimann/Wellenkamp: *Freut euch des
Lebens* (KdF 'Ausstattungsschau')

13 May Kleist *Kätchen von Heilbronn* VB, dir.
Weichert, des. Roethe, mus.
Spies. > w.

14 May Shakespeare *The Merchant of Venice*
Palestine, dir. Jessner, des.
Mokady. 48 perfs.

15 May Spewack *Boys Meets Girl* Vienna
TidJ, dir. Hans Thimig/M.
Schulz, des. A. Schmid.

11 Jun. Toller **No More Peace** (in English)
London, Gate T, dir. N.
Marshall.

28 Jul. Schiller *William Tell* Palestine, dir.
Jessner, des. Sebha. 21 perfs.

2 Aug. Möller **Das Frankenburger
Würfelspiel** Berlin, D-Eckart-
Bühne (Reichssportfeld).
Opening production.

Start of 1936–37 Season

3 Oct. Bethge **Pfarr Peder** Altona StdT.

4 Oct. Schurek *Tulipantjes* Hamburg,
Niederdeutsche Bühne.

8 Oct. Shakespeare *Hamlet* Zurich SH, dir.
Lindtberg. > gb.

? Oct. Vosper *Love from a Stranger* Vienna,
TidJ, dir. Heine, des. Bahner. >
d.

4 Nov. Brecht **Die Rundköpfe und die
Spitzköpfe** Copenhagen,
Riddersalen, dir. Knutzon, mus.
Eisler. (In Danish.)

6 Nov. Giraudoux *La Guerre de Troie n'aura
pas lieu* Vienna TidJ, dir. E.
Lothar, des. Niedermoser. > edt,
fll, th4. 36 perfs

12 Nov. Brecht/Weill *The Seven Deadly Sins*

15 Oct. GorchFock/Balzer **Hein
Godenwind** Altona StdT.

13 Nov. Gräff *Die Heimkehr des Matthias Bruck*

(ballet) Copenhagen, Royal T.,
chor. H. Lander.

20 Nov. Kaiser *Das Los des Ossian Balvesan* Vienna, Burg-T.
2 Dec. Schnitzler *Fräulein Else* Vienna TidJ, dir. Hans Thimig, des. Niedermoser. > b. 22 perfs.

19 Dec. Lasker-Schüler *Arthur Aronymus und seine Väter* Zurich, SH, dir. Lindtberg. > gb, hw, ka, la, st.

29 Dec. Wolf *Das trojanische Pferd* Engels State T, dir. Reich.

1937

7 Jan. Werfel *The Eternal Road* New York, Manhattan O, dir. Reinhardt, des. Bel Geddes, mus. Weill. (In English.)

2 Feb. Ibsen. *A Doll's House* Engels StateT., dir. Vallentin.

2 Apr. Horváth *Figaro lässt sich scheiden* Prague NDT KB, dir. Marlé, des. Schultes.

VB, dir. Klöpfer, des. Sachs. > kl.

5 Dec. Grabbe *Don Juan und Faust* ST, dir. Fehling, des. Gliese. > bt, do, gg, kp, ky, mi, wä.
15 Dec. Warsitz *Genie ohne Volk* Düsseldorf SH, dir. Iltz, des. Neher. > es, k, qf.
17 Dec. Shaw *The Millionairess* VB, dir. Weichert, des. Müller. > pn.
25 Dec. Schiller *Maria Stuart* Düsseldorf SH, dir. Küpper, des. Neher, mus. Zillig. > es, fa, qf.
26 Dec. A. Kehm *Die Eine und die Andere* Chemnitz StdT.

3 Jan. E. Wiechert *Spiel vom deutschen Bettelmann* Danzig ST.
Gurk: *Magister Tinius* DT (Studio).

23 Jan. Klenau *Rembrandt van Rijn* SO.
28 Jan. Dietzenschmidt *Vom lieben Augustin* Essen SH.
1 Feb. Büchner *Woyzeck* Frankfurt SH, dir. Stanchina, des. Neher.
11 Feb. Jones *The Geisha* VB, dir. Paulsen, des. v. Arent. (With lg, pn.)
20 Feb. Bethge *Die Blutprobe* Frankfurt SH.
24 Feb. Heynicke *Frau im Haus* ST KH.
2 Mar. Shakespeare *Richard III* ST, dir. Fehling, des. Müller. > bt, fh, fk, k, kö, kp, mi.
Schoeck *Massimilla Doni* Dresden O.
9 Mar. Sheriff *Journey's End* VB, dir. Kenter, des. Roethe. > ky.
26 Mar. Shakespeare *Coriolanus* DT, dir. Engel, des. Neher, mus. W-Régeny. > bs, dh1, po.

3 Apr. Käutner *Ein Auto geht in See* Frankfurt SH.
7 Apr. Rombach *Andreas Schlüter* Frankfurt, Künstler-T.
8 Apr. Shaw *Pygmalion* VB, dir. Weichert, des. Streiter. > pn.

20 May K. Čapek *Die weisse Krankheit* Zurich
SH, dir. Lindtberg.

15 Apr. Thilo v. Trotha *Engelbrecht* Kiel
StdT.

25 Apr. Möller *Struensee* Frankfurt SH,
des. Neher. Simultaneous
premiere Leipzig.

27 Apr. Dodie Smith *Der erste Frühlingstag*
(ad. Hilpert). DT KS.

25 May O Krauss *Grusinoff, der Rebell*
Düsseldorf StdBühnen.

12 Jun. Lippl *Der Holledauer Schimmel*
Hamburg SH, dir. Wüstenhagen,
des. Neher, mus. List.

13 Jun. Griese *Wind im Luch* Hannover
SH.

8 Jul. Orff *Carmina Burana* Frankfurt O,
dir. Wälterlin, des. Neher, cond.
Wetzelsberger.

Start of 1937–38 Season

19 Sep. Burte *Herzog und Henker* DT, dir.
Hilpert, des. Neher. > bs.
Schweikart *Lauter Lügen* ST KH.

24 Sep. Horváth *Ein Dorf ohne Männer*
Prague NDT, dir. Liebl.

28 Sep. Brecht/Weill *Die Dreigroschenoper*
Paris, Th. de l'Etoile, dir. F. de
Mendelssohn, des. Eugène
Berman. (In French.)

2 Oct. Wagner-Régeny *Der zerbrochene
Krug* SO.

3 Oct. Billinger *Die Windsbraut* Giessen
StdT.

5 Oct. Werfel *In einer Nacht* Vienna TidJ,
dir. Reinhardt, des. Dworsky. >
ed, th1, th4. 31 perfs.

9 Oct. H. Rothe *Die Ausländerin* Leipzig
SH.

11 Oct. Stravinsky *Jeu de Cartes* Dresden O.

16 Oct. Brecht *Señora Carrar's Rifles*
Paris, Salle Adyar, dir. Dudow,
des. Lohmar. > sp, wg.

16 Oct. Pirandello *Trovarsi* Frankfurt SH KH.

20 Oct. Billinger *Der Gigant* ST, dir.
Fehling, des. Gliese, mus.
Lothar. > et, go, kl, kp, wa, wk.

27 Oct. Rehberg *Kaiser und König*
Hamburg SH, dir. Haenel, des.
Neher, mus. Krohn. > kn.

29 Oct. Luce *The Women* Vienna TidJ, dir.
Kalbeck, des. Niedermoser. >
fw. 73 perfs.
Wolf *Peter kehrt heim* Engels State
T, dir. Fahrmann.

14 Nov. Lyndon *The Amazing Dr. Clitterhouse*
Vienna, Kom. > d.

11 Dec. Horváth *Der jüngste Tag* Mährisch
Ostrau (Moravská Ostrava), dir.
P. Marx, des. M. Miller.

16 Dec. Bruckner *Napoleon der Erste.* Zurich
SH, dir. Lindtberg.
21 Dec. Bizet *Carmen* Vienna SO, dir. Ebert,
cond. Walter, des. Neher.

25 Dec. Käutner ***Juchten und Lavandel***
Leipzig SH, mus. Eichhorn.

Also during 1937:
Horváth *Himmelwärts* Vienna.

1938

7 Jan.   F. P. Buch ***Ein ganzer Kerl*** Bremen
SH.
15 Jan. Steguweit ***Streit am Lagerfeuer***
(army play) Giessen StdT.
Graeff Begegnung mit Ulrike
Dresden SH and Karlsruhe StdT.
26 Jan. Housman *Victoria Regina* Ren-T.
27 Jan. Hella Wuolijoki *Die Frauen auf
Niskavuori* (ad. V. Prill) Hamburg
SH.

28 Jan. Shaw *The Doctor's Dilemma* Vienna
TidJ, dir. Kalbeck, des.
Niedermoser. > bn, d, ri.

28 Jan. Shaw *The Apple Cart* DT, dir. Hilpert/
Loos, des. Neher.

11 Feb. Lehár *The Land of Smiles* TamN, dir.
B. Herrmann, des. Streiter.
14 Feb. Künnecke/R. Kessler ***Hochzeit von
Samarkand*** T des Volkes (GS).
25 Feb. Shakespeare *The Tempest* DT, dir.
Engel, des. Neher, mus. Zeller.
> ls, we.

26 Feb. Otway/Hofmannsthal ***Der gerettete
Venedig*** Vienna TidJ.
5 Mar. Brecht *Die Gewehre der Frau Carrar*
Stockholm, Odeon T, dir. Greid.

5 Mar. Shaw *Mrs. Warren's Profession* ST, dir.
Fehling, des. Klein.> kö, mi, wä.
3 Apr. Blunck ***Jacob Leisler (Kampf um
Neuyork)*** Saarbrücken ST.
7 Apr. Rehberg ***Der siebenjährige Krieg***
ST.
20 Apr. E. W. Möller speech in Vienna TidJ,
"Berufung der Zeit."
23 Apr. Calderon *Der Richter von Zalamea*
Sch-T production in TidJ,
Vienna.
28 Apr. Gilbricht ***Letizia*** DT.

21 May Brecht: ***99%*** (scenes from *Fear and
Misery of the Third Reich*) Paris,
Salle d'Iéna, dir. Dudow, des.
Lohmar. > wg.
31 May Verdi: *Macbeth* Glyndebourne, dir.
Ebert, cond. Busch, des. Neher.

8 Jul.   P. Kreuder ***Liebe, Trommein und
Fanfaren*** Munich State
Operetta.
24 Jul. R. Strauss/Gregor ***Friedenstag***
Munich NT.

Start of 1938–39 Season

	6 Sep. Shaw *Man and Superman* DT, dir. Engel, des. Neher. > bn, ri.
	30 Sep. Steguweit **Glück und Glas** Dortmund StdT and Karlsruhe ST.
	4 Oct. Shakespeare *As you Like It* Vienna, TidJ, dir. Hilpert, mus. Mozart. (Opens Hilpert's management.)
	10 Oct. Shakespeare *Hamlet* (ad. Hauptmann) Rose Th.
	15 Oct. Strauss/Gregor **Daphne** Dresden Opera.
	18 Oct. Cremers *1813* Leipzig StdT.
	23 Oct. Möller **Der Untergang Karthagos** Darmstadt LT KH, dir. Everth, des. Neher. Simultaneous premiere in Bremen ST.
	29 Oct. Thilo v. Trotha **Prinzessin Plumpudding** Hamburg-Altona DVT.
17 Nov. Zuckmayer **Bellman** Zurich SH.	
	24 Nov. Egk **Peer Gynt** SO.
	26 Nov. Solms **Zirkuskomödie** Frankfurt a.d. Oder, mus. K. Heuser.
10 Dec. Hans Sahl **Jemand** Zurich, Limmathaus des. W. Roth/R. Furrer, mus. Tibor Kasicz	
	15 Dec. Coward *Gefallene Engel* TamS, dir. Kenter, des. Schmidt. > ky.
	23 Dec. Raimund *Bauer als Millionär* dir. Hilpert. > ms. DT production in TidJ.
28 Dec. Wilder **The Merchant of Yonkers** NY Theatre Guild, dir. Reinhardt.	
	31 Dec. Bolten-Baeckers/Bennecke/P. Lincke **Im Reich des Indra** Chemnitz Opera.

1939

	18 Jan. H. Graedener *Sickingen* Vienna Burg-T.
	27 Jan. Blunck *Kampf um New York* VB, dir. Kenter, des. Klein. > ky, sv.
	28 Jan. Neher/Wagner-Régeny **Die Bürger von Calais** SO, dir. Klitsch, des. Neher, cond. Karajan.
	31 Jan. Racine *Bérénice* (trs. R. A. Schroeder) Giessen StdT.
	5 Feb. Orff **Der Mond** Munich ST.
	6 Feb. Billinger **Am hohen Meer** ST, dir. Fehling, des. Gliese. > et, go, kn, kp, lb, wa, wk.
13 Feb. Zweig *Jeremias* Sweden, émigré self-help.	
	14 Feb. Lernet-Holenia **Glastüren** Vienna TidJ.

20 Mar. Bethge *Rebellion um Preussen* Frankfurt SH.

5 Apr. Graeff *Die Prüfung des Meister Tilman* VB, dir. Weichert, des. Klein. > ky.

6 Apr. Rehberg *Die Königin Isabella* ST.

5 May Shakespeare *Richard II* ST, dir. Fehling, des. Müller, mus. Lothar. > bt, fh, fk, gg, kn, kp, mi.

Pfitzner *Die Rose vom Liebesgarten* Frankfurt O.

6 May Shakespeare *Othello* DT, dir. Engel, des. Neher, mus. Mausz. > bs.

7 May Möller *Der Prinz Eugen* Giessen StdT.

11 May Theo Lingen *Was wird hier gespielt?* ST.

26 May Schiller *William Tell* Los Angeles, El Capitan T., dir. Jessner. > d, gr.

June (collective) *Four and Twenty Black Sheep* London, Arts T.

Start of 1939–40 Season

9 Sep. C. Hauptmann *Die lange Jule* DT, dir. Karchow, des. Neher. > we, fl.

12 Sep. Forzano *Die Morgengabe* TamS, dir. Klein-Rogge, des. Daniel.

21 Sep. Madách *The Tragedy of Man* VB, dir. Kenter, des. Schmidt. > kl.

7 Oct. Shakespeare *Twelfth Night*, DT, dir. Hilpert, des. Neher, mus. W-Régeny. > ls, we. (Moves to TidJ 3 Nov.)

12 Nov. R. Goering/W. Zillig *Das Opfer* Hamburg Opera.

30 Nov. Shaw *Pygmalion* DT, dir. Hilpert, des. Neher. > hy.

6 Dec. Malipiero *Julius Caesar*, ("music drama") Gera, Reuss'sches T.

9 Dec. Calderon *Der Richter von Zalamea* Zurich SH, dir. Steckel, des. Otto.

23 Dec. Shakespeare *The Taming of the Shrew* DT, dir. Hilpert. > wy.

1940

29 Jan. Shaw *St. Joan* VB, dir. Kenter, des. Gliese.

6 Feb. Kleist *Der Prinz von Homburg* Sch-T, dir. Fehling, des. Fenneker, mus. Spies. > g, w, wn.

8 Feb. Büchner *Dantons Tod*. Zurich SH, dir. Lindtberg, des. Otto. > bk, hz, la, py.

23 Feb. Kortner/D. Thompson *Another Sun* New York, National T, dir. Kortner. > hf, ka.

4 Mar. Shaw *St. Joan* Washington, Belasco T, dir. Piscator. > ra.

9 Mar. Shakespeare *King Lear* DT, dir. Hilpert, des. Neher, mus. W-Régeny. > bs, we.

20 Apr. Hofmannsthal *Everyman* Los Angeles, the Max Reinhardt Workshop, dir. Reinhardt.

1 May W. Goetz *Kampf ums Reich* Sch-T, dir. Fehling, des. Fenneker, mus. Spies. < g, kö, lg, w.

12 May Brecht *Das Verhör des Lukullus* (radio play) Radio Beromünster, dir. Bringolf.

21 May Hauptmann *Winterballade* Vienna TidJ, dir. Haenel, des. Neher.

3 Jun. Heinz Kindermann lectures in TidJ, on "Ferdinand Raimund and the German Nation."

Start of 1940–41 Season

9 Sep. Shakespeare *A Midsummer Night's Dream* DT, dir. Hilpert, des. Neher, mus. Mausz. > fl.

15 Oct. Hauptmann *Fuhrmann Henschel* VB, dir. Martin, des. Sachs. > ba, wu. (K.H. Martin's return to directing).

18 Oct. Halbe *Der Strom* Sch-T, dir. Fehling, des. Prätorius. > hö, w.

2 Nov. Kaiser *Der Soldat Tanaka* Zurich SH. > py. 3 perfs. only.

30 Nov. Shakespeare *Richard II* DT, dir. Hilpert, des. Neher, mus. W-Régeny. > f.

14 Dec. Shakespeare *King Lear* New York StudioT, dir. Piscator, des. Heythum. > bh.

19 Dec. Verdi *La Traviata* Vienna SO, dir. Schuh, des. Neher. (Start of Schuh-Neher collaboration).

1941

19 Jan. Bethge *Pfarr Peder* Darmstadt LT, dir. Everth, des. Neher.

7 Mar. Hauptmann *Kollege Crampton* Vienna TidJ, dir. Haenel. > ed.

4 Apr. Neher/Wagner-Régeny *Johanna Balk* Vienna SO, dir. Schuh, des. Neher, cond. Ludwig.

5 Apr. C. Goetz *Der Lügner und die Nonne* Zurich SH, dir. Steckel, des. Otto.

19 Apr. Brecht *Mutter Courage* Zurich SH, dir. Lindtberg, des. Otto, mus. Burkhard. > bi, gie, la, m, py.

27 Apr. Shakespeare *Julius Caesar* ST, dir. Fehling, des. Müller, mus.

1 May   Brecht *Die Mutter* Zurich, Volkshaus,
        dir. Steiner, des. Ferrer.

Lothar. > fk, k, kn, kp, mi.

Start of 1941–42 Season

25 Aug. Winsloe *Girls in Uniform* Los
         Angeles, Max Reinhardt
         Workshop, dir. Helene Thimig.

9 Sep.   Solms *Zirkus Komödie* VB, dir.
         Hanke, des. Daniel.

4 Oct.   Ardrey *Thunder Rock* Zurich SH, dir.
         Steckel, des. Otto. > la.

27 Oct. Mozart *The Marriage of Figaro* Vienna
         SO in Redoutensaal, dir. Schuh,
         des. Neher.

10 Nov. B. von Heiseler **Cäsar** DT, dir.
         Hilpert, des. Neher.
         Simultaneous premieres in
         Darmstadt and Königsberg.

15 Nov. Hauptmann **Iphigenie in Delphi**
         ST, dir. Fehling, des. Gliese,
         mus. Lothar.

12 Dec. Shaw *You Never Can Tell* DT, dir.
         Engel, des. Neher.

20 Dec. Bruckner *Criminals* New York,
         Studio T, dir. Meisner.

1942

7 Feb.   Bruckner *Die Rassen* New York,
         Tribüne, dir. Viertel. (Reading).

6 Feb.   Shaw *Pygmalion* Vienna TidJ, dir.
         Hilpert, des. Neher. > wy.

5 Mar.   Rehberg *Heinrich und Anna* ST, dir.
         Fehling, des. Müller. > fh, fl, hk,
         kp, lb, mi, mü, we.

7 Mar.   Kleist *Amphitryon* DT, dir. Hilpert,
         des. Neher, mus. W-Régeny. >
         bs.

19 Mar. Shakespeare *Richard III* Zurich SH,
         dir. Lindtberg. > py, st.

14 Apr. H. Leip **Idiothea** DT, dir. Seyferth,
         des. Neher, mus. Bachmann. >
         po. Joint premiere with
         Augsburg StdT.

7 May   Tolstoy/Piscator/Neumann **War and
         Peace** New York, Studio T, dir.
         Piscator, des. Condell, film
         Richter.

7 May   Hamsun *Abendröte* ST, dir. Fehling,
         des. Müller, mus. Lothar. > fl, k,
         kp, wä.

28 May   Shakespeare *The Tempest* Zurich SH,
         dir. Steckel, des. Otto.

12 Jun. Brecht *Furcht und Elend des III Reiches*
         (four scenes) New York, Tribüne,
         dir. Viertel. > nm.

Start of 1942–43 Season

	12 Oct. Orff *Carmina Burana* Milan, La Scala, dir. Schuh, des. Neher, cond. Marinuzzi.
	24 Nov. Kolbenheyer *Die Brücke* TamS, dir. Weichert, des. Gliese.

1943

16 Jan. V. Clement *The Marseillaise* Beverly Hills, dir. Jessner, des. R. Feld.

4 Feb. Brecht ***Der gute Mensch von Sezuan*** Zurich SH, dir. Steckel, des. Otto. > bk, gie, py.

　　　　　　　　　　　11 Feb. Shakespeare *Antony and Cleopatra* (trs. R. Gliese) DT, dir. Hilpert, des. Neher, mus. W-Régeny. > hd.

4 Mar. S. Zweig *Die Flucht zu Gott* Sweden, émigré self-help, dir. Trepte.

6 Mar. "Jessner Evening" at Los Angeles, Wilshire-Ebell T. > d, gr, hf, ko, re, wg.
　　　　　"Brecht Evening" at New York Studio T. > bg, lo.

?Mar. Lessing *Nathan der Weise* (ad. Bruckner) New York Studio T, dir. J. Light. > bh.

　　　　　　　　　　　23 Mar. Kleist *Der Prinz von Homburg* DT, dir. Hilpert, des. Neher. > bs.

　　　　　　　　　　　26 Mar. J. Kay ***Vagabunden*** Vienna TidJ, dir. Hilpert. > wy. 251 perfs.

3 Apr. (collective) *We Fight Back* New York, Hunter College, dir. Aufricht. > ka, lj, sk.

15 Apr. "In Memoriam Reinhardt" Los Angeles, Wilshire Ebell T. > d, dh2, di.

　　　　　　　　　　　21 Apr. Shaw *St Joan* ST, dir. Fehling, des. Müller, mus. Lothar. > bt, go, kn, kw, ky, we.

24 Apr. "Brecht evening," New York, Tribüne at Heckscher T. > bg, bh.

Start of 1943–44 Season

9 Sep. Brecht ***Galileo*** Zurich SH, dir. Steckel, des. Otto. > la, st, py.

　　　　　　　　　　　20 Sep. Axel v. Ambesser ***Lebensmut zu hohen Preisen*** DT, dir. Seyferth, des. Neher.

　　　　　　　　　　　27 Sep. Mell *Die Sieben gegen Theben* Vienna TidJ. 38 perfs.

12 Oct. Kaiser ***Die Spieldose*** Basel StdT, dir. R. Trösch, des. Perottet v. Laban.

　　　　　　　　　　　6 Nov. Caragiale *Ein verlorener Brief* ST, dir. Fehling, des. Müller. > bt, fk, w, wä.

15 Nov. Paul Osborn *The Innocent Voyage*
New York Belasco T, dir. Osborn.
> bh, hm.

20 Dec.   C. Goetz *Ingeborg* Vienna TidJ. 89
perfs.

1944

10 Mar. Brecht *Der gute Mensch von Sezuan*
Basel StdT, dir. Steckel, des.
Gunzinger.

15 Apr. Lorca *Blood Wedding* Zurich SH, dir.
Steckel, des. Otto. > bk, gie, py.

29 Apr. Kaiser ***Zweimal Amphitryon***
Zurich SH.

27 Apr.   Shakespeare *A Winter's Tale* DT, dir.
Hilpert, des. Neher, mus.
Mausz. > bs, do.

28 Jun. Shakespeare *Measure for Measure*
Zurich SH, dir. Steckel, des.
Otto.

 5 Aug. Irving Kaye Davis *Last Stop* New
York, Ethel Barrymore T., dir.
Piscator.

On 1 September the German theatres were closed.

30 Sep. Bruckner *Denn seine Zeit ist kurz*
Mexico City, H. Heine Club, dir.
Steffi Spira.

12 Oct. Sartre *Les Mouches* Zurich SH, dir.
Steckel, des. Otto. > bk, gb.

11 Nov. Werfel ***Jacubowsky und der***
Oberst Zurich SH, dir. Steckel,
des. Otto.

1945

25 Jan. Hauptmann *Rose Bernd* Zurich SH,
dir. Steckel, des. Furrer. > gb, la.

22 Feb. Shakespeare *The Taming of the Shrew*
Zurich SH, dir. Steckel.

24 Feb. Kaiser ***Das Floss der Medusa***
Basel StdT.

22 Mar. Synge *The Playboy of the Western
World* Zurich SH, dir. Steckel,
des. Furrer.

 5 May Silone *And He Did Hide Himself*
Zurich SH.

10 May Kisch *Der Fall des Generalstabschefs
Redl* Mexico City, H. Heine Club.
(One perf. with cast of exiled
writers incl. Abusch, Renn,
Seghers, Uhse.)

24 May Shakespeare *Pericles* Zurich SH, dir.
Steckel, des. Otto.

27 May Schönthan *Raub der Sabinerinnen*
Ren-T. (First postwar Berlin
production.)

 7 Jun. Brecht *The Private Life of the Master
Race* (17 scenes from *Furcht und
Elend des III Reiches*) Berkeley,
Wheeler Auditorium, dir. H.
Schnitzler.

12 Jun.   ditto, New York, Pauline Edwards T,
    dir. Viertel, des. Kerz, mus.
    Eisler. > b, nm.
 5 Jul.   Death of Georg Kaiser at Ascona, Switzerland.

First German Theatre Season after Fall of the Third Reich

August	15	Brecht/Weill	*Die Dreigroschenoper* TidK (Hebbel-T), dir. Martin.
	27	'Jurgen-Fehling-Theater' opens in Künstlerhaus Zehlendorf.	
September	7	Lessing	*Nathan der Weise* DT, dir. Fritz Wisten. > m, w, mn.
	8	Gluck	*Orpheus* SO, dir. W. Völker, des. Herlth, cond. Schait.
	13	Bruckner	**Die Befreiten** Zurich SH, dir. Steckel. > gie, la.
	18	Hay	**Der Gerichtstag** DT, dir. Wangenheim.
	25	Hofmannsthal	*Der Schwierige* Vienna TidJ, dir. R. Steinböck. > edt. 107 perfs.
October	6	Goethe	*Urfaust* Jürgen-Fehling-T, dir. Fehling, des. Freese.
	27	Gorky	*The Lower Depths* Zurich SH. > la. Langhoff's last performance before return to Germany.
November		Ardrey	*Thunder Rock* TidK (Hebbel-T), dir. Martin. > bu.
	15	Beethoven	*Fidelio* Munich SO, dir. Rennert, des. Neher. (First postwar prodn.)
December	7	Horváth	**Der jüngste Tag** Vienna TidJ. 59 perfs.
	11	Shakespeare	*Hamlet* DT, dir Wangenheim, des. Schütte.
	?	Wolf	*Dr. Lilli Wanner* Chemnitz (First Wolf play in Germany since 1932.)
	?	Wilder	*Our Town* Munich KS, dir. Engel. (German premiere.)

Appendix 3
Some Relevant Films of the Period

This comprises:

1. Films Relating to Plays or Theatre Productions
2. Some Films Featuring Leading Actors of the Weimar Theatre
3. Some Nazi Films Involving Weimar Actors

NOTE: The same abbreviations for the names of actors apply as in the previous appendix. Date of premiere is given where known. Unless otherwise specified, cinemas named were in Berlin.

Films Relating to Plays or Theatre Productions

1920
Kaiser: *Von Morgens bis Mitternachts.* (Ilag-Film). Dir. Karlheinz Martin, script Martin and H. Juttke, sets Neppach. > ba, d, ri, wa.

1921
Hauptmann: *Die Ratten.* (Grete Ly-Film). Dir. Hanns Kobe, script Julius Sternheim, sets Neppach, cam. K. Freud. > eb, hö, j, kl, lk, tw, vl. (July 1921).

1922
Schiller: *Kabale und Liebe;* new title *Luise Millerin.* (Froelich Film). Dir. Carl Froelich, script Walter Suppe. > dv, ha, k, ko, sz.
Wedekind: *Erdgeist.* (Leopold Jessner-Film, dist. Oswald-Film). Dir. Jessner, script Carl Mayer. > b, eb, f, g, gr.

Wedekind: *Frühlings Erwachen.* (Wiener Kunstfilm). Dir. Luise Kolm/Jacob Fleck, script Lantz/Fleck, sets J. Ballenstedt. > pa, ri.

1923

Schiller: *Wilhelm Tell.* (Atthoff-Amboss-Film). Dir. Rudolf Dworsky, script Dworsky and Walther-Fein, sets Stern/Rudi Feld. > dg, eb, gt, s, v, wn. (23 August 1923, Marmorhaus).

1927

Hauptmann: *Die Weber.* (Friedrich-Zelnik-Film). Dir. Zelnik, script Fanny Carlsen/Willy Haas, mus. Schmidt-Gentner, sets Andrejev, masks Grosz. > di, kk, ls, se, tw, w. (14 May 1927, Capitol).

Zuckmayer: *Der fröhliche Weinberg.* (FPG GmbH). Dir. Jacob and Luise Fleck, script Zuckmayer/Lantz, mus. Schmidt-Gentner. > od, nm. (20 December 1927, Marmorhaus).

Zuckmayer: *Schinderhannes.* (Prometheus-Film). Dir. Kurt Bernhardt, script Zuckmayer/Bernhardt, sets Heinrich Richter. > fh, hm, ri, sr. (1 February 1928, Tauentzien-Palast).

1928

Wedekind: *Büchse der Pandora.* (Nero-Film). Dir. G. W. Pabst, script Vajda, sets Andrejev. > ko, lr. (9 February 1929, Gloria-Palast).

Schnitzler: *Fräulein Else.* (Poetic-Film). Dir. and script Czinner. > b, bg, sr. (8 March 1929, Capitol).

1929

Lampel: *Giftgas über Berlin;* new title *Giftgas.* (Loew & Co.). Dir. Michael Dubson, script N. A. Zarkhi, sets August Rinaldi. > ko. (13 November 1929, Marmorhaus).

Zuckmayer: *Katharina Knie.* (Karl-Grune-Film GmbH). Dir. Grune, script Franz Höllering, sets Neppach. > bu, dg, ett, fo, kl, kw, ri, wä. (13 December 1929, Capitol).

1930

Wolf: *Cyankali.* (Atlantis-Film). Dir. and script Hans Tintner, mus. Schmidt-Gentner. > hk, ku, mo. (23 May 1930).

Joachimson: *Wie werde ich reich und glücklich?* (Emelka). Dir. Max Reichman, mus. Spoliansky.

Kaiser: *Zwei Krawatten.* (Max-Glass-Filmprod., dist. Terra-Film). Dir. F. Basch/R. Weichert, mus. Spoliansky. > gt, li, od. (16 October 1930).

Brecht/Weill: *The Threepenny Opera.* (Warner/Tobis coprod.). Dir. Pabst, script Vajda, Lania, Balázs, sets Andrejev, cost. Neher. > bu, f, lj, ne, sz, th4. (19 February 1931).

1931

Sherriff: *Journey's End*, German title *Die andere Seite.* (Cando-Filmprod.). Dir. Heinz Paul, script H. Reisiger, mus. E. E. Buder. > kw, ls, v. (19 October 1931).

Zuckmayer: *Der Hauptmann von Köpenick.* (Roto-Film, dist. Süd-Film). Dir. R. Oswald, script Zuckmayer/Joseph. > ad, bie, fh, gt, ky, lb, od, ss, st, vl, wm. (22 December 1931).

Some films featuring leading actors of the Weimar theatre

1920

Der Golem, wie er in die Welt kam. (Projektions-AG Union). Dir. Paul Wegener/Carl Boese, script Wegener, sets Hans Poelzig. > d, sa, sr, w.

1921

Danton. (Wörner-Film). Dir. Dimitri Buchowetzki. Script Carl Meyer, sets Dreyer. > j, k, wn.

Hintertreppe. (Henny Porten/Gloria-Film). Dir. Leopold Jessner/Paul Leni, script Carl Meyer. > di, ko.

1924

Wachsfigurenkabinett. (Neptun-Film). Dir. Paul Leni, script H. Galeen, cam. H. Lerski, cost. Ernst Stern. > di, j, k, lg, v. (13 November 1924, Ufa-Palast am K'damm).

Der letzte Mann. (Ufa). Dir. F. Murnau, script C. Mayer. > j, vl. (13 December 1924, Ufa-Palast am Zoo).

1925

Geheimnisse einer Seele. (Neumann-Filmprod). Dir. Pabst, script Colin Ross/Hans Neumann, sets Ernö Maetzner. > k. (24 March 1926, Gloria-Palast).

1926

Metropolis. (Dist. Parafumet). Dir. Lang, script Thea v. Harbou. > g, ls, wg. (10 January 1927).

1929

Atlantik. (British Int. Pictures). Dir. E. A. Dupont, mus. J. Reynders. > fo, ko, le, lr, ma, w. (28 October 1929).

Tagebuch einer Verlorenen. (G. W. Pabst-Film). Dir. Pabst, script Rudolf Leonhardt. > ge, ki.

1930

Der blaue Engel. (Ufa). Dir. J. v. Sternberg, script Liebmann/Zuckmayer/Vollmoeller (from H. Mann's novel *Der Untertan*), mus. Friedrich Holländer. > al, bie, dg, die2, ge, j, va, wn. (1 April 1930).

Dreyfus. (R. Oswald Filmprod). Dir. Oswald, script Goldberg/Wendhausen. > b, bt, g, hk, hm, ka, ko, mo.

Die drei von der Tankstelle. (Ufa). Dir. W. Thiele, script F. Schulz/P. Franck, mus. W. R. Heymann. > br, fo, ge, ks, rü. (15 September 1930).

Das Flötenkonzert von Sanssouci. (Ufa). Dir. Ucicky, mus. Schmidt-Gentner. > as, ky, li, ls, wä.

Eine Stunde Glück. (Cicero-Film). Dir. Dieterle, script Karl Gillmann, mus. Jean Gilbert. > di, pn, w. (16 March 1931).

1931

1914. Die letzten Tage vor dem Weltbrand. (Oswald-Film). Dir. Oswald, script Goldberg/Wendhausen. > b, bt, g, gr, hö, hm, kl, kw, ls, od, re, sz. (20 January 1931).

Der Mann, der seinen Mörder sucht. (Ufa). Dir. R. Siodmak, script Hirschfeld/K. Siodmak/Wilder, mus. Holländer/Wachsman. > bie, lb, rü, ss. (5 February 1931).

Der Mörder Dimitri Karamasoff. (Terra-Film). Dir. Ozep, script L. Frank/Ozep/Trivas, mus. Rathaus/Schröder. > ko, mi. (6 February 1931).

Berlin-Alexanderplatz. (Allianz Tonfilm, dist. Süd-Film). Dir. Jutzi, script Döblin/Wilhelm/K. H. Martin (from Döblin's novel), mus. Gray/Guttmann. > bie, dp, fh, g, mi.

Danton. (Allianz Tonfilm, dist. Süd-Film). Dir. H. Behrend, script H. Goldberg/Rehfisch, mus. Guttmann. > gg, gn, gr, ko, ma, ss, wh.

Der Koffer des Herrn O.F. (Tobis). Dir. Granowsky, script Lania/Granowsky, songs Kästner, mus. Rathaus/Schröder. > bu, ln, lo, pn.

M. (Nero-Film). Dir. Lang, script T. v. Harbou. > bie, gg, gn, hk, hr, lo, lö, ls, mr, od, st, we. (11 November 1931).

Menschen hinter Gittern. (MGM coproduction, dist. Parafumet). Ad. and dialogue Toller/Hasenclever/E. W. Brandes from MGM's *Big House.* > et, g, tw.

Niemandsland. (Resco-Filmprod). Dir. Trivas, mus. Eisler/K. Schröder. > bu, lz, sw. (20 December 1931).

York. (Ufa). Dir. Ucicky, mus. Schmidt-Boelcke. > as, f, gg, hd, hl, k, ky, ls, mo, mü, wb. (23 December 1931).

1932

Fünf von der Jazzband. (Ufa/Tobis). Dir. Erich Engel, mus. Mackeben. > bie, lo. (12 April 1932).

Der träumende Mund. (Pathé and Matador-Film, dist. Emelka). Dir. Czinner, script Czinner and C. Mayer. > bg, edt, f. (13 September 1932).

Das Testament des Dr Mabuse. (Nero-Film). Dir. Lang, script v. Harbou, mus. H. Erdmann. > hk, li, ls, sp, we. (Vienna 12 May 1933, having been rejected by German censorship on 29 March).

1933

Kleiner Mann, was nun? (R. N.-Filmprod., dist. Tobis). Dir. Wendhausen, script Selpin/Wendhausen from Fallada's novel, sets Neher, mus. H. Böhmelt. > er, hk, kw, li, th4. (3 August 1933).

Some Nazi Films with Weimar Actors

Hitlerjunge Quex. (Ufa). Script, K. A. Schenzinger from own novel. > dp, dr, g, ki, ss. (19 September 1933).

Flüchtlinge. Dir. Ucicky, script Gerhard Menzel from own novel, mus. H. Windt/E. E. Buder. > al, gn, gw, hl, hp, ki, kl. Awarded State Prize 1 May 1934. Subject: sufferings of the Volga Germans.

Jud Süss. (Terra-Film). Dir. Veit Harlan, script L. Metzger/E. W. Möller/Harlan, mus. W. Zeller. > fh, g, k, kl.

Appendix 4
Select List of Radio and
Gramophone Recordings

Unless otherwise indicated, these are recordings held in the Deutsches Rundfunk-archiv, Frankfurt-am-Main, i.e., the West German sound archives. Details can be found in their catalogues *(Bild- und Tonträger-Verzeichnisse)* numbers 3 and 14. Recordings of modern performances are excluded. Abbreviation of actors' names follows the list beginning on p. 252.

The list comprises the following sections.

1. Works Recorded in Whole or in Significant Part
   a. Plays or Radio Plays of the Weimar Theatre
   b. Musicals and Revues
   c. From the New Nazi Theatre
   d. Relevant Classics
2. Actors of the Weimar Theatre: Some Sample Recordings
3. Miscellaneous

Works Recorded in Whole or in Significant Part

(a) Plays or Radio Plays of the Weimar Theatre

Bauer, Walter: *Bahnsteig, oder Ein Werk in Deutschland* (5-min. extract). Leipzig 1931.

Brecht: *Saint Joan of the Stockyards*—radio adaptation, dir. Alfred
     Braun for Berlin Radio, 11 April 1932. > bt, bu, gn, ko, lo, ne,
     wg.
Brecht/Weill: *Lindbergflug* (shortened to 19 mins.), cond.
     Scherchen, Berlin 1930. > gb.
Döblin: *Die Geschichte vom Franz Biberkopf*—adapted from novel
     Berlin-Alexanderplatz, dir. Max Bing, mus. W. Goehr. > bie, g,
     kb, tw.
Herzog/Rehfisch: *Die Affäre Dreyfus*. (Gram. recording of
     speeches). > g.
Horváth: *Hin und Her* (Amadeo gram. recording). > th4.
Kästner/Nick: *Leben in dieser Zeit* (extracts).
Moeller: *Douaumont*, dir. Max Bing, mus. Karl Knauer. Berlin
     1932. > g, hk, kp
Schönlank, Bruno: *Bergwerk* (brief extract). Leipzig 1932.
Wolf: *SOS rao rao Foyn. Die Tragödie des Luftschiffs "Italia,"* dir.
     Alfred Braun for Berlin Radio.
Zuckmayer: *Katharina Knie* (Short extract). Recorded 1949. > b.
Zuckmayer: *Der Hauptmann von Köpenick* (one scene). Amadeo
     record > w.

(b) Musicals and Revues

F. W. Bischoff/Nick: *Mittsommernacht* (extracts).> py.
Brecht/Weill: *Die Dreigroschenoper* (i) Original gramophone
     recording December 1931, cond. Theo Mackeben.> ge, lj, po.
     Issued under various labels and numbers. (ii) Condensed
     Electrola selection *Die Songs der Dreigroschenoper*. > ge, ne
Brecht/Weill: *Aufstieg und Fall der Stadt Mahagonny. Querschnitt aus
     der Oper* (Condensed Electrola version of 1931 Berlin
     production), cond. Hans Sommer. > lj.
Seeler/Holländer: *Bei uns um die Gedächtniskirche rum* (extracts on
     record).
Schiffer/Spoliansky: *Es liegt in der Luft* (condensed version and
     two songs). > dh2, ks, ln.

(c) From the New Nazi Theatre

Euringer: *Vögelbunt*. (The Thingspiel author reading from his
     work).
Johst: *Schlageter* (short reading by the author).
Moeller/Blumensaft: *Die Verpflichtung* (cantata).
Rehberg: *Die preussische Komödie*. Berlin 1933. > hd, ls.
Scheller, Thilo: Speech choruses and fanfares for party functions.
     1935.
von Hoerschelmann: *Der Weg in die Freiheit,* dir. Arnolt Bronnen.
     Berlin 1933. > g, ki, mü.

(d) Relevant Classics

Büchner: *Woyzeck* (radio adaptation), dir. Ernst Hardt. Cologne
     1932. > bt, bu, hd, mz, re.

Goethe: *Faust, Part 1* (on three lp records), dir. Gründgens, mus.
   Mark Lothar. > fl, gg, go, ha.
Goethe: *Stella,* dir. Max Bing. Berlin 1931. > ha, s, se, th1.
Hauptmann: *Biberpelz* and *Roter Hahn* (extracts on gram. records).
   > gz, hö.
Hebbel: *Maria Magdalena* (extracts), dir. Bing. > g, gg, th1.
Ibsen: *Ghosts* (extract, gram. recording c. 7 mins.). > ky
Kleist: *Amphitryon* (gram recording c. 12 mins.). > eb, lsn.
Kleist: *Prinz Friedrich von Homburg,* dir. Reinhardt. > ky, th1, w,
   wn.
Wedekind: *Der Kammersänger* (gram, recording, c. 20 mins.). > f

Actors of the Weimar Theatre—Some Recordings

These are almost entirely gramophone recordings. In most cases their date is
unspecified, and some may have been recorded after the Second World War.
The list is not meant to be anything like complete.

Aslan and Balser: From Goethe's *Tasso.*
Bassermann: *Albert Bassermann—Porträt eines Schauspielers.* Teldec
   Telefunken. (And three speeches in the Lautarchiv).
Bergner: From Schnitzler's *Fräulein Else.* (Deutsche
   Grammophon).
Bois: *Sprechen Sie sich aus.* 1930. (Teldec Telefunken).
Deutsch: *Ernst Deutsch—ein grosser Schauspieler.* Teldec
   Telefunken.
Dorsch: *Käthe Dorsch—eine unvergessene Stimme.* (Ariola record).
   Athena.
Durieux: *Tilla Durieux spricht Szenen und Monologe.* (Deutsche
   Grammophon), with comments by Erwin Piscator.
Ebert: Extracts from *Egmont* and *Faust* (record).
Eysoldt: From Hofmannsthal's *Elektra* and Kleist's *Penthesilea*
   (record).
Florath: *Tschekhow Schwanengesang* (record). Teldec Telefunken.
Forster: *Das Spiel, mein Leben.* SM Deutsche Grammophon.
Frank, W.: *Faust* monologues. (ditto). Ditto.
George: *Heinrich George spricht.* Teldec Telefunken,
   and *Heinrich George. Porträt eines Schauspielers.* Ditto, Ditto.
Gold: *Käthe Gold spricht Gedichte, Märchen und Szenen.* Deutsche
   Grammophon.
Gründgens: *Gustav Gründgens, ein Porträt.* With Emmy
   Sonnemann (Goering).
Hartmann: Faust's first speech. Deutsche Grammophon.
Höflich: Two speeches from *Faust* (record).
Kainz: From *Cyrano de Bergerac* (old private recording).
Kayssler: *Faust-Sorge/Fausts Tod.* Teldec Telefunken.
Koppenhöfer: From Schiller's *Braut von Messina* (record).
Krauss: *Werner Krauss. Porträt eines Schauspielers.* Teldec
   Telefunken.
      Also extracts from Schiller's *Wallensteins Tod* (with H. Körner—
      record).

Leibelt: From *Twelfth Night* (record).
Lingen: *Theo Lingen. Porträt eines Schauspielers*. Teldec Telefunken.
Moissi: *In Memoriam*. Deutsche Grammophon.
   From *Faust* (record).
   From *Hamlet* (record—in German)
   —and several other recordings in the Lautarchiv.
Müthel: Prologue to Schiller's *Wallenstein* (record).
Pallenberg: From Leo Fall's *Madame Pompadour,* with Fritzi
   Massary (record).
   Also from Franz Molnár's *1,2,3.*
Thimig, Hugo: From Schiller's *Kabale und Liebe.* (Private
   recording).
Wassmann: From *A Midsummer Night's Dream* and other plays.
Wegener: From *Nathan der Weise* (record).

NB: There are also numerous recordings by famous cabaret or music hall performers such as Claire Waldoff and Karl Valentin, and several have been reissued. In addition Polydor has issued two LP records under the title *Sterne ihrer Zeit—Die Grossen der Kleinkunst*, featuring such performers as Curt Bois, Marlene Dietrich, Trude Hesterberg, Oskar Karlweis, Theo Lingen, and Paul Morgan under nos. 47819 and 47826.

Miscellaneous

Erich Kästner/Edmund Nick: *Gespräch über das Kabaret* (very
   brief). 1952
Alfred Kerr reading "Als Joseph Kainz starb" and other pieces
   (record).
Erwin Piscator on a production of *Nathan der Weise* (short). 1952.
Max Reinhardt: speech in Berlin at the Deutsches Theater 50th
   anniversary celebrations (about 6 mins.)
Richard Weichert on Carl Zuckmayer (about 8 minutes). 1952.

Notes

PAGE	NOTE	
19	7	Cited in Heinrich Bräulich, *Die Volksbühne* (East Berlin: Henschel, 1976), 34.
21	8	Franz Mehring in *Die Volksbühne*, no. 3 (January 1893), cited by Bräulich, 50.
22	9	Figures from *Die Volksunterhaltung* Jg. 8, no. 9 (September 1906), cited by Bräulich, 225, note 55.
23	10	Cecil W. Davies: *Theatre for the People* (Manchester: Manchester University Press, 1977), 30.
25	11	Cited by Denis Bablet, *Esthétique générale du décor de théâtre de 1870 à 1914* (1975 reprint; Paris: CNRS, 1965) 243. From Appia's unpublished "Richard Wagner et la mise en scène," written in March 1925.
25	12	Adolphe Appia, *L'Oeuvre d'art vivant* (Geneva and Paris: Atar, 1921), 31, cited by Bablet, 247.
26	13	Bablet, 273, citing Appia's "Acteur, espace, lumière, peinture" in *Théâtre Populaire*, no. 5, (Jan.–Feb. 1954): 42.
28	14	See Henry van de Velde, *Geschichte meines Lebens* (Munich: Piper, 1962), 268–72. On his theatre project see also 255–58, 264–67, and fig. 72.
28	15	Peter Behrens, *Feste des Lebens und der Kunst* (Leipzig, 1900), 13, cited in Kranich, *Bühnentechnik der Gegenwart* vol. II, 308.
28	16	Cited by Bablet, 362, from p. 47 of Fuchs's book.
30	17	Reinhard Sorge, *Der Bettler: Eine dramatische Sendung* (Berlin: Fischer, 1912, 6. und 7. Auflage, 1928), 30.
30	18	Translated by J. M. Ritchie in *Seven Expressionist Plays* (London: Calder and Boyars, 1968), 25.
30	19	Will Grohmann, *Wassily Kandinsky* (Thames and Hudson, London, 1959), 100. The full text of the play is in the Blaue Reiter almanach (reprint by Piper, Munich, 1965) and a translation by John C. Crawford in *Arnold Schönberg/Wassily Kandinsky: Letters, Pictures and Documents,* edited by Jelena Hahl-Koch (London and Boston: Faber, 1984).

Chapter 3:
Reinhardt, The Bridge to the 1920s

33	1	Max Reinhardt, *Schriften* (East Berlin: Henschel, 1974), 304.
33	2	Ibid., 266, citing an interview in the *Nieuwe Rotterdamse Courant*, 1 May 1916.
34	3	Ibid., 264, from the same interview.
35	4	Cited in Walter Rösler, *Das Chanson im deutschen Kabarett 1901–1933* (East Berlin: Henschel, 1980), 105.
36	5	Arthur Kahane, *Tagebuch eines Dramaturgen* (Berlin, 1926). Cited in Reinhardt, *Schriften*, 64.
36	6	Ibid., 65.
36	7	Ibid., 66.
37	8	Reinhardt, *Schriften*, 65.
37	9	Letter to Berthold Held, 20 July 1902, cited in Reinhardt, *Schriften*, 75.
37	10	Reinhardt, *Schriften*, 76.

PAGE	NOTE	
37	11	Cited in Reich, *Im Wettlauf mit der Zeit* (East Berlin: Henschel, 1970), 121.
39	12	See his instructions to Held in the long letter of 21 July 1904, reprinted in Reinhardt, *Schriften*, 83–91.
39	13	For Reinhardt's basic concept for this play, see Heinz Herald, "Ein Sommernachtstraum," in Ernst Stern and Heinz Herald, eds., *Reinhardt und seine Bühne* (Berlin, 1919), 37–45.
41	14	"Aus dem Regiebuch 'Ein Sommernachtstraum,' " in Reinhardt, *Schriften*, 275.
41	15	"Das Regiebuch," ibid., 257–59.
42	16	Reinhardt, *Schriften*, 258. The present writer feels that, in the English-language theatre at least, this is an abuse which reduces the words to rubbish.
42	17	Reich, *Im Wettlauf mit der Zeit*, 132.
42	18	Entry for June 1905 in Craig's Chronology. Janet Lepper, *Edward Gordon Craig: Designs for the Theatre* (Harmondsworth: Penguin, 1948), 35.
43	19	Letter of 21 July 1904, in Reinhardt, *Schriften*, 91.
43	20	See Kranich, *Bühnentechnik der Gegenwart*, vol. 1, 212 and 289; and vol. II, 23.
43	21	Undated letter from Maeterlinck to F. von Oppeln Bronikowski in Sayler, ed., *Max Reinhardt and His Theatre* (New York: Brentano's, 1924), 331–32.
43	22	In his recollections *Da geht ein Mensch* (Berlin-Grunewald: Non-Stop Bücherei, n.d.), 119.
45	23	Interview in *Nieuwe Rotterdamse Courant* 1 May 1916, reprinted in Reinhardt, *Schriften*, 265.
45	24	Letter to Count Ledebour, ibid., 244.
45	25	According to a note in *Der Sturm*, Berlin (22 April 1911).
45	26	Nicholas Slonimski, *Music since 1900*, 1st ed., entry for 27 September 1921.
46	27	This extract is taken at random from the American "Regiebuch" reproduced in Sayler's *Max Reinhardt and His Theatre*, 315.
46	28	See the illustration in ibid., opposite 193. Also Tim Benton, *Expressionism, Course Book A305 9–10* (Milton Keynes: Open University Press, 1975), 71–72 and illustrations 86–92.
48	29	Fritz Kortner, *Aller Tage Abend* (Munich: DTV, 1959) 136.
48	30	Ibid., 240.
48	31	Ibid., 241.
49	32	Ibid., 115.
49	33	In a letter to Ferdinand Kunzelmann, 21 July 1918, included in Reinhardt, *Schriften*, 182.
49	34	See Herald's description in *Reinhardt und seine Bühne*, 64–72.

Chapter 4:
Revolution and the Establishment of Expressionism

PAGE	NOTE	
53	1	Herbert Jhering, *Berliner Dramaturgie*, (East Berlin: Aufbau-Verlag, 1948), 60.

PAGE	NOTE	
53	2	Huntly Carter, *The New Spirit in the European Theatre 1914–1924* (London: Ernst Benn, 1925), 164.
54	3	Friedrich Schiller, "Die Schaubühne als eine moralische Anstalt betrachtet," in *Schillers sämmtliche Werke in einem Bande* (Stuttgart and Tübingen: Cotta, 1840), 704.
59	4	Kurt Pinthus, "Rede an junge Dichter," in *Die neue Dichtung, ein Almanach* (Leipzig: Kurt Wolff, 1918), 150.
59	5	Jhering, *Berliner Dramaturgie* (East Berlin: Aufbau-Verlag, 1948), 60.
61	6	Kurt Pinthus, ed., *Menschheitsdämmerung. Symphonie jüngste Dichtung* (Berlin: Rowohlt, 1920; reissued 1959), xiii.
61	7	Ernst Toller, *Die Wandlung: Ringen eines Menschen* (Potsdam: Kiepenheuer, 1920).
63	8	See its opening program manifesto, reproduced in Willett, *The Theatre of Erwin Piscator* (1978), 48.
65	9	From *Der neue Weg* Jg 47, no. 43–44 (15 November 1918); reproduced in the catalogue *Theater in der Weimarer Republik* (West Berlin, 1977), 689.
66	10	Ibid., 690.
66	11	Act 3, scene 5.
67	12	Act 3, scene 3.
67	13	Fritz Kortner, *Aller Tage Abend* (Munich: DTV, 1959), 228.
67	14	Ibid., 225.
68	15	Cited in Heinrich Bräulich, *Die Volksbühne* (East Berlin: Henschel, 1976), 103.
69	16	"The Author to the Producer," October 1921, from Ernst Toller, *Masses and Man*, trs. Vera Mendl (London: Nonesuch Press, 1923), ix.
70	17	Bernhard Reich, *Im Wettlauf mit der Zeit* (East Berlin: Henschel, 1970), 111.
70	18	Carl Zuckmayer, *Als wärs ein Stück von mir* (Frankfurt: S. Fischer, 1966), 323.

Chapter 5:
Expressionism Runs Out of Steam

73	1	Harry Graf Kessler, *Tagebücher 1918–1937* (Frankfurt: Insel-Verlag, 1961), 95. (Entry for 6 January 1919).
74	2	Ibid., 104. (Entry for 14 January 1919).
75	3	Alfred Döblin, *Griffe ins Leben: Berliner Theaterberichte* (East Berlin: Henschel, 1974), 214–17.
76	4	Iwan Goll, "Der Expressionismus stirbt," *Zenit*, no. 8 (Belgrade 1921): 8ff.
76	5	Kessler, *Tagebücher*, 141. (Entry for 1 March 1919).
77	6	Siegfried Jacobsohn, *Jahre der Bühne* (Hamburg: Rowohlt, 1965), 212.
77	7	Kurt Tucholsky, *Ausgewählte Briefe 1913–1935* (Hamburg: Rowohlt, 1962), 130, letter to Jhering 21 May 1922.
77	8	Carl Zuckmayer, *Als wärs ein Stück von mir* (Frankfurt: S. Fischer, 1966), 365.

PAGE	NOTE	
77	9	Fritz Kortner, *Aller Tage Abend* (Munich: DTV, 1959), 306.
78	10	Cited in Richard Samuel and R. Hinton Thomas, *Expressionism in German Life, Literature and the Theatre (1910–1924)* (Cambridge: Heffer, 1939), 176.
81	11	Kessler, *Tagebücher*, 360. (Entry for 8 January 1923. This describes meetings with Jean Cocteau and Pierre-Jean Jouve).
82	12	Published by Albert Langen, Munich, n.d., as no. 4 of the Bauhausbücher.
83	13	L. Moholy-Nágy, "Theater, Zirkus, Variété," in ibid., 52–53.
83	14	See Werner Schmalenbach, *Kurt Schwitters* (Cologne: M. Dumont Schauberg, 1967), 36 (illustration) and 201–2 (description)
83	15	Iwan Goll, *Methusalem oder Der ewige Bürger. Ein satirisches Drama* (Potsdam: Kiepenheuer, 1922), 7.
84	16	Iwan Goll, *Die Unsterblichen: Zwei Possen* (Potsdam: Kiepenheuer, 1920), 7.
84	17	Goll, *Methusalem oder Der ewige Bürger*, 8.
86	18	Georg Kaiser, *Nebeneinander: Volksstück 1923 in fünf Akten* (Potsdam: Kiepenheuer, 1923), 136.
86	19	Ibid., 57.
86	20	Siegfried Jacobsohn, *Jahre der Bühne* (Hamburg: Rowohlt, 1965), 224.
86	21	Alfred Döblin, *Griffe ins Leben: Theaterfeulletons* (East Berlin: Henschel, 1974), 223–24.
87	22	Günther Rühle, *Theater für die Republik 1917–1933: Im Spiegel der Kritik* (Frankfurt: S. Fischer, 1967), 296–97.
87	23	Ernst Barlach, *Prosa aus vier Jahrzehnten*, ed. Elmer Jansen (East Berlin: Union-Verlag, 1966), 471, letter to Reinhard Piper.
87	24	Rühle, *Theater für die Republik*, 455.
87	25	Alfred Klaar, in ibid., 457.
87	26	Jacobsohn, *Jahre der Bühne*, 222.
87	27	Jürgen P. Wallmann, *Else Lasker-Schüler* (Mühlacker: Stieglitz-Verlag E. Händle, 1966), 74.
88	28	Rühle, *Theater fur die Republik*, 806.
90	29	Asja Lacis, *Revolutionär im Beruf* (Munich: Rogner und Bernhard, 1971), 38.
91	30	Bertolt Brecht, *Briefe* (Frankfurt: Suhrkamp, 1981), 45, letter no. 33.

Chapter 6:
The Twenties Strike Gold

97	1	Marcellus Schiffer, "Es liegt in der Luft." Foxtrot from the revue of that name by Schiffer and Mischa Spoliansky, in Klaus Budzinski, ed., *So weit die scharfe Zunge reicht* (Munich: Scherz-Verlag, 1964), 268–69.
98–99	2	Bertolt Brecht, *Gedichte aus dem Nachlass* (Frankfurt: Suhrkamp), 128. This is not the text as set to music by Weill.
102	3	On Bruinier see Fritz Hennenberg, ed., *Das grosse Brecht-Liederbuch* (East Berlin: Henschel; and Frankfurt: Suhrkamp, 1984).
102	4	Arnolt Bronnen, *Anarchie in Sillian: Schauspiel* (Berlin: Rowohlt, 1925), 110.

PAGE	NOTE	
103	5	Arnolt Bronnen, *Rheinische Rebellen: Schauspiel* (Berlin: Rowohlt, 1925, 69.
103	6	Günther Rühle, *Theater für die Republik 1917–1933.* (Frankfurt: S. Fischer, 1967), 644.
103	7	Partial text published as epilogue to *Vatermord* in Alfred Wolfenstein, ed. *Die Erhebung zweites Buch* (Berlin: S. Fischer, 1920), 218–37.
104	8	Berthold Viertel, *Schriften zum Theater* (Munich: Kösel-Verlag, 1970).
104	9	*Der fröhliche Weinberg,* in Günther Rühle, *Zeit und Theater. Von der Republik zur Diktatur 1925–1933,* Band 2 (West Berlin: Propyläen-Verlag, 1972), 99.
105	10	Carl Zuckmayer: *Als wärs ein Stück von mir* (Frankfurt: S. Fischer Verlag, 1966), 397.
105	11	Carl Zuckmayer, *Der fröhliche Weinberg,* Rühle, *Zeit und Theater,* 99.
106	12	See "Kommentar" in Rühle, *Zeit und Theater,* 770 ff.
109	13	Ernst Toller, *Hoppla, wir leben!,* in Rühle, *Zeit und Theater,* 185.
109	14	Herbert Jhering, *Von Reinhardt bis Brecht* (Hamburg: Rowohlt), 259.
110	15	Text of Piscator's *Schweik* adaptation is in Herbert Knust, ed., *Materialien zu Bertolt Brechts "Schweyk im zweiten Weltkrieg"* (Frankfurt: Suhrkamp, 1974). For Grosz's drawings and notes for the animator, see the Busch-Reisinger Museum's catalogue *Theatrical Drawings and Watercolors by George Grosz,* compiled by Hedy B. Landman and Herbert Knust, (Cambridge: Harvard University Press, 1973).
118	16	Claude Hill, *Bertolt Brecht* (Boston: Twayne, 1975), 58.
118	17	E. J. Aufricht, *Erzähle, damit Du Dein Recht erweist* (West Berlin: Ullstein), 65.

Chapter 7:
Politics Take Command

122	1	Herbert Jhering, *Die getarnte Reaktion* (Berlin: Rowohlt, 1930). Abridged reprint in Thomas Rietschel, ed., *Kritik in der Zeit: Fortschrittliche deutsche Literaturkritik 1918–1933* (Halle-Leipzig: Mitteldeutscher Verlag, 1983), 408–9.
122	2	Peter Heyworth, *Otto Klemperer, His Life and Times: Vol. 1, 1885–1933* (Cambridge: Cambridge University Press, 1983), 346.
123	3	Tut Schlemmer, ed., *The Letters and Diaries of Oskar Schlemmer* (Middletown, Conn.: Wesleyan University Press, 1972), 305.
124	4	See Karoline Hille's article, "Beispiel Thüringen. Die Machtergreifung auf der Probebühne 1930," in the Staatliche Kunsthalle's catalogue *1933—Wege zur Diktatur* (West Berlin, 1983), 187–217 (especially 204–12).
125	5	Hanns Eisler, "Vom bürgerlichen Konzertbetrieb," in *Die Rote Fahne,* Berlin (15 April 1928), reprinted in his *Musik und Politik, Schriften 1924–1928,* (Leipzig: Deutscher Verlag für Musik, 1973).
125	6	Harry Graf Kessler, *Tagebücher 1918–1937* (Frankfurt: Insel-Verlag, 1961), 589. (Entry for 18 July 1929).
125	7	Ibid., 591 (19 August 1929).

PAGE	NOTE	
128	8	A photograph of this performance is reproduced in John Willett (ed.) *Brecht on Theatre*, later editions, fig. 9, and Willett, *The New Sobriety/Art and Politics in the Weimar Period*, 190.
129	9	Anonymous review in *Die Rote Fahne* (16 December 1930), reproduced in Rainer Steinweg, ed., *Bertolt Brecht: Die Massnahme* (Frankfurt: Suhrkamp, 1972), 338.
129	10	Paul Fechter in the *Deutsche Allgemeine Zeitung* (15 December 1930), in ibid., 331–32.
131	11	In Ludwig Hoffmann and Klaus Pfützner, *Theater der Kollektive*, vol. 1 (East Berlin: Henschel, 1980), 19–23.
132	12	Friedrich Wolf, "Die Fahne tragen . . ." reprinted in ibid., 60.
135	13	Wilhelm Pieck, "Die klassenbewussten Arbeiter auf der Bühne," in *Das Arbeiter-Theater. Neue Wege und Aufgaben proletarischer Bühnen-Propaganda* published by the Deutscher Arbeitertheater-Bund in 1928. Reprinted in Ludwig Hoffmann's *Deutsches Arbeiter-Theater 1918–1933*, vol. 1, 325.
135	14	Ibid., 44. Slightly different figures in *Arbeiterbühne und Film*, no. 1 (1931): 8, cited in the catalogue *Theater in der Weimarer Republik*.
135	15	Herbert Jhering in *Berliner Börsen-Courier* (7 September 1929), reprinted in Rühle, *Theater für die Republik* (Frankfurt: S. Fischer, 1967), 957.
137	16	Details in the catalogue *Theater in der Weimarer Republik*, 915–16.
137	17	In F. Ziege, ed., *Leopold Jessner und das Zeit-Theater* (Berlin: Eigenbrödler-Verlag, 1928), 51. This also contains a tribute to Jessner's "brilliant intuition" by the subsequent Nazi Lothar Müthel.
137	18	As in the Prussian Landtag debate on 17 March 1928.
138	19	Herbert Jhering's review of 2 January 1930 is in his *Von Reinhardt bis Brecht* (Hamburg: Rowohlt), 307–8.
138	20	See Brecht's letter to the *Berliner Börsen-Courier* of 8 March 1931, reprinted in Willett, (ed.) *Brecht on Theatre*, 55–56.
138	21	Rühle, *Theater für die Republik*, 1021.
140	22	The episode is described in Wolfgang Heidelmeyer, *Der Fall Köpenick: Akten und zeitgenössische Dokumente zur Historie einer preussischen Moritāt* (Frankfurt: Fischer-Bücherei, 1967).
140	23	Carl Zuckmayer, *Als wärs ein Stück von mir* (Frankfurt: S. Fischer-Verlag, 1966), 439–41.
140	24	Rühle, *Theater für die Republik*, 1114 and 1118.
145	25	Zuckmayer, *Als wärs ein Stück von mir*, 459.

Chapter 8:
The Continuity of Talent

151	1	Alfred Muhr, *Rund um den Gendarmenmarkt von Iffland bis Gründgens* (Oldenburg: Gerhard Stalling-Verlag, 1965), 242.
151	2	Ibid., 243.
156	3	Jürgen Fehling, "Note on the Production," in Ernst Toller, *Masses and Man: A Fragment of the Social Revolution of the Twentieth Century* (London: Nonesuch Press, 1923), 58.

PAGE	NOTE	
156	4	Caspar Neher to Boleslaw Barlog, 7 May 1951.
157	5	Herbert Jhering, *Von Reinhardt bis Brecht* (Hamburg: Rowohlt), 198.
157	6	Ibid., 348.
158	7	Berthold Viertel, "Die Dramaturgie des Angstes," in his *Schriften zum Theater* (Munich: Kösel-Verlag, 1970), 256.
158	8	Jhering, *Von Reinhardt bis Brecht*, 123.
158	9	Carl Zuckmayer, *Als wärs ein Stück von mir* (Frankfurt: S. Fischer-Verlag, 1966), 387.
160	10	Kurt Tucholsky to Jacobsohn, 10 May 1917, from his *Ausgewählte Briefe 1913–1935* (Hamburg: Rowohlt, 1962), 89
160	11	Bernhard Reich, *Im Wettlauf mit der Zeit* (East Berlin: Henschel, 1970), 142.
162	12	From an article on Werner Krauss written for *Das neue Tagebuch* in 1937, and included in Viertel's *Schriften zum Theater*.
164	13	From Brecht's review, "Schillers Räuber im Stadttheater," on 23 October 1920, in the *Augsburger Theaterkritiken*, included in his *Schriften zum Theater 1* (Frankfurt: Suhrkamp, 1963), 32.
164	14	E. J. Aufricht, *Erzähle, damit du dein Recht erweist*, 132.
164	15	Fritz Kortner, *Alle Tage Abend* (Munich: DTV, 1959) 257.
165	16	Ibid., 254.
168	17	On these matters see Hans Curjel's very well illustrated *Experiment Krolloper 1927–1931* (Munich: Prestel-Verlag, 1975).
169	18	Details in Walter Gropius, *Theaterbau* (Rome: Reale Accademia d'Italia, 1934). (Part of the proceedings of the IV Convegno "Volta," 8–14 October 1934).
169	19	For these and other entries for the Kharkhov competition see Kranich, *Bühnentechnik der Gegenwart*, vol. 2, 339–42 and 349–52.
172	20	In Ernst Stern and Heinz Herald, eds., *Reinhardt und seine Bühne: Bilder von der Arbeit des Deutschen Theaters* (Berlin: Dr. Eysler & Co., 1919). Shortened English version in Sayler's symposium, *Max Reinhardt and his Theater* (New York: Brentano's, 1924), 124ff.
172	21	See Hanns Eisler's table of contrasts in his *Musik und Politik: Schriften 1924–1948*. Abridged English version in Willett, *Brecht in Context* (1984), 174–75.
173	22	Arno Paul, "Theater," in Eberhard Roters, ed., *Berlin 1910–1933* (New York: Rizzoli, 1982).
174	23	Günther Rühle, *Theater für die Republik* (Frankfurt: S. Fischer, 1967), 1173.
175	24	Jhering, *Von Reinhardt bis Brecht*, 255.
175	25	Five of his articles on Soviet theatre dated between 3–23 June 1931 are in Jhering, *Von Reinhardt bis Brecht*, 334–41.
176	26	Rühle, *Theater für die Republik*, 1153.
176	27	Jhering, *Von Reinhardt bis Brecht*, 343.

Chapter 9:
Parting of The Ways

180	1	Kurt Tucholsky to Heinz Pol, 7 April 1933, in his *Ausgewählte Briefe* (Hamburg: Rowohlt, 1962), 226.

PAGE	NOTE	
181	2	*Reichstag–2 Sitzung. Donnerstag den 23 März 1933*, 23. Reproduced in Staatliche Kunsthalle, Berlin, catalogue *1933–Wege zur Diktatur* (Berlin: 1983), 317. This song is by Eckart.
182	3	Ibid., 27–28, reproduced on 321–22.
182	4	See Joseph Wulf, *Theater und Kino im Dritten Reich*, 244ff.
182	5	Ibid., 76. Hitler's speech of 1 September 1933 is in Wulf's *Die Bildenden Künste im Dritten Reich: Eine Dokumentation* (Gütersloh: Sigbert Mohn, 1963),64–67.
183	6	See Laubinger's foreword to the *Deutsches Bühnen-Jahrbuch* for 1935 for his acceptance of the Nazi line.
183	7	Resolution of the Reichstheaterkammer, 21 August 1933, in Wulf, *Theater und Kino*, 39.
184	8	Gustav Gründgens, "Zur Soziologie des deutschen Schauspielers," in *Berliner Hefte*, (1946), reproduced in his *Briefe Aufsätze Reden* (Munich: DTV, 1970), 56.
184	9	Wulf, *Theater und Kino*, 49.
184	10	Ibid., 221, resuming Trotha's article "Rasse und Bühne" ("Race and Stage") in *Deutsche Bühnenkorrespondenz* (21 April 1934). Trotha committed suicide some months later.
185	11	Mary Wigman, *Deutsche Tanzkunst* (Dresden: 1935), 11–12, cited in Wulf, *Theater und Kino*, 158.
186	12	From Euringer's thirteen theses reprinted in ibid., 168–69. See also Jutta Wardetzky, *Theaterpolitik im faschistischen Deutschland* (East Berlin: Henschel, 1983), 304–5.
186	13	Illustrations in Wulf, *Theater und Kino*, plates 5, 6, 7.
186	14	Ibid., 170–71.
186	15	Report in the *Berliner Lokal-Anzeiger* (18 June 1935), summarized by Wulf, 45–46.
187	16	Letter from Count Solms to the Theaterkammer, 27 June 1935, in Wardetzky, *Theaterpolitik im faschistischen Deutschland*.
187	17	Tucholsky to Hasenclever, 5 January 1934. In his *Ausgewählte Briefe* (Hamburg: Rowohlt, 1962), 277.
188	18	Report by Rainer Schlösser to Goebbels, 22 May 1936, in Wardetzky, *Theaterpolitik*, 304–5.
189	19	Letter from the Verlag für Kulturpolitik to Schlösser at the Propaganda Ministry, 27 June 1934, in ibid., 277–78.
189	20	Secret report by Dr. Mahlo to Secretary of State Dr. Naumann, 14 August 1944, in ibid., 353–54.
190	21	Letter of 16 June 1933, "An die Nazionalsozialistische Regierung Deutschlands," in Max Reinhardt, *Schriften* (East Berlin: Henschel, 1974), 222–25.
191	22	Carl Zuckmayer, *Als wärs ein Stück von mir* (S. Fischer-Verlag, 1966) 64.
193	23	So he wrote in Thomas H. Dickinson, ed., *The Theatre in a Changing Europe* (New York: Putnam, n.d.), 176.
194	24	Hans Sahl, *Jemand* (Zurich: Oprecht, 1938), cited in Werner Mittenzwei's *Exil in der Schweiz* (Leipzig: Reclam), 249.
198	25	Reinhardt, *Schriften*, 227.
198	26	Zuckmayer, *Als wärs ein Stück von mir*, 486.
198	27	Fritz Kortner, *Alle Tage Abend* 1st ed. (Munich: DTV, 1959), 320.
198	28	Ibid., 269.

PAGE	NOTE	
199	29	Bernhard Reich, *Im Wettlauf mit der Zeit* (East Berlin: Henschel, 1970) 178.
199	30	Kortner, *Alle Tage Abend*, 200.
200	31	Cited by Wulf, *Theater und Kino*.
200	32	Heinz Hilpert, *Gedanken zum Theater* (Göttingen, 1951), 61f. Quoted by Wardetzky, *Theaterpolitik*, 123.
201	33	Klaus Völker, *Brecht-Chronik*, (Munich: Hanser, 1971), 126.
202	34	"Unterredung mit Herrn Reichsminister Dr Goebbels vom 9 April 1934, 1 Uhr 30," in Gründgens, *Briefe Aufsätze Reden* (Munich: DTV, 1970, 26–27.

Bibliography

The following is a personal attempt to name books that cover the various aspects of this still rather unsystematised subject. It is neither complete nor opinion-free, and it does not include all of those cited in the notes. Being meant primarily for English-speaking readers it omits the great number of plays of the period which have been published in German, whether at the time or more recently, except where such publications contain other useful material. Virtually any play titles that the reader might want can now be found in major library catalogues or the East and West German lists of books in print. This selection does however include other German or French publications which I have found relevant, as there is still too little written in (or translated into) English to make a satisfactory basis for further study.

1. General Accounts and Catalogues

The broadest-based recent English-language work on this subject is Michael Patterson, *The Revolution in German Theatre 1900–1933* (London and Boston, 1981). Hugo Garten's *Modern German Drama* (London 1958; Fair Lawn, N.J., 1959) deals with the playwrights considered important at that date. Peter Jelavich's *Munich and Theatrical Modernism* (Cambridge, Mass., 1985) provides valuable groundwork. Huntly Carter's *The New Spirit in the European Theatre 1914–1924* (London, 1925) communicates the excitement of discovering the Weimar theatre in its early years. Of the two books entitled *German Expressionist Drama*, that by J. M. Ritchie (New York, 1977) is the more general, since Renate Benson's (London, 1984) is confined to the work of Toller and Kaiser, as its subtitle indicates. Arno Paul's chapter in the symposium *Berlin 1910–1933*, edited by Eberhard Roters (English trans. London and New York, 1982) gives a good all-round view of the Berlin theatre in the Weimar period. The best short survey of the whole area is still René Lauret's *Le Théâtre allemand d'aujourd'hui*, published by Gallimard (Paris, 1934); Lauret, a correspondent for the review *Comoedia*, was a regular the-atregoer in Berlin from 1924 to 1933, and his estimate of the leading actors is par-ticularly valuable.

Apart from his book the most thorough and indispensable studies are only available in German. They are first of all the two undertakings by Günther Rühle: (a) his admirably annotated selection of contemporary criticism, *Theater für die Republik 1917–1933* (Frankfurt, 1967) and (b) his three volumes of reprinted and informatively commented plays called *Zeit und Theater* (Berlin 1972–; paperback edition in 6 vols., Berlin, 1980). Equally basic is the large, lavishly illustrated, nearly one-thousand-page catalogue *Theater in der Weimarer Republik*, produced by a team of contributors under Dieter Rückhaberle for the Kreutzberg Kunstamt and the Cologne University Theatre Institute (Berlin, 1977), though over two-thirds of it deals with the social and political background rather than theatre proper. An edited-down version by Paolo Chiarini is available in Italian under the title *Teatro nella republica di Weimar* (Rome, 1978). The international symposium *L'Expressionisme dans le théâtre*, edited by Jean Jacquot and Denis Bablet, is also useful (Paris, 1971); it contains the proceedings of the Strasbourg conference referred to in chapter 1, with good illustrations. Bernhard Diebold's *Anar-chie im Drama* (4th ed., Berlin, 1928) is a considered contemporary view of develop-ments from Wedekind to the arrival of Piscator with his high-tech theatre. Diebold was chief theatre critic of the *Frankfurter Zeitung* from 1917 to 1933.

2. Plays in English

Following Walter Sokel's pioneering *An Anthology of German Expressionist Drama* (Ithaca, 1984), four selections have been published in Calder and Boyars's series 'German Expressionism' under the editorship of J. M. Ritchie. They are *Seven Expressionist Plays* ranging from Wedekind and Sternheim to Barlach's *Der blaue Boll* (London, 1968), *Vision and Aftermath: Four Expressionist War Plays* (London, 1969), *Carl Sternheim: Five Plays*, and *Georg Kaiser: Five Plays* (both London, 1970). Herman Ould, ed., *Seven Plays by Ernst Toller*—from *Die Wandlung* to *Wunder in Amerika*—appeared in the author's lifetime (London 1935); more recently there were two volumes of Georg Kaiser's Works: *Plays* (Riverrun, 1980) and one of *Plays and Stories* by Arthur Schnitzler (Con-tinuum, 1982). See also Eric Bentley, ed., *Before Brecht: Four German Plays* (New York, 1985). A considerable number of other plays by these and such authors as Wedekind, Werfel, Hasenclever, Bruckner and Wolf are listed in the apparatus of Peter Bauland's *The Hooded Eagle: Modern German Drama on the New York Stage* (Syracuse, 1968), though without indication whether the translations and adaptations mentioned have been published. A complete edition of Brecht's *Collected Plays* under the editorship of Ralph Manheim and John Willett is appearing in separate U.S. and U.K. editions (New York 1971–, London 1970–); the former alone contains his adaptations for the Berliner Ensemble, but in other respects the latter has progressed further. Recent U.K. transla-tions of other writers include Schnitzler's *Undiscovered Country* (London, 1980), Zuckmayer's *The Captain of Köpenick* and Horváth's *Tales from the Vienna Woods* (London, 1977) and *Don Juan Returns from the Wars* (London, 1978), translated respectively by Tom Stoppard, John Mortimer and Christopher Hampton.

3. Contemporary Critics

These are perhaps our most valuable single source for reimagining the Weimar theatre. At present their writings are available only in German, and besides Rühle's *Theater für die Republik* (see section 1 above) there are a number of individual collections. Siegfried Jacobsohn's *Jahre der Bühne* edited by Walther Karsch and Gerhart Göhler (Hamburg, 1963) collects the longer reviews of this outstanding critic, taken from the annual *Das Jahr der Bühne* put out by his magazine *Die Schaubühne/Die Weltbühne* between 1912 and 1921; he died in 1926. Herbert Jhering's reviews are available in a number of different collections, of which the paperback *Von Reinhardt bis Brecht: eine Auswahl der Theaterkritiken von 1909–1932*, edited by Rolf Badenhausen (Hamburg, 1963), is the most useful; it gets to the parts some of the other critics never reached. Alfred Kerr's five-volume *Die Welt im Drama* (Berlin, 1917) gives a full picture of the immediately preceding period (including its cabarets), while a selection of his reviews over three decades has been edited by Hugo Fetting under the title *Mit Schleuder und Harfe* (Leipzig, 1982). Diebold's reviews are drawn on by Rühle, and much of his criticism is reworked in *Anarchie im Drama* (see section 1). Alfred Döblin's brief period as a critic is resumed in his *Griffe ins Leben: Berliner Theaterberichte* (East Berlin, 1974). Julius Bab's *Kranze dem Mimen* (Emsdetten, 1954) gives sketches of some 30 leading Weimar actors, with photographs. Fritz Engel and Hans Böhm's *Berliner Theaterwinter: 99 Bilder aus 55 Stücken* (Berlin, 1927) comments on productions in the 1926–27 season, using unposed photographs taken during performance.

4. On Specific Directors and Theatres

(a) Reinhardt

English-language studies include Huntly Carter, *The Theatre of Max Reinhardt* (reprint, New York, 1964), J. L. Styan, *Max Reinhardt* (Cambridge, England, 1982) and Walther A. Vollbach's "Memoirs of Max Reinhardt's Theatres 1920–1922," in *Theatre Survey* (Pittsburgh) 13, no. 1a (1972), while Gottfried Reinhardt's *The Genius* (New York 1979) original German title *Der Liebhaber*, Munich/Zurich 1972) is both vivid and moving about his father's later years. An invaluable chronology of the productions is Heinrich Huesmann's comprehensive *Welt-Theater Reinhardt. Bauten Spielstätten Inszenierungen* (Munich, 1983), which virtually supersedes such earlier works as Franz Horch's *Die Spielpläne Max Reinhardts 1905–1930* (Munich, 1930). Jacobsohn's reviews in *Max Reinhardt* (Berlin, 1921), the symposium *Reinhardt und seine Bühne*, edited and graphically illustrated by Ernst Stern and Heinz Herald (Berlin, 1919), and Paul Legband's introductory *Das Deutsche Theater in Berlin* (Munich, 1909) all help bring the detailed listings to life. Of these the Stern/Herald volume also provided part of Oliver Sayler's English-language symposium *Max Reinhardt and his Theater* (New York, 1924), which however was largely designed to promote that theatre's US tour with *The Miracle* the same year. Hans Böhm, ed., *Die Wiener Reinhardt-Bühne im Lichtbild: Erstes Spieljahr 1924/1925* (Vienna, 1926) contains 125 photographs of productions at the newly re-opened Theater in der Josefstadt. Among the available biographies Helene Thimig Reinhardt, *Wie Max Reinhardt lebte* (Percha, 1973) and that by his former secretary Gusti Adler, *Max Reinhardt–sein Leben* (Salzburg, 1963) are relevant. Two useful selections of Reinhardt's own very occasional writings are the East German Academy's volume *Max*

Reinhardt Schriften (East Berlin, 1974) and Fritz Hadamowsky's *Max Reinhardt: Aus-gewählte Briefe, Reden, Schriften und Szenen aus Regiebüchern,* in the Austrian National Library's 'Museion' series (Vienna, 1963). There are massive Reinhardt archives at the State University of New York at Binghamton.

(b) Piscator

Following Christopher Innes's *Erwin Piscator's Political Theatre* (Cambridge, England, 1972), Hugh Rorrison has translated and annotated *The Political Theatre* (New York, 1978; London, 1980), which sets out Piscator's main ideas and describes his productions up to 1929, the year of its original Berlin publication. This is complemented by my own *The Theatre of Erwin Piscator* (London, 1978; New York, 1979). The West German postwar re-edition of *Das Politische Theater* has been somewhat sanitized as compared with the authentic text now available in Ludwig Hoffmann's two-volume edition of his *Schriften* (East Berlin, 1968), whose second volume contains a selection of Piscator's articles and lectures and a chronology of productions. There are also two *Erwin Piscator* exhibition catalogues available in English (respectively London, 1971 and 1979), of which the second, prepared by the West Berlin Academy of Arts under Walter Huder, is the better illustrated. Maria Ley-Piscator's *The Piscator Experiment* (New York, 1967) is useful on his work in exile, but perhaps underrates the importance of the earlier years.

(c) Brecht

The English-language edition of the plays (see section 2 above), whose notes contain material relating to productions in the Weimar theatre, also embraces a selection of the *Poems* (including the theatre poems), the short stories and the early diaries. My compilation *Brecht on Theatre* (London and New York, 1964) comprises an annotated selection of his theoretical writings, and is complemented by his *The Messingkauf Dialogues* (London, 1965) which set out his ideas of theatre in dialogue form. The flood of writing about Brecht (see *The Year's Work in Modern Language Studies* for the past thirty years) includes biographical studies by Ronald Hayman (London and New York, 1983) and Klaus Völker (London and New York, 1978), neither of them as short and useful as the latter's earlier *Brecht Chronicle* (New York, 1975) or as thorough as James K. Lyon's *Bertolt Brecht in America* (Princeton, 1980; London, 1982), dealing with his exile there. There are of course extensive German editions of Brecht and profuse commentaries on his work, including a new two-volume biography by Werner Mittenzwei, *Das Leben des Bertolt Brecht* (East Berlin, Weimar, and Frankfurt am Main, 1986). There are also three well-illustrated volumes which are valuable to students ignorant of the language: Carl Niessen, *Brecht auf der Bühne* (Cologne, 1959, drawn from the university theatre collection there), and the picture biographies by Werner Hecht (Frankfurt, 1978) and Ernst and Renée Schumacher (East Berlin, 1978; paperback, Leipzig, 1984). For an attempt to establish Brecht's relationship to other theatre people and the other arts see my *Brecht in Context* (London and New York, 1984); for his principal designer and composers see under 7 and 8 below.

(d) Other Directors

The theatrical *Schriften* of Jessner and Erich Engel, edited respectively by H. Fetting and T. Lenk, have been published by the East German Academy in a form not unlike those of Reinhardt and Piscator (East Berlin, 1979 and 1971), while a similar volume for Berthold Viertel has been edited by Gerd Heidenreich under the title *Schriften zum Theater* (Munich, 1970). Hilpert's *Gedanken zum Theater* appeared in 1951, Fehling's *Die Magie des Theaters* in 1965, Gerhard Ahrens's generously illustrated symposium *Das Theater des Regisseurs Jürgen Fehling* in 1985. There are monographs also on Viertel by Fr. Pfäfflin (1970), Weichert by O. Büthe, Wälterlin by M. P. Loeffler (1979) and Dudow—primarily in relation to film—by Hermann Herlinghaus (East Berlin, 1965). There are German dissertations on Jessner by H. M. Müllenmeister (Cologne, 1958) and on Karlheinz Martin by Walter-Jürgen Schorlies (Cologne, 1971).

(e) Other Theatres

On the Volksbühne, Cecil W. Davies: *Theatre for the People* (Manchester, 1977) and Heinrich Bräulich, *Die Volksbühne: Theater und Politik in der deutschen Volksbühnenbewegung* (East Berlin, 1976). On the Staatstheater, Alfred Muhr, *Rund um den Gendarmenmarkt* (Oldenburg, 1965). On the Schiller-Theater, Georg Zivier, *Schiller-Theater, Schlosspark Theater, Berlin* (West Berlin, 1963). On the Grosses Schauspielhaus (including before and after Reinhardt), Wolfgang Carlé, *Das hat Berlin schon mal gesehen* (East Berlin, 1978). On the Rose-Theater W. D. Heinrichs. *Das Rose-Theater* (1965). On the Düsseldorf Schauspielhaus, *Das Schauspielhaus Düsseldorf* (Düsseldorf, 1930). On Frankfurt city theatre, Albert Richard Moor, *Das Frankfurter Schauspiel 1927–44* (Frankfurt, 1974). On Mannheim, Ernst Leopold Stahl, *Das Mannheimer Nationaltheater* (Mannheim, 1929). On the Munich Kammerspiele: Wolfgang Petzet: *Theater: Die Münchner Kammerspiele 1911–1972* (Munich, 1973). On the Vienna Burgtheater, Franz Herterich, *Das Burgtheater und seine Sendung* (Vienna, n.d. ? 1948).

5. Cabaret and Musicals

Lisa Appignanesi: *Cabaret* (London, 1975; paperback, 1984) deals with the international phenomenon but concentrates on Germany, including the post-1933 exiles. Among German publications Klaus Budzinski's *Das Kabarett* (Düsseldorf, 1985) is part of an encyclopaedia, with various relevant entries; he has also written a general account, *Pfeffer ins Getriebe* (Cologne, 1984). Walter Rösler, *Das Chanson im deutschen Kabarett 1901–1933* (East Berlin, 1980) and Franz-Peter Köthes, *Die theatralische Revue in Berlin und Wien 1900–1938* (Wilhelmshaven) are more detailed studies. German anthologies include Helga Bemmann's *Immer um die Litfaßsäule rum: Gedichte aus sechs Jahrzehnten Kabarett* (East Berlin, 1965) and Budzinski's *Soweit die scharfe Zunge reicht* (Munich, 1964). The songs and poems of Tucholsky, Ringelnatz, Kästner, Walter Mehring and Weinert are readily available in German, and there are short monographs in the Rowohlt series on the three first named; while Friedrich Holländer's memoirs (see section 10) also contain useful material. For the Dada 'Cabaret Voltaire' see Hugo Ball's *Flight Out of Time. A Dada Diary* and Richard Huelsenbeck's *Memoirs of a Dada Drummer* in Robert Motherwell's series *The Documents of 20th-Century Art* (both New York, 1974). For Berlin Dada performances see *The Drama Review* (New York) 18, no. 2 (June 1974).

6. Fringe and Political Theatre

For the Bauhaus see Oskar Schlemmer et al., *The Theatre of the Bauhaus* (London and Middletown, 1961); also the theatre section in H. M. Wingler, *The Bauhaus* (Boston,

1969). For Piscator's 'Proletarian Theatre', *RRR* and *Trotz Alledem* see his *The Political Theatre*, section 4b above. For the political collectives, see Ludwig Hoffmann and Klaus Pfützner, *Theater der Kollektive. Proletärisch-revolutionäres Berufstheater in Deutschland 1928–1933*, 2 vols (East Berlin, 1980). For the agitprop groups and examples of their material, Ludwig Hoffmann and Daniel Hoffmann-Oswald, *Deutsches Arbeiter-Theater 1918–1933* (2nd, augmented ed., East Berlin, 1972). On 'Kolonne Links' and its subsequent career in exile see Helmut Damerius, *Über zehn Meere zum Mittelpunkt der Welt* (East Berlin, 1977); on the whole political theatre movement, F. W. Knellessen, *Agitation auf der Bühne* (Emsdetten, 1970); on the broader context of the politicized arts, the Neue Gesellschaft für Bildende Kunst's generously illustrated catalogue *Wem gehört die Welt—Kunst und Gesellschaft in der Weimarer Republik* (West Berlin, 1977).

7. Stage Design and Technology

Here again there is not much in English apart from Denis Bablet's splendidly illustrated *Revolutions in Stage Design of the Twentieth Century* (Paris and New York, 1977), which contains much material on Germany, Hugh Rorrison's 'Designing for Reinhardt: The Work of Ernst Stern' in *New Theatre Quarterly* no. 7. (Cambridge, 1986), and my own monograph *Caspar Neher: Brecht's Designer* (London and New York, 1986). In German see Huesmann on Reinhardt's stage, Piscator's *The Political Theatre* and Niessen's *Brecht auf der Bühne* (all in section 4 above), likewise Niessen's short *Max Reinhardt und seine Bühnenbildner* (Cologne, 1958). The whole Weimar period is usefully and economically covered in Helmut Grosse's catalogue, *Theater in der Weimarer Republik: Eine Ausstellung des Instituts für Theaterwissenschaft der Universität zu Köln* (Leverkusen, 1974). Hans Curjel's *Experiment Krolloper 1927–1931* (Munich, 1975) includes illustrations of the very advanced productions at that institution. The illustrations, some colored, in Oskar Fischel's *Das moderne Bühnenbild* (Berlin, 1923) only take the story up to the decline of Expressionism. As for later designers, there is a useful coffee-table album on *Caspar Neher*, edited by Siegfried Melchinger and Gottfried von Einem (Velber, 1966), with good illustrations, some in color, a full and informative list of productions, and contributions by various hands. *Hein Heckroth 1901–1970* is the catalogue of a memorial exhibition to the Essen designer (at the Frankfurter Kunstverein, 1970). For developments in stage technology and architecture from Wagner to the Kharkhov theatre competition, Friedrich Kranich's *Bühnentechnik der Gegenwart* is a mine of information (2 vols., Munich and Berlin, 1927–31). Design before World War I is well covered in Denis Bablet's *Esthétique générale du décor de théâtre de 1870 á 1914* (Paris, 1965 and 1975), which deals also with the theory and philosophy of the main pioneers.

8. Music and the Theatre

In addition to Curjel's *Experiment Krolloper* (see the preceding section) the first volume of Peter Heyworth's *Otto Klemperer: His Life and Times* (Cambridge, 1983) gives an authoritative account of the innovations of Klemperer and his colleagues. Dietrich Stern, ed., *Angewandte Musik 20er Jahre* (West Berlin, 1977), forbiddingly subtitled *Exemplarische Versuche gesellschaftsbezogener musikalischer Arbeit für Theater, Film, Radio, Massenveranstaltung,* is in fact a stimulating symposium on developments outside the orthodox 'apparatus'. Among the composers featured there, there are English-language studies of Kurt Weill by Kim Kowalke and Ronald Sanders, and a translation of

Albrecht Betz, *Hanns Eisler* (Cambridge, 1982). In German, Weill has been the subject of a number of publications, notably a useful short biography by Jürgen Schebera (Leipzig, 1983) and two paperback collections edited by David Drew (Frankfurt, 1975), while Hanns Eisler's critical writings form section III of the main East German Eisler edition (Leipzig, 1973–83). An English-language selection of these has been published as *Hanns Eisler: A Rebel in Music* (East Berlin, 1978). For this whole musical movement, viewed primarily in relation to Brecht, see also Albrecht Dümling's 736-page *Lasst euch nicht verführen* (Munich, 1985); for cabaret music the works by Rösler and Holländer under sections 5 and 10 respectively, and Drew's *Kurt Weill: A Handbook* (London 1987).

9. After Weimar—the Third Reich

(a) Theatre under the Nazis

See chapters 4 and 5 of J. M. Ritchie's *German Literature under National Socialism* (London and Totowa, N.J., 1983), which also deals with the exiled dramatists. In German the most thorough study of the organisational, financial and political aspects is Boguslaw Drewniak's *Das Theater im NS-Staat* (Düsseldorf, 1983), which is very informative about the involvement of individuals. A contemporary account is Hermann Wanderscheck, *Deutsche Dramatik der Gegenwart* (Berlin, n.d., ca. 1939). Bruno Fischli, *Der deutsche Dämmerung: Zur Geschichte der völkisch-faschistischen Dramas und Theaters* (Bonn, 1976) may be relevant, as is U. K. Ketelsen, *Von heroischem Sein und völkischem Tod* (Bonn, 1970), which gives resumes of forty-four plays. A number of such plays, including Johst's *Schlageter,* are republished in the third (1933–1945) volume of Rühle's *Zeit und Theater* (see section 1), while the better productions are illustrated in K. H. Rüppel, ed., *Grosses Berliner Theater,* (Velber, 1962) dealing with the work of Gründgens, Fehling, Müthel, Hilpert, and Engel after 1933. Gründgens's contribution is the main theme of Alfred Muhr, *Rund um den Gendarmenmarkt* (see 4e above), and is selectively documented in the paperback Gustav Gründgens, *Briefe Aufsätze Reden* (Munich, 1970), edited by Rolf Badenhausen and Peter Gründgens-Gorski. For 'Thing-Spiele' and the like, see *Massenspiele* by Henning Eichberg, Michael Dultz, Glen Gadberry and Günther Rühle (Fromann-Holzboog, 1977), which includes an account in English. Two mainly documentary studies are Josef Wulf's *Theater und Film im Dritten Reich: Eine Dokumentation* (Gütersloh, 1964, paperback West Berlin, 1983) and Jutta Wardetzky, *Theaterpolitik im faschistischen Deutschland: Studien und Dokumente* (East Berlin, 1983). The second of these is based on a study of the Ministry of Propaganda's archives; it accordingly has very little to say about Goering's Staatstheater, but within its limits contains much fascinating material.

(b) Theatre in Exile

The work of the playwrights is now often subsumed under the general heading of 'Exilliteratur', on which much has been published over the past ten years or so, most notably Hans Christoph Wächter, *Theater im Exil* (Munich, 1973) and F. N. Mennemeier and Frithjof Trapp, *Deutsche Exildramatik 1933–1950* (Fink, 1980): following a hundred-page introduction this gives samples of the plays, but says nothing about productions. Wolfgang Elfe et al. have edited a South Carolina symposium on *Deutsches Exildrama und Exiltheater* (Bern, 1977). Two particularly useful paperback series are the seven-volume East German *Kunst und Literatur im antifaschistischen Exil 1933–1945* (Leipzig, 1979–1983) by some two dozen authors under the editorship of Werner Mittenzwei, Ludwig Hoffmann, Wolfgang Kießling and Eike Middell, and the joint project of the Humboldt University and the Academy of Arts called *Deutsches Theater im Exil* (East Berlin, 1978–) among which Mittenzwei's volume *Das Zürcher Schauspielhaus 1933–1945* is particularly relevant. Other publications in this field include David Pike, *German Writers in Soviet Exile 1933–1945* (Chapel Hill, 1982); Hermann Haarman et al., *Das 'Engels' Projekt: Ein antifaschistisches Theater deutscher Emigranten in der UdSSR 1936–1941* (Worms, 1975); John Russell Taylor, *Strangers in Paradise. The Hollywood Émigrés 1933–1950* (London and New York, 1983); Gerhard Hirschfeld, ed., *German Exile in Britain* (Birmingham, 1984); and the well-illustrated West Berlin Academy catalogue *Theater im Exil 1933–1945* (West Berlin, 1973).

10. Individual Memoirs etc.

The principal English translations have been Brecht's *Letters* (in course of preparation) and *Diaries 1919–1922* (London and New York, 1979), Tut Schlemmer, ed., *The Letters and Diaries of Oskar Schlemmer* (Middletown, 1972), Ernst Stern's *My Life, My Stage* (London, 1951), Ernst Toller's *I Was a German* (London, 1934), Alexander Granach's *There Goes an Actor* (Garden City, 1945), and Carl Zuckmayer's *A Part of Myself* (London and New York, 1970, somewhat abridged from the German). Harry Kessler's diaries *In the Twenties* (London and New York, 1971) give valuable background material. In German relevant memoirs or autobiographies have been written by the following [in this listing, * follows the more important works; † those which I have not seen]: Ernst Josef Aufricht,* Ludwig Barnay,† Elisabeth Bergner, Rudolf Bernauer, Curt Bois, Arnolt Bronnen,* Helmut Damerius, Berta Drews,* Tilla Durieux, Rudolf Frank, Valeska Gert,† Julius Hay,* Felix Holländer, Friedrich Holländer,* Herbert Jhering (up to c. 1920 only), Franz Jung,* Arthur Kahane, Fritz Kortner,* Werner Krauss,† Asja Lacis, Mischket Liebermann, Bernhard Reich,* Hans Rodenberg, Heinz Rühmann, Steffi Spira-Ruschin, Agnes Straub,† Aribert Wäscher,† Eduard von Winterstein. In addition Koreya Senda's *Wanderjahre* (East Berlin, 1985) describes his experiences in the German theatre 1927–31. Harry Wilde's biography *Theodor Plievier: Nullpunkt der Freiheit* (Munich, 1965) is likewise personally lived and vividly written.

11. Reference and Miscellaneous

There are two biographical reference works for the German theatre: Wilhelm Kosch's *Deutsches Theaterlexikon* (Klagenfurt-Vienna, 1953–) and Herbert Frenzel et al., eds., *Kürschner's Biographisches Theater-Handbuch* (Berlin, 1956). The first is not yet finished, and is confusingly arranged (e.g. actresses are under their married names); the second only lists living persons. Further information about playwrights and the main critical studies of them can be found in Kosch's *Literaturlexikon* and Kunisch's *Handbuch der deutschen Gegenwartsliteratur* (Munich, 1965), which give bibliographies for each entry. A number are discussed at more length in Wolfgang Rothe, ed., *Expressionismus als Literatur* (Berne, 1969), which again gives useful short bibliographies. On the organisation and personnel of all German-language theatres the annual *Deutsches Bühnenjahrbuch* is invaluable; it lists all German premières. For general history of the theatre I have used Joseph Gregor's *Weltgeschichte des Theaters* (Zurich, 1933), for information about the cinema the three-volume *Geschichte des Films* by Jerzy Toeplitz (East Berlin and Munich, 1975, 1977 and 1980). Some of the theatre magazines and programs of the period are very pertinent, though hardly to be found outside specialist libraries (such as that of the excellent Cologne University Theatre Museum at Porz-Wahn). They include notably the Berlin magazines *Arbeiterbühne und Film* (reprint, Cologne, 1974), *Blätter der Piscatorbühne, Das junge Deutschland, Der neue Weg, Die Szene* and *Volksbühne;* also *Die neue Schaubühne* (Dresden, 1919, reprint Nedeln, 1969), *Der Scheinwerfer* (Essen) and *The International Theatre* (Moscow 1933–35). Finally, for those interested in the larger framework of my interpretation of the period, my books on *Expressionism* (London and New York, 1970) and *The New Sobriety: Art and Politics in the Weimar Period* (London and New York, 1978) try to supply it.

12. Acknowledgments

It would have been difficult to write this book without the help of the Cologne University Theatre Museum at Porz-Wahn, and the use of its photo collection (originally got together by Carl Niessen). I am grateful to its director Helmut Grosse and his photographer Karl Arendt; likewise to the Academy of Arts of the GDR in Berlin and (for items from the Arts Council of Great Britain's Caspar Neher exhibition of 1986) the theatre collection of the Austrian National Library. In London I have used the British and London Libraries and the Goethe Institute; in New York, the Lincoln Centre Library of the Performing Arts; and I am also an old habitué of the Bertolt Brecht Archive in East Berlin. Avro Systems Technology of Hayes have improved my word processing (this being the first book I have done this way). Electrodom of Dieppe gave me a vital connection. Personal friends who have helped with advice and information include Denis Bablet and Professor Arno Paul, while my son Thomas undertook additional photography.

Index

Figures in **bold type** indicate the more important references under a given head. Those in *italic type* denote illustrations. "Cit." before a page reference indicates a quotation. This index relates only to the main text, not to the bibliography or to the appendices covering theatres, actors, films and recordings. Dates are not given for any actors, since they will be found in the list at the beginning of Appendix 2.